The Papacy and World-Affairs

AS REFLECTED IN
THE SECULARIZATION OF
POLITICS

The Papacy and World-Affairs

AS REFLECTED IN
THE SECULARIZATION OF POLITICS

By
CARL CONRAD ECKHARDT
Professor of History
in the University of Colorado

WIPF & STOCK · Eugene, Oregon

Wipf and Stock Publishers
199 W 8th Ave, Suite 3
Eugene, OR 97401

The Papacy and World Affairs
As Reflected in the Secularization of Politics
By Eckhardt, Carl Conrad
ISBN 13: 978-1-4982-9268-9
Publication date 3/22/2016
Previously published by University of Chicago Press, 1937

TO GLORIA, MY WIFE

WHOSE FRIENDLY COLLABORATION HAS BEEN A SIGNIFICANT FACTOR IN THE PRODUCTION AND COMPLETION OF THIS TREATISE

Preface

THE secularization of politics may be said to have taken place when at the Congress of Westphalia the Catholic and Protestant princes agreed to disregard the protest of the pope against the treaties of Münster and Osnabrück, which were, after a long period of turmoil and confusion, to become the fundamental law of Europe. The event called the "secularization of politics" had been a long time in preparation. There had been many individual princes and groups of secular rulers who had flouted papal secular authority in previous centuries, especially during the Reformation. But it was not until the close of the Thirty Years' War that there was a concerted effort in both Catholic and Protestant camps to disregard papal authority in the political affairs of Europe, an authority that had been potently and effectively exercised through much of the medieval period.

But it took the papacy a long time to accept the changed situation. It repeatedly protested, without effect, against all those international treaties and other actions of the secular rulers that injured the interests and claimed legal rights of the church. Its protests were most frequent and vehement after 1860 and 1870, when, through the action of the Italian kingdom, the papacy lost the Papal States, which, according to papal theory, were essential in order to give the pontiff full freedom from secular interference when administering the spiritual affairs of the world.

However, the papacy terminated this attitude of protest when, in 1929, it signed the Lateran Accord with Mussolini and agreed not to participate in the settlement of international disputes of the states of the world unless it were invited to do so by the harmonious action of the states concerned. This marked the secularization of politics in its final aspects, when the papacy itself, after three centuries of protest, recognized the fact that it could no longer exercise any authority in international relations.

To the superficial observer the secularization of politics may seem to imply a defeat for the papacy. But, on the contrary, it was a blessing in disguise, for it freed the papacy from those secular objectives and activities that undermined or paralyzed its leadership in religion and morals, which were its original and true fields of action. The evidence in chapter xix will show that Catholic as well as non-Catholic students of the question agree that the papacy is a more effective spiritual, ethical, and social agent since it has been extruded from politics than during the eight or nine centuries when it not merely was a potent political authority but was, in harmony with the ideals of medieval unity, also the head of a state that can be called at least a "projected totalitarian state." Under papal leadership the medieval church was an attempted totalitarian state, an authoritarian state, in which secular and political affairs were to be subordinated to the spiritual objectives of the *Civitas Dei*, whose goal was preparation of all mortals for life in the next world.

But the European states, which were relatively weak after the disintegration of the Roman Empire and during the feudal period, gradually became assertive in their own secular sphere, and ultimately took over the direction of religious matters when there was a conflict of authority or objective. The national spirit of early modern times, which gave a psychological basis for the development of the state as a dominant institution, has led not merely to the secularization of politics but to the secularization of religion, in this day of the totalitarian or authoritarian states of central and eastern Europe. This is a recent development that has brought new problems not merely to the papacy and the Roman Catholic church, but to the Christian church in all its branches. To the student of contemporary affairs the story of the secularization of politics will afford a historical background that explains the development of the state and its contemporary actions that mean the secularization of religion.

PREFACE

The author knows of no work, in any language, that coordinates and unifies this long story concerning a significant aspect of the relations of church and state. He is aware, however, that in his efforts to control so large a field, covering fifteen centuries, he may easily have made mistakes in judgment and failed to use all the available sources of information. But it is his hope that as a survey of a hitherto neglected field this treatise may find a grateful reception both among specialists and the reading public. It is, however, not merely a survey. In the chapters dealing with the Peace of Westphalia and the secularization of politics (chaps. iv–xvi) an effort has been made to deal with the subject exhaustively, on the basis of the original sources. In the other chapters original sources have been used when possible, but in many cases only secondary sources could be utilized.

The author wishes to express his grateful acknowledgment of the many kindnesses conferred on him by the officers and staff of the libraries of the following universities in this country: Cornell, Harvard, Yale, Columbia, Colorado, Chicago, Illinois, Wisconsin, Kansas, Missouri; also of the Denver Public Library. His further appreciation is also gladly expressed of the special courtesies granted him by the officers and attendants of the following foreign libraries: the Bayerische Staatsbibliothek, the Bayerisches Geheimes Staatsarchiv, the Bayerisches Hauptstaatsarchiv, all of Munich, Bavaria; Munich University Library; the Nationalbibliothek in Vienna; the Vatican Library; the Bibliothèque nationale; and the Library of the British Museum.

The author also wishes to express his obligations and gratitude to Dr. George Lincoln Burr, professor emeritus of history, in Cornell University, who, as a stimulating guide in graduate work, suggested this field of historical investigation; to the late Dr. James Field Willard, of the University of Colorado, and Dr. John Brown Mason, of Colorado Woman's College, who have read the entire manuscript; to Dr. Earl Swisher, of the University of Colorado, who has assisted the author in tracing certain references. Naturally these persons are not to be held responsible for the opinions and conclusions expressed in this work. Appreciation is also due to Dr. Konrad Meyer, of Munich, whose linguistic ability was invaluable to the author in getting control of the seventeenth-century Latin works on the controversial literature (chaps. xiv–xvi).

Special gratitude and appreciation are expressed to the Social Science Research Council, whose generous grant-in-aid for the year 1932–33 made easier for the author his studies in European libraries.

C. C. Eckhardt

Table of Contents

TABLE OF CONTENTS

TABLE OF CONTENTS

TABLE OF CONTENTS

Chapter One

THE CHURCH AND POLITICS IN THE MIDDLE AGES

I. THEORY OF PAPAL CONTROL OF POLITICS

UNDER the Roman Empire the popes had no temporal powers. But when the Roman Empire had disintegrated and its place had been taken by a number of rude, barbarous kingdoms, the Roman Catholic church not only became independent of the states in religious affairs but dominated secular affairs as well. At times, under such rulers as Charlemagne (768–814), Otto the Great (936–73), and Henry III (1039–56), the civil power controlled the church to some extent; but in general, under the weak political system of feudalism, the well-organized, unified, and centralized church, with the pope at its head, was not only independent in ecclesiastical affairs but also controlled civil affairs. The church interfered in secular affairs on the basis of its theory of the relation of church and state, which was formulated in substance by Augustine (354–430) and given wider and more definite application by such popes as Gregory VII (1073–85), Innocent III (1198–1216), Boniface VIII (1294–1303), and others.[1]

[1] Nys, "Le droit international et la papauté," *Revue de droit international*, X (1878), 505–14; Jarrige, *La condition internationale du Saint-Siège avant et après les accords du Lateran*, pp. 30–41; Dunning, *History of Political Theories, Ancient and Medieval*, pp. 131–51; Chénon, *Histoire des rapports de l'église et de l'état du Ier au XXème siècle*, pp. 40–92; Bluntschli, *Die rechtliche Unverantwortlichkeit und Verantwortlichkeit des römischen Papstes*, pp. 22–25; Nys, *Les origins du droit international*, pp. 13–33; Bryce, *Holy Roman Empire*, pp. 64–68, 94, 103–9, 133–39, 150–52, 159–66, 218–20; Gierke, *Political Theories of the Middle Age*, pp. 2, 9–11; Murray, *History of Political Science*, pp. 37–47; Hauck, *Der Gedanke der päpstlichen Weltherrschaft bis auf Bonifaz VIII;* Bernheim, *Mittelalterliche Zeitanschauungen in ihrem Einfluss auf Politik und Geschichtsschreibung*,

2. SOCIETY A DIVINE STATE IN THE MIDDLE AGES

According to the theory of the relation of church and state that was actually applied in western Europe from about the eleventh century to the Reformation, the supreme function of life on earth was preparation for life in the next world. Society was a unit, the *Civitas Dei*, a divine state, dominated by the church. There was no separation of church and state. The state was merely one aspect of society; it was not something external to the church; it had no interests opposed to or pitted against those of the church. Whatever affected the church favorably or adversely had a like effect on the state. The spiritual and temporal powers were two aspects of the same social organization, the City of God, as described by Augustine, elaborated by Thomas Aquinas (1225–74), and expressed in legal form by various popes in the thirteenth and fourteenth centuries.[2]

It was just as natural in medieval times to regard church and state as two aspects of the same organization as it is for us in a modern state to regard the legislative, executive, and judicial functions as three different aspects of the same governing state.[3]

3. AFFIRMATION OF PAPAL AUTHORITY

In the thirteenth and fourteenth centuries a number of popes issued decrees affirming their rights as final authority over secular affairs.[4] These decrees asserted that in political affairs the

---

Part I, pp. 4–5, 10–62, 110–233; Luchaire, *Innocent III, la papauté et l'empire*, pp. 11–15; Luchaire, *Innocent III, Rome et l'Italie*, pp. 31–32; R. W. and A. J. Carlyle, *History of Medieval Political Theory in the West*, I, 164–75; II, 143–52; III, 9–10, 92–105 (misjudges the influence of Augustine, see Bernheim, *op. cit.*, pp. 10–11); Dempf, *Sacrum Imperium*, Part II, chaps. iii, v, viii; Dempf, *Die Hauptform mittelalterlicher Weltanschauung*, pp. 61–77; Schramm, *Kaiser, Rom und Renovatio*, I, 238–50.

[2] Gierke, *op. cit.*, pp. 11–18; Figgis, *From Gerson to Grotius*, pp. 4–5; Bartlet and Carlyle, *Christianity in History*, pp. 400–419; Dunning, *op. cit.*, pp. 156–58, 205–7; Chénon, *op. cit.*, pp. 41–42; Schnabel, *Deutsche Geschichte im neunzehnten Jahrhundert*, I, 8–18; Bernheim, *op. cit.*, I, 119, 213–14; Andreas, *Deutschland vor der Reformation*, pp. 17–18; E. F. Jacob, in Crump and Jacob, *The Legacy of the Middle Ages*, pp. 510–17; Wright, *Medieval Internationalism*, pp. 18–19.

[3] Jarrige, *op. cit.*, p. 40, n. 19; Crump and Jacob, *op. cit.*, p. 516.

[4] See appendix at end of this chapter concerning these decrees.

papacy was superior to all sovereigns, just as the sun is superior to the moon, the spirit to the flesh, gold to lead. The papacy had control over both swords, the temporal and spiritual; it used the temporal sword by making use of the intermediary power of the kings and princes, who were servants of the papacy. These wide claims were asserted not in a spirit of papal self-seeking but as a consequence of the medieval interpretation of the purpose and organization of world-society according to the divine will.[5] Although the popes never fully or continuously exercised these wide claims, they were the bases of the following asserted papal rights, rights that the pope exercised with effectiveness in political and civil affairs until the decline of the papacy in the fourteenth and fifteenth centuries, though some of the incidents cited took place after the close of the Middle Ages.

The pope could judge and verify the powers of the sovereigns; he could confirm their legitimacy, arbitrate concerning opposing claims (*Venerabilem*, *Ausculta fili*).[6] He could depose temporal sovereigns when they were disobedient to papal orders by excommunicating them and releasing their subjects from their oaths of fidelity (*Ad apostolicae*); thus the right of co-ordinate resistance and revolution not only existed for the church but was bestowed on the people by the church.[7]

The pope and his vast church organization had full charge of all civil and criminal cases involving ecclesiasts, except those concerned with feudal affairs. Papal and church jurisdiction was, in civil affairs, exercised also over widows, orphans, crusaders, and students in universities. The students could utilize the civil courts, but that was rarely done because the justice ad-

[5] Bernheim, *op. cit.*, chap. iii, but especially pp. 213–24, 232–33; Luchaire, *Innocent III, la papauté et l'empire*, pp. 11–15.

[6] Bompard, *Le pape et le droit de gens*, p. 4; Chénon, *op. cit.*, p. 91; Chénon, in Lavisse and Rambaud, *Histoire générale*, II, 289; Nys, *Les origins du droit international*, pp. 22–23; Hauck, *Kirchengeschichte Deutschlands*, IV, 686–87; Hauck, *Der Gedanke der päpstlichen Weltherrschaft*, pp. 27–28, 31–41; Bernheim, *op. cit.*, I, 230–31.

[7] Bompard, *op. cit.*, p. 4; Chénon, *Histoire des rapports*, p. 91; Chénon, in Lavisse and Rambaud, *op. cit.*, II, 289; Nys, *Les origins*, pp. 23–24; Hauck, *Kirchengeschichte Deutschlands*, IV, 687; Bernheim, *op. cit.*, I, 194, 220–21; Hauck, *Der Gedanke der päpstlichen Weltherrschaft*, pp. 19–20, 28–29.

ministered in the ecclesiastical courts was superior to that of the lay courts.[8]

The pope could promulgate civil laws applicable in all states in the domain of private law—embracing such matters as betrothals; marriage; the relations of husband and wife, parent and child, guardian and ward; the making of wills, especially with reference to the matter of legacies to the church. In many countries the church had jurisdiction (sometimes merely concurrent and greatly limited) in the making and execution of contracts, since entering a contract was accompanied by taking an oath, which was a religious act. In so far as the secular state took cognizance of these various arrangements, either actively or tacitly, these parts of canon law were an integral part of civil law in each state.[9] The pope could establish special jurisdictions to interpret and apply those laws emanating from Rome. In each state there was a hierarchy of judicial officials, culminating in the pope. He had final jurisdiction in all Christendom. All persons having received Christian baptism were under papal jurisdiction. Even so late as August 7, 1873, Pope Pius IX ventured to affirm in a letter to the German emperor William I that the pope possesses a spiritual authority over the whole of Christendom, not merely over Catholic Christendom, and that all who have received Christian baptism in any form whatsoever are under his jurisdiction. This claim was rejected in the answer of the German emperor of September 3, 1873, with great vigor. The medieval secular princes were enjoined, under pain of excommunication, not to interfere with ecclesiastical juris-

[8] Chénon, *Histoire des rapports*, pp. 93–94; Chénon, in Lavisse and Rambaud, *op. cit.*, II, 256; Poncet, *Les privilèges des clercs au moyen âge*, pp. 81–147; Esmein, *Cours élémentaire d'histoire du droit français*, pp. 320–29; Schröder, *Lehrbuch der deutschen Rechtsgeschichte*, pp. 596–99; Jastrow and Winter, *Deutsche Geschichte im Zeitalter der Hohenstaufen*, I, 86, 102–4. For English practice see Pollock and Maitland, *History of English Law*, I, 130–31.

[9] Jarrige, *op. cit.*, p. 47; Bompard, *op. cit.*, pp. 4–5, 8; Chénon, *Histoire des rapports*, pp. 94–95; Chénon, in Lavisse and Rambaud, *op. cit.*, II, 256–57; Esmein, *op. cit.*, pp. 325–29; Schröder, *op. cit.*, pp. 597–99. For English practice see Pollock and Maitland, *op. cit.*, I, 124–35; II, 197–202; Smith, *Church and State in the Middle Ages*, pp. 57–100.

diction in their own lands; they were not to interfere in appeals to the papal court at Rome.[10]

On the basis of the wide temporal claims asserted by such popes as Gregory VII, Innocent III, and Boniface VIII the papacy aimed to attach all Christian states to the Holy See by means of a feudal bond. By the time of Innocent III the pope had become a sort of spiritual emperor of the world; just as he ruled the church, he aimed to control the secular world as a fief of Peter. The individual states were to be kept in subordination without destroying their independence.[11] With such objectives in mind Innocent III and other popes created or recognized kingdoms, decided disputes between pretenders, transferred the lands of heretical rulers to princes of the true faith, interfered in the internal affairs of kingdoms, became feudal overlord of many princes in central and western Europe.

The popes were appealed to, to decide between pretenders to the throne, as was Alexander III (1159–81) in the case of Poland and as was Innocent III in the case of Hungary and Norway.[12] Innocent III regarded the kingdom of Hungary as having originated by papal action, and the coronation oath of the king recognized the duty of obedience to the Holy See.[13] In Languedoc, during the Albigensian crusade, the legates of Innocent III transferred to the conquerors the seignories of the van-

[10] Mirbt, *Quellen zur Geschichte des Papsttums und des romischen Katholizismus*, pp. 469–71; Bompard, *op. cit.*, p. 5; Bluntschli, *op. cit.*, pp. 8–9; Nys, *Les origins*, p. 140; Hauck, *Der Gedanke der päpstlichen Weltherrschaft*, pp. 39–40; Kaiser, *Deutsche Geschichte im Ausgang des Mittelalters*, II, 350–53; Poncet, *op. cit.*, pp. 13–18; Smith, *op. cit.*, pp. 45–52; Luchaire, *Social France at the Time of Philip Augustus*, pp. 142–206.

[11] Hergenröther, *Handbuch der allgemeinen Kirchengeschichte*, II, 348; Ficker and Hermelink, *Das Mittelalter*, pp. 126–27, in Vol. II of Krüger, *Handbuch der Kirchengeschichte;* Bernheim, *op. cit.*, I, 217–24.

[12] Chénon, in Lavisse and Rambaud, *op. cit.*, II, 289; *Cambridge Medieval History*, VI, 28–29, 454; Luchaire, *Innocent III, les royautés vassales du Saint-Siège*, pp. 68–72.

[13] Luchaire, *Innocent III, les royautés vassales du Sainte-Siège*, pp. 63–64, 66–67, 68–72; *Cambridge Medieval History*, VI, 464, 555; Flick, *The Rise of the Medieval Church*, p. 555; Haller, *Gregor VII und Innozenz III*, in Marks and Müller, *Meister der Politik*, I, 551–52.

quished heretics.[14] In England the same pope on August 24, 1215, forbade the observance of the Great Charter, which King John had been forced to sign by his nobles, [15] Many kings and princes voluntarily offered to the pope their crowns and lands in order to receive them back as papal fiefs, thus strengthening their claims in a time of political uncertainty. The first example of this seems to be that of Countess Mathilda of Tuscany, who, sometime in the years 1077–80, did homage for all her holdings to Pope Gregory VII.[16] In 1088 Count Pierre de Substantion received from Urban II (1088–99), with the title of fief, the county of Maguelonne (Montpellier), which he had previously offered to Gregory VII.[17] When the Count of Barcelona recovered Tarragona from the Moors, he offered his conquest and also his inheritance to Urban II, and received both back as fiefs.[18] In 1179 Alexander III (1159–81) created the kingdom of Portugal and gave it to Duke Alfonso; he and later kings regarded themselves as vassals of the pope and continued to pay him tribute.[19] Poland, which in the eleventh century had paid financial tribute to the papacy, was in the twelfth century declared to be a fief of the papacy by Leszek the Wise (1194–1227), who sought papal protection against the emperor of the

[14] Chénon, in Lavisse and Rambaud, *op. cit.*, II, 289; *Cambridge Medieval History*, VI, 24–28; Luchaire, *Innocent III et la croisade des Albigeois*, chap. iv, especially pp. 143, 145, 189–91.

[15] Mirbt, *op. cit.*, p. 181, bull *Etsi carissimus in*; Roger of Wendover, *Flowers of History*, II, 330–34; Bompard, *op. cit.*, p. 5; Luchaire, *Innocent III, les royautés vassales du Sainte-Siège*, pp. 241–45; Adams, *History of England from the Norman Conquest to the Death of John*, p. 441; Davis, *England under the Normans and Angevins*, p. 383; Lingard, *History of England*, II, 363–65.

[16] Chénon, in Lavisse and Rambaud, *op. cit.*, II, 289; *Cambridge Medieval History*, V, 104, cites A. Overmann, *Gräfin Mathilde von Tuscien*, pp. 143–44, which has not been accessible to the writer.

[17] Chénon, in Lavisse and Rambaud, II, 290; Georges Goyau, "Montpellier," *Catholic Encyclopedia*, X, 545.

[18] *Cambridge Medieval History*, VI, 555; R. R. Amado, "Tarragona," *Catholic Encyclopedia*, XIV, 460.

[19] Hergenröther, *op. cit.*, II, 634; Chénon, in Lavisse and Rambaud, II, 289; Mariejol, in Lavisse and Rambaud, *ibid.*, p. 669; Neher, article "Portugal" in Wetzer and Welte, *Kirchenlexikon*, X, 208; Luchaire, *Innocent III, les royautés vassales*, pp. 5–27.

Holy Roman Empire. The overlordship of the papacy was used by the Polish kings as a means of realizing the international ambitions of the Polish dynasty.[20] In 1204 Peter II (1196–1213) of Aragon transformed all his realm into an apostolic fief and came personally to Rome to be crowned by the pope.[21] Johannitza (Kalojan, 1197–1207), the prince or tsar of Bulgaria, recognized himself as vassal of the Holy See, in hopes of being more successful in overcoming his enemies within his state and resisting the claims of the Byzantine emperor.[22] It is quite clear that, according to papal theory, and to a great extent in practice, "Rome was the source of royal power and regal rights."[23] Even distant Armenia sought protective connection with Rome in the early years of the pontificate of Innocent III, and for a number of years recognized the suzerainty of Rome.[24] In 1213 John Lackland agreed to pay to the pope a tribute of 1,000 marks and to do him homage as suzerain for the crown of England.[25]

It was the pope and his officials who claimed the right to supervise the diplomacy and international relations of the medieval states. Religion was the only bond uniting the medieval peoples of central and western Europe; it permeated all their

[20] Hergenröther, *op. cit.*, II, 415; Kaindl, *Polen*, p. 19; Zivier, *Polen*, pp. 28–29; Phillips, *Poland*, p. 23.

[21] Luchaire, *Innocent III, les royautés vassales*, pp. 50–58; Chénon, in Lavisse and Rambaud, *op. cit.*, II, 290; Hergenröther, *op. cit.*, II, 633; *Cambridge Medieval History*, VI, 411, 555; Haller, *op. cit.*, I, 551.

[22] Chénon, in Lavisse and Rambaud, *op. cit.*, II, 290; Hergenröther, *op. cit.*, II, 510; Luchaire, *Innocent III, les royautés vassales*, pp. 94–106; *Cambridge Medieval History*, VI, 30, 31; Haller, *op. cit.*, I, 551–52; Zöpffel-Mirbt, article "Innocent III," in Herzog-Hauck, *Realencyklopädie*, IX, 118.

[23] Luchaire, *Innocent III, les royautés vassales*, p. 106; Jastrow and Winter, *op. cit.*, II, 239–40.

[24] Haller, *op. cit.*, I, 552; Petermann-Gelzer, article "Armenien," in Herzog-Hauck, *Realencyklopädie*, II, 81; *Cambridge Medieval History*, VI, 16; Flick, *Decline of the Medieval Church*, I, 6.

[25] Roger of Wendover, *op. cit.*, II, 268–70; Chénon, in Lavisse and Rambaud, *op. cit.*, II, 290; Hergenröther, *op. cit.*, II, 488; *Cambirdge Medieval History*, VI, 237, 555; Haller, *op. cit.*, I, 546–47; Zöpffel-Mirbt, in Herzog-Hauck, *op. cit.*, IX, 118–19; Bompard, *op. cit.*, p. 8; Barry, *The Papal Monarchy*, p. 322; Luchaire, *Innocent III, les royautés vassales*, chap. iv, especially pp. 224–25.

relations and was invoked to serve as a guaranty to international contracts. Many treaties between states were concluded under papal mediation, or, when possible, under the high mediation of a council of the church. The place where ambassadors met, or where important treaties were drawn up, or where an important convention was officially or publicly executed, must in the Middle Ages be a place consecrated to religion, whether it be a church, a chapel, a sacristy, an episcopal palace, the great hall of an abbey, or the lighted choir of a cathedral church.[26] As an innovation in this respect Philip IV (1285–1314) of France sometimes received important embassies in his royal residence, the Louvre.[27]

Co-ordinate with papal influence in negotiating and executing treaties was the influence of churchmen in diplomatic negotiations, due partly to the fact that only churchmen (or at least few laymen) could read and write and keep records and partly to the fact that churchmen commanded great respect and influence in their respective communities. The more important an embassy, the higher the rank of ecclesiastical officials that accompanied it; at times all the diplomatic commissioners were clerics. In signing diplomatic documents bishops and clerics, as members of the first estate, had precedence over laymen. Every diplomatic deputation contained a priest with the special title of "chaplain"; it was his rôle to take charge of the religious ceremonies connected with the negotiation and conclusion of treaties. Ambassadorial interviews, the conclusion of treaties, and discussions between several crowned heads were usually placed under the patronage and supreme direction of a prelate, preferably the bishop of the diocese in which the interview or negotiations occurred. Although the prelate did not take part in the negotiations and his name was not mentioned directly in the protocol, his presence might be indicated in the other texts incident to the negotiations.[28]

[26] Funck-Bretano, "Le caractère religieux de la diplomatie du moyen âge," *Revue d'histoire diplomatique*, I, 115–17.

[27] *Ibid.*, p. 116. [28] *Ibid.*, pp. 117–18.

Once the diplomats had assembled, the negotiations were preceded by religious ceremonies or prayers. When the negotiations had been concluded and if the treaty was of great importance, the negotiators met in the choir of a church, richly decorated with flags and abundantly lighted. The bishops appeared in their pontifical garments. Mass was celebrated; all the negotiating officials were absolved from their sins in the name of the sovereign pontiff. In frequent cases the principal negotiators took communion; and, after touching the cross and the Gospels, each swore in the name of the prince he represented to observe faithfully the concluded treaty. The negotiators preferred to complete an important negotiation on a religious feast day.[29] The relations between two enemy crowns were re-established ordinarily under the mediation of the pope, who in this way naturally gave direction to the negotiations. Although Philip IV had been almost constantly in contest with the papacy, he did not neglect, in the course of his long and laborious discussions with the English king, to have recourse to pontifical legates.[30]

Since treaties between sovereigns secured their validity by virtue of being negotiated in the shadow of the church, surrounded by sacred ceremonies and confirmed by an oath, a religious vow, the pope also claimed the right to annul such treaties or free one of the parties from observing his oath (*Novit ille*).[31] The fact that the pope was an international figure, and not connected with the nations concerned, gave greater effectiveness to his claim. When, during the Hundred Years' War, Philip (1419–67), Duke of Burgundy, signed the solemn Treaty of Arras, September 21, 1435, and arranged under the direction of two papal legates to co-operate with Charles VII (1422–61) of France against the English, these two legates released Philip from the oath that he had taken in 1419 to support the Eng-

[29] *Ibid.*, p. 118. [30] *Ibid.*, p. 125.

[31] Mirbt, *op. cit.*, pp. 117–18; Bompard, *op. cit.*, pp. 5–6; Heffter, *Das europäische Völkerrecht der Gegenwart*, p. 20; Nys, *Les origins*, pp. 215, 269–70; W. Ernest Beet, article "Oath," in James Hastings, *Encyclopaedia of Religion and Ethics*, IX, 435.

lish.[32] Although it cannot be proved that Clement VII (1523–34) expressly released Francis I (1515–47) of France from his oath to observe the Treaty of Madrid which he signed, under duress, with Charles V (1519–58) in 1525,[33] the pope did even better: he formed a league with the French king and Venice against the emperor, Charles V, in order to free Italy from imperial domination.[34] Clement VI (1342–52) wrote to the Bishop of Verceil that conventions concluded to the prejudice to the states of the Holy See were null, even when confirmed by an oath, since an oath must not be a bond of iniquity.[35] The same pope granted to the confessors of the kings of France the power to free them from all vows that they found inconvenient to keep.[36] Julius II (1503–13) permitted Ferdinand (1479–1516) the Catholic to violate the obligation that he owed to Louis XII (1498–1515) of France. Charles V begged the pope to release him from his oath to maintain the privileges that were enjoyed by the Spanish Cortes.[37] Papal annulments of treaties were actually so frequent that later the negotiators took the precaution of stipulating that it would not be possible to be freed from one's oath by Rome.[38] The most significant precaution taken by negotiators against papal annulment of oaths accompanying the signing of a treaty occurred in 1648, when the Catholic and

[32] Nys, *Les origins*, pp. 267–69; Lavisse, *Histoire de France depuis les origins jusqu'à la Révolution*, Vol. IV, Part II, p. 78; C. W. Oman, *Political History of England from the Accession of Richard II to the Death of Richard III*, pp. 275–76, 321–23; Leonard V. D. Owen, *The Connection between England and Burgundy during the First Half of the Fifteenth Century*, pp. 55, 71–72; article "Philippe Bourgogne," in Hoefer, *Nouvelle biographie générale*, XXXIX, 983.

[33] Hergenröther, *op. cit.*, III, 430, n. 1; Pastor, *Geschichte der Päpste*, Vol. IV, Part II, p. 208, n. 3; Bompard, *op. cit.*, p. 6.

[34] Nys, *Les origins*, pp. 215–16; Pastor, *op. cit.*, Vol. IV, Part 2, pp. 208–11; Lavisse, *op. cit.*, Vol. V, Part 2, pp. 48–51.

[35] Nys, *Les origins*, p. 215.

[36] Nys, *Les origins*, p. 215. For underlying political reasons for this policy see Hergenröther, *op. cit.*, III, 286–90, 297–98; Wright, *op. cit.*, p. 110.

[37] Hume, *Spain, Its Greatness and Decay, 1479–1788*, p. 82; Klüber, *Europäisches Völkerrecht*, I, 250, n. *b*.

[38] Bompard, *op. cit.*, p. 6; Nys, *Les origins*, p. 271; Klüber, *op. cit.*, I, 250–51.

Protestant princes that signed the Peace of Westphalia agreed that the treaty was to stand regardless of papal protests.[39]

In medieval international relations, canon law and the decisions of the pope were the only authority. Sovereigns and their lay advisers did not, as yet, have any consciousness of their reciprocal relations as leaders and members of individual states in an international political society. The community of religious belief between states was the only bond of union. The Holy See was the sole superior power that had to be obeyed by the kings, princes, and Christian people. The popes were the judges of the law between sovereigns; they gave orders to terminate wars and to submit the disputes in question to the papal tribunal, as when Innocent III in 1199 ordered Philip Augustus (1180–1223) of France and Richard I (1189–99) of England to stop their wars and submit their difference to him.[40] During the Hundred Years' War the popes intervened frequently on behalf of the kings of France, and in the fifteenth century continually exhorted the kings of both England and France to terminate their horrible struggle.[41]

The popes disposed of territories and settled disagreements resulting from the right of occupation and discovery. Alexander VI (1492–1503), by establishing the papal lines of demarcation of 1493 and 1494, partitioned the colonial world between the Portuguese and the Spanish.[42] Such a remarkable exercise of papal secular power had numerous precedents. Alexander II (1061–73) had blessed William the Conqueror's (1066–87) inva-

[39] See below, chaps. iv–x.

[40] Adams, *op. cit.*, p. 385; Lavisse, *op. cit.*, Vol. III, Part 1, pp. 119–20; Bompard, *op. cit.*, p. 6.

[41] Lingard, *op. cit.*, III, 114, 115, 128, 149–50, 161–62, 176, 183–84, 515; IV, 46–47; *Cambridge Medieval History*, VII, 345, 347, 357, 365, 579; *Catholic Encyclopedia*, II, 431; IV, 23; VI, 799; VIII, 19; XV, 217; Nys, *Les origins*, pp. 266–67; Jenkins, *Papal Efforts for Peace under Benedict XII, 1334–1342*, pp. 26–69.

[42] Hergenröther, *op. cit.*, III, 358; Pastor, *op. cit.*, Vol. III, Part 1, pp. 619–22; Abbott, *The Expansion of Europe*, I, 99–101; Bourne, *Essays in Historical Criticism*, pp. 193–217; also in *Yale Review*, I, 35–55; Supan, *Die territoriale Entwicklung der europäischen Kolonien*, pp. 14–18; Nys, *Les origins*, pp. 370–72.

sion of England in 1066, though the English king rejected the idea of feudal dependency on the pope.[43] Adrian IV (1154–59) disposed of Ireland as though it belonged to him and gave Henry II (1154–89) of England permission to conquer it. This grant was later renewed by Alexander III (1159–81).[44] Some authorities state that in gratitude for help against Frederick Barbarossa (1155–90) Pope Alexander III (1159–81) invested Venice with the dominion of the sea by presenting to the doge a ring as a symbol of the union of Venice and the sea, and that the pope instituted the celebrated national Festival of the Wedding of the doge to the Adriatic Sea.[45] This, however, is merely a legend, developed undoubtedly to give added importance to the ring ceremony of the festival. This festival was celebrated long before the pontificate of Alexander III.[46] Nevertheless, the development of the legend is significant; its affirmation is in harmony with the current idea of papal power to bestow such authority. In 1264 Urban IV (1261–64) offered, as an incentive to King Ottokar II (1213–78) of Bohemia, full possession of all lands that he could conquer, through a crusade at the expense of the heathen Slavs on the Baltic Sea (Russians and Lithuanians), to the east of the lands of the Teutonic Order in Prussia.[47] In 1344 Clement VI (1342–52) bestowed on the Castilian prince Louis de la Cerda sovereignty over the Canary Islands,

[43] William of Malmesbury, *Chronicle of the Kings of England from the Earliest Period to the Reign of King Stephen*, p. 273; Stenton, *William the Conqueror and the Rule of the Normans*, p. 161; Hodgkin, *History of England from the Earliest Times to the Norman Conquest*, pp. 475–76; Adams, *op. cit.*, p. 49; James F. Loughlin, article "Alexander II," in *Catholic Encyclopedia*, I, 286; *Cambridge Medieval History*, VI, 554.

[44] Roger of Wendover, *op. cit.*, I, 523; Nys, *Les origins*, pp. 369–70; Bompard, *op. cit.*, p. 7, n. 3; E. A. D'Alton, "Ireland," *Catholic Encyclopedia*, VIII, 101; Arthur W. Clerigh, "Adrian IV," *ibid.*, I, 158–59; Curtis, *History of Medieval Ireland*, pp. 68–69; Dunlop, *Ireland from the Earliest Times to the Present Day*, p. 27.

[45] Smith, *The Seven Ages of Venice*, p. 70; Brown, *Venice, an Historical Sketch of the Republic*, pp. 110–11; Nys, *Les origins*, pp. 379–80; A. J. Valentinelli (Neher), article "Venedig" in Wetzer and Welte, *op. cit.*, XII, 657–58.

[46] A. J. Valentinelli (Neher), *op. cit.*, XII, 657–58; see also H. Reuter, *Geschichte Alexanders III.*, III, 328–29.

[47] Lorenz, *Geschichte König Ottokars II. von Böhmen und seine Zeit*, p. 264; Bompard, *op. cit.*, p. 7, n. 3, gives the date as 1260.

with the title of a prince of Fortunia, in consideration of an annual tribute, although Louis was not able actually to secure possession thereof in the face of the later activities of the Portuguese.[48] The Portuguese prince Henry the Navigator (1394–1460) demanded of Martin V (1417–31) the investiture of the Portuguese discoveries. Compliance with this request occurred under Eugene IV (1431–47), who in 1443 granted the Portuguese all the lands that were to be discovered from Cape Bojadore and Cape Non (in northwest Africa) to the mainland of India. This was confirmed by Nicholas V (1447–55) in 1454, on consideration that Christianity should be introduced in these lands.[49] In 1452 Nicholas V, by virtue of his apostolic authority, granted to Alphonso V (1438–81) of Portugal the right of attacking, subjugating, and reducing to perpetual servitude Saracens, the pagans, and the other infidel enemies of Christ; he permitted the king to seize and appropriate their property.[50]

4. THE POWERS OF CHURCH COUNCILS

International jurisdiction was claimed also by church councils, which could judge an emperor; in 1245 Frederick II was called by Innocent IV before the Council of Lyons and deposed, which deposition was not, however, effective.[51] A council could also depose a heretical prince and dispose of his states; the Fourth Lateran Council in 1215 gave the lands of Raymond VI (1195–1223) of Toulouse to Simon de Montfort.[52]

5. THE CHURCH AND ECCLESIASTICAL LANDS

Besides possessing the Papal States in full sovereignty, the church possessed, and could collect the income from, ecclesiasti-

[48] Nys, *Les origins*, p. 370; Hergenröther, *op. cit.*, III, 354–55; Pastor, *op. cit.*, I, 95; Bourne, *op. cit.*, p. 194, n. 1.

[49] Nys, *Les origins*, p. 370; Hergenröther, *op. cit.*, III, 355; Pastor, *op. cit.*, I, 632, n. 1.

[50] Nys, *Les origins*, p. 370; Bourne, *op. cit.*, pp. 194–95.

[51] Bompard, *op. cit.*, p. 7; Hergenröther, *op. cit.*, II, 590–91; *Cambridge Medieval History*, VI, 105, 108, 159, 356; Jastrow and Winter, *op. cit.*, II, 522–23; Georges Goyau, *op. cit.*, IX, 477.

[52] Bompard, *op. cit.*, p. 7; Hergenröther, *op. cit.*, II, 558–59; *Cambridge Medieval History*, VI, 27, 126; *Catholic Encyclopedia*, XII, 670.

cal lands in each Roman Catholic state. The church could collect tithes on the income from real property. It could raise taxes from the national clergy for crusading purposes. However, the effort of the papacy since the Third and Fourth Lateran Councils (1179, 1215) to secure the exemption of the clergy from state taxes, and culminating in the bull *Clercis laicos* of Boniface VIII in 1296, was not successful.[53]

6. SUMMARY OF PAPAL POLITICAL POWER

Thus, in the fields of public and private law and international relations in medieval times the papacy, although not unlimited, was dominant. Politics were an inseparable part of a unified theocracy. The papacy, although essentially a religious institution, was also a political power,

> having in each state a hierarchy of agents, with numerous privileges, enjoying considerable authority, having special tribunals, owning extensive property, claiming the right to raise taxes, the right to render justice in civil matters, of making laws directly applicable to the subjects of every prince.
>
> This political power, all the more easily obeyed since it was based on a religious faith widely spread, was the preponderating influence that directed the temporal affairs of all European nations, in both internal and external matters. It was with this extensive power of the popes over politics that all sovereigns had to reckon; against it all had to struggle.[54]

7. PAPAL DOMINATION TRANSITORY

It is beyond the purpose of this treatise to discuss whether the dominance of the medieval church over the states was fortunate or not. It is true, as Laurent points out,[55] that from the standpoint of governing efficiency, and broad social and moral outlook, the church was superior to the secular states, whose power during and after the Germanic invasions was based on

[53] Mirbt, *op. cit.*, pp. 208, 209; Bompard, *op. cit.*, p. 8; Hergenröther, *op. cit.*, II, 496, 607–8; Smith, *Age of the Reformation*, pp. 41–42; Seppelt, *Papstgeschichte*, II, 4–7; Willard, *The English Church and Lay Taxes in the Fourteenth Century* ("University of Colorado Studies," Vol. IV), pp. 217–25; Lunt, *The Valuation of Norwich*, pp. 1–169; Viollet, *Histoire des institutions politiques et administratives de la France*, II, 398–406.

[54] Bompard, *op. cit.*, 17.

[55] Laurent, *Etudes sur l'histoire de l'humanité*, Vol. VI: *La papauté et l'émpire*, p. 354; see also Hergenröther, *op. cit.*, III, 361–62; Vogüé, "Pope Leo XIII," *Forum*, XXII, 524.

physical force, and whose lack of constructive ideals and leadership only accentuated the social disorder following the decline of the Roman Empire. The church, through its governing authority, exercised over medieval society a moral, civilizing, and stabilizing influence. But by its very nature this dominance was transitory. The church was carrying on an educative process; it was exercising a tutelage that must terminate when the peoples had reached their majority. The church did not understand it thus; it continued to claim absolute power by virtue of divine law.[56]

Our discussion thus far has been concerned with papal claims and their application to the political life of medieval Europe. The remaining chapters of this treatise will show how, coincident with the internal decline of the church and the papacy, the secular states, becoming more conscious of their power, rejected the claims of the papacy to control their internal and external affairs, and put into practice the theory of secularized politics. We are dealing here with a long struggle, the papacy gradually declining in political power but continuing to assert its claims to political authority for many centuries—in fact, until the third decade of the twentieth century. On the other hand, during these half-dozen centuries the secular states effectively increase their control over politics. The states themselves determine the scope and objectives of politics. The states regulate their own internal affairs and even control religious matters when reasons of state require it, and the states regulate their own international life regardless of papal attitudes and protests.

8. APPENDIX: PAPAL DECREES CONCERNING PAPAL AUTHORITY OVER SECULAR AFFAIRS

The most important papal decrees are the following:

1. By Innocent III (1198–1216): *Solitae* (1200); *Venerabilem* (1202); *Novite ille* (1204); the bull *Etsi carissimus in* (August 24, 1215), which annulled the Great Charter.

2. By Innocent IV (1243–54): *Ad apostolicae* (1245).

[56] Laurent, *op. cit.*

3. By Boniface VIII (1294–1303): *Clericis laicos* (1296); *Ausculta fili* (1301); *Unam sanctam* (1302).

4. By Benedict XI (1303–4): *Quod olim* (1304).

5. By Clement V (1305–14): *Meruit* (1306); *Romani pontificis* (1311); *Pastoralis* (1311).

6. By John XXII (1316–34): *Si futrum* (1316); *De consuetudine* (1322).

7. Most important of all, the bull *In coena domini*, found as early as the pontificate of Honorius III (1216–27) and Gregory IX (1227–49), published annually after the pontificate of Urban V (1362–70) until its publication was discontinued by Clement XIV (1769–74) in 1770, and finally abrogated by Pius IX (1846–78) in the constitution *Apostolicae Sedis* (1869).[57]

[57] See the following: Nys, "Le droit international et la papauté," *Revue de droit international,* X, 510–13; Phillimore, *Commentaries upon International Law,* II, 206–17; Bompard, *op. cit.*, p. 4; Mirbt, *op. cit.*, pp. 175–78, 183, 196–97, 208–9, 210, 211, 211–12, 455–56; in *Catholic Encyclopedia*, VII, 718, article "*In coena domini*," by John Prior; VIII, 14, article "Innocent III," by Michael Ott; I, 127–28, article "*Ad apostolicae*," by M. Riordan; IV, 50, article "*Clericis laicos*," by J. F. Laughlin; II, 112, 666, articles "*Ausculta fili*," by M. Riordan, and "Boniface VIII," by Thomas Oestreich; XV, 126–27, article "*Unam sanctam*," by J. P. Kirsch; Wright, *op. cit.*, pp. 18–50.

Chapter Two

THE DECLINE OF PAPAL CONTROL OF POLITICS

I. THE SPIRITUAL AND MORAL DECLINE OF THE PAPACY

THE papacy could keep control of politics only so long as it remained strong and the European monarchies remained weak. Papal control of secular affairs in the late Middle Ages had often been resented by the monarchs and their supporters; there had been frequent clashes over opposing claims to authority. When, in the fourteenth and fifteenth centuries, the papacy degenerated spiritually and morally, the states were aggressively active in asserting their independence of the church in political affairs, and even assumed control of religious affairs as well. During the Babylonian captivity of the church, the Great Schism, and the era of church councils the papacy declined spiritually and morally; this circumstance gave the aggressive secular rulers an opportunity to assert their independence of the papacy in political affairs and also to assume increasing control of religious matters.

During the Babylonian captivity (1309–77) the papacy was not at Rome but at Avignon, on the southeastern border of France in the Rhone Valley. The French kings dominated and directed papal policy. This roused nationalist opposition in other Roman Catholic countries and undermined the universal, international position of the papacy. Numerous criticisms were directed against the popes, owing to the extravagance and luxury of their court, the increase in papal financial exactions, and papal efforts to further personal and family interests. The theologians at the courts of the secular powers criticized the church and its broad claims; the princes rejected papal claims to authority to judge secular matters and increasingly exercised state jurisdiction over ecclesiastical affairs.[1]

This decline in papal influence was intensified when an attempt was made to take the papacy back to Rome and keep it there. This led to the Great Schism (1378–1417), when for a time there were two popes, a Roman pope and a French pope at Avignon. An effort to heal the Schism by the General Church Council (Synod) of Pisa (1409) resulted in the creation of a third pope, a conciliar pope being added to the other two. It was not until 1417 that a second council, meeting at Constance (1414–18), healed the Schism and once more united Roman Catholic Christendom.

But the Schism had done irreparable damage. It ruined the unity of Roman Christendom. Some nations adhered to one pope; some to the other. The laity, already overburdened, now had two papal courts to maintain. Neither the Roman pope nor the anti-pope conducted himself in an exemplary manner, giving offense by various policies and acts. Each pope, to procure needed revenues, imposed crushing burdens on the churches of the lands obedient to him, or resorted to the sale of church offices. In many dioceses there was doubt as to which of the two bishops (appointed by the two opposing popes) was the legal incumbent. Everywhere could be heard not only complaints from the people against this situation but doubts, and even denials, that the papacy was a divine institution. Learned doctors of law at the University of Paris (such as Heinrich von Langenstein, vice-chancellor, and Jean Charles Gerson) and Cardinal Francesco Zabarella expressed the opinion that only a general council, which is superior to a pope, could heal the Schism or reform the church. This doctrine was maintained also

[1] Pastor, *Geschichte der Päpste*, I, 67–119; Hergenröther, *Handbuch der allgemeinen Kirchengeschichte*, III, 1–50, 61–64; Seppelt, *Papstgeschichte*, II, 9–36; Chénon, *Histoire des rapports*, pp. 113–17; Flick, *Decline of the Medieval Church*, I, 59–245; Hergenröther, article "Avignon," in Wetzer and Welte, *Kirchenlexikon*, I, 1758–59; J. P. Kirsch, article "Reformation," in *Catholic Encyclopedia*, XII, 701; Goyau, *Histoire religieuse*, Vol. VI, in Hanotaux, *Histoire de la nation française*, pp. 280–86, 287–91.

by the Council of Basel (1431–49). A secular ruler, the Emperor Sigismund of Germany (1410–37), had been most influential in persuading the Pisan or conciliar pope, John XXIII (1410–15), to summon the Council of Constance. In many other respects the power of the secular rulers was enlarged at the expense of the ecclesiastical authority and privileges.[2]

Church reform, so imperatively needed after the devastating, blighting influence of the Babylonian captivity and the Great Schism, was not successfully undertaken by either the popes or the councils of Basel (1431–49) and Ferrara-Florence (1438–45), two further councils called to institute reform. Between 1450 and 1521 the popes concerned themselves less with religious affairs than with such Renaissance activities as humanism, the promotion of art and science, the collection of books, manuscripts, works of art, and precious gems, and the building of libraries and palaces. The pontiffs were deeply concerned with the enrichment of their relatives, and especially with Italian and European politics, the aggrandizement of the Papal States. Their neglect of their duties as spiritual leaders was reflected in the general degradation of the clergy. Neither the popes nor the clergy could check the decline that made possible the disruptive Reformation movement.[3]

2. THE STATE AND ITS CONTROL OF RELIGIOUS AFFAIRS BEFORE THE REFORMATION

Coincident with the decline of the papacy in religious and moral influence in the fourteenth and fifteenth centuries, the

[2] Pastor, *op. cit.*, I, 120–227; also article "Papacy," in *Encyclopaedia Britannica* (14th ed.), XVII, 208; Hergenröther, *Handbuch*, III, 62–66, 96–195; Chénon, *op. cit.*, pp. 117–36; Seppelt, *op. cit.*, II, 37–51; Kaser, *Deutsche Geschichte im Ausgang des Mittelalters*, II, 358; Louis Salembier, article "Schism," in *Catholic Encyclopedia*, XIII, 539–41; J. P. Kirsch, article "Reformation," *Catholic Encyclopedia*, XII, 701; Wurm, article "Schisma," in Wetzer and Welte, *op. cit.*, X, 1794–1805; Flick, *op. cit.*, II, 3–397; Goyau, *op. cit.*, pp. 295–304.

[3] Pastor, *op. cit.*, I, 317–25, 335–58, 513–70; II, 23–38, 210–14, 318–54, 655–710; III, Part I, 3–203, 284–99, 317–20, 519–31, 562–656; III, Part II, 896–1041; IV, Part I, 3–8, 55–77, 199–246, 350–558, 608–9; Chénon, *op. cit.*, pp. 135–36; Hergenröther, *op. cit.*, III, 197–252, 257–306; Seppelt, *op. cit.*, II, 51–89; Flick, *op. cit.*, II, 398–483; J. P. Kirsch, article "Reformation," *Catholic Encyclopedia*, XII, 700–701.

nations of western Europe were evolving legal theories of national independence and self-sufficiency. When at the Council of Constance the delegates voted according to nationalities, the medieval idea of unity had come to an end.[4] Hereafter, the nations of France, England, and Spain, and the states of Germany and other western European countries definitely formulated new theories of power. These governments asserted the modern theory of state sovereignty that the state must be absolute and supreme in controlling all domains of human activity. The bases of this assertion lay in the old Roman law, emphasized anew during the Renaissance, and the formulation of the theory of the divine right of kings.[5] Secular society was being permeated with a growing feeling of self-reliance, an increasing claim to full political power. The secular princes declared their desire to have absolute control over their own temporal affairs and also to exert authority over the church and its affairs. The princes had overcome the opposition of the feudal lords; they had restricted the autonomy of the cities; and it was a natural next step to demand that the clergy should also become submissive to state authority.[6] The princes were supported in their designs by writings of such thinkers as Marsiglius of Padua (1270–1342), who, in his *Defensor pacis*, demanded full subordination of the church to the state. During the era of the Great Schism and the church councils, the idea influenced not merely the temporal rulers but also the clergy.[7]

[4] Wylie, *The Council of Constance to the Death of John Huss*, pp. 63–65; Andreas, *Deutschland vor der Reformation*, p. 29; Hergenröther, *op. cit.*, III, 146; Barry, *The Papal Monarchy*, pp. 58–59.

[5] Gierke, *Political Theories of the Middle Age*, pp. 92–95; Pastor, *op. cit.*, II, 103–4; Hergenröther, *op. cit.*, III, 61–62, 294–301; Hill, *History of Diplomacy*, I, 374–75; Kaser, *op. cit.*, II, 245–58, 350, 354, 358; Chénon, in Lavisse and Rambaud, *Histoire générale*, III, 343–44; Figgis, *The Divine Right of Kings*, pp. 1–16, 38–176; Allen, *A History of Political Thought in the Sixteenth Century*, pp. 268–70, 367–93; Esmein, *Cours élémentaire d'histoire du droit française*, pp. 381–85, 390–92.

[6] Kaser, *op. cit.*, II, 376; J. P. Kirsch, article "Reformation," in *Catholic Encyclopedia*, XII, 701.

[7] Previté-Orton, *The Defensor pacis of Marsiglius of Padua*, Introduction, pp. xvii–xxiv; Figgis, *op. cit.*, pp. 28–29; Kaser, *op. cit.*, II, 377; Murray, *The History of Political Science from Plato to the Present*, pp. 81–83, 86–87; L. Salambier, article "Marsiglius of

In harmony with such ideas and tendencies the states, during the Great Schism and the era of church councils, not only restricted the power of the ecclesiasts over secular matters but even assumed control over ecclesiastical affairs themselves. They limited clerical privileges, restricted ecclesiastical taxing powers, deprived the church of its properties, and tried to make the income of the church and the monasteries dependent on the will of the state.[8] Even before the Babylonian captivity the English government enacted the Statute of Mortmain (1279), forbidding (without royal license) the alienation of land from the jurisdiction of the civil power by appropriating it to religious purposes. The withdrawing of land from the obligation to pay taxes and feudal dues was thus checked. In spite of the extravagant claims of Boniface VIII in his bulls *Clericis laicos* and *Unam sanctam*, the English and French monarchs continued to tax the clergy and regulate church affairs. The Statutes of Provisors (1351 and 1390) forbade appointment to English benefices by the pope, and the Statutes of Praemunire (1353, 1366, 1393) took away the right of the English subjects to appeal cases from English courts to the papal court. To be sure, these statutes were not fully executed, and they did not correct the abuses at which they were aimed; but the mere enactment thereof and their partial observance indicate the tendency toward the primacy of the state; they signify that the state was beginning to assume control of church affairs.[9]

The humiliating consequences of the era of the Great Schism

Padua," in *Catholic Encyclopedia*, IX, 719–20; Wurm, article "Marsilius von Padua," in Wetzer and Welte, *op. cit.*, VIII, 907–11; Sander, article "Marsiglius von Padua," in Herzog-Hauck, *Realencyklopädie*, XII, 368–71.

[8] Hergenröther, *op. cit.*, III, 63–66, 295–301.

[9] Smith, *Age of the Reformation*, pp. 41–42; Adams and Stephens, *Select Documents of English Constitutional History*, pp. 71–72, 117–21, 123–24, 150–52, 156–59; Tout, *History of England from the Accession of Henry III to the Death of Edward III*, pp. 377–78, 426; Oman, *History of England from the Accession of Richard II to the Death of Richard III*, pp. 120–21; Lingard, *History of England*, III, 254–65, 538; Capes, *The English Church in the Fourteenth and Fifteenth Centuries*, pp. 89, 91, 161, 170; Charles W. Sloane, articles "Provisors" and "Mortmain," *Catholic Encyclopedia*, XII, 516; X, 580; Herbert Thurston, article "England," *Catholic Encyclopedia*, V, 440.

were manifested in the concessions to the secular rulers made by the popes in various concordats with France in 1516, and with the German emperor in 1448, and especially in the concessions made to many German princes and to the Spanish monarchs. It was necessary for the papacy to make these concessions because it needed political allies. It had lost its prestige as spiritual ruler of the world and wished to maintain its political influence as an Italian and European power.

When, in 1516, Leo X (1513–21) signed the concordat of Bologna with Francis I (1515–47), the French kings were granted the right of presenting candidates for the higher church offices, the pope having the right of approval.[10] To be sure, this concordat abrogated the unilateral Pragmatic Sanction of Bourges (1438), whereby the French king had controlled church affairs to an even greater extent,[11] and it was necessary for Francis I to coerce the parlement of Paris and the Sorbonne to accept the concordat.[12] But the influence of the Pragmatic Sanction of Bourges persisted as an effective factor in the demand for Gallican (or French) church liberties.[13] However, after the concordat of 1516 had been signed, the French king had power to appoint more than six hundred archbishops, bishops, and abbots, who controlled lands, the incomes of which approached that of the state itself.[14] The French king was master of the French church and could exert an influence in matters of belief.[15] Unquestionably, after receiving such concessions, it

[10] Pastor, *op. cit.*, IV, Part I, 580–82; Hergenröther, *op. cit.*, III, 292, 297; Chénon, *op. cit.*, 138; Barry, *The Papacy and Modern Times*, pp. 96–97; Leo A. Kelley, *Catholic Encyclopedia*, IV, 203; Lavisse, *Histoire de France depuis les origins*, V, Part I, 253–54; Esmein, *op. cit.*, pp. 713–15; Smith, *op. cit.*, pp. 42–43; Goyau, *op. cit.*, pp. 326–28.

[11] Pastor, *op. cit.*, I, 342–43; Hergenröther, *op. cit.*, III, 292, 295–97; Chénon, *op. cit.*, pp. 129–32, 138–43; Nys, *Les origins*, pp. 31–43; *Cambridge Modern History*, I, 388; Creighton, *History of the Papacy*, V, 263–66; Esmein, *op. cit.*, pp. 711–12; Smith, *op. cit.*, pp. 42–43.

[12] Pastor, *op. cit.*, IV, Part I, 566–88; Hergenröther, *op. cit.*, III, 297; Esmein, *op. cit.*, p. 716.

[13] Hergenröther, *op. cit.*, III, 728.

[14] Pastor, *op. cit.*, IV, Part I, 589.

[15] *Ibid.*, pp. 589–91; Lavisse, *op. cit.*, VI, Part I, 258–59; Lavisse and Rambaud, *op. cit.*, IV, 175.

was to the advantage of the French kings to remain Catholic; however, as will be shown later in this chapter, the French monarchs abused the privileges granted them in the concordat.[16]

Long before the concordat of 1516 had been concluded with France, the papacy, through its superior diplomatic skill, and by exploiting the lack of unanimity of the German princes and the selfishness of the emperor Frederick III (1440–93), was able to negotiate the concordat of Vienna (1448), which was designed to regulate the religious affairs of the German Empire. Unlike the French concordat, the concordat of Vienna did not greatly restrict the rights of the church, but guaranteed to the cathedral and monastic chapters the right freely to elect bishops and abbots, gave the papacy the right of confirming such elections, and re-established papal financial rights.[17]

Nevertheless, the concordat of Vienna did not prevent Frederick III from subsequently securing great powers of nominating candidates for bishoprics and other benefices. The papacy was likewise compelled to make concessions to many of the individual German princes and secure their support by granting them a share in filling benefices and power to tax and judge the clergy. In Brandenburg, Jülich-Cleve, Saxony, the Austrian hereditary lands, in the lesser German states, and the free cities the secular power secured influence in the administration of church lands. The temporal rulers, before the Reformation, increasingly controlled church affairs, thus preparing the way for the confiscation of church lands in Reformation times. During the era of the church councils (1409–49) the need for reform was so great that only the state seemed capable of adequately looking after church interests. With the consent of the church the German secular rulers tried to root out clerical avarice, immorality, and neglect of duty. They forbade the sale of the sac-

[16] Pastor, *op. cit.*, IV, Part I, 590; Lavisse and Rambaud, *op. cit.*, IV, 174.

[17] Hergenröther, *op. cit.*, III, 238; Andreas, *op. cit.*, pp. 32–33; *Catholic Encyclopedia*, IV, 203; Hergenröther, in Wetzer and Welte, *op. cit.*, III, 826–28; G. Voigt, article "Frederick III," *Allgemeine deutsche Biographie*, VII, 449; Kraus, *Deutsche Geschichte im Ausgang des Mittelalters*, I, 199–200; Smith, *op. cit.*, p. 45.

raments, regulated the charges for church services, used threats of force to elevate monastic life, and supervised and regulated the economic life of the monasteries.

The secular rulers and the German cities also assumed increasing control over affairs that had formerly been under the exclusive control of the church, such as matters pertaining to wills and marriage, the regulation of beggars, the care of the poor and sick, supervision of morals, social life, parochial and monastic education, and the rigorous prosecution of blasphemers. These states maintained purity of the faith by taking measures against religious improprieties, such as excesses in pilgrimages, the sale of indulgences, and belief in alleged miracles. It was no longer unusual for the temporal authorities to insist that their assent (*placet*) was necessary for the publication of ecclesiastical decrees. Some rulers, such as the dukes of Jülich and Berg, arranged religious thanksgiving and memorial services without consulting the ecclesiastical authorities. They even went so far as to determine religious ceremonial details, such as restricting the length of sermons or regulating the tolling of church bells. Although in many respects the administration of ecclesiastical affairs became an integral part of the administration of the secular state, the sovereigns had no intention of weakening the rights of the ecclesiastical authorities; the aim was to co-operate with the clergy in achieving church reform.[18]

By the end of the Middle Ages the church no longer exercised complete monopolistic control over education; efforts were already under way to restrict ecclesiastical supervision of schools. It was apparent that the state would become increasingly assertive in its control over education.[19]

In the fifteenth century the "Catholic Kings" of Spain skillfully exploited the circumstances of the times to achieve extensive control of church affairs. Ferdinand V (1479–1516) secured the right to nominate all the higher church officers and used the

[18] Kaser, *op. cit.*, II, 354–83; Andreas, *op. cit.*, pp. 33–34; Pastor, *op. cit.*, II, 616–19; Smith, *op. cit.*, pp. 45–46.

[19] Andreas, *op. cit.*, pp. 34–35.

Inquisition for political purposes; Ferdinand's prime minister, Cardinal Ximenez, conducted in Spain the most thoroughgoing reform of the church in pre-Reformation times.[20]

In Italy the secular powers assumed great responsibility in the administration of ecclesiastical matters, especially in Venice, Milan, Florence, and Naples. The papacy had to be willing to make such concessions in order to secure the political aid of the Italian states in regaining and keeping control of the Papal States during the uncertain times of the Babylonian captivity, the Great Schism, the era of the church councils, and the rivalries of the French and Spanish houses for dominance in Italy during the fifteenth and sixteenth centuries.[21]

3. THE REFORMATION AND STATE CONTROL OF THE CHURCH

The pre-Reformation tendencies in the direction of state control of church affairs were naturally heightened during the Reformation, not only in Protestant lands but in Catholic countries as well. In Germany, through the influence of Luther, the idea was applied that the right of ecclesiastical oversight belongs to the supreme territorial secular authority, this including provisions for state support of the ministry, for the maintenance of schools, and for the care of the poor. It was felt that only the state, through its supervision and final authority, could prevent the ecclesiastical abuses and excesses of the past. This idea was based on the Roman civil code. In other countries of the Reformation (in Scandinavia, Switzerland, Holland, England) the church became more or less subject to the state.[22] In England the Reformation under Henry VIII (1509–47) was a forcible reform of the church by the state. Henry VIII's wish was to make himself emperor and pope. In the later changes, in the time of Edward VI (1547–53) and Elizabeth (1558–1603), it

[20] Hergenröther, *op. cit.*, III, 297–98; Pastor, *op. cit.*, II, 623.

[21] Hergenröther, *op. cit.*, III, 42–46, 65, 298.

[22] Kaser, *op. cit.*, II, 1–31; Hergenröther, *op. cit.*, III, 432; Lindsay, *History of the Reformation*, I, 400–416; II, 7–9; Pfannkuche, *Staat und Kirche*, pp. 2–11; Waring, *The Political Theories of Martin Luther*, pp. 61–134.

was the state that determined religious institutions and practices.[23]

The Reformation led to caesaropapism in Catholic lands as well as in those breaking away from papal control. In France the state soon went beyond the powers granted by the concordat of 1516.

Before and during the Council of Trent (1545–63) complaints were made that the French secular power hindered the execution of papal rescripts; imposed, on its own authority, a tithe on the clergy; settled disputes concerning church benefices; and subjected church decrees to state approval.[24] Francis I tried to prevent the calling of the Council of Trent; that having failed, the French delegates assumed an arrogant, presumptuous attitude during the sessions of the Council and did their best to thwart its purpose. The Council's disciplinary decrees were condemned by the French government as being contrary to Gallican church liberties.[25] French ecclesiastical assemblies, which were usually held every two years, frequently requested the king and the Estates-General fully to recognize the decrees of the Council of Trent; but the third estate, represented by advocates, objected.[26] In the time of Louis XIII (1610–43) and Richelieu (1624–42) the French government fixed the place and date of the clerical assemblies, changed the course of the de-

[23] Fisher, *The History of England from the Accession of Henry VII to the Death of Henry VIII*, pp. 309–29; Pollard, *The History of England from the Accession of Edward VI to the Death of Elizabeth*, pp. 14–24, 66–79, 201–18, 354–72; Lingard, *op. cit.*, IV, 557–60; V, 19–23, 49–57, 91–123, 249–58; VI, 6–8; in *Catholic Encyclopedia*, articles "England" and "Henry VIII," V, 442–44, 445–49; VII, 223–75; Smith, *op. cit.*, pp. 288–94, 310, 329.

[24] Ehses, "Franz I. von Frankreich und die Konzilsfrage in den Jahren 1536–1539," *Römische Quartalschrift*, XII, 313; Hergenröther, *op. cit.*, III, 728.

[25] Ehses, "Franz I., etc.," *Römische Quartalschrift*, XII, 306–23; Hergenröther, *op. cit.*, III, 728; Pastor, *op. cit.*, VI, 61–62, 65–66, 76–77, 157–62, 169–70, 236–37, 362; J. P. Kirsch, article "Trent," *Catholic Encyclopedia*, XV, 30–35; Knöpfler, article "Concil von Trent," in Wetzer and Welte, *op. cit.*, XI, 2038–2115, especially col. 2114; Goyau, *op. cit.*, pp. 370, 392.

[26] Hergenröther, *op. cit.*, III, 728.

liberations, and forbade the holding of church assemblies and councils without royal permission.[27]

Louis XIV (1643–1715) regulated church affairs almost as if he were a Justinian. His parlementary courts and his Grand Council adjudicated all ecclesiastical affairs, except questions of dogma and purely spiritual matters. The church was treated with favor and enjoyed numerous privileges only by reason of yielding to the state all authority in temporal or mixed affairs.[28]

The culmination of state control of religious affairs in France occurred in 1790, when the National Constituent Assembly drew up and applied the Civil Constitution of the Clergy.[29]

In Spain the successors of Ferdinand the Catholic augmented royal control over ecclesiastical affairs. Charles V (king of Spain, 1516–56) secured a complete and permanent right of presentation and patronage for all archiepiscopal and episcopal offices in Spain. The Spanish state secured the right of appointing most of the other holders of profitable benefices. The state increased its power of supervising ecclesiastical jurisdiction. The royal authority tenaciously held the right of examining every papal decree concerning Spain and Naples, and to declare those decrees invalid that were contrary to the laws and customs of these kingdoms. Such offending papal decrees were merely withheld. The Spanish monarchy greatly increased the wealth of the church, and, with papal consent, taxed it for state purposes, often for crusades; and at times such income was diverted to other purposes. The Inquisition was also used to keep the Spanish clergy obedient to the state. Philip II (1556–98) misused the Inquisition for political purposes. Since two-thirds

[27] Lavisse and Rambaud, *op. cit.*, V, 345; Boudinhon, article "Laicization," *Catholic Encyclopedia*, VIII, 746.

[28] A. Boudinhon, "Laicization," *Catholic Encyclopedia*, VIII, 746; Lavisse and Rambaud, *op. cit.*, VI, 205–6; Lavisse, *op. cit.*, VII, Part II, 1–37, especially pp. 16, 17, 36–37; Hergenröther, *op. cit.*, IV, 19, 24–33; Esmein, *op. cit.*, pp. 734–37; Grant, *The French Monarchy, 1483–1789*, II, 55–57; Goyau, *op. cit.*, pp. 445–49.

[29] Hergenröther, *op. cit.*, IV, 281–83; Pastor, *op. cit.*, XVI, Part III, pp. 430–502; Goyau, *op. cit.*, pp. 504–10.

of the income resulting from its activities went to the state, the Inquisition became an important source of royal revenue.

Philip II enjoyed almost unrestricted sovereignty over the Spanish church. He interfered in many purely ecclesiastical affairs, greatly to the prejudice of church independence. At one time, in his effort to maintain royal authority over the Spanish church, he expelled a papal nuncio from the country. He was also partially successful in asserting similarly broad claims to ecclesiastical control in Milan, Naples, and Sicily. At the Council of Trent his royal agents fought to preserve royal control of the Inquisition, and he accepted the decrees of the Council of Trent in so far as they did not conflict with his regal rights.[30]

It is not the purpose of the author of this treatise to pursue any farther the phase of this subject that is concerned with state control of church affairs in Catholic lands, a tendency which, since the sixteenth century, has been carried on with increasing intensity not only in France and Spain but practically in all Catholic lands to the present time. The purpose of the writer in presenting this section of this chapter has been merely to indicate how state control of church affairs forms a part of the general subject—the secularization of politics, whereby medieval conditions have been reversed. Instead of the papacy determining the sphere of the activity of the states, and controlling them, the states, after the fifteenth century, increasingly asserted their authority to determine for themselves their sphere of activity. That is, they, in spite of repeated papal protests, conditioned the nature and scope of politics, making it include the regulation of church affairs whenever such action would increase the power and prestige of the states and overcome any check to their absolute power.

The remainder of this treatise will be concerned with an even more important aspect of the subject, the secularization of international politics.

[30] Pastor, *op. cit.*, VII, 362, 542–45; VIII, 279–331; IX, 253–58, 264–69; Hergenröther, *op. cit.*, III, 297–98, 732–33; Hume, *Spain, Its Greatness and Decay*, pp. 15–16, 82–83, 93–95, 128–30, 142–43, 172–73; *Cambridge Modern History*, I, 353–54, 355–56; II, 99.

4. THE STATE AND INTERNATIONAL POLITICS FROM THE FIFTEENTH TO THE SEVENTEENTH CENTURY

Along with the rise of the national states and the development of the absolute power of the kings there emerged the modern feeling that the state has interests that must be fostered regardless of all rival considerations, including religious, sacred, or ecclesiastical matters. Machiavelli's ideas that the state is an end in itself and that the end justifies the means were being adopted and applied. The two centuries from 1453 to 1648 were an era of keen international rivalries. The powers in their struggle for supremacy, or for mere existence (in their wars for self-realization or self-preservation), not only disregarded religious interests but furthered political interests at the cost of religion.

The emperor Charles V did not immediately attempt to crush the Lutheran religion, but temporized with it in order to deal more effectively with his great rival, the French house of Valois and its ally, the Ottoman Empire.[31] Religious interests did not seem to be of supreme importance—at least they could not be allowed to jeopardize the political interests of Charles. Even the popes seemed more intent on maintaining their political power in Italy than they were in crushing the Reformation movement.[32] Both Charles V and his devout son Philip II had to wage wars against the political pretensions of the pope in Italy. This happened during the Reformation movement, when religious interests should have transcended political considerations.[33] In many of the dynastic and international wars religion was merely a secondary consideration or was used as a screen for political ambitions at home and abroad. During the Reformation, when Charles V was trying to root out the Lutheran heresy in Germany, and while the popes were attempting to call

[31] Hergenröther, *op. cit.*, III, 407, 414–15, 436, 460–61, 464, 469–70, 481–82, 491–92; Pastor, *op. cit.*, IV, Part I, 333–40; IV, Part II, 177–94, 212–382, 437–59; Spahn, article "Charles V," *Catholic Encyclopedia*, III, 626–29.

[32] Pastor, *op. cit.*, V, 164–65, 205–6, 587–88, 594–98, 613, 624.

[33] Hergenröther, *op. cit.*, III, 430–32, 580; Pastor, *op. cit.*, IV, Part II, 212–382; VI, 382–443; Hume, *op. cit.*, 57–60, 119–21; Spahn, article "Charles V," *Catholic Encyclopedia*, III, 626; Kurth, article "Philip II," *Catholic Encyclopedia*, XII, 3.

the Council of Trent in order to unify at least all the Catholic powers in support of a united church, Francis I of France ceased to be guided by the interests of Catholicism at large and sought only the good of the French nation. He went so far as to make a political alliance with the infidel Suleiman the Magnificent (1520–66), sultan of the Turkish Empire, in order to have an effective ally against Charles V; and one clause of the treaty of 1536 even made provisions for the alliance of the pope with the sultan provided the pontiff ratified the agreement within eight months.[34] In 1540 Francis I persuaded the declining republic of Venice to detach herself from her alliance with Charles V and make a treaty of alliance with the Turks; this was done in spite of repeated papal efforts to dissuade Venice from such a policy.[35] Venice was merely stressing her trade in the Levant and was also fearful of the possibility of Hapsburg dominance in the Mediterranean.[36] The actions of France aroused general indignation at the time;[37] but by 1579 England was anxious to make a treaty of commerce and good will with Turkey, and by 1580 she had succeeded in her negotiations. The papacy had forbidden trade between Catholics and Turkey, and both Turkey and Protestant England were glad to make a commercial treaty, which was the first of many.[38] In 1602 the Netherlands, and in 1615 Austria, made similar treaties with the infidel Turks.[39]

[34] Zinkeisen, *Geschichte des osmanischen Reiches in Europa*, II, 759–61; Hammer-Purgstall, *Geschichte des osmanischen Reiches*, II, 122; La Jonquière, *Histoire de l'empire ottoman*, I, 174–75; Schevill, *History of the Balkan Peninsula*, p. 223; Egelhaff, *Deutsche Geschichte im sechzehnten Jahrhundert*, II, 309; Moritz Brosch, in *Cambridge Modern History*, III, 104–5; Bourrilly, "L'ambassade de la Forest et de Marillac à Constantinople, 1535–1538," *Revue historique*, LXXVI, 297–328; Lavisse, *op. cit.*, V, Part II, p. 79; George Goyau, article "France," *Catholic Encyclopedia*, VI, 170, also article "Francis I," *ibid.*, p. 208; Ehses, "Franz I., etc.," *Römische Quartalschrift*, XII, 311, 319–23.

[35] Zinkeisen, *op. cit.*, II, 796–808; Hammer-Purgstall, *op. cit.*, II, 163–64; Schevill, *op. cit.*, p. 224; Pastor, *op. cit.*, V, 209; Brosch, *op. cit.*, III, 115–17.

[36] Pastor, *op. cit.*, VIII, 541.

[37] Zinkeisen, *op. cit.*, II, 804–5; Egelhaaf, *op. cit.*, II, 309; Brosch, *op. cit.*, III, 104–5; *Catholic Encyclopedia*, VI, 208; Pastor, *op. cit.*, IX, 260.

[38] Pollard, *op. cit.*, pp. 389–90; Zinkeisen, *op. cit.*, III, 418–27; Hammer-Purgstall, *op. cit.*, II, 464; Sax, *Geschichte des Machtverfalls der Türkei*, p. 43.

[39] Zinkeisen, *op. cit.*, III, 654; IV, 265; Sax, *op. cit.*, p. 54.

In the twelfth and thirteenth centuries the popes had been able to rouse much of Catholic Christendom to undertake crusades against the infidel Seljukian Turks. But after the fall of Constantinople in 1453, the popes made vain appeals to the princes to undertake the expulsion of the Ottoman Turks; and for this action the pontiffs were merely suspected of greed for money.[40] The papacy had lost its spiritual leadership, it was treated merely as a secular power.[41]

However, one pope, Pius V (1566–72), in the face of tremendous difficulties, succeeded in uniting the Catholic maritime powers—Spain, Venice, and Genoa—to attack and defeat the Turks in the great naval battle of Lepanto in 1571.[42] The successor of Pius V, Gregory XIII (1572–85), tried to keep the anti-Turkish league intact and secure even greater victories over the infidel enemies of Christendom. But in 1573 Venice signed a separate treaty of peace with Turkey; this agreement virtually reversed the outcome of the battle of Lepanto; Venice ceded important lands and paid Turkey a large war indemnity, but retained valuable trading privileges.[43]

In 1580, in spite of vigorous papal opposition and in the face of papal effort to reorganize the anti-Turkish league, Philip II of Spain signed a nine months' truce with Turkey, renewed it for a year and later for five years—an agreement that lasted until the end of his reign. Philip took such action because he wished to be free to deal with the rebellious Netherlands; because he feared France, the ally of the Turks; and, above all, because he wished to keep his hands free in 1580 to take over the throne of

[40] Flick, *op. cit.*, II, 237, 402, 406, 415, 470; Pastor, *op. cit.*, II, 623–32; III, Part I, 256–79, 546–61; IV, Part I, 146–74; IV, Part II, 119–25, 129–31, 437–59; IX, 235—74; X, 381–94; Bréhier, article "Crusades," *Catholic Encyclopedia*, IV, 555.

[41] Flick, *op. cit.*, II, 415.

[42] Hergenröther, *op. cit.*, III, 627; Seppelt, *op. cit.*, II, 118–19; Pastor, *op. cit.*, VIII, 539–610; Zinkeisen, *op. cit.*, II, 930–34; Hammer-Purgstall, *op. cit.*, II, 419–24; Brosch in *Cambridge Modern History*, III, 134–35.

[43] Du Mont, *Corps universel diplomatique*, V, Part I, 218–19; Brosch in *Cambridge Modern History*, III, 137–38; Hammer-Purgstall, *op. cit.*, II, 426; Zinkeisen, *op. cit.*, II, pp. 934–35.

Portugal, his legal claim to the succession of that crown meeting with opposition from the Portuguese. Philip's truce with the Turks was, as Pastor says, "a further step toward the pursuit of private advantage without reference to general interests." All further efforts of Gregory XIII to revive the anti-Turkish league were futile. Venice feared it as a means of strengthening Spanish dominance in Italy; and, although Philip continued to collect from the Spanish church the *cruzada* (money for crusading purposes), he had no desire to embark on such an enterprise.[44]

Let us mention one final point as evidence of the disregard of the European states for papal political pretensions, namely, the fact that not only such Protestant powers as England, Holland, Sweden, and Denmark, but Catholic France, acquired colonies in the sixteenth and seventeenth centuries regardless of the monopoly on colonial rights granted by Alexander VI through the papal lines of demarcation.[45]

5. SUMMARY OF CHANGES IN THE POLITICAL OUTLOOK OF EUROPE FROM THE THIRTEENTH TO THE SEVENTEENTH CENTURY

In these four centuries a great change had taken place in the scope and objectives of European politics. Instead of the medieval idea of unity, with the objectives and destinies of the secular states being guided and controlled by the pope as divinely appointed chief of Christendom, the secular states were now pursuing their own interests and policies. State or secular interests transcended all other interests; the objective of the secular princes of expanding the power and prestige of the state, of maintaining state sovereign authority on the basis of Roman law, surpassed all other considerations, including religious inter-

[44] Pastor, *op. cit.*, IX, 235–74; Zinkeisen, *op. cit.*, III, 500–501, 507–8, 510; Jorga, *Geschichte des osmanischen Reiches*, III, 160–61.

[45] Abbott, *The Expansion of Europe, a Social and Political History of the Modern World, 1415–1789*, I, 327–57; Leroy-Beaulieu, *De la colonisation chez les peuples modernes*, I, 60–187; Supan, *Die territoriale Entwicklung der europäischen Kolonien*, pp. 46–60, 61–67, 75.

ests and claims as shaped by the papacy. The papacy, after its humiliations of the fourteenth and fifteenth centuries, had ceased to be a great moral force; it was stressing secular objectives in Italy, in Europe, and was treated by the European rulers as a mere secular power. Even dependable, loyal Catholic states, like Austria and Spain, waged war against the popes and refused to undertake crusades or to antagonize the Ottoman Empire if state interests demanded the signing of truces or commercial treaties with that empire.

The new system of state or secular control of religion and matters of conscience, which had been quite well developed by the sixteenth century, was not, however, given the final stamp of approval until the signing and execution of the Peace of Westphalia in the seventeenth century, when Catholic princes co-operated with the Protestant princes to regulate the ecclesiastical affairs of Germany in the great international Treaty of Westphalia, regardless of papal interests and in the face of papal protest. But before discussing that most important phase of this movement we must concern ourselves with the Peace of Augsburg as a forerunner of the Peace of Westphalia in the long movement called the "secularization of politics."

Chapter Three

THE PEACE OF AUGSBURG A STEP IN THE SECULARIZATION OF POLITICS

I. THE PEACE OF AUGSBURG INCOMPATIBLE WITH PAPAL THEORY

THE popes could never be expected to recognize as legal or permanent the Peace of Augsburg (September 25, 1555), which closed the era of sixteenth-century Lutheran wars in Germany. This Peace injured Catholic interests as follows: (1) it tolerated Lutheran princes and town councils and gave them the right to determine their own religion and that of those over whom they ruled; (2) it gave to the Lutheran princes of Germany legal title to those ecclesiastical lands (archbishoprics, bishoprics, abbacies) that they had held in 1552; (3) it sanctioned the fact that three of the imperial electors (Brandenburg, Saxony, the Palatinate) were heretics; (4) it granted the evangelical princes equality of rights with the Catholic princes for an indefinite period; (5) this treaty, a supposedly binding legal document, attempted to regulate church affairs and did so to the detriment of church interests.[1] To be sure, this Peace, merely corroborating the Peace of Passau (1552), which had closed the era of Lutheran wars in Germany (1547–52), was regarded by both Catholic and Protestant princes as a truce. Its terms were not final; a compromise was effected solely because both

[1] Ritter, "Der Augsburger Religionsfriede, 1555," *Historisches Taschenbuch*, I, 259–60; Gustav Wolf, *Der Augsburger Religionsfriede*, p. 170; Hergenröther, *Handbuch der allgemeinen Kirchengeschichte*, III, 496–97; Pastor, *Geschichte der Päpste seit dem Ausgang des Mittelalters*, VI, 564–67; Ritter, *Deutsche Geschichte im Zeitalter der Gegenreformation und des dreissigjährigen Krieges*, I, 79–88.

sides were worn out. The Catholic princes could not permanently accept the principle of parity in religious affairs; nevertheless, they feared that a continuance of the struggle might lead to a worsening of their own situation. Moreover, by waiting indefinitely some fortunate turn of affairs might enable the Catholic secular powers completely to crush the Protestants and fully to restore Catholic authority. The Lutheran princes, on the other hand, took great satisfaction in having achieved their political independence and the power to regulate religious affairs, and hoped ultimately to exclude Catholicism entirely from Germany.[2]

2. INEFFECTIVE PROTEST OF THE BISHOP OF AUGSBURG AGAINST THE PEACE

Against this compromise Peace there had been two protests: (1) that of Otto Truchsess von Waldburg, Bishop of Augsburg (1543–73); and (2) a private epistolary protest of Paul IV (1555–59) to Ferdinand, the king of Rome, who, as representative of his brother Charles V (1519–58), was responsible for the signing of the Peace of Augsburg.

Otto Truchsess, or the Cardinal of Augsburg, as he was usually called, was one of the most courageous and consistent defenders of undiminished church and papal rights in Germany. He had opposed the conciliatory policy of Charles V toward the German Protestants, and regarded him as being responsible for all mistakes made in Germany's affairs since the Schmalkald War (1547–52). Bishop Otto took part in various Reichstags and always vigorously defended the interests of the Catholic church; opposed all concessions to the Protestants by Emperor Charles V; and resisted all attempts on the part of the emperor and the secular princes to regulate ecclesiastical and religious affairs. He thought the papacy should withstand this last ac-

[2] *Cambridge Modern History*, III, 140; Maurenbrecher, "Beiträge zur deutschen Geschichte, 1555–1559," *Historische Zeitschrift*, L, 8; Ritter, "Der Augsburger Religionsfriede, 1555," *Historisches Taschenbuch*, I, 260; Ritter, *Deutsche Geschichte*, I, 81–85; Pastor, *op. cit.*, VI, 568, n. 1.

tion of the secular rulers, even through the use of force.[3] On March 23, 1555, in the early part of the sessions of the Diet of Augsburg, Bishop Otto presented to that body a most emphatic protest against the Religious Peace of Augsburg. He did this undoubtedly with the approval of Cardinal Morone, the cardinal legate at the Diet. In the protest Bishop Otto declared that, although he was in favor of peace, he must protest against the Peace in order to maintain the full rights of the pope and the church intact. He would rather lose his life and all else that is earthly than refrain from doing his duty as he saw fit in this respect.[4]

This declaration of Bishop Otto was the only formal protest made against the Peace, but it called forth such consternation and confusion at first that it was feared the Reichstag or Diet would be dissolved. There arose rumors that Otto, who, immediately after depositing his protest, had gone to Rome as cardinal to help elect a new pope to succeed Julius III (1550–55), was planning to negotiate an alliance between the pope and the emperor in order to break the Peace of Augsburg and renew the war against the Protestants.[5] But the rulers of Austria and Bavaria succeeded in persuading the other ecclesiastical princes

[3] Stauffer, article "Otto Truchsess von Waldburg," *Allgemeine deutsche Biographie*, XXIV, 636–37; Druffel, *Briefe und Akten zur Geschichte des sechzehnten Jahrhunderts*, IV, 604, 607; Specht, *Geschichte der ehemahligen Universität Dillingen*, p. 5; Specht, "Cardinal Otto Truchsess von Waldburg, Bischof von Augsburg (1543–1573)," *Beilage der Augsburger Postzeitung*, 1897, No. 51, pp. 354–55; Duhr, "Die Quellen zu einer Biographie des Kardinals Otto Truchsess von Waldburg," *Historisches Jahrbuch*, VII, 188; A. Weber, in Wetzer and Welte, *op. cit.*, XII, 115; Janssen, *Geschichte des deutschen Volkes*, III, 724.

[4] Lehenmann, *De Pace Religionis acta publica et originalia*, pp. 24–25; Braun, *Geschichte der Bischöfe von Augsburg*, III, 433–34, contains the protest; also condensed in Duhr, "Die Quellen . . . . ," *Historisches Jahrbuch*, VII, 194–95; Bucholtz, *Geschichte der Regierung Ferdinand des Ersten*, VII, 178; Egelhaaf, *Deutsche Geschichte im sechzehnten Jahrhundert bis zum Augsburger Religionsfrieden*, II, 591; A. Weber, "Cardinal Otto Truchsess von Waldburg," *Historische-politische Blätter*, CX, 785; Janssen, *op. cit.*, III, 788; Specht, "Cardinal Otto Truchsess," *Beilage der Augsburger Postzeitung*, 1897, p. 355 (wrongly gives the date as December 23 instead of March 23); Pastor, *op. cit.*, VI, 564; Menzel, *Neuere Geschichte der Deutschen*, II, 260–61.

[5] Maurenbrecher, *Karl V und die deutschen Protestanten, 1545–1555*, p. 331; Druffel, *op. cit.*, IV, 610; Specht, "Cardinal Otto Truchsess," *Beilage der Augsburger Postzeitung*, 1897, p. 355; Janssen, *op. cit.*, III, 788; Braun, *op. cit.*, III, 434.

to ignore Otto's protest, and saw to it that the Lutheran princes understood the actual situation.[6] Ferdinand, the brother of Charles V, sent a message to Cardinal Otto taking him to task for registering such a protest. He thought that the Cardinal, in his capacity of imperial commissioner, should think of extinguishing the existing fire rather than rekindling it. On the contrary, through his protest, he had accentuated the already existing tragedy.[7] Thus, in spite of the protest of Cardinal Otto, the effort of the German secular and ecclesiastical princes to regulate ecclesiastical and religious affairs went on unchecked. But the protest was long remembered, and in 1648 it was used as a pattern for a similar protest against the Peace of Westphalia by the Archbishop of Salzburg.[8]

3. PAUL IV AND THE PEACE OF AUGSBURG

Far more significant than the protest of Cardinal Otto is the papal attitude toward the Peace of Augsburg. Pope Paul IV (1555–59) in a letter of December 18, 1555, had expressed to King Ferdinand his deep disappointment over the Augsburg settlement, which was contrary to the wishes of the pope, the king of Germany, and all Catholics.[9] On the same date Paul wrote to Wolfgang, Bishop of Passau, deploring the Augsburg settlement, alluding to it as a disgraceful example of unbridled wilfulness.[10] Similar letters were written on the same day to Cardinal Madruzzo (prince bishop of Trent), to four German archbishops, to five German bishops, to Duke Albert V of Bavaria, and to various members of the Hapsburg house.[11]

But it was not until March, 1558, that Paul IV took any definite and vigorous action concerning the Peace of Augsburg, and

[6] Druffel, *op. cit.*, IV, 610; Janssen, *op. cit.*, III, 788, n. 2; Braun, *op. cit.*, III, 434.

[7] Braun, *op. cit.*, III, 434–35; Bucholtz, *op. cit.*, VII, 179.

[8] See below, chap. xi.

[9] Raynaldus, *Annales ecclesiastici ab anno MCXCVIII ubi Card. Baronius desinit, Opus Posthumum*, Vol. XXI, Part II, Doc. 51; Pastor, *op. cit.*, VI, 586, n. 1.

[10] Raynaldus, *op. cit.*, Doc. 53; Pastor, *op. cit.*, VI, 568, n. 1.

[11] Pastor, *op. cit.*, VI, 568, n. 2.

then only (incidentally) in connection with some special problems arising out of the resignation of Charles V from the emperorship. Moreover, it should be mentioned, in anticipation, that the two successors of Paul IV, namely, Pius IV (1559–65) and Pius V (1566–72), owing to practical considerations, carried out a policy of inactivity with reference to the Peace.

Early in 1558 Charles V formally abdicated as emperor of the Holy Roman Empire. When on March 24, 1558, the electors, meeting at Frankfurt, elected Ferdinand I, the brother of Charles V, as emperor, there began a struggle between Paul IV and Ferdinand that lasted until the close of the year 1559. Although Paul was inspired with the idea of church reform and the re-establishment of the Catholic faith, he was impetuous, vehement, extreme in his claims concerning papal authority, politically unsagacious, incapable of making concessions, and, above all, a passionate enemy of the Spanish and Austrian Hapsburgs.[12]

4. PAUL IV'S GRIEVANCES AGAINST FERDINAND I

Paul IV felt aggrieved at Ferdinand I, the emperor-elect, for various reasons: (1) Since 1556, when Charles V had divulged his plan of abdicating the emperorship, Ferdinand had withheld all information thereof from the pope; moreover, a similar secrecy was observed concerning the plan of the electors to elect Ferdinand as Charles's successor when they met in Frankfurt in February–March, 1558. (2) Ferdinand had permitted a theological discussion to take place at Worms in 1557 between Protestant and Catholic divines. (3) Ferdinand had refused the papal secretary Linterius admission to the meeting of electors at Frankfurt under the pretense that Ferdinand wished in this meeting to secure the aid of the Protestants against the Turks and that the presence of a papal nuncio would be merely a

[12] Reimann, "Papst Paul IV und das Kaiserthum," *Abhandlungen der schlesischen Gesellschaft für vaterländische Cultur, Philosophische-historische Abtheilung*, 1871, p. 28; article "Paul IV," in Wetzer and Welte, *op. cit.*, IX, 1640; Benrath, article "Paul IV," in Herzog-Hauck, *Realencyklopädie*, XV, 43; Brandenburg, *Kaiser Karl V*, in Marcks and Müller, *Meister der Politik*, II, 148; Pastor, *op. cit.*, VI, 569–71, 573, 624–25.

hindrance. Of course, Ferdinand actually feared that the presence of a papal nuncio would make difficult the support of the three Protestant electors (Brandenburg, Saxony, the Palatinate) in his election to the emperorship. Therefore the nuncio was doomed to a position of mere observer. (4) The election of Ferdinand in March, 1558, was a specially important one. Never before had an emperor abdicated voluntarily as Charles V had done in February, 1558. Since Charles was, by papal and imperial law, responsible to the pope, his abdication could not be regarded as legal without papal sanction. (5) Moreover, when, in 1531, Ferdinand had been elected as king of the Romans, there had been carried on a correspondence with the Roman court to ascertain whether the election might be valid when a heretic, the elector of Saxony, had participated therein. Pope Clement VII (1523–34) had uttered his opinion that such participation did not alter the legality of the election of the king; but now, in 1558, three Protestant or heretical electors participated in the election of Ferdinand to the emperorship without any consultation with the pope whatever. (6) Paul IV held Ferdinand most responsible for the negotiations leading to the Peace of Passau and its acceptance as the Religious Peace of Augsburg by the Imperial Diet in 1555. Ferdinand, in his election capitulation, or agreement, in March, 1558, had once more obligated himself to observe and maintain intact the terms of the Peace of Augsburg in spite of its injury to Catholic interests. (7) Ferdinand permitted his son, Maximilian, the Archduke of Austria and probable successor, to hold Protestant views. (8) Ferdinand had appointed bishops in Hungary and had transferred bishops from one diocese to another without such bishops having sought papal confirmation in Rome.[13] Of all these grievances the two most important, in the mind of Paul

[13] Reimann, "Der Streit zwischen Papstthum und Kaiserthum im Jahre 1558," *Forschungen zur deutschen Geschichte*, V, 299–302; Schmid, "Die deutsche Kaiser und Königswahl und die römische Curie in den Jahren 1558–1620," *Historisches Jahrbuch*, VI, 5–6; Pastor, *op. cit.*, VI, 571–73; W. Maurenbrecher, "Beiträge zur Geschichte Maximilians II. 1548–1562," *Historische Zeitschrift*, XXXII, 266.

IV, were Ferdinand's responsibility for the Peace of Augsburg and Maximilian's heterodoxy.[14]

5. PAUL IV'S UNCOMPROMISING VIEWS AND ACTIONS

Paul IV, insisting on his plenary rights in the matter, presented the situation to his cardinals with instructions to report fully after consulting the papal archives thoroughly concerning all legal aspects of the situation. The cardinals, responsive to the pope's views and wishes, after exhaustive inquiry presented the following opinions: (1) Although the electors have the legal right to elect an emperor, it is the pope who examines and then approves an election; and through the papal anointing, blessing, and coronation the emperor receives his title, power, dignity, and jurisdiction. (2) An emperor wishing to resign must turn back all these dignities and powers to the pope. The pope alone may freely resign; he has no earthly superior and is therefore superior to the emperor. (3) Only the pope can depose an emperor; he alone can relieve an emperor from office if the reasons advanced are satisfactory. (4) The emperor Charles V at his coronation had promised allegiance to the pope and protection to the church; the emperor cannot unilaterally release himself from this agreement. Neither can the electors release him. Only the pope can do so. If the emperor withdraws from his duties without consulting the pope, the pope can depose him. Hence Charles V is still emperor, or, rather, through his one-sided resignation he has lost his imperial power; but no one has been legally elected to succeed him. The proceedings of the electors at Frankfurt are null and void. (5) But even had Charles's resignation been valid, Ferdinand could not succeed him; rather, he ought to be deposed as Roman king because he permitted his son, Maximilian, to hold heretical views and especially because he had broken his oath to maintain the true interests of the church when signing the Peace of Augsburg. (6) Even if Ferdinand were capable of holding the emperorship,

[14] Maurenbrecher, "Beiträge zur Geschichte Maximilians II. 1548–1562," *Historische Zeitschrift*, XXXII, 266.

his election is null and void because it had been participated in by three heretical electors, quite apart from the consideration that the electors had no right to elect an emperor during the lifetime of the present incumbent, Charles V.[15]

The statement of such a comprehensive view of papal power gave promise of a papal-imperial contest of the thirteenth-century type. But the actual break did not occur, largely because Ferdinand avoided everything that might lead to an open break.[16] Martin Guzman, who had been sent as Ferdinand's emissary to render veneration and obedience and secure papal recognition of his master's imperial election, was kept waiting for two months in Rome without being granted an official interview. When, on July 13, 1558, a papal interview was finally granted, it was only a semiofficial audience, in which the pope merely stated that when the papal court arrives at a decision in this difficult question a special messenger will be sent to inform Ferdinand as to what action and attitude he would be expected to take.[17] Even when Charles V died, September 21, 1558, a few months after the beginning of the dispute, and the question of resignation had therefore been settled, Paul persisted in demanding that Ferdinand be required to have special papal ratification in order to enter into his imperial governmental duties.[18]

6. THE COUNTERACTION OF FERDINAND I

Thus far Ferdinand had conducted himself calmly and patiently, hoping that a peaceful solution would save the dignity of both the pope and himself. But now, after the death of Charles V had left the situation unchanged in papal eyes, Ferdinand took a more aggressive stand. It seemed necessary to re-

[15] Schmid, *op. cit.*, pp. 13–17; Reimann, "Der Streit zwischen Papstthum," *Forschungen*, V, 305–7; Pastor, *op. cit.*, VI, 574–76.

[16] Maurenbrecher, "Beiträge zur Geschichte Maximilians II," *Historische Zeitschrift*, XXXII, 266–67.

[17] Reimann, "Papst Paul IV," *Abhandlungen*, 1871, pp. 29, 30; Pastor, *op. cit.*, VI, 576–77.

[18] Ritter, *Deutsche Geschichte*, I, 143.

port to the electoral college a full account of what had thus far taken place. The three secular electors (Brandenburg, Saxony, and the Palatinate)—all Protestants—whose legitimacy was therefore also attacked by the papal attitude toward Ferdinand, advised him not to worry about papal ratification, not to be frightened by any threats and anathemas, and especially not to be worried about the coronation. Finally they declared that in case of further papal attack he could count on their support. But the Catholic electors (Mainz, Trier, Cologne), even though they had to consider their double capacity of allegiance to the pope and emperor, declared themselves ready, in case of further papal action, to consider preventive measures to maintain respect for the emperor and the Empire.[19] Manifestly, in the empire in which the princes had achieved parity, the papal claims could no longer be expected to find champions. It was just this consideration that determined the attitude of foreign powers. France did not wish, through her support of the pope, foolishly to destroy her good relations with the Protestant states of Germany, which it needed to hold the Hapsburg house in check. Philip II, on whose Catholic loyalty Rome could, above all, depend, informed Paul IV, during the long and fruitless negotiations on behalf of Ferdinand, that Spain needed the alliance of Ferdinand against the Protestants, who had become so powerful in Germany. Paul IV was wholly deserted in his ill-advised attack on Ferdinand, who remained in undisturbed possession of the emperorship.[20]

At the request of the emperor the imperial vice-chancellor Sigmund Seld, the statesman most responsible for formulating imperial policies, undertook to express the legal aspects of the controversy in question. In a well-formulated document he said that German law, established by the emperor and the states, is in sharp contrast with the papal demands and decrees. According to German law the government of the Empire, as well as the

[19] Reimann, "Der Streit zwischen Papstthum," *Forschungen*, V, 316; Schmid, *op. cit.*, pp. 34–35; Ritter, *Deutsche Geschichte*, I, 143–44.

[20] Ritter, *Deutsche Geschichte*, I, 140.

titles of a Roman king and of an elected emperor, are conferred solely through the regular election by the electors. Papal authority could verify the election and even refuse recognition and imperial coronation, but the conferred recognition does not confirm the election; the papal coronation does not add to the powers that the emperor-elect already has. The pope does not possess power to confer or rescind the emperor's right to conduct the imperial government. The right to dethrone the emperor belongs to the electors or to all the states.

From the secular standpoint these affirmations cut the ground under all the claims of Paul IV. Seld went even further in stating the nature and limits of papal power. Appealing to the decisions of the councils of Constance (1414–18) and Basel (1431–49), he declared that the power of all bishops, like that of the pope, had originally come down from the universal church. The bishops are the servants of the church; the church can, through a council, control even the pope.[21]

This assertion that the pope was dependent on the power of a church council was especially significant since the Council of Trent, which had been in session in the years 1545–47 and 1551–52, had not yet completed its work; and this question as to where final authority lay was still unsolved.[22]

7. THE CONCILIATORY POLICY OF PIUS IV ENDS THE DISPUTE

Seld's clearly stated claims concerning papal limitations as to the emperorship and the church were not given the test that might have been expected. On August 18, 1559, the disturbing reign of Paul IV came to an end. The majority of cardinals felt the new pope must break with the policy of his predecessor; first of all, there must be a reconciliation with Emperor Ferdinand. Pius IV (1559–65), chosen after a prolonged conclave of four months, was prepared to make peace with Ferdinand, for

[21] Ritter, *ibid.*, pp. 144–45; Reimann, "Der Streit zwischen Papstthum," *Forschungen*, V, 309–10; VIII, 3–4; Pastor, *op. cit.*, VI, 577–78.

[22] Ritter, *Deutsche Geschichte*, I, 147–48.

whom a reconciliation was essential for his personal comfort and the stability of his policies. On December 30, 1559, Pius IV declared to his cardinals that he did not find it expedient to object to Ferdinand's election. For, although some electors not members of the Catholic church had participated in the election, there were others present who were members. He added that he wished to show favor to Ferdinand, who was very religious and an earnest defender of Christianity against heretics. Soon the court of Pius IV granted Ferdinand what Paul IV had refused, the imperial title and first rank for his representative in Rome.[23] Nothing was said concerning the legality of Ferdinand's election or the wisdom of his accepting the Peace of Augsburg. The only point on which Pius IV insisted was that Ferdinand should see to it that his son Maximilian, his heir apparent, should desist from holding Protestant views.

Ferdinand, to secure papal recognition, sent a representative to Rome to assure the pope of his reverence and homage. But the pope demanded in addition a promise of obedience. This difficulty was solved when the imperial representative, Count Scipio von Arco, on the advice of two cardinals to whom Ferdinand had referred him, in an audience of February 17, 1560, exceeded his authority and conformed to the wishes of the pope.[24] Pius IV also had previously, in December, 1559, expressed the wish to the imperial representative Count Franz von Thurm, who had come to Rome to present the interests of Ferdinand, that, when the emperor sends his new representative to the papal court, he should, for the satisfaction of several cardinals, present an apology concerning the Peace of Passau and other recesses of the Imperial Diet. Ferdinand, when sending an expression of gratitude to Pius for his recognition of the imperial title, promised that his new representative would offer the desired apology.[25] But concerning the apology that the new

[23] Reimann, "Papst Paul IV," *Abhandlungen*, 1871, p. 37.

[24] Ritter, *Deutsche Geschichte*, I, 147.

[25] Reimann, "Papst Paul IV," *Abhandlungen*, 1871, pp. 37–38.

representative, the Count von Arco, had to make, nothing is known. It was probably not exhaustive or humble. In any case, in harmony with the earlier advice of Philip II to Ferdinand, it was made merely orally, not only for the reason that Philip indicated (namely, that this concession was a matter of necessity) but probably for the more significant reason of avoiding the possibility of a copy of this document ever straying into Germany to embarrass the Hapsburgs when dealing with the Protestant princes.[26]

8. PAPAL POLICY AS RELATED TO THE SECULARIZATION OF POLITICS

The difficulties between Paul IV and Ferdinand I, and all events related thereto, were clearly an important step in the secularization of politics; and in this final section of this chapter the significant consequences of this sixteenth-century state of this struggle will be presented.

a) *A conflict between old and new political ideals.*—Manifestly this was a contest between the old papal ideals of supreme political control and the new political ideals that were striving to free themselves from papal control, and the contest eventuated to the advantage of the new secular forces. On the one hand, it was inevitable that Paul IV should take the action he did. By his indirect protest against the Peace of Augsburg he was endeavoring to maintain the dependence of the emperor on the papacy in a time of great church losses to the papacy. If the Protestants were ever to be brought back into the fold of the Catholic church, the emperorship would need to be kept in a state of dependence such as had resulted from the earliest victories of the hierarchy over the Empire. To keep such historic control over the emperorship the papacy had to check or destroy the power of the Protestant electors in choosing the emperor.[27] Under the circumstances the papacy would not merely need to

[26] *Ibid.*, pp. 32–33, 39.

[27] Reimann, "Die römische Königswahl von 1562 und der Papst," *Forschungen zur deutschen Geschichte*, VIII, 3.

retain what power it formerly had, but would even need to strengthen its power. Therefore Paul IV made claims that were wider than any ever stated in medieval times.[28] On the other hand, these times were also favorable to wide-reaching claims and bold actions on the part of the Protestants. As a result of the Reformation movement it was in the air to test papal claims of the past and present, to criticize them in the light of historic knowledge that was the fruit of the studies of the humanists and reformers. It was in this spirit that Seld uttered his significant political opinions concerning the limited powers of the popes. In a similar spirit the electors and the kings of France and Spain acted in consideration of their own interests, irrespective of how the church or religion would be affected. This was clearly a step in the secularization of politics.

b) *Pius IV tactfully remedies the mistake of Paul IV.*—Once the contest was begun, it became evident, in view of existing circumstances, that the papacy had made a mistake; it did not wholly reverse itself, but it changed its tactics, and, like the secular princes, and in reflection of the spirit of the times, acted from the standpoint of expediency. Paul IV, by indirectly protesting against the Peace of Augsburg in his contest with Ferdinand I, made a tactical mistake. Pius IV, in bringing about an adjustment with Ferdinand, said nothing at all about the Peace of Augsburg. To be sure, the papacy had never formally, after a full consideration, uttered a special protest or issued a breve (bull) against the Peace as did Innocent X in 1650 (antedated 1648) against the Peace of Westphalia. Such an action of protest was considered in 1566, when in the Reichstag the Catholic estates of the Empire entered a formal confirmation of the Religious Peace of Augsburg.

c) *Pius V withholds a protest against the peace in 1566.*—Pius V (1566–72), who held views like those of Paul IV,[29] was of the opinion that, since the Council of Trent, which had completed

[28] Reimann, "Der Streit zwischen Papstthum," *Forschungen zur deutschen Geschichte*, V, 307; Schmid, *op. cit.*, pp. 13–17.

[29] Pastor, *op. cit.*, VIII, 465.

its work in 1563, had clarified all matters concerning religion, every good Christian should accept the decisions of the Council.[30]

Therefore he instructed Commendone, his nuncio at the Reichstag in question, that if the confirmation of the Peace of Augsburg occurred, and if that Peace were really in conflict with the dogmatic decrees of the Council of Trent, he should protest against such confirmation.[31] Pius V had also sent instructions to the archbishops of Mainz and Trier, and to all German bishops, to prevent a consideration of ecclesiastical affairs at the Diet and to preserve the rights of the pope and the bishops.[32] The situation confronting the legate was embarrassing. The Calvinists, who were not recognized by the Peace of Augsburg, wished to have it modified to include them.[33] The Calvinists and Lutherans, although opposed to each other in religious affairs, were united in their aim to do away with the ecclesiastical reservation clause and to uproot what remained of Catholicism.[34] The Catholic states wished to have the Peace ratified as it stood, for they feared they might, through the actions of the Protestants, lose the rights guaranteed by the Peace.[35] A papal protest against the Peace through the legate would merely have results advantageous to the Protestants and would cause disagreement with Emperor Maximilian II (1564–76), who was sympathetic with Protestantism.[36] If the situation had not been properly handled, a strained condition, or even a rupture between the Catholic states of Germany and the Curia, might have resulted; it is clear that under these circumstances an acceptance of the decrees of the Council of Trent, which was

[30] Ritter, "Der Augsburger Religionsfriede, 1555," *Historisches Taschenbuch*, I, 261.

[31] *Ibid.*

[32] Braunsberger, "Pius V und die deutschen Katholiken," in *Stimmen aus Maria-Laach, Katholische Blätter*, XXVII, 5–7; Pastor, *op. cit.*, VIII, 461–63; Janssen, *op. cit.*, IV, 223.

[33] Braunsberger, *op. cit.*, p. 7; Pastor, *op. cit.*, VIII, 465.

[34] Braunsberger, *op. cit.*; Pastor, *op. cit.*, VIII, 464; Janssen, *op. cit.*, IV 224–27.

[35] Braunsberger, *op. cit.*, p. 8; Pastor, *op. cit.*, VIII, 465.

[36] Pastor, *op. cit.*, VIII, 465.

the matter of greatest importance to the papacy, could not have occurred.[37]

The nuncio, Commendone, now asked advice from three Jesuits who, as theological experts, accompanied him; one of these was Petrus Canisius, the first German Jesuit (who was canonized in 1864). These three Jesuits held that, since the Peace of Augsburg did not assert positively that Protestants should disregard the Council of Trent, no action would need to be taken by the church. The Peace was concerned with political affairs, not with dogmatic matters. That Peace was imposed by insurmountable conditions of force; it was merely an expedient, a preliminary armistice. To be sure, the pope could not regard it as a good peace; but he and the Catholics could endure it until the Catholics, through a successful use of force, might be able to secure a complete return of their rights. For the pope to insist on issuing a protest might result in a new war in Germany, a conflict that might jeopardize what remained of Catholic rights in the fatherland.[38] Commendone, presented with an opinion so contrary to papal directions, sent to Rome for instructions. But the pope left the decision to his legate, which meant that a protest against the Peace would not be necessary. This papal action was due in large part to the intervention of the Jesuit general Franz Borgia (Borja) (1510–72), whom the Augsburger Jesuits, the advisers of Commendone, had asked to intervene.[39] The Catholic states of the Diet of Augsburg had in the meantime ratified the Peace of Augsburg in harmony with their best interests.[40]

[37] Drews, "Petrus Canisius der erste deutsche Jesuit," *Schriften des Vereins für Reformationsgeschichte*, X, 122.

[38] Braunsberger (ed.), *Beati Petri Canisii Societatis Iesu Epistolae et Acta*, V, 229–55; Braunsberger, *Petrus Canisius, ein Lebensbild*, pp. 162–65; Braunsberger, "Pius V," in *Stimmen aus Maria-Laach*, XXVII, 9; Metzler, *Der Heilige Petrus Canisius und die Neuerer seiner Zeit*, p. 34; Drews, "Petrus Canisius," *Schriften des Vereins für Reformationsgeschichte*, X, 121–23; Pastor, *op. cit.*, VIII, 465–66.

[39] Braunsberger, *Canisii Epistolae*, V, 250–55; Braunsberger, "Pius V," in *Stimmen aus Maria-Laach*, XXVII, pp. 10–11; Pastor, *op. cit.*, VIII, 466.

[40] Pastor, *op. cit.*, VIII, 466; Ritter, "Der Augsburger Religionsfriede," *Historisches Taschenbuch*, I, 262.

So the vigorous policy of Paul IV (1555–59) in condemning the Peace was a mere temporary spurt, ignored by Pius IV (1559–65) and, for the reasons just described, not resumed by Pius V (1566–72). It is clear that the advice of the three Jesuits was sophistry *sui generis*, designed to support the policy of doing nothing, the time being regarded as unfavorable. This situation showed that the papacy was also carrying out the same policy of expediency as were the Catholic and Protestant secular powers. The Jesuits, however, did not abide by the decision of their three members as expressed in 1566. By about 1608 they were already bold enough to deny the validity of the Peace of Augsburg; they maintained that it could not have been properly ratified without the consent of the pope; that in any case it was valid only until the Council of Trent had authoritatively regulated church affairs, and must be considered as only a sort of interim, or temporary, arrangement.[41]

In 1630, after imperial victories had in the recent preceding years strengthened the Catholic cause in Germany, the Jesuits signified their determination to pay no regard even to the Treaty of Augsburg.[42]

d) *Weakening of the bonds between the Empire and papacy.*—The actions of the papacy in the years 1558–60 did much to dissolve the bonds that long had bound the papacy and Empire together. Fully to understand what is here implied, we must consider the general change in attitude toward papal coronation of emperors since the time of Maximilian I. Maximilian I (1493–1519) had been elected Roman king in 1486 and emperor in 1493. Owing to internal and external problems, he had never been crowned emperor by the pope. In the years 1505 and 1506 he especially felt the need of having the imperial title; but, being at war with France and Venice, he could not easily reach Rome to secure papal coronation. So, in February, 1508, Maximilian himself took the title of emperor-elect in the city of Trent. The ceremony occurred in a church without even the presence of a

[41] Ranke, *History of the Popes*, II, 186.

[42] Steinberger, *Die Jesuiten und die Friedensfrage*, pp. 11–12; Ranke, *op. cit.*, II, 303.

papal legate. This unprecedented step was looked upon as an act of necessity, and within a week Pope Julius II (1503–13), the ally of Maximilian against Venice, quite willingly sanctioned and blessed the assumption of the title as being justified in order to give the German warriors an incentive to fight more enthusiastically in their further march toward Rome; but the pope evidently did not regard this as a substitute for papal coronation in Rome. Maximilian himself had the intention of later having himself crowned in Rome by the pope, when conditions were favorable. But that time never came, and in the last year of his reign there occurred a significant incident. In August, 1518, Maximilian I had secured the preliminary pledge of four electors to elect his grandson Charles as king of Rome. When the news of this proposed action reached the papal court, Pope Leo X (1513–21) became extremely excited and remarked, among other things, that he was surprised that the electors would so easily and quickly proceed to the election of a Roman king since Maximilian himself was still Roman king, never having been crowned emperor. The pope remarked further that he did not recall that a similar situation had ever occurred. But Maximilian's early death in January, 1519, solved this problem; Charles was elected emperor later in the year.[43]

However, the eventuation in the mind of subsequent imperial supporters was as follows: (1) it was held that Maximilian had virtually assumed the imperial title himself, (2) his successors followed the practice of taking the title of emperor-elect at Aachen immediately after the election, (3) when later difficulties with the pope occurred, these historic facts were interpreted as a step in the long and varied process of weakening the agelong political power of the pope, and history has corroborated Ranke's view that "the German crown had been emancipated from the pope" by Maximilian I's action.[44] As just observed,

[43] Baumgarten, "Die Politik Leos X. in dem Wahlkampf der Jahre 1518 und 1519," *Forschungen zur deutschen Geschichte*, XXIII, 531; Goetz, *Maximilians II. Wahl zum römischen Könige, 1562*, p. 197, n. 3.

[44] Leopold Ranke, *Deutsche Geschichte im Zeitalter der Reformation*, I, 177–78; VI, 90–93; Kaser, *Deutsche Geschichte*, II, 110, 112; F. Schneider, in Gebhardt, *Handbuch der*

one of the considerations of Maximilian I in seeking imperial coronation was the embarrassment of not having been crowned emperor when he was trying to have his grandson, the later Charles V, elevated to the Roman kingship. But Ferdinand I, fifty-four years later, seemed to find no embarrassment at all in not being crowned emperor, although Pius IV would gladly have sent the imperial crown over the Alps and although he repeatedly urged Ferdinand to secure papal coronation.[45] Ferdinand did not seek this honor, because he wished to avoid taking the oath of obedience to the pope, such as had been forced into the ceremony in connection with securing papal confirmation of his election to the emperorship in February, 1560. Moreover, any change in the imperial oath as demanded by the pope required the sanction of the electors.[46] Furthermore, Maximilian II (1564–76) had become Roman king without the official co-operation of the pope and without the reigning emperor, Ferdinand I, having been previously crowned.[47] So, as Reimann asks, what necessity was there hereafter for imperial successors to trouble themselves about this coronation? They were less inclined to request this of their own accord since they had to fear the evangelical princes. Indeed, they had to fear becoming involved with the pope in a contest over the oath of obedience, which was unequivocally demanded of them. So, through the influence of the new ideas, the bonds that had for centuries bound the emperorship to the papacy were being completely dissolved.[48]

---

deutschen Geschichte, I, 543; Ulmann, article "Maximilian I," in *Allgemeine deutsche Biographie*, XX, 722–23.

[45] Schmid, "Die deutsche Kaiser- und Königswahl," *Historisches Jahrbuch*, VI, 63, 165, 170.

[46] *Ibid.*, pp. 176–77; Reimann, "Die römische Königswahl von 1562 und der Papst," *Forschungen zur deutschen Geschichte*, VIII, 3–17.

[47] Schmid, "Die deutsche Kaiser- und Königswahl," *Historisches Jahrbuch*, VI, 161–64; Wilhelm Maurenbrecher, "Beiträge zur Geschichte Maximilians II," *Historische Zeitschrift*, XXXII, 290–95; Reimann, "Die religiöse Entwicklung Maximilians II in den Jahren 1554–1564," *Historische Zeitschrift*, XV, 54–61.

[48] Reimann, "Die römische Königswahl," *Forschungen*, VIII, 17; see also Goetz, *op. cit.*, pp. 197–98.

9. SUMMARY

In various respects the Peace of Augsburg and its consequences, as portrayed in this chapter, had done much to undermine papal dictation with reference to political affairs. But this did not mean that the Catholic powers in Germany were quite ready to disregard papal leadership altogether. The Catholic princes, as well as the papacy, hoped that the existing situation was a temporary one and that the truce imposed on the two contending groups in 1555 would give the Catholic powers time to recuperate for a final struggle that would abrogate the parity in religious affairs that had been granted to the Protestants and would re-establish religious uniformity in Germany. In such a struggle the papacy would be a useful ally of the Catholic princes. But that hoped-for success never came. At the close of the Thirty Years' War the defeated Catholic powers needed peace. To secure a permanent peace and to protect their own secular interests regardless of papal interests, they agreed to co-operate with the Protestant princes to nullify the papal protest against the Peace of Westphalia. When that happened, international politics may be said to have been secularized. This final step in this movement will be the subject of the following chapters.

Chapter Four

THE EVANGELICALS AND THE CLAUSE AGAINST PROTESTS

I. THE PROBLEM OF CONCLUDING PEACE AT WESTPHALIA

THE Congress of Westphalia, meeting in the years 1644–48, after preliminary but futile peace efforts dating back to 1635, had as its main task to bring to a close an era of religious wars. Since Luther's disturbing break with the Roman Catholic church, Protestant and Catholic Europe had been troubled with civil and international wars that had bred deep hatreds, profound distrusts, and suspicions similar in bitterness and intensity to those that we of the World War and post-war period know only too well. The Thirty Years' War (1618–48), apart from its long duration, was in some respects quite as catastrophic in its results as the World War. It had produced uncertainties as to territorial boundaries in Germany and central Europe and had raised knotty problems as to the future status of Catholicism and the two great Protestant religions of Germany, Lutheranism and Calvinism; it had left scores of other problems, national and international rivalries, to be adjusted. The physical and mental exhaustion of the belligerent peoples was the most potent factor in inducing the governments to negotiate at all concerning these exceedingly vital problems. But even the substitution of pen and tongue for sword and cannon proved too tiring for the negotiators; after four years of negotiating they adjourned with part of their task uncompleted.[1]

[1] Heigel, "Das westfälische Friedenswerk von 1643 bis 1648," *Zeitschrift für Geschichte und Politik*, V, 414.

The plenipotentiaries, after prolonged and childish bickerings over questions of diplomatic precedence, and after numerous discouragements, finally gave Europe an arrangement embodied in the two treaties of Münster and Osnabrück, which together are called the "Treaty of Westphalia," the two places Münster and Osnabrück being two cities about thirty miles apart in the province of Westphalia, where the Treaty was negotiated because it was impossible to have all negotiators meet in one place since Catholics and heretics refused to negotiate together. So the emperor had to negotiate with the Catholics at Münster and with the Protestants at Osnabrück. This Treaty of Westphalia corresponds in the public law of Europe to the Treaty of Vienna of 1815 and to the treaties of Versailles and St. Germain, Neuilly, Trianon, and Sèvres of 1919–20. The fundamentals of this arrangement of 1648 remained in force for almost a century and a half, until 1792. It would have been a great comfort to many of the plenipotentiaries at Westphalia to have had the assurance that they were producing a peace of such stability. Once the solution of the numerous political, economic, and religious problems had been attained, it was highly important to the negotiators and their governments that the peace providing for such solutions and fundamental adjustments should be permanent and stable, and not be jeopardized by any effective protest from whatever source. In this chapter we shall discuss the negotiations concerning the clause against protests, around which centers the problem of secularizing politics during the negotiations at Westphalia.

2. A PROTEST FROM THE POPE INEVITABLE

If the Swedes had succeeded in securing all or even a part of their demands, they might surely have expected a protest from the pope declaring null the treaty whereby all the Swedish gains were guaranteed. Throughout the negotiations the plenipotentiaries of Queen Christina of Sweden (1632–54) had demanded four things: first, that an amnesty be extended to all that had participated in the war since 1618, and that all parties be reinstated in the condition that they had enjoyed at the outbreak of the war;[2] second, that the Calvinists, as well as Lutherans, be allowed freedom of worship;[3] third, that the secularized ecclesiastical lands remain in the hands of the princess;[4] and fourth, that Sweden be given a "satisfaction," or land indemnity in Germany, which very probably would include several ecclesiastical states.[5]

That a protest from the pope against such concessions was inevitable could be assumed from the actions of the pope and his nuncios since the meeting of the Congress of Cologne in 1636, when the first efforts were made to bring about a termination of the war.[6]

To this Congress Urban VIII had sent his nuncio, Cardinal Ginetti, who was to have the status of legate and mediator among the Catholic princes.[7] By June, 1638, over papal signature, instructions were sent to the Cardinal to oppose the revocation, or even any weakening, of the Edict of Restitution (1629)[8] and the establishment of a Protestant prince as elector of the Palatinate unless he marries a Catholic.[9] He must ener-

[2] J. G. von Meiern, *Acta Pacis Westphalicae publica, oder westphälische Friedens-Handlungen und Geschichte*, I, 436, 743, 804–5, 807; II, 185, 299–300; III, 151, 408, and elsewhere.

[3] *Ibid.*, II, 10; III, 166; IV, 98.

[4] *Ibid.*, I, 821–31; II, 572, 614; III, 167, 256–65.

[5] *Ibid.*, II, 187–88, 196–98, 835–39; III, 78, 151.

[6] Adami, *Arcana Pacis Westphalicae*, pp. 12–24; Adami, *Relatio historica de pacificatione* (ed. Meiern), pp. 15–28; Bougeant, *Histoire du traité de Westphalie*, I, 401–8; *Cambridge Modern History*, IV, 396; Gindely, *Geschichte des dreissigjährigen Krieges*, III, 84.

[7] Bougeant, *op. cit.*, I, 401.

[8] *Instruttione del Cardinale Ginetti per un congresso de pacificazione general*, Staatsbibliothek, München, Codex italiano, 98, fol. 60, copy of the original manuscript in Vatican Secret Archives, XXXIX, 1049. See *Codices Manuscripti, Bibliothecae Regiae Monacensis* (Munich), VII, 177; for two copies in Bibliothèque nationale, Paris, see A. Marsand, *I Monoscritti italiani della regia biblioteca Parigina*, I, 337, 656, which gives the date as 1636; Pastor, *Geschichte der Päpste*, XIII, Part I, 484, n. 2, gives date of Urban's signature as June 25, 1638. Brosch, in *Cambridge Modern History*, IV, 688; Richard, "Origins et développements de la secrétairerie d'état apostolique (1417-1823)," *Revue d'histoire ecclésiastique*, XI, 744, n. 2.

[9] *Instruttione del Cardinale Ginetti*, fol. 56.

getically oppose everything that gives an advantage to the heretics and a disadvantage to the Catholic religion. He must oppose especially anything that could be unfavorable to the regaining of the ecclesiastical lands, which must be politically controlled by the church so Catholicism can exist therein.[10] He must see to it that the secular powers of the papacy are not jeopardized.[11] Above all, he must not co-operate in the formulation of any treaties of peace agreed to between Catholic and heretical powers.[12] Copies of this original manuscript of papal instructions to Ginetti are today found in fourteen European libraries, including Stockholm,[13] which would suggest that the contents must have been well known to the negotiators in both Catholic and Protestant ranks, even if Cardinal Ginetti exerted very little active influence as mediator, owing to his frugality.[14]

When the question of granting an amnesty was being considered by the emperor and the Nürnberg Diet of Electors (1640), and was also to be considered at the Regensburg Diet (1640–41), Pope Urban VIII sent a breve to the emperor and to each of the Catholic princes urging them to consider Catholic interests most carefully.[15] In addition he commissioned Gaspare Mattei, the cardinal nuncio in Vienna, orally to caution the emperor against making any sacrifice of church lands.[16] When it became clear that the amnesty was going to be sanctioned by the emperor and the Diet of Regensburg in 1641, Bishop Henry V of Augsburg protested against the amnesty in the same spirit in which Cardinal Otto Truchsess protested against the Peace of Augsburg in 1555;[17] and the papal nuncio at Vienna, Gaspare Mattei, pro-

[10] *Ibid.*, back of fol. 59. [11] *Ibid.*, fol. 61. [12] *Ibid.*, fol. 61.

[13] Pastor, *op. cit.*, XIII, Part I, 484, n. 2.

[14] Ranke, *Die römischen Päpste*, II, 373.

[15] Brockhaus, *Der Kurfürstentag zu Nürnberg im Jahre 1640*, pp. 110–24, 241–57; Pastor, *op. cit.*, XIII, Part I, 492.

[16] Pastor, *op. cit.*, XIII, Part I, 492.

[17] Protest of Bishop Henry V, in Conring, *Opera*, II, 508; in Ernestus de Eusebiis (i.e., Wangnereck), *Judicium Theologicum*, sec. 4, point 8, Part III; Steinberger, *Die Jesuiten und die Friedensfrage, 1635–1650*, pp. 10, 37.

tested against the amnesty because it was contrary to the interest of the church.[18] But Emperor Ferdinand III, already acting somewhat in the spirit of secularized politics, as manifested later during the Congress of Westphalia, issued an imperial decree on August 20, 1641, providing for an amnesty, which, however, was only partial.[19]

Soon after Innocent X (1644–55) succeeded to the pontificate, he wrote to Fabio Chigi, the papal nuncio at Münster, on October 5, 1644, commanding him to see that the dignity of the Roman church suffer no prejudice during the peace negotiations. The nuncio was "to safeguard the rights and liberties of the church in resisting with all his force any agreement that could be prejudicial to it, and he should rather leave the Congress than consent to such an agreement, were it merely by his presence; [he was] to consider the cause of God before all things."[20] Chigi was also instructed to place a similar document into the hands of Bishop Henry V of Augsburg as well as the other ecclesiastical princes of Germany.[21] In consequence the nuncio announced to the plenipotentiaries that he would fill his office of mediator only on condition that the interests of religion were fully guaranteed.[22]

When the Protestant and Catholic princes were considering where the ecclesiastical grievances (*gravamina*) could be handled, it was decided that, because of the attitude of Chigi, it would be difficult to handle them at Münster, for he had in December, 1645, expressly declared that because of his position

[18] Conring, *op. cit.*, II, 505–6, in Ernestus de Eusebiis, *op. cit.*, sec. 4, point 8, Part II; Adami, *Arcana Pacis*, pp. 23–24; Adami, *Relatio historica*, pp. 28–29; Steinberger, *op. cit.*, p. 37; Laurent, *Etudes sur l'histoire de l'humanité*, X, 282.

[19] Londorp, *Acta publica*, V, 579–81; *Theatrum europaeum*, IV, 449–552; Bougeant, *op. cit.*, II, 127–29; Pastor, *op. cit.*, XIII, Part I, 493–94; Meiern, *op. cit.*, II, 3; Steinberger, *op. cit.*, p. 37.

[20] Meiern, *op. cit.*, IV, 861–62, contains the letter in full; also Adami, *Arcana Pacis*, pp. 37–38; Adami, *Relatio historica*, pp. 46–47; also Brom, *Archivalia in Italië*, III, 388–89; Pastor, *op. cit.*, XIV, Part I, 74.

[21] Meiern, *op. cit.*, II, 861, 862–63.

[22] Adami, *Arcana Pacis*, p. 38; Adami, *Relatio historica*, p. 47; Laurent, *op. cit.*, X, 282.

and office he could not meddle with the negotiations, much less give his consent to them, but that in this matter he would be constrained at all times to manifest his dissent, and that he must preserve the virginity (*virginitas*) and intact rights (*jus integer*) of the Catholic church; but, as for the rest, he would have to let the negotiations take their course.[23] Because of this attitude most of the negotiations concerning religious affairs were transacted at Osnabrück. But this was done for policy's sake; it did not prevent the execution of terms prejudicial to the interests of the church.

Chigi did his best to encourage the Catholic deputies to remain firm in their opposition to the demands of the Protestants.[24] He repeatedly warned Trauttmannsdorff, and also the French, against making concessions that were detrimental to the church.[25] On November 29, 1647, he wrote to the Bishop of Augsburg that, if the peace terms were to contain any arrangements contrary to the laws of the church fathers, councils, and popes, one might expect, not the sanction, but the vigorous protest of the Holy See against such a treaty.[26]

A nineteenth-century Belgian jurist and historian, François Laurent, sums up the attitude of Chigi as follows:

> The nuncio declared in the name of the pope that, if the Congress endeavored to decide affairs concerning ecclesiastical lands and religion, the Holy See would protest and would utter censures against the Catholic princes. In fact, the mediation of the nuncio passed in protests; he declared in advance that all the conventions contrary to the honor of God would be null, that the treaty that sanctioned them would not be a peace but an abominable monster of horrible confusion; he wished his protest to be repeated at the beginning, in the middle, at the end of all acts that they drew up, and that it [his protest] should remain until all the signatories should appear before the tribunal of God, on the day of judgment.[27]

[23] Meiern, *op. cit.*, II, 138.

[24] Pastor, *op. cit.*, XIV, Part I, 79.

[25] *Ibid.*, XIV, Part I, 81–85.

[26] Meiern, *op. cit.*, IV, 862–63; Heigel, "Das westfälische Friedenswerk," *Zeitschrift für Geschichte und Politik*, V, 436.

[27] Laurent, *op. cit.*, X, 283, cites a work that has not been accessible to me, Meiern, *Emblemata ad historiam de pacificatione Westphalica*, pp. 44, 45, 54, and which, to my knowledge, is referred to nowhere else.

So there was ample indication that the pope would protest against anything done by the Congress that was prejudicial to the interests of the Catholic church. Knowing this attitude of the pope and his nuncio, it behooved the Protestants to make arrangements that would safeguard the peace against any protest.

3. THE EVANGELICAL PRINCES AT OSNABRÜCK INSERT THE CLAUSE AGAINST PROTESTS

Besides the ordinary guaranties against the breaking of the Peace that were finally inserted in both the treaties of Münster and Osnabrück,[28] much negotiation was required to make the Peace protest-proof against all possible antagonists; but naturally the protest that was most feared was that of the pope, for the treaty terms contemplated by the Protestants would do most injury to the interests of the Catholic church, and, moreover, the pope was the most powerful and influential of those that would sustain any injury at the hands of the Congress. In the instructions that the royal Swedish government sent its plenipotentiaries in the latter part of the year 1645, they were told to mention as possible territorial satisfaction (or indemnity) such ecclesiastical lands as Magdeburg, Halberstadt, Minden, Osnabrück, Bremen, Verden, or Cammin.[29] Keeping in mind the possibility of papal protests against such cessions and other arrangements detrimental to Catholic church interests, the evangelical princes under the leadership of Sweden, when discussing the means of negotiating peace September 4, 1645, resolved that "no reservation or protest shall be valid at the present time or in the future, neither shall it be heard."[30] This clause against reservations and protests was inserted in every peace project that the Swedes subsequently handed to the imperial

[28] Peace of Osnabrück, Art. XVII, pars. 4–7; Peace of Münster, pars. 115, 116, in Walther, *Universal Register*, pp. xlviii, xlix, lxxxvi.

[29] Breucker, *Die Abtretung Vorpommerns an Schweden und die Entschädigung Kurbrandenburgs*, p. 36; Geijer, *Geschichte von Schweden*, III, 371.

[30] Meiern, *Acta Pacis Westphalicae publica*, I, 601, 606.

plenipotentiaries, and its insertion was insisted on as an essen tial to peace.[31] That the evangelicals wished to make certain that no protest against the peace should be valid, whether made by the pope or by any other ecclesiastical officer, is seen quite clearly in their reply submitted to the imperial plenipotentiaries in December, 1646. They declare:

> This clause must not merely be repeated but also all contradictions and protests that may already have been made, must be expressly invalidated and declared void, and this without exception of persons, and not excepting members of religious orders or their provincials, whatever their title, who are resident in the Holy Roman Empire, or their generals, and immediate superiors, who, although they may be found outside the Roman Empire are, nevertheless by reason of their properties situate within the Empire, subject to the Empire and to its ordinances [*constitutionibus*], and are especially to be bound by this treaty.[32]

Around the negotiations concerning this clause against protests centers the secularization of politics at the Congress of Westphalia.

[31] *Ibid.*, I, 705 (October 2, 1645); III, 425 (November 21, 1646); IV, 17 (December 22, 1646).

[32] *Ibid.*, IV, 17.

Chapter Five

AUSTRIA AND THE CATHOLICS INSERT THE CLAUSE AGAINST PROTESTS

1. TEMPORARY CATHOLIC OPPOSITION TO THE CLAUSE AGAINST PROTESTS

NATURALLY the chief opposition to the Swedish declaration against protests would come from the Catholic ranks, which in all important matters were led by the emperor. We find that until January, 1647, the Catholic or imperial plenipotentiaries refused to insert the clause against protests;[1] but after that date, as will be seen later, the clause was always inserted in the imperial peace projects. According to the available records, the Catholic princes did not always express what must have been their real motive for refusing to insert such a clause. On September 10, 1645, the Bishop of Bamberg, in discussing the Swedish proposals, objected to the insertion of a clause against protests inasmuch as such a declaration would hinder discussion.[2] In the electoral council at Münster, September 21, 1645, it was declared that the insertion of the clause "was entirely too premature, for, when the peace negotiations draw to a close, the crowns will of their own accord desire means of securing a guaranty for the treaty, and, moreover, such clauses are not to be found in any ordinance of the Imperial Diet [*Reichsabschied*]."[3]

[1] Meiern, *Acta Pacis Westphalicae publica*, I, 681 (September 10, 1645), 685 (September 21, 1645); III, 356 (September 19, 1646), 369 (September), 422 (November, 1646).

[2] *Ibid.*, I, 681.

[3] *Ibid.*, p. 685.

Far more to the point are the objections made a year later. In September, 1646, the Catholics at Münster declared:

> Although all protests and contradictions are to be counted null by those of the Augsburg Confession, yet it cannot be doubted that many of the Catholics, and especially those that have been most interested in this work, will be unwilling to be deprived of this privilege [*beneficium*], pitiable though it be and allowed to everyone, and often used, moreover, by those of the Augsburg Confession themselves; but they [the Catholics] will reserve to themselves this privilege: since it is in every way fair and should remain free for all and each to use it as he may think best for his future protection.[4]

In November, 1646, the Catholics again declared that they would not permit that their right to protest be taken from them, and that all should be left free to act as they thought best in this respect.[5]

These assertions plainly showed that the Catholic princes did not expect to be bound by the treaty. They were all hoping for a favorable turn in the war; and, if that did not come, they did not wish to be bound by the terms of this treaty if it became possible subsequently to disregard them. Besides the motives of self-interest and self-preservation that actuated them, these princes must have been somewhat influenced by the declarations that the nuncio repeated so often and also by the work of the Society of Jesus. Not only did the members of this order labor secretly, at both Münster and Osnabrück, trying to influence the Catholic plenipotentiaries, but the whole machinery of this order was used for the purpose of collecting information and bringing pressure to bear where needed. Letters were sent to members of the order at such Catholic courts as Vienna, Munich, and Mainz, where, in the capacity of confessors, they could secure valuable information; in accordance with the rules of the order, this information was all sent to the general of the Society at Rome, by whom it was utilized to the desired end.[6]

At Münster the Jesuits closely watched all Catholic ambassadors, especially those that had been converts to Catholicism,

[4] *Ibid.*, III, 356. [5] *Ibid.*, p. 422.

[6] Pütter, *Geist des westphälischen Friedens*, p. 53; Steinberger, *Die Jesuiten und die Friedensfrage, 1635–1650*, pp. 2–3.

such as the imperial representatives Nassau, Volmar, and chiefly Trauttmannsdorff.[7] The Jesuits were particularly dissatisfied with Trauttmannsdorff because he had been too yielding concerning Catholic interests. However, it was Trauttmannsdorff's ill health, and not the influence of the Jesuits, that caused his departure from the Congress in July, 1647, fifteen months before the conclusion of peace.[8] The Jesuits had no confidence in him. The Swedes intercepted and published a significant letter, dated July 12, 1647, written by a Jesuit from Münster to the confessor of Ferdinand III; in this letter it was stated that the extreme Catholic party longed for the departure of Trauttmannsdorff from the Congress. The writer, Johannes Mulmann, also urged the imperial confessor to persuade Emperor Ferdinand III to make no concessions to the Protestants and to continue the war to a victorious end. Another member of the order, Gottfried Coeler, added a postscript testifying that he had in vain tried to stir the conscience of Aesculapius, as they called Trauttmannsdorff, for he continued to work for peace in a yielding spirit even though no reciprocal gains were secured.[9]

The anti-peace activities of the Jesuits were so persistent, and, as it was feared, likely to prolong the already devastating war, that at the conference of the evangelicals, November 7, 1645, the Mecklenburg representative recommended that the order be dissolved, or at least driven out of Germany.[10] In March, 1646, when the evangelicals were discussing means of making the Peace permanent, it was pointed out that the

Emperor, kings, princes, and lords were not obliged to observe any agreement that had been negotiated and concluded with others not recognizing the Roman pope; and that, since the republic of Venice had for these and other

[7] Meiern, *op. cit.*, IV, 703; Pütter, *op. cit.*, pp. 53–54.

[8] Egloffstein, article "Trauttmannsdorff," *Allgemeine Deutsche Biographie*, XXXVIII, 535; Pütter, *op. cit.*, p. 54.

[9] Meiern, *op. cit.*, IV, 703–4; Pütter, *op. cit.*, pp. 55–56; Odhner, *Die Politik Schwedens*, p. 224.

[10] Meiern, *op. cit.*, I, 781; Pütter, *op. cit.*, p. 57.

grievances driven the members of this order out forever, just so there would be a secure and stable peace in Germany if the Jesuits were expelled.[11]

Some of the Jesuits also entered the field of public controversy, vigorously opposing Catholic acceptance of any permanent peace with the heretics. Foremost among these Jesuit pamphleteers was Heinrich Wangnereck, whose various works, especially the *Judicium theologicum*, stirred up much hostility in the ranks of the Protestants and the moderate Catholics. But, as we shall see in subsequent chapters, responses to Wangnereck were written by other members of the Jesuit order, notably by Johann Vervaux, the confessor of Maximilian of Bavaria.

2. AUSTRIA AND THE CATHOLIC PRINCES INSERT THE CLAUSE AGAINST PROTESTS AFTER JANUARY 28, 1647

So, until the beginning of the year 1647 the Catholics refused, for the reason mentioned, to insert the clause against protests; but in the conference of January 28, 1647, between the imperial and the Swedish plenipotentiaries at Osnabrück, the imperialists agreed to the insertion of the clause.[12] In all subsequent peace projects and negotiations the clause was retained;[13] and, as will be observed later, after the treaties of Münster and Osnabrück were signed (October 24, 1648), provisions were made for the execution of this clause, and the emperor remained true to his agreement. Owing to the frequently expressed attitude of the papacy and the nuncio Chigi, the Catholic princes must have known precisely what consequences their action would have, that they would ultimately be forced to disregard the protest of the nuncio and the pope. The question arises: Why did the emperor's plenipotentiaries at this particular time sanction the insertion of this clause against the protests, and why did the

[11] Meiern, *op. cit.*, II, 489; Pütter, *op. cit.*, p. 57; Duhr, *Geschichte der Jesuiten in den Ländern deutscher Zunge*, II, Part I, 452–56, which gives a corrective view. For the expulsion of the Jesuits from Venice in 1606 see Pastor, *op. cit.*, XII, 100–101.

[12] Meiern, *op. cit.*, IV, 36, 39.

[13] *Ibid.*, IV, 118 (March 5, 1647), 181 (April 4, 1647), 835 (December 16, 1647); V, 468 (April, 1647), 765 (April 24, 1648), 936 (June, 1648); VI, 5 (June, 1648), 110 (July 27, 1648), 170 (August 6, 1648), 393 (September, 1648).

emperor subsequently find it to his profit to adhere to and execute the agreement? The answer lies undoubtedly in the trend that the imperial negotiations were taking between Sweden and her allies from November, 1646, to February, 1647. The war had been going against the emperor; the French and Swedish generals, though not constantly victorious, were, on the whole, able to defeat the imperial and Bavarian troops most of the time.[14] Bavaria had been devastated; by March 14, 1647, Maximilian of Bavaria had signed the armistice of Ulm with Sweden and France; his brother, the elector Ferdinand of Cologne, was given the privilege of adhering to the armistice, which he did early in May, 1647.[15] Thus Ferdinand III had lost his last and only effective ally in Germany; it looked as though the imperial cause were lost.[16] The superiority of the French and Swedish troops was generally manifest.[17] These victories enabled the Swedes and the French to press their claims to "satisfaction"; Mazarin realized that a close co-operation with Sweden in making these demands was necessary. France had in May and September, 1646, made fairly definite arrangements concerning the question of territories to be annexed by her at the expense of Germany;[18] these arrangements might be jeopardized if the strong support of Sweden were lacking. The Spanish were trying then, as later, to hinder the conclusion of peace with the Empire,[19] and were attempting, through separate peace negotia-

[14] Ritter, *Deutsche Geschichte*, III, 606–10, 620–21; *Cambridge Modern History*, IV, 391; Riezler, *Geschichte Baierns*, V, 598–612; Huber, *Geschichte Österreichs*, V, 584–87.

[15] Meiern, *op. cit.*, V, 6–12; Londorp, *Acta publica*, VI, 186–91; Egloffstein, *Baierns Friedenspolitik von 1645 bis 1647*, pp. 149–76; Riezler, *op. cit.*, V, 611–13; Huber, *op. cit.*, V, 585; Ennen, "Ferdinand von Köln," in *Allgemeine deutsche Biographie*, VI, 696; *Cambridge Modern History*, IV, 391.

[16] Katt, *Beiträge zur Geschichte des dreissigjährigen Krieges*, 99; Ritter, *op. cit.*, III, 620.

[17] Ritter, *op. cit.*, III, 621; *Cambridge Modern History*, IV, 391; Heigel, "Das westfälische Friedenswerk," *Zeitschrift für Geschichte und Politik*, V, 424; Fischer, *Beiträge zur Kenntnis der päpstlichen Politik während der westphälischen Friedensverhandlungen*, pp. 27, 28.

[18] Meiern, *op. cit.*, III, 28–29, 723–27; Heigel, *op. cit.*, V, 423; Odhner, *op. cit.*, p. 159.

[19] Le Clerc, *Négociations secrètes*, III, 262, 270; Meiern, *op. cit.*, IV, 352, 800; Bougeant, *Histoire du traité du Westphalie*, V, 111.

tions, to detach Holland from her allies, the French and the Swedes.[20] Moreover, the arrangements that the emperor had conceded were advantageous not only to Sweden but also to the other allies of France, namely, Brandenburg and Hesse, whose good will France wished to keep.[21]

With the war constantly going against the imperial forces, which now had to bear the entire burden of carrying on the struggle,[22] and with the Swedes and the French persistently asserting their claims, the emperor was compelled to yield. On the other hand, the French and the Swedes were able, through the skilful use of bribes, to break down the resistance of the lesser German princes represented at Münster; as a consequence more and more imperial princes were pressing the emperor to bow to the inevitable and make the requisite concessions.[23] The policy that the emperor adopted under these circumstances caused him to feel the necessity of inserting into the treaty projects the clause that declared all protests to be null and void. In December, 1645, and January, 1646, Sweden demanded Silesia, among numerous other territories, as a satisfaction.[24] This demand for one of his choice hereditary lands distressed the emperor greatly.[25] But if Sweden were to be satisfied without giving her Silesia, some other compensatory means must be found; if Sweden received Pomerania, whose ruling line had died out in 1637, and which was claimed by Brandenburg by virtue of the Treaty of Grimnitz made in 1529,[26] the elector of Brandenburg must be indemnified elsewhere; so in May, 1646, the French suggested that Brandenburg be indemnified with part of Silesia.[27]

[20] Chéruel, *Lettres du Cardinal Mazarin*, II, 359–64, 366–67, 396, 407, 426, 439, 447; Bougeant, *op. cit.*, V, 111, 163; Odhner, *op. cit.*, p. 179.

[21] Chéruel, *op. cit.*, II, 358, 422.

[22] *Cambridge Modern History*, IV, 391.

[23] Heigel, *op. cit.*, V, 423; Wild, *Johann Philipp von Schönborn*, pp. 10, 11.

[24] Meiern, *op. cit.*, II, 188; Gärtner, *Westphälische Friedens-Cantzley*, VIII, 380–411, but especially p. 403; Breucker, *Die Abtretung Vorpommerns an Schweden*, p. 36; Geijer, *Geschichte von Schweden*, III, 371.

[25] Meiern, *op. cit.*, II, 188.

[26] *Ibid.*, II, 939; Odhner, *op. cit.*, p. 34; *Cambridge Modern History*, IV, 104.

[27] Meiern, *op. cit.*, III, 30; Hanser, *Deutschland nach dem dreissigjährigen Kriege*, p. 65.

This suggestion offended the imperial plenipotentiaries;[28] but this proposal, like the demand that Sweden be given Silesia, undoubtedly helped the emperor and his plenipotentiaties and adviser, Trauttmannsdorff, to be willing to insert the clause against the protests. If Sweden were to receive Wismar and the island of Poël at the expense of Mecklenburg, the Duke of Mecklenburg must be indemnified for his loss. If Hesse-Cassel were to be indemnified as France insisted in her "satisfaction project" of June 1, 1645,[29] some means must be found for this purpose. Unless Austria wished to give up Silesia and other hereditary lands, she must consent to the only other means of indemnification, the secularizing of ecclesiastical states. That was precisely what she did.

3. THE SECULARIZATION OF ECCLESIASTICAL LANDS WITH AUSTRIA'S CONSENT

During the latter part of the year 1646 and the early part of 1647 the imperial negotiators were granting the demands for "satisfaction" and indemnities at the expense of the church lands, thus saving Austria's own territories. The completion of these negotiations practically coincided with the date of Austria's insertion of the clause against protests. (*a*) By November 21, 1646, it had been agreed by the imperialists and Catholics that the archbishopric of Bremen and the bishopric of Verden should remain with the evangelicals.[30] By the middle of February, 1647, both territories had been ceded to Sweden as immediate imperial fiefs.[31] (*b*) On January 22, 1647, the bishopric of Cammin was offered to Brandenburg as an equivalent for Pomerania.[32] By February 20, 1647, the bishopric of Minden had been offered also.[33] In February, 1647, Brandenburg was granted both of these ecclesiastical lands, and final confirmation of the cession occurred in June, 1647.[34] In the same month Bran-

[28] Meiern, *op. cit.*, III, 93–94.

[29] *Ibid.*, I, 419, 445.

[30] *Ibid.*, III, 436.

[31] *Ibid.*, IV, 332.

[32] *Ibid.*, p. 281.

[33] *Ibid.*, pp. 329–30.

[34] *Ibid.*, pp. 329, 334, 582.

denburg was also granted the archbishopric of Magdeburg as a hereditary possession, though with the reservation that such acquisition was to be deferred until the death of the administrator of that time, Prince August of Saxony.[35] By January 29, 1648, the bishopric of Halberstadt was also granted to Brandenburg.[36] (*c*) As early as November 21, 1646, the bishoprics of Schwerin and Ratzeburg had been declared by the imperial and Catholic party to belong to Mecklenburg,[37] and by the end of January, 1647, the imperial and Swedish ambassadors agreed that the bishoprics should be given to Mecklenburg.[38] (*d*) The abbey of Hirschfeld, which had been demanded by the Landgravine of Hesse-Cassel on November 8, 1646,[39] was ceded to that princess by the imperial ambassadors on February 8, 1647.[40]

4. THE NEW SPIRIT IN INTERNATIONAL POLITICS

Emperor Ferdinand, to prevent the deeding of his own territories to his successful enemies, ceded those of the church as a substitute. He, his advisers, his moderate Catholic associates, together with the French, were manifesting a new spirit in international affairs; they were showing an indifference to the historic material interests of the church that was in striking contrast to the spirit manifested in the previous half-millennium. But it was not an absolute or necessarily a voluntary break with the past; the emperor made an attempt for a long time to avoid it; but when he saw the probability of needing to sacrifice church lands to protect his own, he requested a number of court theologians to give their opinion as to the permissibility of such action.[41] This document was shown officially to the important Catholic powers of the Empire, especially to electoral

[35] *Ibid.*, pp. 314, 319.

[36] *Ibid.*, p. 962; Geist, *Die Säkularisation des Bistums Halberstadt im westfälischen Friedenskongresse*, p. 90 and passim.

[37] Meiern, *op. cit.*, III, 436.

[38] *Ibid.*, VI, 513.

[39] *Ibid.*, III, 755.

[40] *Ibid.*, IV, 423, 424.

[41] Steinberger, *op. cit.*, pp. 58–59; Gärtner, *op. cit.*, IX, 874–84; Koch, *Geschichte des deutschen Reiches unter der Regierung Ferdinands III*, II, 188.

Mainz and electoral Bavaria.[42] The theological opinions of these courts were sent to Vienna; and the imperial theologians, after full consideration, concluded that the emperor could, with or without the consent of the Catholic princes of the Empire, agree unconditionally to the permanent cession of the ecclesiastical lands to the Protestants.[43] All efforts of the Catholic extremists under the leadership of the nuncio Chigi and Franz Wilhelm von Wartenberg, bishop of the occupied bishoprics of Minden and Verden, to prevent such concessions were fruitless.[44] Both Trauttmannsdorff and Maximilian of Bavaria stood firm, and continued to do so until the end of the negotiations.[45] The emperor, having succeeded in securing theological support for a policy of making concessions to Protestants at the expense of the church, was still acting in harmony with the historic principles that had been applied in the sixteenth century; but he was following a theological opinion that was based on expediency, an opinion that did much to promote the secularization of politics.[46]

It was all the more easy for Ferdinand and his minister Trauttmannsdorff to apply this theological opinion because the Swedes and French had demanded the cession of Silesian lands, not necessarily in hopes of securing them for Brandenburg, but in order to persuade the imperial court to give its consent to the project of secularizing church lands.[47] It was also recorded that on February 12, 1646, Trauttmannsdorff experienced great joy when he learned that he had succeeded, through Salvius, whom he had probably bribed, in inducing the Swedish government to omit from its utmost demands the Hapsburg hereditary land of Silesia, "the apple of the eye" of the emperor, as the Austrian minister called it during the negotiations. After receiving news of this advantageous arrangement, he had no hesitancy in offering the Swedes Hither Pomerania and the bishoprics of Bremen

[42] Meiern, *op. cit.*, III, 150–55; Steinberger, *op. cit.*, p. 60.

[43] Steinberger, *op. cit.*, p. 61. [44] *Ibid.*, pp. 58, 61–62. [45] *Ibid.*, pp. 61–62.

[46] See chapters xi-xiii on the controversial literature of the period.

[47] Heigel, *op. cit.*, V, 424; Pütter, *op. cit.*, p. 167.

and Verden as a part of their satisfaction.[48] Moreover, as soon as it was clear that the imperial court would not need to lose any of its own possessions, a secularization of ecclesiastical lands to the advantage of Brandenburg was all the more easily promoted.[49]

Once the emperor and Trauttmannsdorff had decided to regard church lands the "great cloth from which all equivalents must be cut,"[50] they were no longer hesitant and embarrassed. They boldly disposed of the ecclesiastical territories. The pious ecclesiasts and their supporters denounced such action by saying that the imperialists "are for amusement playing with ecclesiastical foundations and monasteries as boys would play with nuts and marbles." To this the accused replied: "Every régime (including the ecclesiastical) has its fatal period [*periodum fatalem*] and is subject to change."[51] While the emperor was carrying out his decision to cede the lands of the church to his victorious enemies in order to protect his own hereditary lands, his action was so striking that the French plenipotentiary at Münster, the Duke de Longueville, in a letter addressed to the king of France, January 25, 1647, made the following illuminating comment:

> And truly the imperial negotiators think little of the property of the church, and, provided one does not touch the hereditary property of the house of Austria, they have no great concern for those of St. Peter. All the Catholics in the Empire perceive this truth more clearly than ever, and this consideration will some day prompt the electors and Catholic princes to form a closer connection with France, seeing themselves abandoned by the emperor, who easily sacrifices the interests of the church, when it is a matter of preserving his own.[52]

However, responsibility for the spoliation of the church of its lands lay not alone at the door of the imperialists. The French, on the whole, had refrained from demanding church lands as in-

[48] Chemnitz, *Geschichte des schwedischen in Deutschland geführten Krieges*, Part IV, Book 6, p. 41, col. 1; Odhner, *op. cit.*, p. 138; Breucker, *op. cit.*, p. 44.

[49] Pütter, *op. cit.*, p. 167; Breucker, *op. cit.*, pp. 90, 93.

[50] Heigel, *op. cit.*, V, 424; Geist, *op. cit.*, pp. 17–18.

[51] Hanser, *op. cit.*, pp. 65–66.

[52] Le Clerc, *op. cit.*, IV, 76.

demnification for their Protestant allies, since such action would be "disadvantageous to their religion and salvation."[53] But the Duke de Longueville demanded that the Landgravine of Hesse-Cassel be given a part of the bishopric of Paderborn and Fulda, the abbey of Hirschfeld, and other ecclesiastical lands. Thereupon the Bishop of Osnabrück, Franz Wilhelm von Wartenberg, in the presence of many representatives, objected, in a very neat speech, that His Most Christian Majesty, the French king, was exposing himself to serious criticism if he plundered the church to the advantage of a heretic, the Landgravine of Hesse-Cassel. It is just as though he were using the coat of Christ and Mary to cover a heretical woman. To this the Duke replied complacently but cynically, that "for a woman as virtuous as the Landgravine it is necessary to do much. Why, gentlemen, are you not willing to endure sacrifices yourselves in order to give the full satisfaction desired by Madame Landgravine?"[54] With such representatives pleading her cause it was not surprising that the Landgravine was allowed to incorporate the abbey of Hirschfeld with Hesse-Cassel.[55] The French, who criticized the Austrians for despoiling the church to protect their own secular interests, also insisted on the spoliation of the church to reward and please their ally, by which action they were also protecting their own interests and, as we shall amplify later, were co-operating in the secularization of politics.

[53] Meiern, *op. cit.*, IV, 419.

[54] *Ibid.*, IV, 419; Hanser, *op. cit.*, p. 65; Heigel, *op. cit.*, V, 425.

[55] Heigel, *op. cit.*, V, 425.

Chapter Six

WHY AUSTRIA WAS WILLING TO IGNORE PAPAL PROTESTS

I. THE AUSTRIAN RULERS AND URBAN VIII

ALTHOUGH a good Catholic, extremely rigid in observing the precepts of the church, Emperor Ferdinand III was milder in spirit, more independent in thought, and less fanatical than his father, Ferdinand II (1619–37), had been.[1] His education had been given him by Jesuits, but they were not much in his good graces.[2] He allowed them no influence whatever in his government.[3] He loved peace and was eager to secure a cessation of war.[4] From his father's career he had learned the danger of placing religious above political interests.[5] Such an attitude was undoubtedly taken by him to a large extent as a result of his own relations, as well as those of his father, with Urban VIII (1623–44).

It is difficult to come to a correct and final verdict concerning Urban VIII and his relations to the emperors Ferdinand II and

[1] Gindely, *Geschichte des dreissigjährigen Krieges*, III, 98; Koch, *Geschichte des deutschen Reiches unter der Regierung Ferdinands III*, pp. 1, 9; Huber, *Geschichte Österreichs*, V, 516; *Cambridge Modern History*, IV, 397.

[2] Fiedler, *Die Relationen der Botschafter Venedigs über Deutschland und Österreich im siebzehnten Jahrhundert* ("Fontes Rerum Austriacarum," Zweite Abth.), XXVI, 189; Steinberger, *Die Jesuiten und die Friedensfrage*, pp. 16, 17.

[3] Gindley, *op. cit.*, III, 98; Koch, *op. cit.*, I, 4.

[4] Fiedler, *op. cit.*, XXVI, 389; Stieve, "Ferdinand III," *Allgemeine deutsche Biographie*, VI, 665; Würzbach, *Biographisches Lexikon des Kaiserthums Österreich*, "Ferdinand III," VI, 188; Hanser, *Deutschland nach dem dreissigjährigen Kriege*, p. 48.

[5] Krones, *Handbuch der Geschichte Oesterreichs*, III, 537.

Ferdinand III.[6] One must reject as false the statements: (1) that Urban was almost hostile toward Spain and Austria, and that he wished to humiliate these powers and promote the welfare of France;[7] (2) that, in order to weaken the House of Austria, he tolerated the French alliance with the German Protestants and Swedes, and that Gustavus Adolphus was the natural ally of the pope;[8] (3) that he advocated the dismissal of Wallenstein, Ferdinand II's successful general;[9] (4) that he prevented the election of Ferdinand (later Ferdinand III) as king of the Romans in 1630 at the Diet of Ratisbon (Regensburg);[10] (5) that he rejoiced over the victories of Gustavus Adolphus and mourned over his death.[11] But, in spite of these corrections to the advantage of Urban's character, his relations with the Hapsburgs were full of incidents that caused Ferdinand III to harbor such an ill will toward the pope that it was easier to disregard church and papal interests when sanctioning the final provisions of the Peace of Westphalia. Ferdinand III remembered not only his own vexatious experiences but those of his

[6] Pastor, *Geschichte der Päpste*, XIII, Part II, 1020–31, where is presented a bibliographical account of the older and newer views concerning Urban's policies during the Thirty Years' War; Michael Ott, *Catholic Encyclopedia*, XV, 218–21; Leman, *Urbain VIII et la rivalité de la France et la maison d' Autriche de 1631 à 1635*, pp. v–viii, 524–27.

[7] Gregorovius, *Urban VIII im Widerspruch zu Spanien und dem Kaiser*, p. 7; Ranke, *Die römischen Päpste* (4th ed.), II, 539–40; Pastor, *op. cit.*, XIII, Part I, 266–67, 299–300, 366–67, 370–71, 381–86, 453–54, 463–66, *et al.;* Wurm, in Wetzer and Welte, *Kirchenlexikon*, XII, 451–52.

[8] Ranke, *op. cit.*, II, 558; Leman, *op. cit.*, pp. vi–vii, 72–118, but especially pp. 100–118; Pastor, *op. cit.*, XIII, Part I, 430–31; Wurm in Wetzer and Welte, *op. cit.*, XII, 452.

[9] Ranke, *op. cit.*, II, 555; Gregorovius, *op. cit.*, p. 17; Pastor, *op. cit.*, XIII, Part I, 415–16.

[10] Gregorovius, *op. cit.*, pp. 20–22; Pastor, *op. cit.*, XIII, Part I, 416.

[11] Ranke, *op. cit.*, II, 558; Gregorovius, *op. cit.*, pp. 41, 80; Ward, in *Cambridge Modern History*, IV, 681–82; Benrath, in Herzog-Hauck, *Realencyklopädie*, XX, 327–28; Pastor, *op. cit.*, XIII, Part I, 459–61; Pieper, "Beiträge zur Geschichte des 30jährigen Krieges," Part III (review of Gregorovius, *Urban VIII*), *Historisch-politische Blätter*, XCIV (1884), 471–92; Ehses, "Papst Urban VIII und Gustav Adolf," *Historisches Jahrbuch*, XVI (1895), 336–41; Schnitzer, *Urban VIII. Verhalten bei der Nachricht vom Tode des Schwedenkönigs, Festschrift zum elfhundert jährigen Jubiläum des deutschen Campo Santo in Rom*, pp. 280–83; Schnitzer, *Zur Politik des heiligen Stuhles in der ersten Hälfte des dreissigjährigen Krieges*, pp. 238–41; Leman, *op. cit.*, pp. 245–49; Wolf, review of Leman's work, *Zeitschrift für Kirchengeschichte*, XLIV, 140.

father, with whom he was closely associated in affairs of state.[12]

The Vienna court had been annoyed because, when Ferdinand II was planning and executing the Edict of Restitution (1629), which would restore many German ecclesiastical lands to Catholic control, Urban preserved an attitude of great reserve. Ferdinand II requested that the pope arrange in Rome a public demonstration of joy, processions, and other ceremonies, such as had occurred after the capture of La Rochelle by Richelieu in 1628; but Urban restricted himself to issuing a breve of thanks to the emperor and to mentioning the Edict of Restitution in a praising and acknowledging way in a papal consistory.[13] This papal coldness is easy to understand. Ferdinand was carrying out a policy of state control of church affairs, whereby the restored church lands were, in a preliminary way, to be distributed to the pecuniary and political advantage of Austria without consulting the pope.[14] Moreover, the emperor presented the proposed plan to the Catholic electors but did not present it to Urban VIII; the name of the pope was not mentioned in the entire document; when the commissioners were selected to execute the Edict, the Holy See was ignored entirely.[15] When Urban demanded that the returned lands be taken from the hands of the imperially appointed commissioners and turned over to bishops, who would be more considerate of church interests, the Vienna government warned the bishops not to appeal to Rome concerning the matter, and told the nuncio in Vienna not to meddle in the affair. The government asserted the principle that the kings and princes had to observe papal decisions only in matters of faith, whereas in matters of

[12] Stieve, "Ferdinand II," *Allegmeine deutsche Biographie*, VI, 664.

[13] Pastor, *op. cit.*, XIII, Part I, 410–11, 442; Duhr, *Geschichte der Jesuiten in den Ländern deutscher Zunge in der ersten Hälfte des XVII. Jahrhunderts*, II, Part I, 463; Weech, *Urban VIII*, p. 53.

[14] Stieve, "Ferdinand II," *op. cit.*, VI, 664; Ritter, *Deutsche Geschichte*, III, 425–35.

[15] Tupetz, *Der Streit um die geistlichen Güter und das Restitutionsedict, 1629*, p. 443; Pastor, *op. cit.*, XIII, Part I, 410–11.

church government they may vigorously resist the pope.[16] We see here a manifestation of the spirit of the secularization of politics. Just as Ferdinand I and his father had in 1555 regarded themselves as authorized to negotiate the Peace of Augsburg, even though prejudicial to the church, just so Ferdinand II regarded himself as having authority to settle the question of ecclesiastical lands, especially after the regaining of those lands had been the fruits of a victorious imperial war, waged with only meager papal financial aid.[17]

2. URBAN VIII'S ATTITUDE CONCERNING THE THIRTY YEARS' WAR

In the latter aspects of the Thirty Years' War the Austrians felt that Urban did not always take the correct position concerning the rivalry of the great Catholic powers—France as opposed to Austria and Spain.[18] Ferdinand II and Philip IV (1621–65) of Spain had regarded the Thirty Years' War as a religious war.[19] Both Paul V (1605–21) and Gregory XV (1621–23), acting in harmony with such a view, had heartily supported Ferdinand, Maximilian of Bavaria, and the Catholic League during the beginnings of the war, such action appearing to be to the advantage of the church and the Catholic Restoration.[20] The Austrians naturally counted on a continuation of such a papal policy, but Urban took a different view. As the war proceeded, it became less religious and more political; and Urban shrewdly observed this tendency and was less co-operative with the Austrians.[21] But in doing so he was committing an error in judgment, especially when he underestimated the danger that the invasion of Gustavus Adolphus was to the Catholic cause;[22] he thus offended Hapsburg sensibilities, for the

[16] Tupetz, *op. cit.*, pp. 443–45; Pastor, *op. cit.*, XIII, Part I, 412.

[17] See next section in this chapter.

[18] Pastor, *op. cit.*, XIII, Part I, 119. [19] *Ibid.*, p. 20.

[20] *Ibid.*, XII, 572–75; XIII, Part I, 15; *Cambridge Modern History*, IV, 31, 673.

[21] Pastor, *op. cit.*, XIII, Part 1, 500; Huber, *op. cit.*, V, 399.

[22] Pastor, *op. cit.*, XIII, Part I, 20, 414.

Austrian and Spanish courts felt that Urban should have been more energetic in dissuading Richelieu from co-operating with the Swedes and their German allies.[23] It is true that in the years 1632–34 Urban had sent about two million francs to the Catholics in Germany, the League receiving some of it, but most of it going to the emperor.[24] However, the Austrians had repeatedly asked him for financial aid in the common Catholic cause,[25] but his contributions were by no means as large as had been requested and expected.[26] If the pope had based his ungenerous contributions on the fact that the court of Vienna was guilty of financial extravagance and mismanagement in carrying on the war, as had been manifest until the year 1624,[27] such an excuse could not have made any chastening and corrective impression in Vienna, since Urban was squandering money on his nephews and lavishly providing for his own army and fortifications.[28] Added to this, he frequently showed a distrustful attitude toward the Hapsburg courts at Vienna and Madrid,[29] whereas he continued to have friendly relations with Louis XIII and Richelieu, whom the Hapsburgs regarded as fosterers of heresy.[30]

3. PAPAL POLITICAL AMBITIONS AND THEIR CONSEQUENCES

The fundamental factor in explaining the ill will between the courts of Rome and Vienna lay, however, in the fact that Urban VIII, like his predecessors, had the idea that he must rule independently as a political prince, as ruler of the Papal States, in

[23] *Ibid.*, p. 19; Huber, *op. cit.*, V, 399.

[24] Pieper, "Beiträge zur Geschichte des 30jährigen Krieges," *Historisch-politische Blätter*, XCIV, 480; Pastor, *op. cit.*, XIII, Part I, 21; Ott, *Catholic Encyclopedia*, XV, 220.

[25] Pastor, *op. cit.*, XIII, Part I, 179, 299–300, 443, 447, 448, 450, 451, 466.

[26] *Ibid.*, pp. 299–301, 431, 441–42, 447, 450; Leman, *op. cit.*, pp. 50, 146–65, Schnitzer, *Zur Politik des heiligen Stuhles*, pp. 226–35, 237.

[27] Duhr, *op. cit.*, II, Part II, 698; Pastor, *op. cit.*, XIII, Part I, 21.

[28] Pastor, *op. cit.*, XIII, Part I, 260–61; Part II, 848–52; Ott, *op. cit.*, XV, 219–20; Benrath, in Herzog-Hauck, *op. cit.*, XX, 328; Weech, *op. cit.*, pp. 90, 91.

[29] Pastor, *op. cit.*, XIII, Part I, 266, 267, 417, 419, 425–26.

[30] Leman, *op. cit.*, p. 525.

order that he might be independent as religious head of the church. This position of political independence was difficult to maintain, since more than half of Italy was in the possession of the king of Spain. Therefore Urban looked to France, which had no possessions in the Italian peninsula, as a sort of counterweight to Spain; this would enable him to retain his political independence in Italy.[31] In the years 1620–35 there had been a number of serious international contests in north Italy between Spain and France, in which Spain had been supported by Austria.[32] Richelieu skilfully exploited all the resulting unpleasant friction between Spain and the pope and succeeded in giving the impression that Urban was being surrounded and oppressed.[33]

It was unfortunate that Austria was supporting Spanish aggression in north Italy just at this critical time during the Thirty Years' War, especially in the years 1629–35. This implied Hapsburg plans to dominate Italy, thus jeopardizing the cherished independence of the Papal States. But even more important was Urban's fear that Spain and Austria would dominate the whole church. This, together with Ferdinand II's disregard of papal wishes in planning and executing the Edict of Restitution, caused the pope to feel that Hapsburg political influence was a real menace to the church.[34]

Urban repeatedly, between 1633 and 1642, made genuine efforts to reconcile the Bourbons and Hapsburgs in order to give peace to Europe; he wished to be *padre commune* to all Catholics. But both Richelieu and Mazarin continued the struggle against the Hapsburgs for political reasons. Urban received no thanks from the courts of Vienna and Madrid, where he was regarded as friendly to France. The French, however, regarded him as being too friendly toward the Hapsburgs. He was plead-

[31] Pastor, *op. cit.*, XIII, Part I, 20; Part II, 1031; Schnitzer, *Zur Politik des heiligen Stuhles*, pp. 241, 245–46.

[32] Pastor, *op. cit.*, XIII, Part I, 21, 266–98, 366–407; *Cambridge Modern History*, IV, 35–63.

[33] Pastor, *op. cit.*, XIII, Part I, 21.

[34] *Ibid.*, pp. 21–22.

ing a lost cause; none of the courts wished an impartial mediator; each desired the pope to become an unconditional, submissive ally.[35]

It is easy to agree that Urban VIII was misjudged by his contemporaries and later critics. It is clear that he possessed a shrewd insight into actuality and made honest efforts to induce the Catholic powers to cease their fratricidal war and establish peace. But by so doing he was seriously injuring Austrian interests and playing into the hands of French politics.[36] It is not surprising that the Austrians came to regard him less as a spiritual leader than as a political monarch; to them he was disregarding religious interests and fostering political interests in a partisan way.

It is undoubtedly true that the reports of the Venetian ambassadors must be used with caution by the historian of the seventeenth century,[37] but no criticism can explain away entirely the manifest ill will of Ferdinand III toward Urban VIII as portrayed in the reports of the Venetian ambassadors at Vienna in the years 1638 and 1641. In the first year two ambassadors, Zeno and Contarini, report that the emperor complains because the pope shows himself so partial to the French, is such a declared enemy of the House of Austria, and that one cannot hope for anything from him. Furthermore, the emperor is disgusted because the pope did not send a nuncio extraordinary to congratulate him upon his election to the emperorship, as all other princes had done that were not in open war or on bad terms with him. The emperor ascribes this to the pope's ill will and his wish to second the claims and pretensions of the French, with whom he shows himself so united in support of their empty

[35] *Ibid.*, pp. 19–20, 23, 462–66, 464–71, 473–74, 480–84, 489–92, 495; Leman, *op. cit.*, pp. vii, 390–489, 524–25; Wurm, in Wetzer and Welte, *op. cit.*, XII, 451.

[36] Pastor, *op. cit.*, XIII, Part I, 19; Wolf (review of Leman's work), *op. cit.*, XLIV (1925), 140.

[37] Hübner, *Sixte-Quint*, I, 11–12; Pieper, "Beiträge zur Geschichte des 30jährigen Krieges," *Historisch-politische Blätter*, XCIV, 491–95; Ehses, "Papst Urban VIII," *Historisches Jahrbuch*, XVI, 336; Pastor, *op. cit.*, XIII, Part II, 1021.

pretexts. It is also papal opinion that the imperial election was not well grounded but took place in a disorderly way. The emperor's greatest bitterness comes from the pope's showing himself so partial to the French.[38]

In 1641 another Venetian ambassador in Vienna, Johann Grimani, records that the emperor is expecting the death of Pope Urban VIII and that the emperor is still offended because Urban keeps his favorable attitude toward France and is ill disposed toward all the House of Austria; "if the pope would only do his duty, Christendom would soon have good peace."[39]

4. FERDINAND III AND INNOCENT X

Ferdinand's feeling of dissatisfaction with the papacy under Urban VIII was changed very little, if at all, during the pontificate of his successor, Innocent X (1644–55). The Austrian court manifested only a slight interest in the conclave when the election occurred, giving no instructions in spite of requests for such information by Giulio Savelli, the papal nuncio in Vienna, Cardinal Colonna, the new protector of the German nation, or Cardinal Harrach, Archbishop of Prague. Hapsburg interests were represented only by a Spanish plenipotentiary, Count Sirvela, who arrived shortly before the beginning of the conclave.[40] Innocent X was a weak, dependent, politically unimportant man, with a rather inglorious pontificate.[41] Although he was not unfavorable to Spanish and Austrian interests, his fear of the French prevented him from giving any financial aid to the emperor.[42]

[38] Fiedler, "Die Relationen der Botschafter Venedigs," *Fontes Rerum*, XXVI, 195–96.

[39] *Ibid.*, p. 285.

[40] Wahrmund, *Das Ausschliessungs-Recht der Katholischen Staaten Österreich, Frankreich und Spanien bei den Papstwahlen*, p. 129; Pastor, *op. cit.*, XIV, Part I, 18–19.

[41] Wetzer and Welte, *op. cit.*, VI, 752; Pastor, *op. cit.*, XIV, Part I, 29, 277; Ott, in *Catholic Encyclopedia*, VIII, 21.

[42] Koch, *op. cit.*, II, 37–39.

5. THE SECULAR INTERESTS OF FERDINAND III

To what extent these feelings toward Urban VIII and Innocent X influenced Ferdinand III in sanctioning terms of peace detrimental to the interests of the church it is impossible to estimate. Surely the preservation of his own estates was uppermost in causing him to consent to paying his war losses with church property, more especially because the unfavorable treatment given him by the papacy had been a factor in causing the House of Austria to lose the war.

Such a momentous decision was made all the easier for him by virtue of the advice of several court theologians, the confessor of the empress, the Capuchin Diego Quiroga, and the Cistercian Johann Caramuel y Lobkowitz, whose literary justification of a policy of compromise will be considered later.[43] These theologians sanctioned the permanent cession of ecclesiastical lands to the secular powers in the face of the opposition of the Catholics at Münster, led by the nuncio Chigi, who tried, through the nuncio at Vienna, Camillo Melzio, to thwart Ferdinand's willingness to make concessions.[44]

If the outcome of the war had been favorable to Austria, Ferdinand III would surely have been more considerate of church interests than he was. But in losing the war he felt the need of protecting his own interests as much as possible, even if he had to sacrifice church interests. As early as March 5, 1646, the emperor was quoted as having said that in case of extreme necessity one would need to accept what was unalterable.[45] No one can be quite certain as to what arrangements would have been made if there had been an Austrian victory. But one must recall that the spirit of secularizing politics had already been manifest in the Austrian monarchy in 1629 when Ferdinand II,

[43] See below, chap. xvi.

[44] Krones, *Österreichische Geschichte, Sammlung Göschen*, II, 166; Steinberger, *op. cit.*, p. 62.

[45] "Ein anders wirdt es seyen, wann man nit anderst kan dass man per conveniantam zulasse, was man für diesmal nit wehren kann." Israel, *Adam Adami und seine Arcana Pacis Westphalicae*, pp. 39–40, who cites Vienna archives.

in formulating and applying the Edict of Restitution, disposed of ecclesiastical lands according to a secular policy. Now, in 1646–48, when defeat was certain, the Hapsburgs went even farther in the direction of secularizing politics; to save state interests, church interests had to be sacrificed. By October 15, 1647, Ferdinand III had become so certain of the need of making the concessions in question that he instructed his representatives at the Congress, Lamberg and Crane, to inform the extreme Catholics that if they did not yield he would use his sovereign imperial power to coerce them to yield. He had done all he could in the face of a superior enemy; he would have to yield.[46]

6. THE PEACE POLICIES OF TRAUTTMANNSDORFF DETERMINATIVE

In carrying out a policy of concessions disadvantageous to the church Ferdinand III was ably supported by his chief minister, Count Maximilian von Trauttmannsdorff (1584–1650). He was the emperor's representative at Münster and Osnabrück from November 29, 1645, until July 16, 1647; and it was he that shaped the policies and conducted the negotiations that finally led to the conclusion of a conciliatory peace. He had served under four Austrian emperors and had the full confidence of his master, Ferdinand, whose policy he shaped while in Vienna; and, while at the Peace Congress, he virtually was the source of his own instructions.[47] Like two other of his diplomatic colleagues at the Congress, the Count of Nassau and Isaac Volmar, he was a convert from Protestantism to Catholicism.[48] But his conversion may not have been one of conviction; his

[46] Pastor, *op. cit.*, XIV, Part I, 89; Israel, *op. cit.*, pp. 67–68.

[47] Egloffstein, article "Trauttmannsdorff," *Allgemeine deutsche Biographie*, XXXVIII, 532–34; Koch, *op. cit.*, I, 18; II, 376; Braun, "Skizzen aus dem diplomatischen Leben und Wirken des Sachsen-Altenburgischen Gesandten am westphälischen Friedenskongresse, Wolfgang Conrad von Thumbshirn," *Mittheilungen der Geschichts- und Alterthumsforschenden Gesellschaft des Osterlandes*, IV, 399–400; Odhner, *Die Politik Schwedens*, p. 105.

[48] Walther, *Universal Register*, pp. 6, 8, 9; Pütter, *Geist des westphälischen Friedens*, pp. 53, 54; Koch, *op. cit.*, I, 15.

parents, who had become Protestants before his birth, returned to Catholicism before he had grown up, probably for the purpose of securing a government appointment, and he changed his creed with them.[49] At any rate, he was regarded as being only a mild convert to Catholicism, bearing no hatred toward Protestants and always tolerant of those differing in opinion with him.[50] He was the most capable and unprejudiced of the counselors of Ferdinand, and for that gloomy age he had an unusually elevated, tolerant, and moderate viewpoint.[51]

For his unimpressive exterior, lean figure, and sallow complexion he possessed compensatory qualities that caused him to become the center of negotiations of Westphalia. He manifested an innate earnestness, readiness in speech, calmness and fixity of purpose. In his negotiations he was frank and friendly but was firm when handling important questions. He could see the heart of a problem without obscuring it with nonessentials. He succeeded in many things in which others would have failed. When treated arrogantly and even insultingly by the enemy negotiators, he always preserved an even temper and a shrewd and resolute bearing. He conquered through his superior mentality, his sagacious evasion whenever his opponents sought to drive him into an embarrassing situation. His freedom from religious prejudice and his insight and experience as a statesman account for the confidence that his presence aroused in the members of the Congress.[52] He knew how to secure the good will of the Swedish representative Oxenstierna; he secured the

[49] Egloffstein, "Trauttmannsdorff," *Allgemeine deutsche Biographie*, XXXVIII, 532; Würzbach, *op. cit.*, XLVII, 77; Koch, *op. cit.*, I, 14–15.

[50] Droysen, *Geschichte der preussischen Politik*, III, Part I, 211; Odhner, *op. cit.*, p. 119.

[51] Egloffstein, article "Volmar," *Allgemeine deutsche Biographie*, XL, 265; Koch, *op. cit.*, I, 17; Odhner, *op. cit.*, p. 119; Huber, *op. cit.*, V, 595.

[52] Le Clerc, *Négociations secrètes*, I, 468; Heigel, "Das westfälische Friedenswerk von 1643 bis 1648," *Zeitschrift für Geschichte und Politik*, V, 419; Huber, *op. cit.*, V, 595; Würzbach, *op. cit.*, XLVII, 78; Odhner, *op. cit.*, pp. 120, 224; Koch, *op. cit.*, II, 528; Hansen, "Briefe des Jesuitenpaters Nithard Biber an den Churfürsten Anselm Casimir von Mainz," *Archivalische Zeitschrift*, Neue Folge, IX, 133; Gindely, *op. cit.*, III, 181–82; Charvériat, *Histoire de la guerre de trente ans*, II, 538.

friendship of the Protestant representatives by manifesting a yielding attitude concerning questions of amnesty and the ceding of ecclesiastical possessions.[53] Oxenstierna called him the "soul" of the Austrian delegation; in general by friend and foe he was paid a high tribute for his zeal for peace, his good will toward everyone, and for his moderation and rectitude.[54] He had been unremitting in his efforts to terminate the Thirty Years' War; he had been intrusted by Ferdinand II to negotiate the Conciliatory Peace of Prague in 1635 with the evangelical princes.[55] He now had a policy of conciliation when undertaking peace negotiations in Westphalia.

Into the intricacies of his varied negotiations we cannot go. It is enough to point out that he regarded it as his first and most important duty to bring about a reconciliation of the German princes by making far-reaching concessions to them rather than cede German territory to foreigners. He hoped to make some arrangements with France, Sweden, and their Protestant allies that would not require a cession of Silesia or other Hapsburg hereditary lands.[56] To accomplish this he had to use church lands, "Pfaffengut," "the great cloth from which all equivalents must be cut," to use his own expressions.[57] He felt that such a policy alone would save the Catholic church in Germany; only by signing a conciliatory peace at any cost could the dreadful devastating war be brought to a conclusion.[58] His yielding policy caused the Protestants, Swedes, and French merely to in-

[53] Heigel, *op. cit.*, V, 419.

[54] Meiern, *Acta pacis Westphalicae publicae*, IV, 112, Egloffstein, "Trauttmannsdorff," *Allgemeine deutsche Biographie*, XXXVIII, 536; Würzbach, *op. cit.*, XLVII, 78.

[55] Würzbach, *op. cit.*, XLVII, 77; Odhner, *op. cit.*, p. 119; *Cambridge Modern History*, IV, 252–54; Pastor, *op. cit.*, XIII, Part I, 477–80.

[56] Heigel, *op. cit.*, V, 419; Egloffstein, "Trauttmannsdorff," *Allgemeine deutsche Biographie*, XXXVIII, 534; Geist, *op. cit.*, p. 17.

[57] Heigel, *op. cit.*, V, 424; Geist, *Die Säkularisation des Bistums Halberstadt*, p. 17.

[58] Pastor, *op. cit.*, XIV, Part I, 81; Huber, *op. cit.*, V, 601; Koch, *op. cit.*, II, 365, quotes letter of Trauttmannsdorff to Ferdinand III, dated June 15, 1646, which is in the Vienna archives; Israel, *op. cit.*, pp. 61–62; Reumont, "Fabio Chigi—Papst Alexander VII in Deutschland," *Zeitschrift des Aachener Geschichtsvereins*, VII, 8.

crease their demands; and it was necessary to make further con cessions in order to attain peace. This was especially necessary after Bavaria had signed the armistice of Ulm with France and Sweden on March 14, 1647.[59] However, he refused to concede that the Protestants in the Austrian hereditary lands should have religious autonomy. In April, 1647, he remarked to the Swedish representative Salvius that he would not sign such a provision even if he were sitting in prison in Stockholm.[60] The significant fact in this connection is that it was he, who in the months of November, 1646, to February, 1647, had agreed to the cessions of ecclesiastical lands as indemnification to Austria's victorious enemies and had agreed to the insertion of the clause against all protests that might aim to invalidate the treaty arrangements.[61]

Trauttmannsdorff's yielding attitude naturally caused criticism by Innocent X, Chigi, and the extreme Catholics; they had no appreciation for his moderation when ceding church lands and sanctioning toleration of heretics.[62] Even before Trauttmannsdorff's arrival at Münster, Chigi wrote to Pamfili, the papal secretary of state, October 27, 1645, "Trauttmannsdorff is coming, as is believed, to make peace, even though unfavorable, if nothing else is possible; and he is not too greatly concerned over religious matters, as one can see from the Peace of Prague," which the Count had negotiated in 1635.[63] In contrast with the favorable opinion that history has conceded Trauttmannsdorff, the extreme Catholics regarded him as being only moderately gifted, credulous, timid, apprehensive, and not

[59] Pastor, *op. cit.*, XIV, Part I, 80–81, 83; Egloffstein, "Trauttmannsdorff," *Allgemeine deutsche Biographie*, XXXVIII, 535.

[60] Meiern, *op. cit.*, IV, 488; Odhner, *op. cit.*, pp. 202–4; Huber, *op. cit.*, V, 605; Pastor, *op. cit.*, XIV, Part I, 86–87; Ritter, *op. cit.*, III, 275–76.

[61] See chap. iv.

[62] Hansen, *op. cit.*, letters of Biber to Anselm Casimir, dated Rome, February 3, 10, and March 24, 1646, pp. 158–59, 160–61, 170–71; Steinberger, *op. cit.*, pp. 51, 52, 58–61, 92; Pastor, *op. cit.*, XIV, Part I, 79–80.

[63] Steinberger, *op. cit.*, p. 58, n. 10; letter in Vatican archives.

shrewd in his ardor to come to an understanding with the Swedes and Protestants.[64]

At the papal court also, Trauttmannsdorff was held in low esteem. He was regarded as "a traitor to the Catholic church," as "betraying the Catholic religion," as being "demented." His actions at the Congress were not only "sharply condemned" but "cursed"; he was "scorned as a human being that was born under an evil star for the purpose of destroying the faith in Germany and the House of Austria"; he was a "faithless minister who contemns the true religion and grants everything to the heretics." It was hard to convince the court "that the Count was guiltless."[65] The Spanish, whose interests coincided with those of the extreme Catholics, regarded him as being too sanguine, too easily blinded by the highly colored presentations of his opponents, and too willing to let them view his cards. Peñaranda at one time described Trauttmannsdorff as being a man that had little courage in time of misfortune and one who would purchase peace at any price in order to escape the embarrassment of handling a difficult problem.[66] Trauttmannsdorff left Münster July 16, 1647, to return to Vienna, owing to ill health.[67] There is probably no truth in the affirmation that he left or was recalled as a result of Jesuit and Spanish influence. He went of his own free will.[68] But his departure gave great joy to the extreme Catholics, to Chigi, and to the Spaniards.[69] However, when he left Münster, he felt that peace was assured, or else he would not have left. Chigi had learned from Trautt-

[64] Pastor, *op. cit.*, XIV, Part I, 80–82.

[65] Hansen, *op. cit.*, letters of February 3, 10, and March 24, 1648; *Archivalische Zeitschrift*, Neue Folge, IX, 158–59, 160, 170.

[66] *Coleccio de documentos ineditos*, LXXXII, 245; LXXXIII, 324; Pastor, *op. cit.*, XIV, Part I, 80, n. 1.

[67] Koch, *op. cit.*, II, 528, Egloffstein, "Trauttmannsdorff," *Allgemeine deutsche Biographie*, XXXVIII, 535; Huber, *op. cit.*, V, 606.

[68] Meiern, *op. cit.*, IV, 703; Bougeant, *Histoire des guerres*, V, 345; Pütter, *op. cit.*, pp. 53–56; Koch, *op. cit.*, II, 342, 375–76, 528.

[69] Meiern, *op. cit.*, IV, 654; Odhner, *op. cit.*, p. 224; Egloffstein, "Trauttmannsdorff," *Allegmeine deutsche Biographie*, XXXVIII, 535.

mannsdorff's son that the Count had said that he could not permit himself to be seen at the imperial court except as a bearer of peace.[70]

After Trauttmannsdorff left Münster, the Austrian delegation was in the hands of his colleague, Isaac Volmar, Baron von Rieden (1582–1657), who was a very able man;[71] but he had less diplomatic ability than Trauttmannsdorff, and his great efforts to secure increased concessions for Austria were not realized.[72] Although the military successes of the emperor prolonged the war for over a year, the final arrangements were fundamentally those that Trauttmannsdorff had secured during his stay of almost twenty months at the Congress (November 29, 1645—July 16, 1647).[73]

The essential to keep in mind is that he was the most potent factor in bringing about a cessation of war and the establishment of a conciliating peace. He placed the political welfare of his emperor and country above the ecclesiastical and temporal interests of the pope and church. He negotiated a peace that he hoped would be permanent, and made certain that papal and all other protests against it would be regarded by all contracting parties as null and ineffective.

[70] Pastor, *op. cit.*, XIV, Part I, 88; Koch, *op. cit.*, II, 369.

[71] Walther, *op. cit.*, p. 10; Wicquefort, *L'ambassadeur*, II, 215; Meiern, *op. cit.*, I, 50–51; Würzbach, *op. cit.*, LI, 269; Egloffstein, "Volmar," in *Allgemeine deutsche Biographie*, XL, 536.

[72] Egloffstein, "Volmar," *Allgemeine deutsche Biographie*, XL, 267; Pastor, *op. cit.*, XIV, Part I, 90; Braun, "Skizzen, etc.," *Mittheilungen, etc.*, IV, 400–401.

[73] Koch, *op. cit.*, II, 528: Egloffstein, "Trauttmannsdorff," *Allgemeine deutsche Biographie*, XXXVIII, 535–36; also article "Volmar," *Allgemeine deutsche Biographie*, XL, 267.

Chapter Seven

FRENCH INTERESTS IN THE SECULARIZATION OF POLITICS

1. RICHELIEU, THE MAN OF STATE, THE "REALPOLITIKER"

IN THE opinion of the able Catholic historian, Ludwig Pastor,[1] two cardinals of the Roman Catholic church, Richelieu and Mazarin, did most to secularize politics in the seventeenth century and to make it impossible for the church to complete the Catholic Renaissance or Reformation and thus once more unite Europe religiously. Leopold von Ranke says:

> Among all non-Protestants that ever lived, none rendered a greater service to Protestantism than this Cardinal [Richelieu], who broke its political power in France. On the other hand, he rejuvenated it in Germany, and directed it in England into the path that would secure for him the greatest world-influence.[2]

As a churchman Richelieu had led such a strictly moral life and performed his ecclesiastical function so well that even his most bitter enemies could find nothing to criticize in him.[3] One of his greatest ambitions had been to secure the cardinal's hat, but he regarded himself as a cardinal not by the grace of the pope but by the grace of the king, who had urgently recommended his appointment; the cardinalate was merely a step toward political power and inviolability in his own country.[4] He never even

[1] *Geschichte der Päpste*, XIII, Part I, 23.

[2] Ranke, *Französiche Geschichte*, II, 509.

[3] Pastor, *op. cit.*, XIII, Part I, 504; Lavisse, *Histoire de France depuis les origins jusqu' à la Révolution*, VI, Part II, 368–69; Federn, *Richelieu*, p. 146.

[4] Mommsen, *Richelieu, politisches Testament und kleinere Schriften*, pp. 56–57; Federn, *op. cit.*, pp. 79–80; Hanotaux, "Richelieu cardinal et première ministre," *Revue des deux mondes*, VIII (1902), 106; Pastor, *op. cit.*, XIII, Part I, 502; Lodge, *Richelieu*, pp. 52–53.

went to Rome to secure the cardinal's hat; he was one of the few cardinals in history that did not have a titular church in Rome.[5] Richelieu was primarily a Frenchman; "he was everywhere the man of state, not the Catholic, let alone the man of the church."[6] He coldly and calculatingly pursued his state objectives by pushing into the background all religious and moral viewpoints; he was truly a *Realpolitiker*.[7]

His ideal was the absolute state, with all authority centering theoretically in the hands of the king[8] but practically in the hands of himself as prime minister. The rights of the state were superior to feudal interests, parlements, class interests, church interests, and all moral considerations. "To achieve his ends all means were permitted, yes, even commanded: deceit, cunning, harshness, cruelty."[9] In that section of Richelieu's "Political Testament" in which he discusses the obedience the ruler must show the pope, he advises King Louis XIII as follows:

> Although, on the one hand, the princes are bound to recognize the authority of the church, to comply with its sacred ordinances, and to render complete obedience with reference to the spiritual power that God has put into its hand for the salvation of mankind, and although, furthermore, it is the princely duty to uphold the honor of the popes as successors of Saint Peter and Vicar of Jesus Christ, so, on the other hand, they must not yield to the efforts of the church if it presumes to extend its power beyond the church's own limits.
>
> If the kings are obligated to respect the tiara of the highest priests, even so are they bound to maintain the power of their crown untouched. This truth is recognized by all theologians, but there is no small difficulty in differentiating precisely the dividing line between the independence and the subordination of these two powers.[10]

[5] Pastor, *op. cit.*, XIII, Part I, 502, n. 2; Hanotaux, "Richelieu," *Revue des deux mondes*, VIII, 106; Federn, *op. cit.*, p. 147.

[6] Mommsen, *op. cit.*, p. 54.

[7] Pastor, *op. cit.*, XIII, Part I, 502, n. 4; Mommsen, *op. cit.*, pp. 13–14, 29, 32, 38–39, 58; Federn, *op. cit.*, p. 148; Lodge, *op. cit.*, pp. 184–206; Andreas, *Geist und Staat, Historische Porträts*, p. 64; Andreas, in Marcks, *Meister der Politik*, II, 201–3.

[8] Kerviler, *Able Servien, négociateur des traités de Westphalie*, p. 9.

[9] Pastor, *op. cit.*, XIII, Part I, 502–3; Avenal, *Richelieu et la monarchie absolue*, I, 118–41, 226–47; Andreas, *Geist und Staat*, p. 64; Andreas, in Marcks, *op. cit.*, II, 211–13; Mommsen, *op. cit.*, pp. 16, 17, 29.

[10] Mommsen, *op. cit.*, pp. 88–89.

Richelieu here recognizes the problem of the relation of the state to the church; but he clearly shows that, if there is a conflict of jurisdiction, the state determines where its own interests lie and it is justified in taking the action necessary to sustain them.

Quite as important as establishing France as an absolute monarchy, Richelieu wished to give France security in Europe by establishing a balance of power;[11] to achieve this it was necessary to humiliate the Spanish and Austrian branches of the Hapsburg house, which had been dominant in the sixteenth century under Charles V (1519–58) and Philip II (1555–98). If Richelieu had been genuinely loyal to the Catholic church and the papacy, he would, as cardinal, have co-operated with Austria and Spain to stamp out Protestantism in Germany and the Netherlands. By so doing, he would have given a great impetus to the Catholic Reformation or Renaissance movement, and possibly, if not probably, enabled it to succeed. But that was contrary to his main foreign policy. To him the Thirty Years' War was not a religious war but a political opportunity which enabled him to make France, if not supreme, at least strong in Europe, to establish a balance of power.[12] The French cue was to aid the enemies of the Hapsburgs. Therefore Richelieu aided the German Protestant princes, the Danes, the Swedes, the Dutch, the Portuguese, and the German Catholic princes, such as the ruler of Bavaria and the Catholic electors, if they were willing to accept French, instead of Austrian, leadership; he even threatened to carry on a war against Pope Urban VIII in 1624 because the latter was siding with the Spanish in the matter of the Valteline passes in north Italy; finally he actively entered the Thirty Years' War by declaring war against Spain in 1635 and against Austria in 1638.[13] This *Machtpolitik* of the

[11] *Ibid.*, pp. 35–37.

[12] *Ibid.*, p. 37; Leman, *Urbain VIII*, pp. 4–8, 61; Laurent, *Etudes sur l'histoire de l'humanité*, X, 273.

[13] Mommsen, *op. cit.*, pp. 38, 40–50; Leman, *op. cit.*, pp. 62–63, 91–92, 325–35, 396–400, 439–41, 444–67, 490–520; Stieve, *Abhandlungen, Vorträge und Reden*, "Gustav

French Cardinal prime minister, free from all considerations of religion, had made France the first power in Europe; but it contributed potently to the paralysis and final wrecking of Catholic hopes to restore unity in Germany. Whatever chance the papacy had of exercising any unifying moral and religious force was finally destroyed by the policy of Richelieu's France, now the most powerful state, in its deadly political contest with Austria and Spain, the two other of the most powerful Catholic states of Europe.

After Richelieu's death in 1642 his policy was carried out in foreign affairs and at the Congress of Westphalia quite thoroughly and precisely by his successor, Cardinal Mazarin (1642–61), in accordance with purely secular principles. Such being the case, the other great Catholic powers—Austria, Bavaria, Spain, and even the ecclesiastical princes of Germany (Mainz, Trier, Cologne, Bamberg, Würzburg)—found it quite easy and natural to follow the same policy when papal and church affairs were being decided in Westphalia.[14] When Catholic princes were shaping their policies on the basis of secular interests, regardless of the expressed authoritative interests of the papacy and the church, we can say that the secularization of politics had been achieved.

2. FRANCE AND THE RELIGIOUS PROBLEMS AT THE CONGRESS

When Richelieu's policy of aiding the Protestants against the Catholic Hapsburgs during the Thirty Years' War was criticized by a Catholic called "Mars Gallicus,"[15] the Sorbonne eagerly condemned these views; and the action was supported by the clergy of France. The clergy, assembled in Paris, asserted the

Adolf," p. 207; Schnitzer, *Zur Politik des heiligen Stuhles in der ersten Hälfte des dreissigjährigen Krieges*, p. 249; Vossler, *Jean Racine*, p. 43; Meaux, *La réforme et la politique française en Europe jusqu'à la paix de Westphalie*, II, 463–564; *Cambridge Modern History*, IV, 58–129, 141–46; Lodge, *op. cit.*, chaps. iv, vi, vii; Lavisse, *op. cit.*, VI, Part II, 237–40, 290–316, 338–55; Federn, *op. cit.*, pp. 98–99, 135; Laurent, *op. cit.*, X, 255–71.

[14] Pastor, *op. cit.*, XIII, Part I, 23.

[15] Laurent, *op. cit.*, X, 273–75.

right of the king to make alliances, conduct war, and carry on his foreign policy as he thought best.[16] But if, during the war, France could take an attitude openly hostile to the interests of the Catholic religion and of the Catholic princes that were most intent on aiding the church, she could not be so bold in the peace negotiations. At Münster, where the French negotiated with the emperor and the Catholic princes, their representative had to be extremely cautious. France had allies among both Catholics and Protestants. Without the help of Sweden and the Protestant princes she could not secure the territorial satisfaction that she demanded.[17] If, in return for that aid, she favored the ecclesiastical claims of the Protestants under Swedish leadership, she would offend the nuncio and the Catholic princes. It was to her interest to be on good terms with the nuncio, for he had great influence as mediator in conducting the negotiations; his friendship was not to be despised, for he supposedly controlled all the votes of the ecclesiastical states.[18]

If France offended either the lesser Protestants or the lesser Catholic princes, she would be unable to secure their aid against the imperialistic plans of Austria, against whom alone she had waged war.[19] She was especially anxious to obtain the good will of Bavaria; her constant aim was to detach the elector Maximilian from his alliance with Austria; this turned out to be possible, owing to Maximilian's fear that Austria and Spain would sacrifice his interests in the final peace arrangements.[20] Moreover, one of the French representatives, the Count d'Avaux, was looked upon as a man affecting piety; he was clerical in his attitude and not friendly to the German Protes-

[16] *Ibid.*, X, 275–76.

[17] Bougeant, *Histoire des guerres*, II, 35; Odhner, *Die Politik Schwedens*, p. 129; Meaux, *op. cit.*, II, 578–79.

[18] Laurent, *op. cit.*, X, 283.

[19] Gebhardt, *Handbuch der deutschen Geschichte*, I, 729; Gindely, *Geschichte des dreissigjährigen Krieges*, III, 179.

[20] Gindely, *op. cit.*; Heigel, "Das westfälische Friedenswerk," *Zeitschrift für Geschichte und Politik*, V, 421.

tants;[21] he was anxious, by his actions, to make himself agreeable to the pope, in the hope of being appointed to the cardinalate.[22]

So, under the circumstances, the French plenipotentiaries carried out a policy that could be offensive neither to the Catholics nor to the Protestants; they skilfully avoided giving any support to the ecclesiastical claims of the evangelicals, but they also did very little, if anything, effective to prevent the evangelicals from securing a satisfactory adjustment of the religious gravamina. They played between the Catholic and the Protestant princes, cautiously avoiding entanglements in religious questions and assuming no responsibility in their negotiations. In April, 1645, upon being asked by the nuncio whether or not they would aid the Protestants in the adjustment of their ecclesiastical gravamina, they adroitly evaded a straightforward answer, fearing that they might turn their allies against themselves. They stated

> that they could declare neither for the Catholics nor for the Protestants in this respect, but they would never aid the Protestants in doing anything hostile to the Catholic religion; however, if they should now publicly declare against the Protestants [to the Catholics], they feared that the Protestants might combine and openly attack the Catholic religion. The French therefore preferred to suspend their decision until they saw whether the Protestants would propose anything prejudicial to the Catholic religion.[23]

In December, 1645, when the French proposals for peace were made, D'Avaux prevented the insertion of the ecclesiastical gravamina of the evangelicals.[24] In December, 1646, when the gravamina were being discussed, the French agreed to help expedite the negotiations concerning the Empire, "but in ecclesiastical affairs they could give no assistance; their queen, Anne

[21] Jacob, *Die Erwerbung des Elsass durch Frankreich im westfälischen Frieden*, pp. 17–18; Odhner, *op. cit.*, pp. 99, 118; Gebhardt, *op. cit.*, I, 726.

[22] Pütter, *Geist des westphälischen Friedens*, p. 143, n. 1.

[23] Meiern, *Acta pacis Westphalicae*, I, 389; Pastor, *op. cit.*, XIV, Part I, 80, 93.

[24] *Meiern, op. cit.*, II, 102.

of Austria, being a woman and superstitious, in France the pope and the Catholics must be given due respect."[25]

This is the attitude that the French plenipotentiaries maintained throughout the Congress. They would not give any aid to the Protestants in securing redress of their religious grievances. Twice they even tried to persuade the evangelicals to accept the Catholic proposals. In May, 1646, they advised the evangelicals to be satisfied with the Catholic propositions to hold the ecclesiastical lands seventy or eighty years or more.[26] In February, 1647, an attempt to secure D'Avaux's aid in influencing the Catholics to take a more favorable attitude toward the religious grievances of the Protestants proved of no avail.[27] In February, 1648, the French declared

> that they would co-operate with the Swedes in political matters and affairs of justice, but in matters concerning religion they would support them only in general but not in any particular instance. . . . . For the Spaniards had made the French crown odious to the pope as though it were facilitating a rupture concerning religious matters; and, furthermore, they must be cautious because of the clergy in France.[28]

So the French took a negative attitude toward those matters that most concerned the church. This was significant; they did it solely for political purposes. They wished to offend neither the Catholic princes nor the Swedes and the other Protestants; they needed the aid of both sides to accomplish their political ends. Above all, France needed Swedish support to secure satisfaction for her sacrifices. All efforts at Münster to detach France from Sweden were of no avail; and the defeat of the policy of the Roman Curia was made possible by the merely negative attitude of France.[29]

3. FRANCE ACCEPTS THE CLAUSE AGAINST PROTESTS, JULY, 1647

Though the French diplomatically took an attitude of indifference toward the ecclesiastical gravamina that did not concern

[25] *Ibid.*, IV, 3. The reference to the queen is to Anne of Austria, who was regent during the minority of Louis XIV, during the years 1643–51.

[26] *Ibid.*, II, 637. [27] *Ibid.*, IV, 77. [28] *Ibid.*, p. 988. [29] Pütter, *op. cit.*, pp. 340, 341.

France, they did not hesitate to guard the interests of their own country against any possible protests from the pope. In the peace project of the French of July, 1647, which was really the first project containing in substance the majority of the final provisions of the Peace of Westphalia, the clause that declared protests null was included.[30] The reasons for this are obvious; the proposed treaty provided for the cession of the bishoprics of Metz, Toul, and Verdun to France.[31] These territories had been held *de facto* by the French since 1552; as early as December, 1645, Trauttmannsdorff had offered them to France as part of her "satisfaction."[32] The French were as much concerned about the permanence of these possessions as were the Swedes about their ecclesiastical possessions, for they could expect the pope or his nuncio to issue a protest, an action which occurred in October, 1647 (the nuncio protested against the cession of these territories to the French).[33] Moreover, the proposed treaty granted France Alsatian lands at the expense of Austria and the Empire.[34] It provided also for the granting of the electoral dignity and the Upper Palatinate to the Duke of Bavaria,[35] who had, in March, 1647, done France the great military and political service of signing the armistice of Ulm.[36] The establishment of the eighth electorate and the disposal of the Upper Palatinate had been one of the knottiest problems the Congress had had to solve. Then, furthermore, the Swedes, the elector of Brandenburg, and the Landgravine of Hesse, all French allies, had been given their territorial satisfactions at the expense of church lands.[37] Under the circumstances France accepted the clause against protests which would insure her and her allies of having undisturbed possession of their advantageous war gains.

[30] Meiern, *op. cit.*, V, 160. [31] *Ibid.*, p. 151. [32] *Ibid.*, II, 213.

[33] Fiedler, *Die Relationen*, XXVI, 325; Adami, *Arcana Pacis Westphalicae*, p. 250; Fischer, *Beiträge*, p. 38.

[34] Meiern, *op. cit.*, V, 151–52. [35] *Ibid.*, p. 143. [36] *Ibid.*, pp. 2–17.

[37] Heigel, *op. cit.*, V, 424–27; Fischer, *op. cit.*, pp. 8–9.

4. THE AFFAIR OF THE TWO DOCUMENTS, JUNE–JULY, 1647

Just before the French had inserted the clause against protests in their peace project, there occurred an incident that was very important as marking the tactful respect that both the imperial and the French plenipotentiaries paid to the wishes of the papal nuncio, while at the same time disclosing that fundamentally they were disregarding the principles that outwardly they were pretending to observe. In June, 1647, the imperial plenipotentiaries had given their peace propositions to the mediators, who were to hand the document to the French. However, the imperialists had provided two projects: the first contained all matters both ecclesiastical and political pertaining to the Empire; in the second all ecclesiastical matters were omitted, because the papal nuncio hesitated to place his name to the clause relating to religious matters. Because of these circumstances the two crowns agreed that their negotiations were to stand nevertheless, and that to the project that the papal nuncio was to sign was to be added a provision that all points contained in the other copy were to be nonetheless valid and were to have just as much force as though they were incorporated word for word.[38] This incident merely shows that, though the two Catholic powers regarded the feelings of the nuncio, they did not hesitate to incorporate in their documents the very things that were most opposed by him and against which he had repeatedly protested. They did it probably to save the dignity and feelings of the nuncio and to avoid any unnecessary friction in the remainder of the negotiations, but it is an excellent manifestation of the spirit that pervaded the movement termed "the secularization of politics." If the French were to be certain of the fruits of their efforts in the war and the peace negotiations, they would need to take precautions against papal protests. The spirit that actuated them in the negotiations is apparent;

[38] Meiern, *op. cit.*, V, 130–61 (pages 130–40 contain the peace project without reference to ecclesiastical matters; pages 141–61 contain the references to ecclesiastical matters); Le Clerc, *Négociations secrètes*, IV, 136–37; Fischer, *op. cit.*, p. 42.

they were desirous of achieving political and material advantages through the aid of both Catholic and Protestant allies, and did not wish to offend either. Such an attitude is accountable for a comment in March, 1646, by Leuxelring, a leader of the Catholic extremists; in writing to Abbot Dominikus, he said that the French were leaving the Catholics in the lurch, they talked much, but their achievements amounted to nothing.[39]

5. FRENCH MOTIVES FOR INSERTING AND OBSERVING THE CLAUSE AGAINST PROTESTS

By the time that the French had inserted the clause against protests (July, 1647), all the fundamental characteristics of the Peace of Westphalia had been determined.[40] Let us consider more fully than has thus far been possible, why the French inserted the clause against protests and later participated in its execution, once the Treaty had been signed. The Treaty of Westphalia gave to France results even more far-reaching than those for which she had been striving for a century and a quarter, that is, the ruination, or at least the weakening, of the Spanish and Austrian Hapsburgs and the thwarting of the Hapsburg ideal of the German Empire as a unified, centralized political power. By this Treaty the Holy Roman Empire had virtually ceased to exist. Each of the three hundred and fifty princes was guaranteed in his local sovereign rights; all the princes could conclude alliances with each other and with foreign powers, so long as no injury was done to the interests of the emperor or Empire, which was merely a formal restriction. In legislative affairs all German states were placed on an equality of rights. These Treaty provisions meant the frustration of the Austrian Hapsburg ambitions to control Germany as a centralized, national monarchy. So far as the governmental structure was concerned, France had accomplished her purpose

[39] Israel, *Adam Adami und seine Arcana Pacis Westphalicae*, p. 31, n. 18.

[40] Heigel, *op. cit.*, V, 427.

of politically paralizing the great threatening state to the east.[41]

Territorially Germany had been weakened by the loss of Holland and Switzerland; moreover, France herself had acquired full sovereignty over the bishoprics of Metz, Toul, and Verdun, which she had held as fiefs of the Empire since 1552; she now added in the Rhine country the new territories of Breisach, Philippsburg, and Upper and Lower Alsace,[42] which were strategically important in keeping better control of Germany and preventing Spain from using the Rhine Valley as a means of communication between the Spanish Netherlands and Italy. Sweden, the powerful ally of France, by her territorial gains in north Germany controlled the mouths of Weser, the Elbe, and the Oder rivers, while Holland possessed the mouths of the Rhine. The outlets of all the important rivers flowing northward in Germany were under the rule of foreign, non-German powers.

Such important Protestant states of Germany as Brandenburg, Hesse-Cassel, and Brunswick-Lüneburg had increased their possessions through French and Swedish aid. Charles Louis, although losing part of the lands of his father, the unfortunate Frederick V of the Palatinate, was given the title of elector of the Palatinate. The Catholic Duke of Bavaria had, through French support, gained the Upper Palatinate and the title of elector. Both Bavaria and the Palatinate, if successfully influenced politically by France, could act as buffer states between France and Austria. France would be regarded as the protector of the political rights of both the Protestant and Catholic German princes against the centralizing efforts of Austria, which would make France appear as a great political liberator. France, as a national, European state, had never exercised such power before. She had more friends and allies than

[41] *Cambridge Modern History*, IV, 416–17; Gebhardt, *op. cit.*, I, 732; Odhner, *op. cit.*, pp. 90–102; Onno Klopp, *Der Fall des Hauses Hannover in Gross-Britannien und Irland, im Zusammenhange der europäischen Angelegenheiten von 1660–1714*, I, 81–83.

[42] Jacob, *op. cit.*, pp. 196–201.

at any time in the past. One of her great enemies, Austria, was, by virtue of the Treaty, out of the scene; she had agreed not to intervene when France continued her war with Spain (which was to be prolonged until 1659 with a victory for France).[43]

Since the early sixteenth century France had been using any means to carry out a policy of national egotism. Although her sovereign bore the title of "His Most Christian Majesty" and was an autocrat as a result of the work of Richelieu and Mazarin, he had allied himself with Protestant heretics and Turkish infidels, with Dutch, Portuguese, Hungarian, and Neapolitan rebels—anything to injure the great enemy, the Hapsburgs, and to make useful friendships with the enemies of the Hapsburgs. Having, by 1648, realized this goal of national egotism, France could not afford to jeopardize results by ignoring the possibility of Catholic protests against the Peace. She had entered the war for political purposes, with utter disregard for the interests of the Catholic church and religion; nothing was to be permitted to threaten these results. Losing the three bishoprics of Metz, Toul, and Verdun, would be of small consequence compared with the general results just indicated, results achieved with the co-operation of her heretical allies, the Swedes and the German Protestant princes. Not only was the protesting attitude of the papal nuncio and the pope a threat, but Innocent had even gone farther, in the summer of 1647, and stated that any treaty that the nuncio was to sign dare not contain even the names of the Swedes or other heretical parties.[44]

Under the circumstances any treaty signed by France with Sweden and other Protestant states would be invalid, and this helps account for the French attitude that was a contributing factor in bringing about the secularization of politics. Other reasons of less importance may have played a part in inducing France to insert a clause against protests. A protest might be

[43] Lavisse, *op. cit.*, VII, Part I, 23–24; Cheruel, *Saint-Simon considéré comme historien de Louis XIV*, pp. 202–7; Odhner, *op. cit.*, pp. 90–102; Ritter, *Deutsche Geschichte*, III, 626, 643–44.

[44] Fischer, *op. cit.*, p. 42.

expected from the Duke of Lorraine, a German prince, friendly to Austria, who had been excluded from the Treaty and whose territory was still held by France. This protest actually was made after the Peace was signed.[45] Furthermore, the French desired to continue the war with Spain single-handed and were very anxious that the Treaty should contain a clause prohibiting the emperor's giving aid to Spain. At the same time that France inserted the clause against the protests in the Treaty, Mazarin was giving instructions to his plenipotentiaries to insist that the emperor be prevented from giving aid to the Spanish.[46] In the Treaty was finally inserted the clause providing that "neither power shall ever assist the enemies of the other at the present time or in the future."[47] Such a formal clause is found in almost every modern treaty terminating a war; but in this case special significance is to be attached to the clause, for it was only after much pressure and urging that the emperor consented to desert his ally, the king of Spain, and to refrain from hostile acts on his behalf if France should continue the war against Spain.[48] If the pope could release the emperor and his allies from their oath to observe the Treaty in one respect, the whole structure of the Congress might fall to the ground, and war would continue, French gains would be insecure, and the prosecution of the war with Spain would be hindered.

Another consideration, difficult to determine, is the influence of the Fronde (1648–53), the approaching revolt against the absolute highly centralized government in France. There had been many manifestations of antagonism to Mazarin and his government before 1648; Spain gladly supported these enemies

[45] B. Erdmannsdörffer, *Deutsche Geschichte vom westphälischen Frieden bis zum Regierungsantritt Friedrichs des Grossen*, I, 6.

[46] *Lettres du Cardinal Mazarin, recueilliés et publiés par M. A. Cheruel* ("Collection de documents inédits sur l'histoire de France"), II, 925, letters to A. M. d'Avaux and to the Duke of Longueville, July 19, 1647.

[47] *Instrumentum Pacis Caesareo—Gallicum*, par. 3, in Walther, *Universal Register*, p. lxv.

[48] Bougeant, *op. cit.*, III, 492–95; Huber, *Geschichte Österreichs*, V, 609; Cheruel, *Histoire de France pendant la minorité de Louis XIV*, III, 103.

of Mazarin. It was a relief to the French prime minister to be able to bring the war in central Europe to a close so as to have a freer hand in dealing with the Fronde and Spain.[49] To the later generations the Peace of Westphalia, with all its political advantages for France, looms up as the most significant event of a number of decades; but the signing of the Peace of Westphalia was not heralded in France as a great event. France was much more concerned with internal conditions at the opening of the Fronde movement. When it was announced in Paris that a general peace had been signed in Münster with the Empire, concluding the Thirty Years' War, the news was received with profound indifference. All the memoirs of the time manifested a disdainful silence concerning the most important treaty of a century, the Peace of Westphalia, which terminated one of the most terrible wars in history, of three decades' duration, but which did not at any point touch the privileges of the French parlement or the powers of the barricades or the exactions of the French financiers,[50] which shows that signing a treaty prejudicial to the interests of the pope and the church was a minor, if not a nonexistent, consideration of Mazarin.

[49] Hassall, *Mazarin*, pp. 20–21, 41; Debidour, in Lavisse and Rambaud, *Histoire générale*, VI, 9–16; Lavisse, *op. cit.*, VII, Part I, 29–41; Coville, *Étude sur Mazarin et ses démêlés avec le Pape Innocent X*, pp. 184–86; Ritter, *op. cit.*, III, 620.

[50] Bazin, *Histoire de France sous Louis XIII et sous le ministère de Mazarin*, III, 450.

Chapter Eight

WHY MAZARIN, A CARDINAL, IGNORED PAPAL PROTESTS

THE considerations observed thus far would be pertinent in the case of a layman acting as determinative, controlling head of the French government. But why should a *cardinal* have been one of those, if not the one, most responsible for the secularization of politics?

I. MAZARIN'S PERSONAL CHARACTERISTICS

Mazarin, who, as successor of Cardinal Richelieu, served France as prime minister from 1642 to his death in 1661, was more of a politician than a churchman. Religiously, he himself believed in little or nothing; in fact, he was completely indifferent toward matters of religion.[1] He used his great power as cardinal to personal and political advantage in the bestowing of French benefices and church offices. He employed bishops and other French churchmen to raise church funds that were used to wage the Thirty Years' War, contrary to Catholic interests. He assured the French Protestants at all times of his good wishes and appointed the best of them to high offices. To achieve his personal ends he kept cardinals in his pay at the Roman court. He used ecclesiasts as political spies in French society.[2] Although he had been a cardinal since 1641, he seems never to have visited Rome thereafter; and he never received the cardinal's hat.[3] He had become a naturalized Frenchman in 1639,

[1] Federn, *Richelieu*, p. 146; Federn, *Mazarin*, pp. 91, 100.

[2] Federn, *Mazarin*, pp. 100–101; Fischer, *Beiträge*, pp. 43, 44.

[3] *Catholic Encyclopedia*, X, 92.

but always continued to speak French badly;[4] and he continued to sign his name in Italian form, "Mazarini," thus wishing to preserve his Italian characteristics for possible future advantage, such as the contingency of being elected pope.[5] Nevertheless, he was in spirit completely a Frenchman and conducted French affairs thoroughly in accordance with the policies of his predecessor, Richelieu.[6] It was Mazarin who shaped all French policies at Münster, and all other courses of action as well; he was fully responsible for the creation and execution of French policies.[7] He never did anything without a plan, and nothing from motives of love.[8] These personal characteristics of Mazarin help us understand why he had strained relations with Innocent X in the four years preceding the signing of the Peace of Westphalia; they also explain why he, a cardinal in the church, was not deterred in signing a peace detrimental to papal and church interests, a peace significant in the achievement of French national egotism and the secularization of politics.

2. MAZARIN'S STRAINED RELATIONS WITH INNOCENT X, 1644–48

Mazarin had been greatly disappointed in the election of Innocent X to the papacy in 1644.[9] Upon the death of Urban VIII, who had been so friendly to France,[10] Mazarin hoped, and made all possible plans, to have the election go to either Cardinal Bentivoglio (who died before the conclave terminated) or to Cardinal Sachetti, both of whom were friendly to France. If

[4] Federn, *Mazarin*, p. 54.

[5] Lavisse, *Histoire de France depuis les origins*, VII, Part I, 8.

[6] *Ibid.*, p. 24; Cheruel, *Histoire de France sous le ministère de Mazarin, 1651–1661*, I, 3; Bazin, *Histoire de France sous Louis XIII*, III, 192; Federn, *Mazarin*, p. 75; Hassall, *Mazarin*, pp. 23, 24, 52; Meaux, *La réforme et la politique française*, II, 569.

[7] Aubery, *Histoire du Cardinal Mazarin*, I, 382, 401; H. M. Stephens, *Encyclopedia Britannica* (11th ed., XVII, 940; Fischer, *op. cit.*, p. 68.

[8] Federn, *Mazarin*, p. 106.

[9] Pastor, *Geschichte der Päpste*, XIV, Part I, 39; Bazin, *op. cit.*, III, 286; Lavisse, *op. cit.*, VII, Part I, 12.

[10] See above, chap. v.

necessary, Mazarin was prepared, even publicly, to oppose the election of Cardinal Pamfili, who later became Innocent X.[11] However, through the dominant influence of the Spaniards in the conclave Innocent X was elected.[12] Mazarin's indignation over the defeat was so great that he recalled and disgraced St. Chamond, the French ambassador at Rome, because he had not succeeded in controlling the outcome of the conclave.[13] Cardinal Antoine Barberini, who had been intrusted with French interests during the election, and who had finally, for practical purposes, consented to the election of Innocent, had the title of "protector of France" taken away and was forced to remove the French coat-of-arms from his palace in Rome.[14] Cardinal Theodoli Barberini and also his brother had to remove the French coat-of-arms from their palaces and were deprived of their French pensions.[15] Mazarin's manifestations of anger became quickly known in Rome and were embarrassing to Innocent X.[16] Nevertheless, the cardinal knew it would be well to have the good will of the new pope; so he sent Innocent a letter congratulating him on his elevation.[17] The friendship of the new pope was a matter of great importance to Mazarin, not only from the standpoint of international politics but because he had personal ends in view.

Like his predecessor, Richelieu, Mazarin greatly desired to secure honors for members of his family, and therefore wished to have his brother Michel appointed to the cardinalate to throw

[11] Coville, *Etude sur Mazarin*, pp. 5–9; Pastor, *op. cit.*, XIV, Part I, 19; Federn, *Mazarin*, p. 95; Perkins, *France under Mazarin*, I, 341.

[12] Coville, *op. cit.*, pp. 19–26; Cheruel, *op. cit.*, II, 146–51; Pastor, *op. cit.*, XIV, Part I, 22; von Reumont, *Geschichte der Stadt Rom*, III, Part II, 623.

[13] Fontenay-Mareuil, *Memoires de*, p. 274; Cheruel, *op. cit.*, II, 151; Pastor, *op. cit.*, XIV, Part I, 39; Coville, *op. cit.*, pp. 40–45; Federn, *Mazarin*, pp. 95–96.

[14] Fontenay-Mareuil, *op. cit.*, pp. 274–75; Cheruel, *op. cit.*, II, 151–52; Pastor, *op. cit.*, XIV, Part I, 39; Federn, *Mazarin*, p. 96; Coville, *op. cit.*, pp. 37–40.

[15] Coville, *op. cit.*, p. 45; Cheruel, *op. cit.*, II, 152.

[16] Coville, *op. cit.*, p. 46.

[17] *Letters du Cardinal Mazarin*, II, 88-90; Coville, *op. cit.*, pp. 28–29; Pastor, *op. cit.*, XIV, Part I, 39–40; Federn, *Mazarin*, p. 96.

luster on the family name.[18] However, Innocent did not hold Michel in high regard, actually detested him, and all negotiations having this appointment in view proved in vain until October, 1647, when Michel became cardinal.[19] The intervening time was filled with many events and incidents that tended to keep up the ill feeling between Mazarin and the pope. An attempt of Mazarin to exchange ecclesiastical favors with the pope was entirely unsuccessful. Innocent accepted a French abbey for his nephew but did nothing for the brother of Mazarin.[20] In March, 1645, Innocent X appointed eight cardinals, all friendly to Spain; but Mazarin's brother was not appointed.[21] Innocent, when asked for an explanation, replied that, according to papal rule, two brothers could not be given the cardinalate at the same time.[22] This was an explanation that was irritating to Mazarin, for the rule had been broken for royal and princely families, and Richelieu's brother François had been made cardinal for his services in the capture of La Rochelle.[23] The anger of Mazarin, of the queen regent, and of French official circles was so great over this rebuff that there was some consideration of the possibility of a national break with Rome such as had occurred under Henry VIII of England.[24]

In 1645 a Portuguese bishop, who was in Rome under the protection of France, was attacked by some bandits at the instigation of the Spanish ambassador. The bandits killed one and wounded another of the persons accompanying the bishop. Because the pope refused to force Spain to give up these assas-

[18] Bougeant, *Histoire de traités de Westphalie*, II, 404; Cheruel, *op. cit.*, II, 157, 392; Pastor, *op. cit.*, XIV, Part I, 40–51.

[19] Coville, *op. cit.*, pp. 61, 163; Cheruel, *op. cit.*, II, 401; Pastor, *op. cit.*, XIV, Part I, 51.

[20] *Letters du Cardinal Mazarin*, II, 223; Fontenay-Mareuil, *op. cit.*, p. 275; Coville, *op. cit.*, pp. 54–57; Pastor, *op. cit.*, XV, Part I, 49–50; Cheruel, *op. cit.*, II, 159.

[21] Coville, *op. cit.*, p. 57; Pastor, *op. cit.*, XIV, Part I, 40; Cheruel, *op. cit.*, II, 160–61; Perkins, *op. cit.*, I, 346.

[22] Fontenay-Mareuil, *op. cit.*, p. 275; Cheruel, *op. cit.*, II, 160; Perkins, *op. cit.*, I, 346.

[23] Fontenay-Mareuil, *op. cit.*, p. 275; Perkins, *op. cit.*, I, 346.

[24] Coville, *op. cit.*, pp. 57–58.

sins, Mazarin recalled the French ambassador; and for over a year (March 27, 1646—May 24, 1647) France had no ambassador at the papal court,[25] although other remaining French officials conducted French negotiations, which were limited to creating difficulties for Innocent X.[26] A French noble, De Beaupuis, who had participated in a plot against Mazarin in 1643, took refuge subsequently in Rome. All efforts to have De Beaupuis extradited for trial by the French parlement failed; the pope, in refusing, explained that the offense had been against a prince of the church (Mazarin). To which the French replied that the attacked person was undoubtedly an ecclesiast but was exercising secular power.[27] These various incidents aroused in Mazarin a spirit of revenge and led him to break with the pope.[28] At this point various acts were committed by both Mazarin and Innocent, each purposing to irritate the other. Mazarin again became friendly to, and contracted an alliance with, the three Barberini brothers, whom Innocent was treating with ingratitude in spite of the fact that he owed, in part, his election to them.[29] Because they were called to account for the mismanagement of their numerous church offices for personal profit, they fled to France for safety. Mazarin was glad to give them protection and allowed them once more to put the arms of France on their palaces.[30] This was done in a spirit of personal vengeance;[31] all attempts of the French plenipotentiaries at Münster and of the nuncio Chigi to induce Mazarin to

[25] *Ibid.*, pp. 59–60; Pastor, *op. cit.*, XIV, Part I, 41; Cheruel, *op. cit.*, II, 2, 161–63; Perkins, *op. cit.*, I, 346.

[26] Coville, *op. cit.*, pp. 60–61; Pastor, *op. cit.*, XIV, Part I, 41.

[27] Coville, *op. cit.*, pp. 61–64.

[28] Cheruel, *op. cit.*, II, 166, 167.

[29] Fontenay-Mareuil, *op. cit.*, p. 275; Coville, *op. cit.*, pp. 69–72, 83, 87–88; Cheruel, *op. cit.*, II, 163; Pastor, *op. cit.*, XIV, Part I, 41.

[30] Fontenay-Mareuil, *op. cit.*, p. 275; Bougeant, *op. cit.*, II, 405; Cheruel, *op. cit.*, II, 168; Coville, *op. cit.*, pp. 88–89, 95–108; Pastor, *op. cit.*, XIV, Part I, 42–44; Federn, *Mazarin*, p. 97; von Reumont, *op. cit.*, III, Part II, 623–24.

[31] Coville, *op. cit.*, pp. 89–90; Pastor, *op. cit.*, XIV, Part I, 43; Cheruel, *op. cit.*, II, 168.

control his resentment and adopt a policy of conciliation were futile.[32]

The pope, irritated by this display of friendship toward his enemies, on February 19, 1646, issued a bull that prohibited cardinals from leaving Rome without papal authority. Transgressing cardinals were to lose the income of their charges and benefices in the first six months. In the second six months they were to lose their charges and benefices. If the offenders did not return at the end of fifteen months, they were to lose their cardinalates if the pope desired.[33] This bull was formulated by the pope on his own responsibility, without consulting the College of Cardinals. It was not expressly aimed at any stated situation in the church but was clearly a weapon, quickly forged, to be used against Mazarin,[34] who felt that it was aimed directly at himself.[35] If the bull were carried out, Mazarin would have to give up either his position as French minister or as cardinal. To irritate Mazarin further, Innocent X offered the cardinal's hat to the Abbé de la Riviera, a favorite of the Duke of Orleans, who was the political enemy of Mazarin,[36] in the hope of getting Orleans to declare that he desired peace in spite of Mazarin, in order to make it seem that Mazarin was obstinate.[37] But the Abbé refused the title of cardinal.[38]

For these acts Mazarin had his revenge. He consulted the parlement of Paris, whose leading members he had previously bribed; he also consulted the assembly of the French clergy. Although neither of these groups had any affection for the French minister, they both favored him with an opinion against the papal bull.[39] In order to strike a more effective blow to in-

[32] Bougeant, *op. cit.*, II, 405, 406.

[33] Le Clerc, *Negociations secrètes*, II, 137; Coville, *op. cit.*, pp. 108–9; Pastor, *op. cit.*, XIV, Part I, 45–46; Sismondi, *Histoire des Français*, XVI, 406.

[34] Coville, *op. cit.*, p. 110.

[35] *Ibid.*, p. 109; Martin, *Histoire de France*, XII, 220.

[36] Coville, *op. cit.*, pp. 137–40; Martin, *op. cit.*, XII, 220.

[37] Coville, *op. cit.*, pp. 138–39, 147–48; Bougeant, *op. cit.*, II, 401–2.

[38] Martin, *op. cit.*, XII, 220.

[39] Le Clerc, *op. cit.*, III, 156; Coville, *op. cit.*, pp. 111–14; Martin, *op. cit.*, XII, 220; Sismondi, *op. cit.*, XVI, 407.

sure respect for France in Rome, Mazarin sent an expedition to attack Spain in Naples, and especially in the Tuscan Presides, five coastal points that had been owned by Spain since the time of Philip II and which controlled access to central Italy.[40] Although the Italian campaign was not an unqualified success, it prepared Innocent for a reconciliation; and Mazarin reciprocated.[41] A French ambassador was once more sent to Rome in May, 1647; the Barberini were no longer persecuted, their property was restored.[42] The negotiations for the coveted honor, the cardinalate, were continued with much persistence. Mazarin arranged for a marriage between a French princess and the king of Poland, Wladislaus II. Not only was political influence in Poland gained thus, but the Polish ruler used his right as a Catholic king to nominate a cardinal by proposing the brother of Mazarin.[43] However, finally, October 7, 1647, Innocent X conferred the cardinalate on Michel Mazarin, ostensibly of his own free will, but actually to please the French queen regent and Mazarin.[44] This news was very gratifying to the French prime minister. It meant that France now had another cardinal and that the influence of the prime minister had been increased thereby. It signified further that the pope had finally submitted to Mazarin, had renounced the struggle against him and preferred to make an ally of him. This eventuation constituted a remarkable diplomatic success.[45]

[40] Pastor, *op. cit.*, XIV, Part I, 46–48; Perkins, *op. cit.*, I, 346.

[41] Coville, *op. cit.*, pp. 138, 146, 149–60; Pastor, *op. cit.*, XIV, Part I, 48–49; Perkins, *op. cit.*, I, 347–50; Sismondi, *op. cit.*, XVI, 417–18.

[42] Coville, *op. cit.*, pp. 142, 143, 148; Pastor, *op. cit.*, XIV, Part I, 48–49; Perkins, *op. cit.*, I, 350; Sismondi, *op. cit.*, XVI, 428.

[43] *Lettres du Cardinal Mazarin*, II, 235, n. 2, 283–84, 477; Le Clerc, *op. cit.*, II, Part II, 156–57; III, 486; Coville, *op. cit.*, pp. 163–64; Cheruel, *op. cit.*, II, 394; Pastor, *op. cit.*, XIV, Part I, 51; Perkins, *op. cit.*, I, 350–52; Fischer, *op. cit.*, p. 70.

[44] *Lettres du Cardinal Mazarin*, II, 511–12; Coville, *op. cit.*, pp. 178–79; Pastor, *op. cit.*, XIV, Part I, 51; Fischer, *op. cit.*, pp. 70–71; Perkins, *op. cit.*, I, 353.

[45] Coville, *op. cit.*, pp. 181–83. This author (pp. 180–81) undermines the testimony of Fontenay-Mareuil, the French ambassador in Rome, that Mazarin affected an air of indifference on hearing of his brother's appointment, delayed expressing his gratitude to Innocent X, censured the ambassador for making a national affair of the appoint-

The outcome of this struggle over the cardinalate was a great proof of the strength of Mazarin. The ultramontane section of the French church and the pope had tried to overthrow him. Now Mazarin showed the French clergy and all his even more bitter political opponents that he was master of France. The papal court had regarded him merely as the subordinate, minor clerk of his early days; but he, through his vigorous, bold action, had forced the papacy to capitulate.

The important aspects of the hostility between Mazarin and Innocent closed in 1648, but troubles of comparative minor importance continued.[46] Innocent was absolutely right when in November, 1651, he said that since the beginning of his pontificate Mazarin had been the stumbling-block in the relations between France and Rome; he had been the cause of all the unpleasantnesses and quarrels; the minister would finally ruin France and also the papacy.[47] We must keep in mind that these personal and political wrangles between the pope and Mazarin show the latter's ill will toward Innocent and help explain why the French were unwilling to uphold papal efforts in support of Catholic interests in the negotiations at Münster.[48] However, the essential consideration was undoubtedly the fact that the Peace of Westphalia, as finally formulated, gave France such an advantageous arrangement politically that she could run no risk of having it jeopardized by papal protest. And one might be quite safe in saying that, even if friendly relations had prevailed between France and the papacy, Mazarin would have felt impelled, for political reasons, to make papal protests against this advantageous peace ineffective.

---

ment, and merely sent some trifles to the pope's sister-in-law. See *Memoirs de Marquis de Fontenay-Mareuil*, p. 286; Cheruel, *Histoire de France pendant la minorité de Louis XIV*, II, 402; Perkins, *op. cit.*, I, 354. For a statement corroborating that of Coville, see Fischer, *op. cit.*, pp. 70–71.

[46] Pastor, *op. cit.*, XIV, Part I, 51–52.

[47] *Ibid.*, pp. 52–53.

[48] Fischer, *op. cit.*, pp. 19–22.

3. FRENCH RESENTMENT OF INNOCENT'S SYMPATHY FOR SPAIN

Besides the ill will arising out of the strained relations between Mazarin and Innocent in the years 1644–48, Mazarin gives further testimony of his resentment over the pope's sympathy for Spain and disregard for France in his letters. As early as November 25, 1644, two months after Innocent's election, in a letter to his brother, Mazarin says:

> To speak frankly, the whole court and all the parlements of the realm believe that today we have a Spanish pope. Their opinion is based on the partiality that His Holiness has always shown to Spain during his prelacy and his cardinalate, and, as is generally known, on the joy that the ministers of the House of Austria have shown upon the news of his election. They think that His Holiness, in spite of his protestations of friendship, which he has made since his elevation, for the crown of France, dissimulates his sentiments and in the depth of his heart preserves a profound spite for the exclusion that has been given him on our part. There has been no lack of people that have called into question whether we must accept the mediation of His Holiness. The following has been written to Münster: "It is necessary that His Holiness first give us at least a moral guaranty proving to us by facts that he is disposed to conduct himself as a common father of the faithful."[49]

Again in a letter of March 25, 1645, to Cardinal Grimaldi, Innocent is regarded as being entirely devoted to the Spaniards, and Mazarin speaks of strange propositions that have been made to the queen concerning the election of Innocent.[50] In another letter to Cardinal Grimaldi (May 8, 1645) Mazarin makes complaint against the pope who favors other nations and does nothing for France.[51] Once more in a letter of January 2, 1645, Mazarin declared that the pope is acting by caprice or by devotion to the Spaniards.[52] On another occasion, in a letter of July 15, 1645, Innocent is accused "of supporting all [doing anything] providing he can secure the fall of Mazarin."[53] In a letter to Cardinal Grimaldi, February 9, 1646, on the eve of the departure of the fleet for Italy, Mazarin gives expression to the grievances of France against the pope.[54]

[49] *Lettres du Cardinal Mazarin*, II, 103.

[50] *Ibid.*, p. 135.

[51] *Ibid.*, pp. 161, 162.

[52] *Ibid.*, p. 182.

[53] *Ibid.*, p. 204.

[54] *Ibid.*, Introduction, pp. xxiii–xxvi.

4. PAPAL LENIENCY TOWARD THE DUTCH-SPANISH TREATY OF MÜNSTER, JANUARY 30, 1648

An additional and much more important cause of French irritation was the lenient papal attitude toward the Dutch-Spanish Treaty of Münster (January 30, 1648), which recognized Dutch independence and whose terms ultimately became an integral part of the Peace of Westphalia. French irritation was manifested later in the year 1648, when Chigi and the French diplomat Servien were negotiating concerning the nuncio's protest against the Peace of Westphalia. The nuncio Chigi had sent Servien a copy of his own protest against the terms of the Treaty of Westphalia that were injurious to Catholic interests,[55] requesting that the receipt of it be acknowledged by letter. Servien responded, December 4, 1648, stating that he was instructed by his king to ascertain "if the nuncio has made a similar protest against the treaty that was made earlier in the same place between Spain and the United Provinces . . . . and that the treaty made with the United Provinces is without comparison more prejudicial to the Catholic religion than is the treaty made by the Empire."[56] This letter indicates French resentment over the partiality of the pope and the nuncio toward the Spanish. This resentment was justifiable, as the following facts will establish.

The United Provinces (or Holland) had been the allies of France and Sweden against Spain in the Thirty Years' War.[57] But the Dutch government disregarded the wishes of France and negotiated a separate treaty with Spain because it had come to fear Spain less than France. Moreover, by negotiating without France it was able to secure better terms from Spain, whose aim was to weaken France by detaching Holland from her as an ally.[58] Chigi, the papal nuncio, worked hard to keep

[55] Pastor, *op. cit.*, XIV, Part I, 95, 96.

[56] René Kerviler, *Abel Servien, négociateur des traités de Westphalie*, pp. 132, 133.

[57] *Cambridge Modern History*, IV, 142, 144, 220.

[58] Bougeant, *op. cit.*, V, 418–23; Edmundson, in *Cambridge Modern History*, IV, 715; also in *Encyclopaedia Britannica* (11th ed.), XIII, 599; Fischer, *op. cit.*, pp. 67, 75, 77.

the Spanish from signing a peace with Holland that would, by the very nature of things, have to be prejudicial to the interests of the Catholic church; but the papacy suffered a defeat.[59] The Spanish, wishing to avoid embarrassment, kept the negotiations with the United Provinces (Holland) practically secret from Chigi, because it was impossible for them to negotiate a peace with Holland that would be in harmony with the wishes of the papacy.[60] In the end Spain signed a treaty that was, like the treaties of Münster and Osnabrück (i.e., the Treaty of Westphalia), prejudicial to the interests of the Catholic church and religion. A heretic was recognized as ruler of Holland, and this implied that a heretical religion would be tolerated. Moreover, Spain ceded to Holland the almost wholly Catholic parts of Brabant, Flanders, and Limburg. By Article XVII of the Treaty the king of Spain granted to the subjects and inhabitants of the United Netherlands liberty of conscience in his territories.[61] Finally, according to Article XIX the subjects of the king of Spain, when in the United Provinces, were not, in matters of religion, to give any offense by their actions; and, reciprocally, the Dutch were to show the same consideration when sojourning in the territories of the king of Spain.[62]

If the nuncio protested against one peace, he should have protested against the other. No public protest was issued at the time; however, the nuncio issued a protest privately,[63] but its contents were not known until published in 1885.[64] This publi-

[59] Fischer, *op. cit.*, pp. 66–77; Brosch, in *Cambridge Modern History*, IV, 688.

[60] Pastor, *op. cit.*, XIV, Part I, 107; G. Brom, *Archivalia in Italië*, III, 425, 426; Fischer, *op. cit.*, p. 77.

[61] Du Mont, *Corps universelle diplomatique du droit des gens*, VI, Part I, 431; Londorp, *Acta publica*, VI, 333; Pastor, *op. cit.*, XIV, Part I, 107; Hubert, *Les Pays-Bas Espagnols et la République des Provinces—Uniés, La question religieuse et les relations diplomatiques* ("Mémoires d'Académie Royale de Belgique, Classe des lettres et des sciences morales et politiques et class des beaux arts," deuxième serie), II, 113.

[62] Du Mont, *op. cit.*, VI, Part I, 431; Londorp, *op. cit.*, VI, 333; Hubert, *op. cit.*, p. 113.

[63] Brom, *op. cit.*, III, 437.

[64] *Coleccion de documentos ineditos para la historia de España*, LXXXIV (Madrid, 1885), 228.

cation does not seem to have caused any widespread attention at the time, for so careful a scholar as Ludwig Pastor states that "this protest, whose contents were guarded so very secretly, were first made known by Brom (III, 437 f.)," a work that appeared in 1914.[65] During the negotiations the Dutch would concede nothing in the religious field, and the Spanish representatives had to adjust themselves to that situation.[66] The pope and the nuncio were less energetic in opposing this Dutch-Spanish peace than they were when protesting against the later peaces of Münster and Osnabrück.

In appraising French attitude toward the conclusion of peace between the Dutch and the Spanish we must keep in mind the following significant facts:

1. That Adami, the historian of the Congress, who was favorable to the papacy and the nuncio, says he had never seen any protest from Chigi, the nuncio, but he knew that the nuncio had not seen the articles of the Dutch-Spanish peace before they were published, and that, when he heard of it, he orally and privately had expressed his disapprobation of the Dutch-Spanish peace.[67]

2. That although Innocent X had told Chigi in a letter of November 20, 1647 (that is, before the Dutch-Spanish peace had been signed), fearlessly to safeguard the best interests of the church and solemnly to protest against the cessions that were proposed to the advantage of the heretics and to the great detriment of the Catholic faith,[68] it was not until May 16, 1648 (three and a half months after the peace had been signed), that the nuncio wrote a letter to the Spanish ambassador, the Count of Peñaranda, and inclosed a copy of the admonitory letter of Innocent X.[69]

[65] *Op. cit.*, XIV, Part I, 107, n. 2.

[66] Hubert, *op. cit.*, II, 110.

[67] Adami, *Arcana Pacis Westphalicae*, p. 398; Adami, *Relatio historica* (Meiern ed.), pp. 542, 543; see also Fischer, *op. cit.*, pp. 73–77.

[68] Garampi, *Ragguaglio della Paca di Vestfalia, e delle varie Proteste fattesi dalla S. Sedi contro la medisima*, Fondo Garampi 94, p. 1; Brom, *op. cit.*, III, 438; *Coleccion de documentos ineditos para la historia de España*, LXXXIV, 228, 229.

[69] Garampi, *op. cit.*, p. 7; Brom, *op. cit.*, III, 437–38 (which gives the date as May 18); *Coleccion de documentos*, LXXXIV, 228.

3. That Chigi's letter to the Spanish ambassador was milder than the papal letter to the nuncio, and expressed the nuncio's appreciation of the services that Peñaranda and the other Spanish plenipotentiaries had given to the Catholic religion. However, Chigi protested against the Dutch-Spanish peace in harmony with his papal instructions. He also gave the impression that he had not seen the treaty but had heard that it had been ratified and published.[70]

4. That when Peñaranda, two days later (Mary 18, 1648), reported on these communications to the Spanish sovereign, he indicated that the nuncio had been exceedingly considerate in the way he had negotiated concerning this matter. In carrying out the commands of the papal brief and notifying the Spanish plenipotentiaries of the desire of the pope, Chigi did it "with so great prudence and caution and secrecy that (so far as I [Peñaranda], can learn) the counselor Brun and I alone have knowledge of it."[71] In speaking further of Chigi's conduct of this case, Peñaranda commends the nuncio especially for prudently having made no disturbance, or demonstration, or any other sort of protest, because he recognized that such action might greatly harm the treaties by arousing fear and distrust in the Dutch Estates-General and might also give the French and their partisans an opportunity of fomenting sedition, quarrels, and complaints by the Protestant preachers.[72]

In the same letter Peñaranda indicated that the information that he had given Chigi in a previous conference might have had some weight in softening the attitude of the nuncio and the pope. The ambassador showed that he had acted in harmony with the instructions from his king and in conformity with the advice of the Catholic universities of Louvain and Douay and of the bishops and prelates, who, by order of the lord Archduke Leopold, had assembled to discuss the matter in Flanders. All

[70] *Coleccion de documentos*, LXXXIV, 228.

[71] *Ibid.*, p. 226, letter of Peñaranda to the Spanish king, Philip IV. Brun was also a Spanish plenipotentiary at Münster.

[72] *Ibid.*, p. 227; Hubert, *op. cit.*, p. 114.

that he, as plenipotentiary, had done was adequately justified and on the basis of complete knowledge of the situation. He had acted in accordance with his royal master's mandate. Therefore he had an easy conscience. He was of the opinion that the demands of the Dutch had to be met in order to avoid wrecking the prospective peace or ultimately making even greater concessions.[73]

If we recall Innocent X's friendship for Spain,[74] we can understand why he would not press the point and protest publicly and disturbingly against a treaty, the conclusion of which would enable Spain to carry on her struggle with France more advantageously. The Dutch treaty may not have affected the interests of the Catholic church as deeply as the later treaties of Münster and Osnabrück, but certainly a protest should have been made publicly and with equal rigor in both cases if the papacy were acting consistently. But from the evidence presented, above, it is apparent that the papacy itself, conducting its affairs in the spirit of the times, stressed expediency and made concessions to Spain to enable her to carry out more vigorously her policy of antagonism to France, another Catholic power. The evidence also indicates that Spain, although the most loyal of the great powers toward the papacy, had placed her secular interests above those of the church. She also had contributed to the secularization of politics during the negotiations in Westphalia.

[73] *Coleccion de documentos*, LXXXIV, 226, 227; Hubert, *op. cit.*, p. 114, n. 1; Fischer, *op. cit.*, p. 76.

[74] See chap. vii.

Chapter Nine

THE ATTITUDE OF BAVARIA AND THE ECCLESIASTICAL PRINCES CONCERNING THE CLAUSE AGAINST PROTESTS

ALTHOUGH Austria was the leader of the Catholic powers of Germany, it is also important to note the attitude of Bavaria and the German ecclesiastical princes toward the clauses against protests. Bavaria was next to Austria in importance as a German Catholic power. Actually the final conclusion of peace was due largely to Maximilian of Bavaria and Johann Philipp von Schönborn, who was Bishop of Würzburg and Worms, and, after November, 1647, Archbishop-elector of Mainz. Both these princes desired peace most sincerely. They organized a middle party composed of Catholics and Protestants, and through the conciliatory proposals of this party the peace negotiations eventuated successfully. Once these princes had achieved the termination of the war, they were not sympathetic toward a protest that would undo all their work. In most cases these Catholic princes were benefited by the conclusion of the Peace, either in a political and material way or merely by the termination of a war that had, in the minds of many, ceased being a religious war and was doing nothing but injury to church and temporal interests.

1. MAXIMILIAN I, ELECTOR OF BAVARIA, 1597–1651; RELIGIOUS TRAINING AND POLITICAL VIEWS

Maximilian, the first elector of Bavaria, living in a period of remarkable personalities, was himself one of the most remarkable of these noteworthies. His reign was the longest and most eventful of all the Bavarian reigns.[1] Of all the European rulers reigning at the opening of the Thirty Years' War, he was the only one that lived long enough to witness its close. In many ways he was typical of the Catholic rulers of the time. Although deeply religious, he did not permit the interests of the Catholic church to overshadow his political interests.

Maximilian was pious, earnest in observing all religious formalities and practices. In early life he had been impregnated with the idea that every Protestant was destined to suffer the torments of hell. He was an affiliate of various religious orders. He followed the example of his father in engaging daily in religious devotions, and frequently chastised himself to secure peace of mind. He devoted several hours a day to prayer, and heard at least one mass a day, even when on military campaigns. He was deeply interested in pilgrimages and religious relics.[2] He desired religious uniformity to such an extent that he established an ecclesiastical police system unequaled elsewhere in Germany. When the prayer bells rang, everyone must kneel, whether he be on foot or riding in a wagon or on a horse. During religious worship on Sunday people were forbidden to frequent inns or take walks. It was the duty of every subject, even the highest state officials, to present a certificate of having been to confessional at Easter time.[3] He wished to keep Protestantism absolutely out of his lands in every respect. His subjects were forbidden to marry Protestants. No Protestant was to possess lands; all communication with the heretical neighbors was to be avoided. Parents not favoring a Catholic education for their children were imprisoned. Heretical books were prohibited; those in the ducal library were kept in sealed security.[4] He required every one of his subjects to possess a rosary. He

[1] Doeberl, "Maximilian I., Bayerns grosser Kurfürst, in neuester Beleuchtung," *Forschungen zur Geschichte Bayerns*, XII, 208.

[2] Riezler, *Geschichte Baierns*, V, 6–8.

[3] Doeberl, "Maximilian I," *Forschungen*, XII, 211; Brandi, *Gegenreformation und Religionskriege*, p. 152; Doeberl, *Entwicklungsgeschichte Bayerns*, III, 524.

[4] Brandi, *op. cit.*, pp. 150–51; Doeberl, *Entwicklungsgeschichte*, III, 522–23.

employed no official that would not take an oath to the Tridentine creed; his officials were forced to go to church every day and to participate in the weekly religious processions or pay a fine. Spies were used to see to it that his officials conducted themselves religiously and morally as he desired. He himself could hardly participate in processions and pilgrimages enough. He preferred to take important political and military actions on the day of Our Lady Mary.[5]

The Jesuits had trained him in his youth, and he always preserved a fondness for them; to him they were the most perfect representatives and most successful champions of Catholicism. Therefore he favored them and used them as confessors and as counselors in ecclesiastical matters. He also consulted them in state affairs to learn whether his proposed measures were contrary to the commands of God and the church, in hope of being able to conform to their wishes.[6] However, he did not permit them to formulate his governmental and political plans, and in ecclesiastical affairs he even refused their urgent desires. He was never a tool of the Jesuits or of the papal hierarchy.[7]

In all affairs he preserved a rare independence of mind and judgment. As a member of the church he regarded himself as subject to the hierarchy, and he always showed all honor and respect to the church as the representative of God. However, he distinguished between the person and the office; and in his relation to the person (even when bearing the tiara) he preserved a free, and occasionally a subtle, judgment.[8] He acknowledged all the rights of the ecclesiasts, and especially of the pope, that were sanctioned by the canonical rights and the curial system; but, on the other hand, he repelled with rugged determination

[5] Riezler, *op. cit.*, V, 684–85; Stieve, *Der Ursprung des dreissigjährigen Krieges, 1607–1619*, I, 60–68; Doeberl, *Entwicklungsgeschichte*, III, 522, 524–26.

[6] Steinberger, *Die Jesuiten und die Friedensfrage*, pp. 19–20, 60, 94–97, 100–101, 103; Riezler, *Bayern und Frankreich*, p. 502, n. 3; Doeberl, *Entwicklungsgeschichte*, III, 507–8.

[7] Stieve, *Churfürst Maximilian I von Bayern*, pp. 5–6; Riezler, *Geschichte Baierns*, V, 685–86; Steinberger, *op. cit.*, 19, 20; Doeberl, *Entwicklungsgeschichte*, III, 509.

[8] Stieve, *Churfürst Maximilian I*, p. 5; Doeberl, *Entwicklungsgeschichte*, III, 526.

all efforts of the churchmen to interfere in state affairs, and, when he felt that his princely position and prerogatives gave him justification, he unhesitatingly used his authority over the ecclesiasts of his land, even when such acts were absolutely denied to laymen by papal theory.[9] He did not in the least share the presumptuous view, so frequently held by other Catholics, that God would finally grant a triumph to his church. He had no hesitation in sacrificing the claims or rights of the church if, by stubbornly supporting those claims and rights, he seemed to endanger the stability of the church or the Empire.[10] In other words, he was an adherent of the idea of secularized politics. The interests of the state and the church required that he protect them both; he was a judge of what was best for the church. But he took measures contrary to the desires of the churchmen only when all other resources seemed exhausted and he was by duty bound to make his own decisions to save the church and the Empire.[11]

Moreover, he clung firmly to the ecclesiastical rights that had been turned over to him, and extended them to the advantage of himself and the state when possible. He determined the appointment to the bishoprics of Freising and Regensburg as thoroughly as though he had freehold rights over them. His brother Ferdinand was not only Archbishop of Cologne but was, at the same time, Bishop of Liège, Osnabrück, Paderborn, Hildesheim, and Münster.[12]

Time and again Maximilian seemed to place personal interests above that of religion; but he did so because his broad political interests, his love of peace, and the demands of state policy required that he stress religious interests less. As proof of this

[9] Stieve, *Churfürst Maximilian I*, p. 6; Stieve, "Beiträge zur Geschichte des Verhältniss von Staat und Kirche in Baiern unter Maximilian I (1595–1651)," *Zeitschrift für Kirchenrecht*, XIII, 372–96; XIV, 59–64; Stieve, *Ursprung des dreissigjährigen Krieges*, I, 69–73; Doeberl, *Entwicklungsgeschichte*, III, 526, 527.

[10] Stieve, in *Allgemeine deutsche Biographie*, XXI, 21.

[11] *Ibid.*

[12] Doeberl, "Maximilian I," *Forschungen*, XII, 211; Doeberl, *Entwicklungsgeschichte*, III,, 526, Ennen, "Ferdinand, Erzbischof und Kurfürst von Köln," *Allgemeine deutsche Biographie*, VI, 691-97.

may be cited his treatment of the monasteries in the Upper Palatinate, which had come under Bavarian control in 1628. The former secular rulers of the sixteenth century had secularized these monasteries; and Maximilian, with papal consent, continued to keep the income from these monastic properties because these funds were necessary for state purposes, the continuance of the war against heresy. While he was fighting in the north to undo the secularization of ecclesiastical lands by supporting the Edict of Restitution, he was quite willing to continue using the benefits of secularization in his own lands for the better prosecution of the war. As early as 1628 the pope had sanctioned such an arrangement for twelve years; this arrangement was repeatedly prolonged, and it was not until 1669, sixteen years after Maximilian's death, that most of the monastic lands in the Upper Palatinate were once more occupied by the members of the religious orders.[13] In shaping all his policies he exercised full independence of judgment. He believed in the divine-right-of-kings theory; he enjoyed his princely position by divine choice. He wished his counselors to give their advice freely and unhesitatingly, a practice that he regarded as necessary, even for the counselors of an absolute sovereign. However, all his acts were based on his own decisions.[14] He had the strongest regal self-consciousness and became a forceful representative of the princely right of controlling church affairs and of the independence of the state as opposed to the church; he thoroughly believed in absolutism.[15]

2. OBJECTIVES AND METHODS OF MAXIMILIAN'S FOREIGN POLICY

In Maximilian's foreign policy he also stressed his personal and territorial interests regardless of how such action affected Catholic and imperial interests. To be sure, during the Thirty

[13] Riezler, *Geschichte Baierns*, V, 318, 319, 678, n. 3.

[14] Stieve, *Churfürst Maximilian I*, p. 7; Doeberl, "Maximilian I," *Forschungen*, XII, 211.

[15] Riezler, *Geschichte Baierns*, V, 679; Doeberl, *Entwicklungsgeschichte*, II, 61; Pflugk-Harttung, *Weltgeschichte*, *Neuzeit*, *1650–1815*, p. 102.

Years' War he had naturally played an important part as chief of the Catholic League, co-operating against the Protestants, the Swedes, and the French. But in supporting the Catholic emperor he was far from wishing to strengthen the imperial authority so it could oppress the individual German princes. Although he wished to secure the triumph of Catholicism in Germany, he desired also to maintain the old liberties of the German princes in the face of imperial pretensions. He wished, moreover, to create for himself in south Germany a state strong enough to be able to oppose both Austria and France. To insure this with greater certainty, and also to throw luster on his own ducal house, he wished to keep the electorate, which he had acquired in 1623 at the expense of Frederick of the Palatinate, and the territory called the Upper Palatinate.[16]

From the beginning of the war Maximilian had fought valiantly for the cause of the emperor and the interests of the church. But after the signing of the Peace of Prague (1635) and after the entry of the French into the war as the ally of Sweden and the Protestant princes, Maximilian gave up his zeal for the continuance of the war. It was clear that the purpose of France was to humiliate the Austrian and Spanish Hapsburgs and to keep Germany divided politically. In other words, the religious interests of the war were being overshadowed by political considerations. Therefore, he was now willing to bring about peace by making concessions to the Protestants.[17] In the last years of the war his actions were such as fully to substantiate the shrewd estimate of Cardinal Mazarin, who, in writing to his ambassadors D'Avaux and Servien at Münster June 14, 1644, said, in referring to Maximilian, that he "is extremely crafty and adroit, and there is no artifice that he will not resort to in

[16] Cheruel, *Lettres du Cardinal Mazarin*, I, xliv; Stieve, *Churfürst Maximilian I*, pp. 18, 19; Katt, *Beiträge*, pp. 25, 94, 101; Riezler, *Bayern und Frankreich*, pp. 494, 497; Stieve, "Maximilian I., Kurfürst von Baiern," in *Allgemeine deutsche Biographie*, XXI, 10; Pastor, *Geschichte der Päpste*, XIII, Part I, 200–202.

[17] Riezler, *Geschichte Baierns*, V, 646; Stieve, "Maximilian I., Kurfürst von Baiern," in *Allgemeine deutsche Biographie*, XXI, 9; Jacob, *Die Erwerbung des Elsass durch Frankreich im westfälischen Frieden*, p. 15; Doeberl, *Entwicklungsgeschichte*, III, 603.

order to gain his ends."[18] So under the circumstances he would use religion when it suited his purposes,[19] he would co-operate with the emperor and his allies, or enter a truce with France and Sweden, or endeavor to become an ally of France, or revert to his original imperial alliance, in accordance with the needs and conditions confronting him. Maximilian's execution of this tortuous but shrewd policy from 1635 to 1648 can best be followed by considering the following steps:

a) *From French entry into the war until the armistice of Ulm, 1635—March, 1647.*—When in 1635 France intervened in the Thirty Years' War on behalf of the Swedes and Protestants, there occurred what Maximilian had tried to prevent since the beginning of the war. However, in the military campaigns that ensued, Maximilian's generals had succeeded in keeping the French armies beyond the Bavarian frontier until 1645. Thereafter both the imperial and Bavarian forces suffered defeats, and the French entered Bavaria. Consequently, Maximilian's objective was to obtain peace, a peace advantageous to himself. He was filled with the fear that ultimately he might be left isolated between the emperor and Spain on the one hand and France, Sweden, and the German Protestants on the other.[20] From 1635 to 1647 he had loyally co-operated with the emperor, but each mistrusted the other.[21] The long war had exhausted Bavaria's resources.[22] Maximilian needed peace most imperatively; and he regarded the emperor as being the chief deterrent to peace, especially because he insisted on including Spain in the peace that was being haltingly negotiated at Münster.[23] Therefore, in conjunction with Cologne and Hesse-Cassel, and after

[18] Le Clerc, *Négociations secrètes*, II, 62, 63; also Cheruel, *op. cit.*, I, 754; Riezler, *Geschichte Baierns*, V, 678; Doeberl, *Entwicklungsgeschichte*, III, 509.

[19] Riezler, *Bayern und Frankreich*, pp. 500–518.

[20] *Ibid.*, p. 494. [21] *Ibid.*, p. 494; Riezler, *Geschichte Baierns*, V, 646.

[22] Riezler, *Geschichte Baierns*, V, 660–66; Riezler, "Die Meuterei Johann's von Werth," *Historische Zeitschrift*, LXXXII, 40; Egloffstein, *Baierns Friedenspolitik von 1645 bis 1647*, p. 130.

[23] Riezler, *Bayern und Frankreich*, pp. 494, 498–99; Doeberl, *Entwicklungsgeschichte*, III, 602.

long negotiations and with the support of theological opinions,[24] Maximilian signed the armstice of Ulm with France and Sweden, March 14, 1647. This meant that Bavaria would henceforth be neutral.[25]

b) *Maximilian's failure to form an alliance with the French.*—Maximilian's signing the armistice of Ulm with France was an affront to his former ally, Emperor Ferdinand III. The elector tried to justify his action in a note to the emperor,[26] but feared, quite rightly, that Ferdinand would ultimately take vengeance on him and deprive him of the electorate and the Palatinate. Therefore, to safeguard himself against such a misfortune, he negotiated, between March and September, 1647, to effect an alliance with France.[27] Mazarin, the French prime minister, might conceivably have been ready to enter such an agreement; but he had to face the opposition of his ally, Sweden, which feared that such an alliance might be merely the beginning of the formation of a Catholic league contrary to Swedish and Protestant interests.[28]

c) *Maximilian resumes co-operation with the emperor, from September, 1647, to the end of the war in 1648.*—But by September, 1647, Maximilian was once more ready to join forces with the emperor. In his fluctuating policy thus far his objective had been to hasten the conclusion of peace. However, he soon came to realize that the Swedes and the French were using his armistice with them to promote their own interests; the Swedes were demanding greater concessions than ever at the Peace Congress. Moreover, the Catholic forces were regarding Maximilian as a

[24] Riezler, *Bayern und Frankreich*, p. 502, n. 1; Steinberger, *op. cit.*, pp. 94–96.

[25] Meiern, *Acta pacis Westphalicae*, V, 2–17; Riezler, *Bayern und Frankreich*, pp. 500–518; Riezler, *Geschichte Baierns*, V, 612; Riezler, "Die Meuterei Johann's von Werth," *Historische Zeitschrift*, LXXXII, 41; Egloffstein, *op. cit.*, pp. 130–76; Stieve, "Maximilian I., Kurfürst von Baiern," *Allgemeine deutsche Biographie*, XXI, 18; Fischer, *Beiträge*, pp. 26, 27.

[26] Meiern, *op. cit.*, V, 18–24; Londorp, *Acta publica*, VI, 193–96; Fischer, *op. cit.*, p. 27.

[27] Riezler, *Geschichte Baierns*, V, 613–16; Riezler, *Bayern und Frankreich*, p. 519; Riezler, "Die Meuterei Johann's von Werth," *Historische Zeitschrift*, LXXXII, 41–42.

[28] Meiern, *op. cit.*, V, 17–18; Riezler, *Bayern und Franreich*, 510; Riezler, "Die Meuterei Johann's von Werth," *Historische Zeitschrift*, LXXXII, 42–43.

traitor to the Catholic cause because he had signed the armistice of Ulm.[29] On the other hand, Bavaria (which had demobilized its army after signing the armistice) was being unjustly suspected of foul play by Sweden and France, because, under the leadership of the disgruntled Johann von Werth, a Bavarian military group took service with Emperor Ferdinand III.[30] Furthermore, the emperor was now temporarily having encouraging victories; and, in order once more to secure Bavaria's much needed military support, he guaranteed the electorate and the Upper Palatinate to Maximilian with greater assurance. So, by September 7, 1647, the elector signed the Treaty of Pilsen and again joined the imperial forces.[31] In taking this step, it was Maximilian's hope that he could persuade the French that he was merely attacking the Swedes to secure an early peace;[32] for over three months he was able to remain at peace with France. However, by December 29, 1647, France was forced, on the urging of Sweden, to declare war on Maximilian.[33] In the 1648 campaign, Bavaria, already exhausted by repeated invasions, was overrun once more by French troops.[34] However, during the last half-year of the peace negotiations and immediately afterward Mazarin, now free from the need of considering the sensibilities of the Swedes, made efforts to promote friendly negotiations with Maximilian. Bavaria, with French help, received the electorate and the Upper Palatinate; and France, with Maximilian's support, secured the advantages that she demanded.[35]

[29] Fischer, *op. cit.*, pp. 8, 15, 29–30; Steinberger, *op. cit.*, pp. 117, 150; Riezler, *Geschichte Baierns*, V, 628, 629; Doeberl, *Entwicklungsgeschichte*, III, 602.

[30] Riezler, "Die Meuterei Johann's von Werth," *Historische Zeitschrift*, LXXXII, 38–97, 193–239, but especially p. 92; Riezler, *Geschichte Baierns*, V, 615–26, but especially p. 621.

[31] Meiern, *op. cit.*, V, 48–50; Riezler, *Geschichte Baierns*, V, 628–30; Riezler, *Bayern und Frankreich*, pp. 518–20; Egloffstein, *op. cit.*, p. 176; Lorentzen, *Die schwedische Armee im dreissigjährigen Kriege*, p. 121, n. 2; Doeberl, *Entwicklungsgeschichte*, III, 602.

[32] Meiern, *op. cit.*, V, 61.

[33] *Ibid.*, pp. 117–20.

[34] *Cambridge Modern History*, IV, 393; Riezler, *Geschichte Baierns*, V, 635–46.

[35] Cheruel, *op. cit.*, III, 1079, letter of January 1, 1649; Meaux, *La réforme et la politique française en Europe*, II, 678–79; Riezler, *Geschichte Baierns*, V, 655; Riezler, *Bayern und Frankreich*, pp. 540–41; Doeberl, "Maximilian I.," *Forschungen*, XII, 218–19.

It is quite clear that Maximilian was working mainly, if not solely, for his own interests. His religiosity was not so deep as to proscribe from his statecraft all methods that would be contrary to morals. He would outwit his opponents or even his allies although he had to sacrifice uprightness and honesty.[36] Moreover, in his peace policy, especially toward the end of the War, he was willing to disregard the historic interests of the church if thereby he could secure a permanent and advantageous settlement. He refused to be guided by the appeals of the nuncio Chigi and Innocent X, as the next two sections of this chapter will recount.

3. MAXIMILIAN'S DESIRE FOR PEACE

During the early part of the Thirty Years' War Maximilian was devoted to the cause of the church and was desirous of extirpating heresy.[37] In fact, throughout the war, except when he negotiated the truce of Ulm with France, March 14, 1647, the religious motive was constantly at work in his mind. Before the truce of Ulm the idea that the Thirty Years' War was a religious war had been nowhere so impressed on any belligerent camp as on the Bavarian.[38] Nevertheless, when, after 1635, as already observed, political interests overshadowed religious interests in the war, he worked in the direction of peace, regardless of how the settlement might affect the church, though he was not uniformly persistent in his desire for peace.[39] As early as February 23, 1636, he had ordered prayers and works of penitence for the sake of bringing about peace.[40] The effects of the repeated devastations of his lands at the hands of the Swedes and the French accentuated his peace efforts.[41] After 1641 he pressed

[36] Riezler, *Geschichte Baierns*, V, 678; Fischer, *op. cit.*, pp. 29, 30; Pastor, *op. cit.*, XIV, Part I, 80.

[37] Riezler, *Geschichte Baierns*, V, 6.

[38] *Ibid.*, V, 675.

[39] Mentz, *Johann Philipp von Schönborn*, I, 34; Jacob, *op. cit.*, p. 15.

[40] *Bayerischer literärischer und merkantilischer Anzeiger*, No. 17, April 23, 1828, p. 138, attributed by Riezler, *Geschichte Baierns*, V, 646, n. 3, to Deutinger.

[41] Riezler, *Geschichte Baierns*, V, 414–15, 498, 600–601, 660–66; Egloffstein, *op. cit.*, p. 130.

Emperor Ferdinand III with increasing vigor to bring an end to the war.[42]

In 1645 Maximilian had sent his Jesuit confessor, Johann Vervaux, to Paris to seek an armistice for the emperor and Bavaria, or, failing that, an armistice for Bavaria alone, and, if possible, a Bavarian alliance with France. But no success attended these efforts.[43] When negotiating the armistice of Ulm (March, 1647) with France and Sweden, Maximilian was doing so in the interests of peace.[44] When he gave up the short armistice of Ulm (March–September, 1647) and once more joined forces with the emperor, he declared that Ferdinand III could use Bavaria's alliance only to promote the re-establishment of peace as soon as that was humanly possible.[45]

With such manifest desire to bring about peace it is not surprising to find Maximilian, who was the most powerful and ardent patron of the Society of Jesus, writing to Caraffa the General of the Order, January 3, 1648, requesting that he restrain Heinrich Wangnereck, who had written an extreme pamphlet, the *Judicum theologicum*, against the Peace. Maximilian pointed out that Wangnereck and his Jesuit associates were, through their extreme opposition to a moderate peace, doing injury to the general good and to the Order as well.[46] Moreover, at the instigation of Maximilian, his Jesuit confessor, Johann Vervaux, wrote a sharp reply to the irritating pamphlet of Wangnereck, in which he attacked the extreme uncompromising views of his

[42] Stieve, "Ferdinand III," *Allgemeine deutsche Biographie*, VI, 666.

[43] Cheruel, *op. cit.*, II, 140–44, 147–48; Steinberger, *op. cit.*, pp. 39–45; Egloffstein, *op. cit.*, pp. 20–25; Riezler, *Geschichte Baierns*, V, 589–92; Pfülf, "Ein Beitrag zur Geschichte der bayrischen Friedensbestrebungen an der Neige des dreissigjährigen Krieges, Stimmen aus Maria-Laach," *Katholische Blätter*, LVI, 522–24; Bougeant, *Histoire des guerres*, III, 366–67; VI, 457.

[44] Meiern, *op. cit.*, V, 61; Riezler, *Baiern und Frankreich*, pp. 520–21; Brandi, *Gegenreformation und Religionskriege*, pp. 288–89; Doeberl, *Entwicklungsgeschichte*, III, 602.

[45] Meiern, *op. cit.*, V, 61; Riezler, *Baiern und Frankreich*, pp. 520–21; Riezler, *Geschichte Baierns*, V, 646; Doeberl, *Entwicklungsgeschichte*, III, 602.

[46] Steinberger, *op. cit.*, pp. 132–33, also p. 198, which contains Maximilian's letter to Caraffa; Doeberl, *Entwicklungsgeschichte*, III, 603; see also chap. xv, below.

brother-Jesuit and made a sort of apology for Bavaria's separate armistice with France and Sweden of March 14, 1647.[47]

Having gone over to the side of the emperor once more, in September, 1647 (as observed in section 2), Maximilian pursued a vigorous peace policy. In October, 1647, one of the Bavarian ambassadors at Münster, Dr. Ernst, went to each of the Catholic representatives and stated that his master did not wish to continue the war under any circumstances; and he implored them, even with threats, not to hinder the conclusion of peace any longer.[48] In the same month, October 21, 1647, Maximilian wrote a personal letter to Ferdinand III, his cousin and brother-in-law, urging him to make all possible efforts to secure a resumption of effective peace negotiations at Münster and Osnabrück at once, even before the termination of the military campaign then in progress. He reported that the Swedes and French had wrongly concluded that Bavaria's rejoining Austria meant a resumption of the war to extirpate Protestantism, and that the Spaniards, who were formerly inclined toward peace, were rejoicing over the probable prolonging of the war. To save Catholicism from complete destruction, the emperor should desert the peace-resisting Catholic extremists and begin aggressive negotiations with the Swedes and the French, who were willing to consider an early peace.[49]

Six days later, October 27, 1647, Maximilian wrote a second and similar appeal to Ferdinand III, but added, in closing, that if the Austro-Bavarian recess were to result in the emperor's continuing the military campaign, then he, Maximilian, would take measures to protect his own interests, which meant, as explained in the earlier part of the note, that he would sign a separate peace with France and Sweden.[50] Owing to these ap-

[47] Steinberger, *op. cit.*, p. 103; Doeberl, *Entwicklungsgeschichte*, III, 603; see also chap. xvi, below.

[48] Meiern, *op. cit.*, IV, 780; Riezler, *Geschichte Baierns*, V, 646.

[49] Meiern, *op. cit.*, V, 106–10; Sattler, *Geschichte des Herzogthums Würtenberg unter der Regierung der Herzogen*, Vol. VIII, Appendix 62, pp. 196–201; Riezler, *Geschichte Baierns*, V, 646–47.

[50] Meiern, *op. cit.*, V, 110–13; IV, 787; Fischer, *op. cit.*, p. 55.

peals, Ferdinand III showed a more conciliatory attitude; as a consequence the stagnating peace negotiations could be resumed.[51] Since the departure of the imperial representative, Trauttmannsdorff, from the Congress (July 16, 1647) the peace negotiations had come to a complete standstill. Now, through the pressure of Maximilian of Bavaria, Ferdinand III sent instructions to his representatives at Münster and Osnabrück to endeavor to secure an agreement on the basis of the peace plan drawn up by Trauttmannsdorff.[52]

Maximilian, in his great desire for peace, even used his court preacher, Jacob Balde, who was also a Latin poet, called the "German Horace." He wrote a ninth book to his *Lyrical Forests* and dedicated it to the French plenipotentiary D'Avaux, in hope that he would work for an early peace between France and Bavaria; this gesture was not without success, for it is regarded as a factor in bringing about the armistice between France and Bavaria in March, 1647.[53]

Maximilian also used Balde to present an apology for Bavaria's signing the Treaty of Ulm with France in March, 1647; Balde wrote a drama, *Georgicus*, in old Latin. The main political idea expressed was that Bavaria, in the interests of self-preservation, could not permit itself to be ruined in order to continue to aid Austria, which unfortunately was dominated by Spanish influence.[54]

4. MAXIMILIAN'S PEACE EFFORTS AND THE PAPAL CURIA

The papal *Curia* had for thirty years praised Maximilian as a staunch supporter of the church, but now disliked his willingness, in the interests of peace, to make the concessions demanded by the Protestants, and therefore made bitter accusations against him. So, early as December 30, 1645, the elector had

[51] Riezler, *Geschichte Baierns*, V, 647.

[52] Huber, *Geschichte Oesterreiches*, V, 606.

[53] Westermayer, "Balde," *Allgemeine deutsche Biographie*, II, 2; Westermayer, *Jacobus Balde*, p. 177; Steinberger, *op. cit.*, p. 48; Bach, *Jakob Balde*, pp. 37, 38.

[54] Westermayer, *Jacobus Balde*, p. 177; also in *Allgemeine deutsche Biographie*, II, 2; Steinberger, *op. cit.*, p. 96; Bach, *op. cit.*, pp. 36, 108–9.

appealed to Innocent X through a memorandum composed by P. Laurenz Forer and handed by him to the pope. This document maintained that "the Catholic religion was in extreme danger" and that "the German Catholics cannot persist in defending themselves"; and that, "if foreign Catholics do not come to their support," "they will be forced to accept a peace under the most unjust conditions." The pope was implored "to hasten the conclusion of peace through his legate as much as possible; delay is aggravating the situation for the Catholics from day to day."[55] But the appeal was in vain. In an accompanying letter Forer recorded the outcome as follows: "After three months I received from the pope nothing more than 'We shall see.' "[56] When the nuncio Chigi admonished Maximilian for his attitude, he said it was hopeless to continue the struggle; it were better to save what could be saved than to run after the lost with the obvious danger of losing all. He said that he had done his best and that, if those in religious affairs had done as much, conditions would be different.[57] He wrote in the same tone to the pope, as is revealed in the two manuscript volumes of instructions to Crivelli, the Bavarian ambassador at Rome. In December, 1647, Maximilian instructed his emissary to inform the pope that, since "I have attempted all human means" and "since there is no further possibility for me to defend myself and the interests of religion against the enemy, I feel free from all guilt in the eyes of God."[58]

In a further letter to Crivelli, January 2, 1648, Maximilian instructed his ambassador to request the pope for subsidies, explaining that "never has it been more necessary to receive the support of His Holiness for imperiled religion than under the present circumstances; never has the means to defend that re-

[55] *Memoriale in manus oblatum Smo Dno No Innocent X, etc.*, Reichsarchiv (now Hauptstaatsarchiv), Munich, Jesuitica in genere fasc. 25, No. 370; Riezler, *Geschichte Baierns*, V, 648, n. 2.

[56] *Memoriale in manus, etc.*, Jesuitica in genera fasc. 25, No. 370.

[57] Riezler, *Geschichte Baierns*, V, 648.

[58] Crivelli, *Corrispondenza di Roma, 1612–1656* (manuscript volume), instructions to Crivelli, December 11 and 27, 1647, in Bavarian Secret Archives, K. Schw. 515/25.

ligion been more yearned for than now."[59] On January 17, 1648, the elector wrote similarly, "I foresee the certain collapse not only of the Empire but also of the Catholic religion if His Holiness does not definitely and as soon as possible send the requested help to enable me to maintain my armies."[60] In a letter of the Archbishop of Mainz, and imperial chancellor, dated Osnabrück, June 4, 1648, there is noted a remark of the elector of Bavaria's representative, this being made in the Catholic council:

> The Supreme Shepherd of the Catholic Church . . . . has thus far excused himself and confessed not to be able to provide assistance and aid, and has found no other remedy to check this evil; and he [Maximilian] of necessity would have to let those things eventuate that cannot be prevented without an even greater degree of danger and disadvantage to the Catholic religion.[61]

Similar statements are to be found in many of the letters of Maximilian to Crivelli in this manuscript volume of 396 pages, from which we infer that the Bavarian elector felt that, since he had appealed in vain for papal aid and had received relief from no other source, there was no possibility of opposing the enemy and guarding the interests of the church. Maximilian believed that, since the church had neglected her own interests in this time of crisis, he would be justified in bringing about a peace even though the interests of the church might suffer thereby.

Chigi, however, resented Maximilian's supporting the peace plans of Trauttmannsdorff, which were disadvantageous to the church; the nuncio felt that the elector was less intent on safeguarding the interests of the church than in furthering the welfare of his own house.[62] This is undoubtedly a correct view. Maximilian was in his seventy-fifth year when the Peace of Münster was signed. That Peace, negotiated with so much difficulty, secured to his young sons the electoral dignity and the

[59] Crivelli, *Corrispondenza di Roma, 1648, 1649* (manuscript volume) in Bavarian Secret Archives, Munich, K. Schw. 313/13, p. 4.

[60] *Ibid.*, p. 13. [61] *Ibid.*, p. 105; see Riezler, *Geschichte Baierns*, V, 648, n. 3.

[62] Fischer, *op. cit.*, pp. 47–48.

Upper Palatinate. To obtain these he had detached himself from his former political associates, Spain and the ultra-Catholics, and in their place had had the support of France.[63] Having achieved these gains, he wished then to be secure against any papal protests. Circumstances made it compulsory for him, although personally a very devout Catholic, to favor a policy implying the secularization of politics.

5. THE MIDDLE PARTY WORKS FOR PEACE

After Ferdinand III's actions in urging the consideration of Trauttmannsdorff's peace plans, no progress could be made because the extreme Protestants and the extreme Catholics insisted on having their full demands embodied in the Treaty; and for weeks Dr. Isaak Volmar, who was in charge of imperialist interests after Trauttmannsdorff's departure, failed to get support for any compromise proposals.[64] The delay in the peace negotiations alarmed Maximilian, for he feared that the Swedes would, in the spring of 1648, take vengeance on him for having broken the armistice of Ulm.[65] Maximilian was willing to make concessions to the French and Swedes; he was willing to sacrifice his national and religious sentiments, and came to feel that peace could be secured in no other way.[66] For some time he had tried to form a party of compromise, a third or middle party, or political group that would oppose the extreme views of the ultra-Catholic princes of Germany and of Spain and the emperor, and thus come to terms with the well-disposed Protestants. This party was also called by one of the organizers, Vorburg, the "uninterested" party, since it had no interest in further continuing the war.[67] By January 29, 1648, after long and difficult negotiations, the organization of the party was accomplished, largely through the work of (1) Johann Philipp Vorburg, the

[63] Doeberl, *Entwicklungsgeschichte*, III, 603; Odhner, *Die Politik Schwedens*, p. 122; Jacob, *op. cit.*, p. 15.

[64] Huber, *op. cit.*, V, 606. [65] *Ibid.* [66] Riezler, *Geschichte Baierns*, V, 647.

[67] Heigel, "Das westfälische Friedenswerk," *Zeitschrift für Geschichte und Politik*, V, 437; Wild, *Johann Philipp von Schönborn*, p. 67; Doeberl, *Entwicklungsgeschichte*, III, 603.

representative of Johann Philipp von Schönborn, the Bishop of Würzburg, and of (2) Wolfgang Conrad von Thumbshirn, the representative of Sachsen-Altenburg.[68] The Catholic members were Mainz, Trier, Bavaria, Bamberg, and Würzburg; the Protestant members were Brandenburg, Brunswick-Kalenberg, electoral Saxony, Coburg, Brunswick-Lüneburg, Strassburg, Altenburg, and Weimar.[69]

Maximilian had placed himself at the head of this middle party;[70] and through its influence, after overcoming the opposition of the emperor and his representatives, it was possible to bring about an agreement on a number of previously insoluble problems such as the religious gravamina and the year of amnesty; the Swedes and French wished the amnesty to date from the year 1618, the imperialists and the Catholics preferred a later date. There now existed a well-organized party of German states who were bent on securing peace; through the further pressure of Maximilian and Johann Philipp von Schönborn, Emperor Ferdinand III was finally induced to abandon Spain and sign a separate peace with France, without the other member of the Hapsburg house.[71] The moderate party were assisted in their peace policy also by the French, who, after the Spanish had concluded a separate peace with Holland, January 30, 1648, were anxious to conclude a peace with the Empire in order to be able to attack Spain single-handed.[72]

[68] Meiern, *op. cit.*, IV, 939; Braun, "Skizzen aus dem Leben und Wirken des Sachsen-Altenburgischen Gesandten am westphälischen Friedenscongress, Wolfgang Conrad von Thumbshirn, 1645–1649," *Mittheilungen der Geschichts- und Alterthumsforschenden Gesellschaft des Osterlandes*, IV, 413; Wild, *op. cit.*, pp. 67–73; Heigel, "Das westfälische Friedenswerk," *Zeitschrift für Geschichte und Politik*, V, 437; Jacob, *op. cit.*, pp. 264–66.

[69] Mentz, *op. cit.*, I, 36–37; Riezler, *Geschichte Baierns*, V, 647; Wild, *op. cit.*, pp. 67–73; Mentz omits Weimar, Riezler omits Strassburg and Brunswick-Kalenberg. See also Huber, *op. cit.*, V, 606–7; Droysen, *Geschichte der preussischen Politik*, III, Part I, 329–34, which undervalues the work of the middle party; Odhner, *op. cit.*, p. 242.

[70] Doeberl, *Entwicklungsgeschichte*, III, 603; Riezler, *Geschichte Baierns*, V, 647; Steinberger, *op. cit.*, p. 132.

[71] Mentz, *op. cit.*, I, 38–40; Odhner, *op. cit.*, pp. 280–81; Riezler, *Geschichte Baierns*, V, 647–48; Huber, *op. cit.*, pp. 607, 610; Heigel, "Das westfälische Friedenswerk," *Zeitschrift für Geschichte und Politik*, V, 437–38; Doeberl, *Entwicklungsgeschichte*, III, 603.

[72] Mentz, *op. cit.*, I, 40.

6. THE PEACE ACTIVITIES OF JOHANN PHILIPP VON SCHÖNBORN

An even more active agent for peace and the secularization of politics than Maximilian of Bavaria was Johann Philipp von Schönborn. He had been Bishop of Würzburg in the years 1642–47, during which his main policy had been to bring about a cessation of the war.[73] As early as 1644–45, when Maximilian still held to strictly Catholic views, Johann Philipp felt that the war had nothing to do with religion; and even as early as September, 1643, his representative Vorburg at Frankfurt expressed his master's willingness to give up the "ecclesiastical reservation" clause, whereas Maximilian thought it better to continue the war a hundred years longer than make such a concession.[74] When, in November, 1647, he had been elected Archbishop of Mainz to succeed Anselm Kasimir, he felt that it was his special task to use his new influence and increased authority to hasten the peace negotiations at Osnabrück and Münster; and in the minds of some writers he deserves the chief credit for closing the Westphalian peace negotiations.[75] In spite of his rank he was free from religious prejudices and had a yielding attitude when matters of religion were considered by the Congress.[76] He had been a realist in his policies, playing a vacillating policy, supporting first France and Sweden, then Austria and Spain.[77] The war had devastated his territories to the point of exhaustion.[78]

Politically, as Bishop of Würzburg and as Archbishop of Mainz, he wished to maintain the princely rights of the separate states of Germany. He opposed the Austrian policy of imperial centralized political control. He opposed the Austrian alliance with Spain, preferring friendliness with France and co-operation

[73] *Ibid.*, p. 16. [74] *Ibid.*, p. 34.

[75] Wild, *op. cit.*, p. 1; Bockenheimer, "Johann Philipp von Schönborn," *Allgemeine deutsche Biographie*, XXXII, 274; Lavisse, *Histoire de France*, VII, Part I, 69.

[76] Mentz, *op. cit.*, I, 41–42; Pastor, *op. cit.*, XIV, Part I, 90.

[77] Bockenheimer, *op. cit.*, XXXII, 274.

[78] Wild, *op. cit.*, p. 46.

with the German Protestants and Sweden to achieve his political ends to establish peace.[79] While Bishop of Würzburg, he had, among other instructions, advised Vorburg, his representative at Münster, "to foster peace in any way possible."[80] In November, 1647, through the death of Anselm Kasimir, a sympathizer with the emperor and Spain, the archbishopric of Mainz became vacant.[81] Johann Philipp was elected with Bavarian and French support.[82] The newly elected archbishop showed great politeness to the French and manifested his gratitude by supporting their policies at the Peace Congress. This course was, however, not difficult for him, since his interests almost always coincided with their wishes,[83] that is, antagonism to the Hapsburgs and maintaining the independence of the German princes. At any rate, because of Johann Philipp's tolerant attitude and desire for peace, his elevation to the important position of Archbishop of Mainz was very significant for the ultimate securing of peace. He had asserted as his working idea, "Not before the fire that threatens all homes is extinguished, may the individual think of his own property."[84]

7. THE INTERESTS AND ACTIONS OF THE ECCLESIASTICAL PRINCES

We have observed why Catholic Austria and Bavaria, and even the Archbishop of Mainz, fostered peace policies at Münster that were injurious to Catholic interests. Let us further consider why the other German ecclesiastical princes in large part adopted a similar policy. As bishops, archbishops, and abbots these churchmen might well be expected to do the bidding

[79] *Ibid.*, p. 5 and chaps. iii–vi; Baur, *Philipp von Sötern*, II, 137–38.

[80] Wild, *op. cit.*, pp. 47–48.

[81] Mentz, *op. cit.*, I, 46.

[82] Cheruel, *op. cit.*, II, 510–11; Vautorte, in Le Clerc, *op. cit.*, III, 506–7, 512, 519, 521–22; Mentz, *op. cit.*, I, 47–49; Pastor, *op. cit.*, XIV, Part I, 90.

[83] Mentz, *op. cit.*, I, 50.

[84] Heigel, "Das westfälische Friedenswerk," *Zeitschrift für Geschichte und Politik*, V, 437.

of the pope and his nuncio and refuse to support a treaty prejudicial to church interests. But almost all ecclesiastical princes regarded themselves primarily as secular rulers.[85] Most of them were tired of the war; their lands had suffered as a result of invasions, the quartering of troops, and forced contributions. The princes' revenues from their lands had been greatly reduced, if not wholly annihilated; consequently, they were no longer able to maintain troops in an active campaign. Peace alone would enable them to reconstruct their lands and once more enjoy the income therefrom.[86] Therefore they co-operated with the Protestant and moderate-Catholic secular princes in the insertion of the clause against protests that would make the anticipated papal protest illegal and ineffective.[87] Moreover, these ecclesiastical princes could not carry out an independent policy. Some of them were younger members of the Hapsburg and Wittelsbach (Bavarian) houses.[88]

The bishoprics of Passau, Strassburg, and Olmütz were in the hands of Leopold Wilhelm, Archduke of Austria, whose main activities during the war were in the military and administrative service of Emperor Ferdinand III.[89] If his father, Ferdinand II (1612–37), had succeeded in his plans, Leopold Wilhelm would also have possessed the bishoprics of Magdeburg, Bremen, Halberstadt, and Verden as an Austrian secondogeniture.[90] The elector Ferdinand, Archbishop of Cologne, was a brother of Maximilian of Austria. Ferdinand had been a seeker after benefices, for, besides holding lesser offices, he was also Bishop of Liège, Münster, Hildesheim, and Paderborn; in other

[85] Schafmeister, *Herzog Ferdinand von Bayern, Erzbischof von Köln als Fürstbischof von Münster (1612–1650)*, p. 137.

[86] Le Clerc, *op. cit.*, I, 155; Mentz, *op. cit.*, I, 16.

[87] Zwiedeneck-Südenhorst, *Deutsche Geschichte im Zeitraum der Gründung des preussischen Königtums*, I, 67.

[88] Brandi, *op. cit.*, p. 292.

[89] Krones, article on "Leopold Wilhelm," *Allgemeine deutsche Biographie*, XVIII, 402–3; Würzbach, *Biographisches Lexikon des Kaiserthums Oesterreich*, VI, 444–45.

[90] Stieve, "Ferdinand II," *Allgemeine deutsche Biographie*, VI, 664; Ritter, *Deutsche Geschichte*, III, 422–23.

similar ambitions he had not succeeded.[91] In large part his brother, Maximilian, controlled his policies whenever Bavarian interests were involved. To take only one example, when, in October, 1647, the delegates at Münster were to vote on the question of granting the electorate to Maximilian, Maximilian forced Ferdinand to deprive his representative, Franz Wilhelm von Wartenberg, of his vote in the Congress, since he had been leader of the extremists opposing moderate Catholic proposals.[92]

The Archbishop of Trier, Philipp Christoph von Sötern, who was also Bishop of Speyer, had during the war carried on an anti-Spanish and pro-French policy because this seemed to meet his material or political interests better.[93] He instructed his representatives at the Congress that "Your Electoral Grace regards this war as being absolutely no religious war."[94] His liberty of action and political fortune depended on the early establishment of peace.[95] The Bishop of Bamberg, Melchior Otto Voit von Salzburg,[96] stood to lose more by further devastation of his lands than he could gain by refusing to accept the Protestant demands; hence, he too favored peace, even though it be hostile to papal and general church interests.[97]

One can readily see why the lesser ecclesiastical princes, in order to achieve any material or ecclesiastical advantage during the peace negotiations, would need to be attached to either Austria or Bavaria; but the policies of these two powers were, as already shown, hostile to Catholic interests when their own dynastic interests would be jeopardized by supporting Catholic interests. The other German ecclesiastical princes therefore played an indecisive part; only Wartenburg and

[91] Riezler, *Geschichte Baierns*, V, 31-33; Ennen, *op. cit.*, VI, 691–97.

[92] Meiern, *op. cit.*, IV, 777; Ennen, *op. cit.*, VI, 693–96; Odhner. *op. cit.*, p. 242.

[93] Baur, *op. cit.*, II, 149–51, 404–7; P. Wagner, "Philipp Christoph von Sötern, *Allgemeine deutsche Biographie*, XXVI, 61, 66.

[94] Baur, *op. cit.*, II, 151; Gebhardt, *Handbuch der deutschen Geschichte*, I, 727–28.

[95] Le Clerc, *op. cit.*, II, 155.

[96] A castle near Neustadt, Lower Franconia, Bavaria.

[97] Gebhardt, *op. cit.*, I, 727; Meaux, *op. cit.*, II, 679.

Adami vigorously defended the interests of the church in the papal sense during the peace negotiations.[98] Furthermore, it should be stated that the representatives of the Archbishop of Salzburg, Count Paris von Lodron (1619–53), did not sign the Peace of Münster, October 24, 1648, although one of them, Dr. Johann Krebs, was present.[99] But he, along with other Catholic represesentatives, submitted a protest against the terms of the Peace because its terms were prejudicial to church interests.[100]

[98] Brandi, *op. cit.*, p. 292; Le Clerc, *op. cit.*, I, 155; Pastor, *op. cit.*, XIV, Part I, 91.

[99] Meiern, *op. cit.*, VI, 621; Zauner, *Chronik von Salzburg*, VIII, 217–18; Widmann, *Geschichte Salzburgs*, III, 297.

[100] Adami, *Relatio historica* (ed. Meiern), chap. xxix, par. 13, p. 564; Adami, *Arcana Pacis* (1648 ed.), p. 415; Zauner, *op. cit.*, VIII, 217–18, also pp. 248–50, which contain the protest; dated October 12–22, 1648; Widmann, *op. cit.*, III, 297–98.

Chapter Ten

THE CLAUSES AGAINST PROTESTS AS FINALLY INSERTED IN THE TREATIES

WE HAVE considered the reasons for the insertion of the clauses against protests on the part of the Protestant princes, the imperial party, leading German Catholic princes, and the French. When once inserted in the peace projects, they never were omitted, and are found in all subsequent drafts of the treaties.[1] In the Treaty of Osnabrück as finally signed, October 24, 1648, the following statement is to be found: "And notwithstanding the contradiction or protest made by whomever it may be, cleric or layman, whether within or without the Empire, in whatever time it may be; all the said oppositions are declared null and void and without any force."[2]

As a confirmation of the clause found in the Peace of Osnabrück the French and the emperor inserted the following article in the Treaty of Münster:

> Since, in order to re-establish the greatest tranquillity in the Empire, there has been made in this same universal Congress of Peace a certain accord between the emperor, the electors, the princes, and the states of the Empire, which has been inserted in the Treaty of Peace drawn up with the plenipotentiaries of the crown of Sweden concerning the differences relating to ecclesiastical properties and the liberty and exercise of religion, we find it well to confirm and ratify by this present Treaty the same agreement, and likewise

[1] Meiern, *Acta pacis Westphalicae,* V, 468, 765, 936; VI, 5, 110, 170, 393.

[2] "*Instrumentum Pacis Caesareo-Suecicum,* or Peace of Osnabrück," Art. V, par. 1, in Walther, *Universal Register über die westphälischen Friedens- und Nürnbergerischen Executions-Handlungen und Geschichte,* p. xii; Londorp, *Acta publica,* VI, 387; Dumont, *Corps universelle diplomatique du droit des gens,* VI, Part I, 473; Woltmann, *Geschichte des westphälischen Friedens,* Vol. II, Appendix, p. 16.

that which has been agreed upon between the same respecting those that are called Reformed, just as though they had been inserted word for word in the present treaty.[3]

Thus France bound herself to support the terms relating to the Protestants.

The following clause is found word for word in both treaties:

That there shall never be alleged, heard, or allowed, neither against this Treaty nor any of these articles or clauses, any canon or civil law, nor any general or special decrees of councils, whether privileges, indults, edicts, commissions, inhibitions, mandates, decrees, rescripts, pendencies, sentences, rendered at any time whatsoever, [any] verdicts, imperial capitularies, or other rules or exemptions of religious orders, whether former or future protests, appellations, investitures, transactions, oaths, renunciations, all sorts of pacts, still less the edict of 1629, or the Transaction of Prague with its appendixes, or the concordats with the popes, or the interim of the year 1548, or any other statutes, whether political or ecclesiastical decrees, dispensations, absolutions, or any other thing which can be imagined under whatever name or pretext; nor shall there anywhere ever be decreed against this transaction indictments or commissions either from the side of seeker or possessor.[4]

The motives of the negotiators to make ineffective any protests against the Peace of Westphalia will be interesting to consider. Anyone familiar with recent modern history is much more aware than were the negotiators at Münster and Osnabrück that, in spite of the invariable practice among diplomats to insert an affirmation in every treaty of importance that this treaty is to provide for a durable and permanent peace, the observance thereof endured only for a short time. Both the treaties of Osnabrück and Münster in their first articles declared this to be a "Christian, universal, and perpetual peace."[5] The Peace of Augsburg, the most important previous treaty in German history, in its initial paragraph declared it to be a "persistent and

[3] "*Instrumentum Pacis Caesareo-Gallicum*, or Peace of Münster," par. 47, in Walther, *op. cit.*, p. lxxi; Londorp, *op. cit.*, VI, 410; Dumont, *op. cit.*, VI, Part I, 453.

[4] "*Instrumentum Pacis Caesareo-Gallicum*, or Peace of Osnabrück," par. 113, in Walther, *op. cit.*, p. lxxxv; Londorp, *op. cit.*, VI, 417; Dumont, *op. cit.*, VI, Part I, 488; Woltmann, *op. cit.*, Vol. II, Appendix, p. 69; "*Instrumentum Pacis Caesareo-Suecicum*, of Peace or Münster," Art. XVII, par. 3, in Walther, *op. cit.*, p. xlviii; Londorp, *op. cit.*, VI, 403–4; Dumont, *op. cit.*, VI, Part I, 459; Hanser, *Deutschland nach dem dreissigjährigen Kriege*, pp. 78–79; Koch, *Geschichte des deutschen Reiches*, II, 522–23.

[5] Walther, *op. cit.*, pp. ii, lxiv.

permanent peace";[6] but it had not been observed by either Protestants or Catholics. The pope had been the most feared opponent of the Peace of Augsburg; he had declared that the emperor may not observe it and had released the emperor from his oath to observe it. At the Congress of Westphalia the papal nuncio had, at various times during the negotiations, protested with papal sanction against the Peace that was being formulated;[7] and it was quite to be expected that the pope himself would protest against the Peace, as he did under the date of November 26, 1648.[8]

The negotiators, in anticipation of this protest, might have declared null and void the various expected protests, including that of the pope. But this last would have been "odious," or embarrassing, for it would have meant an imperial refutation of what the pope had hitherto done through his nuncio and was certain to do on his own authority later. Furthermore, a protest might be anticipated from Spain, which was not included in the Peace. Therefore a general formula against protests was adopted.[9]

[6] "Beharrlichen und beständigen Friden" [*sic.*]; "duratura et Constant Pace," *In Pacis Compositio inter principes et ordines Imperii Romani Catholicos atque Augustanae Confessioni adherentes in comitiis Augustae Anno M.D. LV* (ed. Dillingen), 1629, Appendix, pp. 38, 47.

[7] See below, chap. xi.

[8] See below, chap. xi.

[9] Gundling, *Vollständiger Discours über den westphälischen Frieden*, p. 257; Riezler, *Geschichte Baierns*, V, 651.

Chapter Eleven

THE PROTESTS AGAINST THE PEACE OF WESTPHALIA

I. THE PROTESTS OF LESSER IMPORTANCE, 1648

DURING the last days of the Congress and soon afterward there appeared a number of protests, meant more or less seriously. Each was opposed to one or more articles of the Peace, not against the Peace as a whole.[1] Duke Charles III of Mantua (1637–65) protested against the clause confirming the Treaty of Chierasco that gave part of Montferrat, a part of his duchy, to the Duke of Savoy.[2] Duke Charles of Lorraine (1645–75), through his representative, protested against the Peace because he had been excluded from it and because his lands were still held by the French, a situation that persisted until the latter, under Louis XIV, incorporated the duchy in 1670.[3] The reader recalls that the French and the Swedes had insisted that the emperor sign a peace that did not include the Spanish Hapsburgs.[4] The Spanish king, Philip IV (1621–65), protested because the Peace of Münster had been signed without regard to Spain or the Burgundian Circle of the Empire, meaning the Spanish Netherlands or Belgium, which Spain still controlled.[5]

[1] Pastor, *Geschichte der Päpste*, XIV, Part I, 100.

[2] Erdmannsdörffer, *Deutsche Geschichte vom westphälischen Frieden bis zum Regierungsantritt Friedrichs des Grossen, 1648–1740*, Vol. I, p. 6; Pastor, *op. cit.*, XIV, Part I, 100.

[3] Londorp, *Acta publica*, VI, 425–27; Erdmannsdörffer, *op. cit.*, I, 6; Pastor, *op. cit.*, XIV, Part I, 100; Lavisse, *Histoire de France depuis les origins*, VII, Part I, 73; Part II, 301.

[4] Odhner, *Die Politik Schwedens*, pp. 280–82. See also chap. vii, §5.

[5] Dumont, *Corps universelle diplomatique*, VI, Part I, 464–67; Londorp, *op. cit.*, VI, 425–29; Erdmannsdörffer, *op. cit.*, I, 6; Pastor, *op. cit.*, XIV, Part I, 100.

The Archbishop of Salzburg, through his representative, Dr. Krebs, submitted a protest against the Peace, October 12–22, 1648, because its terms were prejudicial to the interests of the church.[6] Adam Adami, the historian of the Congress, submitted two protests against the Peace, one in the name of the prelates and one in the name of the abbey of Corvey, whose interest in both cases he had persistently but futilely represented during the negotiations.[7] Count Palatine Wolfgang Wilhelm, Duke of Neuburg and Jülich-Berg (1609–53), protested September 1, 1648, against the transfer of the electorate to the House of Bavaria.[8] He, being the nearest male relation in the Palatine-Zweibrücken line and also a Catholic, had objected, as early as 1623, to the electoral title of the Palatinate being bestowed by Emperor Ferdinand II on Maximilian of Bavaria.[9] But his protest was fruitless in both cases. None of the protests here mentioned had any effect at the time or later. They are of far less importance than those of the nuncio and the pope, which are an inseparable part of the story of the secularization of politics.

2. THE PROTESTS OF THE NUNCIO, 1645–49

As early as October 5, 1644, Innocent X had sent the nuncio, Fabio Chigi, a brief giving him full authority to protest at whatever time and in whatever form he found it advisable against any agreement that was injurious to the interests of the Catholic church.[10] In conformity with such instructions he submitted a protest in December, 1645, against every injury that might be sustained by the church directly or indirectly through

[6] Zauner, *Chronik von Salzburg*, VIII, 217–18, 248–50, contains the protest; Widmann, *Geschichte Salburgs*, II, 297–98; Adami, *Relatio historica*, 564; Adami, *Arcana Pacis*, p. 415.

[7] Israel, *Adam Adami*, p. 81.

[8] Meiern, *Acta pacis Westphalicae*, VI, 229–39; Riezler, *Geschichte Baierns*, V, 649.

[9] Doeberl, *Entwicklungsgeschichte Bayerns*, I, 552–55; Breitenbach, "Wolfgang Wilhelm," in *Allgemeine deutsche Biographie*, XLIV, 95, 98–99.

[10] Meiern, *op. cit.*, IV, 861, contains breve, as does Müller, *Das Friedenswerk der Kirche*, I, 171–72; Pastor, *op. cit.*, XIV, Part I, 95; Fischer, *Beiträge*, pp. 64–65.

the actions of the Congress.[11] As a pattern he used a similar writing in which Cardinal Otto Truchsess von Waldburg, Bishop of Augsburg (1543–73), had protested, on March 23, 1555, against religious concessions made by the Peace of Augsburg to the Protestants in the German Empire.[12] For almost two years Chigi remained silent, awaiting developments in the Congress. When by the latter half of 1647 the negotiations had gone counter to the wishes of the church, in part because the new Archbishop of Mainz, Johann Philipp von Schönborn, was favoring peace policies in opposition to those favored by his predecessor, Anselm Kasimir, the nuncio concluded that he would give up his attitude of silence and protest emphatically in letters and breves against all actions that were prejudicial to the interests of the Catholic church. On November 24, 1647, he wrote a letter of protest to the dean of the chapter at Augsburg; on November 25, 1647, he wrote to Emperor Ferdinand III himself; on the same day he addressed a letter to Count von Trauttmannsdorff and to the elector Maximilian of Bavaria; and on November 29, to the imperial plenipotentiaries, to the elector of Mainz, the elector of Cologne, and to the representatives of the Catholic states.[13]

In his letters to the representatives of the Catholic states Chigi earnestly summoned his faithful instruments to do their utmost for the welfare of the Catholic cause, even to the point of sustaining injury to themselves. Their well-being, he said, was so intimately associated with the cause of the Catholic religion that it would sustain injury precisely when they diverged from the interests of the church ever so slightly. In closing, he safeguarded himself against an eventual reproach that he had ever said anything in his protests that could have been an offense against the holy fathers, the councils and popes, and as-

[11] Pastor, *op. cit.*, XIV, Part I, 77.

[12] *Ibid.*, p. 77, also VI, 564; Braun, *Geschichte der Bischöfe von Augsburg*, III, 433–34, contains the protest of Truchsess. See chap. iii.

[13] Fischer, *op. cit.*, pp. 60–61, cites Chigi's letters in the Vatican archives.

sures his Catholic friends that he will implore God to sustain them in their deliberations.[14]

Many of the Catholic princes regarded the nuncio's letters as a comfort; others ignored them. The imperial representatives, after waiting a long time to reply, deplored that, owing to circumstances shaped by others, presumably the elector of Bavaria, a compromise peace was necessary; but no response of consequence ever followed the sending and receipt of these letters.[15] The nuncio continued in various ways to labor against a peace injurious to church interests.[16] But the ultimate outcome did not prevent the conclusion of a peace that was quite out of harmony with the objectives for which he had been active.

Between October, 1648, and February, 1649, he issued three protests. The first was issued October 14, 1648, before the negotiations had been concluded; it was especially aimed at the negotiations taking place at Osnabrück, where the imperial party was negotiating with the Swedes and their Protestant allies to the detriment of the church. This protest was immediately made known to the Director (*Directorium*) and Chancery of Mainz, and was registered in the acts of the Empire. It was directed against every injury that could arise to religion and the Holy See.[17]

The second solemn protest was issued October 26, 1648, two days after the signing of the Peace of Münster and the Peace of Osnabrück by the respective plenipotentiaries at the two Westphalian towns. Before making public this second protest Chigi celebrated mass in the audience chamber of the monastery in Münster where he had lived during his stay at the Congress; the protest was destined for the Congress and was signed in the presence of a notary public and many other witnesses.[18] This second protest was directed against all those parts or clauses of the Peace of Westphalia (Münster-Osnabrück) that were preju-

[14] *Ibid.*, p. 61. [15] *Ibid.*, pp. 61–62, 78. [16] *Ibid.*, pp. 62–64.

[17] Garampi, *Raggualio della Paca di Vestfalia*, p. 8.

[18] *Ibid.*, p. 8.

dicial to the interests of the Catholic church.[19] Chigi, in his reports to Rome on October 16 and 30, 1648, states the considerations actuating him in issuing his protests. His first protest was against the disadvantages that the church suffered according to the terms of the Peace of Osnabrück as shaped by the Catholic princes under the leadership of Mainz and Bavaria. He sent a copy of his protest to Rome and expressed the intention of submitting a further protest if the treaties in question were ultimately ratified, as it seemed they would be. In sending a copy of his second protest to the papal court he said that such a protest was the only means that could be applied in dealing with these people in order to prevent injury to the church and preserve its rights.

At least such action "would to some extent be a comfort to His Holiness because otherwise he cannot rejoice in his heart over this Peace."[20] In Chigi's letter of October 30, 1648, he states that the plenipotentiaries of the Catholic princes had no difficulty in receiving copies of the second protest from him. He immediately sent this protest, together with the breve of October 4, 1644, which authorized him to make protests, to the Directory of Mainz. But from his later correspondence nothing appears from which one could conclude that he had received any kind of communication that acknowledged or confirmed the insertion of the protest in the imperial acts.[21] Through these protests Chigi merely manifested the same spirit that had actuated him when at various times he had withdrawn from the negotiations in order not to give any validity or tacit sanction to them by his presence. By this action he made certain that the Catholic princes and Contarini, the Venetian mediator, were fully

[19] Du Mont, *op. cit.*, VI, Part I, 462–63, contains both protests, as do the following: Conring, *Pro pace perpetua*, pp. 116–20; Conring, *Opera*, II, 565–66; the protest of October 26, 1648, is in Londorp, *op. cit.*, VI, 423; and Brom, *Archivalia en Italië*, III, 448–49; Pastor, *op. cit.*, XIV, Part I, 95–96; Bougeant, *Histoire des guerres*, VI, 412–13; Hanser, *Deutschland nach dem dreissigjährigen Kriege*, p. 79.

[20] Pastor, *op. cit.*, XIV, Part I, 96, n. 1.

[21] Garampi, *op. cit.*, p. 8.

aware of his attitude of constant protest and his refusal to affix his signature to the Peace documents.[22]

The ratification of the Treaties of Peace had been completed by February 8, 1649.[23] On February 9, 1649, Chigi issued a third and final protest with the same formalities that were observed in the two former cases. Beyond this he added another special protest in hopes of preserving the right of free collation (bestowing of benefices) which the Holy See possessed concerning the bishoprics and benefices of the dioceses of Metz, Toul, and Verdun, and the benefices within them, which had been ceded to France by the Empire in the Treaty of Münster.[24]

In all these protesting activities during and after the Congress of Westphalia, Chigi had full approval of Innocent X; all his protests were sanctioned also by all the cardinals.[25] The course he took at the Congress also met with complete approval at the papal court. Most of his actions were based on very general instructions sent him in a breve of October 5, 1644, by Innocent X;[26] for the intricate details of his work he had to depend on his own judgment and experience.[27] Although he must be regarded as having stood for the principles of the extreme Catholics,[28] and although he naturally was not exactly an impartial mediator when laboring to prevent the moderate Catholics and Protestants from making arrangements that would injure church interests,[29] he was able, because of his personality and tact, to re-

[22] Hanser, *op. cit.*, p. 79; Pastor, *op. cit.*, XIV, Part I, 96.

[23] Meiern, *op. cit.*, VI, 854–65.

[24] Garampi, *op. cit.*, p. 10; Pastor, *op. cit.*, XIV, Part I, 97; Reumont, "Fabio Chigi–Papst Alexander VII—in Deutschland, 1639–1651," *Zeitschrift des Aachener Geschichtsvereins*, VIII, 9.

[25] Pastor, *op. cit.*, XIV, Part I, 96–97.

[26] Meiern, *op. cit.*, IV, 861–62; Reumont, "Fabio Chigi," *Zeitschrift des Aach. Gesch.*, VIII, 9.

[27] Reumont, "Fabio Chigi," *Zeitschrift des Aach. Gesch.*, VIII, 9.

[28] Steinberger, *Die Jesuiten und die Friedensfrage*, p. 104.

[29] Meiern, *op. cit.*, II, 138; IV, 861–62; Fischer, *op. cit.*, pp. 52–53.

main on good terms with all his colleagues.[30] As a reward for his services Innocent X appointed him secretary of state in 1651, and created him cardinal in February, 1652;[31] and when in February, 1655, he became pope, with the title of Alexander VII, many Protestants in Germany and France welcomed his election.[32]

3. THE PAPAL ATTITUDE. THE BREVE "ZELO DOMUS DEI," AUGUST 20, 1650

Although the pope and his cardinals thoroughly approved his nuncio's actions in Münster, Innocent X took no hasty action of his own. It was not until January, 1649, that a meeting of cardinals, under the presidency of the pope, decided that Chigi's protests were to be solemnly confirmed by a bull; but Chigi was instructed January 9, 1649, to remain silent concerning such a plan; he observed this advice when presenting his third protest, February 9, 1649, when the Peace treaties were ratified.[33] The papacy feared to publish a bull of protest against the Peace because such action was fraught with great danger as long as the Swedish troops were still on German soil. The imperial representative in Rome, Savelli, made imploring excuses for the emperor, who was in great distress owing to the great strength of the occupying Swedish army; he also called attention to the military weakness of the German Catholics. If the pope were to suspend the publication of the proposed bull, it would be an advantage to the emperor in his hereditary lands; this must be regarded as offsetting the loss of the bishoprics in north Germany, which could be held by the Catholics only by waging constant war. Savelli believed that the pope would gradually become reconciled to the Peace Treaty. Savelli also stated that the responsibility for the terms of the Treaty so unfavorable to

[30] Meiern, *op. cit.*, IV, 861; Reumont, "Fabio Chigi," *Zeitschrift des Aach. Gesch.*, VIII, 11; Meaux, *La réforme et la politique française*, II, 596–97.

[31] Pastor, *op. cit.*, XIV, Part I, 313; Richard, "Origines et développements," *Revue d'histoire ecclésiastique*, XI, Part I, 736.

[32] Pastor, *op. cit.*, XIV, Part I, 313. [33] *Ibid.*, pp. 96–97.

the church was to be attributed to Bavaria, which forced the emperor to yield, and also to the elector of Mainz, Johann Philipp von Schönborn.[34]

Such considerations caused the papacy to delay until after the Swedish and imperial representatives had completed the negotiations at Nürnberg in June, 1650, for the withdrawal of the Swedish troops.[35] By August 20, 1650, Innocent X commanded that his protest *Zelo Domus Dei*, against the injurious terms of the Peace, be sent to all nuncios, wherever they may be, so that they might make known the decision of the Holy See.[36] But the protest was not issued as originally planned in the form of a solemn bull, but by means of a simple breve. Officially the papal protest was not a bull, as most writers have stated,[37] but merely a breve, or brief, which is a briefer, less solemn, simpler, and less important papal decree than a bull.[38] The papal Curia declined at this time to sanction Chigi's proposal that he issue a fourth protest.[39] It is interesting to note that the breve was antedated November 26, 1648.[40] This was probably done to give the appearance that the papacy had not been negligent in waiting more than a year and eight months to protest against so injurious a peace. It is curious that Garampi, in his "Report concerning the Peace of Westphalia and the Various Protests That Were Issued by the Holy See against the Same," placed his account of the protest of Innocent X chronologically where it naturally would belong, in the year 1648, but in this single instance omits giving the year.[41] In giving all other dates in his

[34] *Ibid.*, p. 99.

[35] Meiern, *Acta pacis executionis publica*, II, 347–51; Pastor, *op. cit.*, XIV, Part I, 94.

[36] Brom, *op. cit.*, III, 462–63; Pastor, *op. cit.*, XIV, Part I, 99.

[37] Meiern, *Acta pacis executionis publica*, II, 781; Steinberger, *op. cit.*, p. 161; *Cambridge Modern History*, IV, 688; Hanser, *op. cit.*, p. 79; Philipps, *Kirchenrecht*, III, 476; Philippson, in Pflugkh-Harttung, *Weltgeschichte, Neuzeit, 1650–1815*, p. 101; Seppelt, *Papstgeschichte*, II, 154; Hergenröther, *Handbuch der allgemeinen Kirchengeschichte*, III, 744.

[38] Pastor, *op. cit.*, XIV, Part I, 99, n. 5; *Catholic Encyclopedia*, III, 56. Since the decree of Leo XIII of December 29, 1878, the chief difference between bulls and breves has been removed (Meyers, *Lexikon*, III [1925], 867).

[39] Pastor, *op. cit.*, XIV, Part I, 99. [40] *Ibid.*, p. 99. [41] Garampi, *op. cit.*, p. 7.

report he meticulously gives the year. Whether in this case his omission was accidental or intentional must remain conjectural, but it seems to have been intentional. Professor Ludwig Andreas Veit is guilty of the same omission.[42]

4. CONTENTS OF THE BREVE "ZELO DOMUS DEI"

The breve *Zelo Domus Dei*[43] was the papal protest not against the whole Peace of Westphalia but merely against those articles that were prejudicial to the interests of the Roman Catholic church. The specific points against which he protested were:

(1) That "very great prejudices had been caused to the Roman Catholic religion, to the inferior churches, and to the ecclesiastical order, as also to their jurisdictions, immunities, franchises, liberties, exemptions, privileges, affairs, possessions, and rights"; (2) that "to the heretics and their successors have been abandoned in perpetuity the ecclesiastical properties that they have formerly occupied"; (3) that "those heretics, to whom the term 'Confession of Augsburg' is applied, are allowed the free exercise of their heresy in many places, and that they are given sites on which to build churches"; (4) that "they [the heretics] are admitted with the Catholics to public charges and offices, and to some archbishoprics, bishoprics, and other ecclesiastical dignities and benefices, and to the participation in the first expectancies that the Apostolic See has granted to the said Ferdinand, king of the Romans, emperor-elect"; (5) that "annates, the rights of the pallium, confirmation, the papal months, and similar rights of reservation in the ecclesiastical possessions of the said Confession of Augsburg have been abolished; to the same secular power is attributed the confirmations of the elections or the application for dispensations of the pretended archbishops, bishops, or prelates of the same Confession"; (6) "that many archbishoprics, bishoprics, monasteries, provostships, bailliages, commanderies, canonries, and other benefices and properties of the church have been given to heretical princes as perpetual fiefs, under the title of secular dignities, with suppression of the ecclesiastical domination"; (7) "that it is ordered that against this Peace or any of its articles there must not be alleged, heard, or admitted any canonical or civil laws, general or special, decrees, dispensations, absolutions, or other exemptions"; (8) that "the number of seven electors of the Empire, formerly decreed by apostolic author-

[42] Veit, *Kirchengeschichte*, IV, Part I, 12.

[43] *Bullarium Romanum* (Taurinensis ed.), XV, 603–6; Conring, *Consultatio Catholica*, pp. 108–20; Conring, *Opera*, II, 563–65; Londorp, *op. cit.*, VI, 423–25; Meiern, *Acta Pacis Executionis*, II, 781–84; Müller, *op. cit.*, I, 176–80; in French, Le Clerc, *Négociations secrètes*, IV, 510–11; also, though less accurate, Du Mont, *op. cit.*, VI, Part I, 463–64; Pastor, *op. cit.*, XIV, Part I, 99–100; Steinberger, *op. cit.*, p. 161; Hergenröther, *Katholische Kirche und christlicher Staat*, pp. 703–9; Menzel, *Neuere Geschichte der Deutschen*, VIII, 240–41.

ity, has been agumented without our consent and that of the said Holy See, and an eighth electorate has been erected in favor of Charles Louis, Count Palatine of the Rhine, a heretic"; (9) that "there have been ordained many other things that would be shameful to report, very prejudicial and harmful to the orthodox religion, to the said Roman See, to the inferior churches, and to others above-named."[44]

The pope reiterates the contents of Chigi's protest, and states that "each transaction or agreement made concerning ecclesiastical things without the authority of the said See is null, and without force and validity"; that all articles contained in these treaties "that in any manner whatsoever, harm or cause the least prejudice, or that can be said, understood, pretended, or estimated to be able to harm or having harmed in any manner the Catholic religion," and all that pertains to the Catholic church and religion, "have been by law, are, and shall be perpetually null, vain, invalid, iniquitous, unjust, condemned, reproved, frivolous, without force and effect, and that no one is bound to observe them or any of them although they be fortified by an oath"; ". . . . and for all that for the sake of the greatest possible precaution, ... we condemn, reprove, break, annul, and deprive of all force and effect the said articles and all the other things prejudicial to the above as has been said, and protest against and declare their nullity before God; and wherever it is also necessary we restore, replace, and reinstate in full powers the affairs of the church to that condition in which they were before the said transactions. This protest shall remain valid for all time to come in spite of all agreements, laws, decrees, and publications to the contrary, and shall be binding on all. All ordinary judges and all officers of the church and all others in authority must acknowledge this breve and judge in accordance with it, notwithstanding all ecclesiastical laws of any sort or all secular laws of any kind."

In this breve the pope protested against, and declared null, all that had been done by the Congress of Münster and Osnabrück concerning religious affairs. All things harmful to the church that had been done since the Reformation or at any

[44] The enumeration is the author's.

other time were undone. All persons were commanded to observe this breve; it was to hold notwithstanding any ecclesiastical laws, and was declared superior to all secular laws. This statement declared religious matters to be solely in the hands of the church; it was a reiteration of the papal theory, as opposed to the new theory, that the state was sovereign and could control not only politics but religious and ecclesiastical affairs.

5. THE VALIDITY OF THE PAPAL PROTEST

The question of the validity, at least of one aspect of the protest (i.e., point 8, concerning the origin of the college of seven electors), was the subject of archival research in Rome at the time. It was conducted by an expert in church history, Felice Contelori, Urban VIII's custodian of the Vatican Library; under Innocent X he had fallen into disfavor, but the many important papal matters requiring archival research necessitated his reappointment.[45] His researches indicated that, according to the viewpoint of the papal court, the founding of the imperial college of electors, composed of seven men, dated back to the time of Gregory in the year 1002;[46] but this date falls within the pontificate of Sylvester II (999–1003), which may be somewhat illuminating as to the accuracy of both the papal archivist and the views of the papal court. Contelori concludes that the electoral college of seven men had been established by the pope and therefore is an institution based on ecclesiastical, and not secular, law.[47] This idea was embodied in the papal protest of August 20, 1650; the wording of the breve (*Zelo Domus Dei*) was executed by various unnamed papal diplomats, and this was the occasion of very serious differences among them.[48] It is needless here to indicate that this official view of the papal court is quite

[45] Beltrani, "Felice Contelori e i suio studi negli Archivi vel Vaticano," *Archivio della Società Romana di Storia Patria*, II, 165–208 (especially, pp. 165, 166, 190, 191), 257–80; III, 1–47 (especially pp. 19, 20, 23–25, 27–28); Pastor, *op. cit.*, XIII, Part II, 914–15; XIV, Part I, 258–79.

[46] Beltrani, *op. cit.*, III, 27, 28; based on manuscript volume, XXXIII, 138 v. Bibliografica, n.o. in Biblioteca Barberini.

[47] *Ibid.*, p. 29.

[48] *Ibid.*, p. 30.

out of harmony with the accepted historical view of the origin of the college of electors held in Germany at the time or since, namely, that it was of purely secular origin.[49]

6. THE JUSTIFICATION OF THE PAPAL PROTEST

It was inevitable that the pope should issue a protest against those articles of the Peace of Westphalia that caused such great injury to the Catholic church. The Peace confirmed the Peace of Passau (1552) and the Peace of Augsburg (1555), which had never been accepted by the church; it also provided that January 1, 1624, should be the normal date for determining the possession of ecclesiastical lands by the German states. This arrangement placed into the hands of the Protestants the control of the greater part of the free imperial cities; in five such cities authority was shared equally by the Catholics and Protestants. The Catholic church had saved the archbishoprics of Mainz, Trier, Cologne, and Salzburg and about twenty bishoprics, and less than ten abbeys exercising sovereign rights. The Catholic church had lost two archbishoprics, thirteen bishoprics, six abbeys, besides a great number of mediate church lands. Aside from these material losses, two heretical religions were legalized.[50] The protest was also justified, at least on the basis of fear, inasmuch as it was now not impossible for the emperor of the Holy Roman Empire to be a Protestant. During the war the success of Frederick V, the elector palatine, might have had that eventuation; Gustavus Adolphus had harbored thoughts of his becoming emperor through the creation of a Swedish, a ninth, electorate; in April, 1647, the French feared the possibil-

[49] Quidde, *Die Entstehung des Kurfürstencollegiums*, p. 110; Lindner, *Die deutschen Königswahlen und die Entstehung des Kurfürstentums*, p. 214; Maurenbrecher, *Geschichte der deutschen Königswahlen vom zehnten bis dreizehnten Jahrhundert*, pp. 243–44; Meister, *Deutsche Verfassungsgeschichte von den Anfängen bis 15. Jahrhundert*, pp. 99, 160–63; Wunderlich, "Die neueren Ansichten über die deutsche Königswahl und der Ursprung des Kurfürstenkollegiums," in Ebering, *Historische Studien*, Heft 114, especially pp. 98, 148, 216–22; Vigener, "Kaiser Karl IV," in *Meister der Politik*, II, 15–18; Gebhardt, *Handbuch der deutschen Geschichte*, I, 382; Schäfer, *Deutsche Geschichte*, I, 377; Seppelt, *op. cit.*, II, 30.

[50] Pastor, *op. cit.*, XIV, Part I, 94–95; Hergenröther, *Katholische Kirche und christlicher Staat*, p. 709.

ity of a Protestant emperor.[51] Actually at a later time, in 1657, when the successor of Ferdinand III was to be elected, the elector of the Palatinate demanded the election of a Protestant emperor.[52] Throughout the seventeenth century such an idea had been held in Protestant ranks; for if there were Protestant electors there could be a Protestant emperor.[53] Under the circumstances the head of the church would have been guilty of neglect of his high duties if he had not followed up the protests of his nuncio with a solemn protest of his own.[54] Practically it merely meant a papal censure and condemnation of the Peace.[55]

Ultimately, even the non-Catholics accepted the view that the pope could not act differently. The German historian Menzel says that the pope wished "merely to content himself by doing what his position as head of the church required, what the head of no other institution in a similar circumstance would dare to neglect, without laying himself open to the criticism of neglect of duty."[56]

But surely the pope must have known that it was impossible to overthrow the power of Protestantism, that his political policy had failed, and that his protest must therefore be without effect.[57] The protest was not made therefore with any immediate results in view; it was made rather in harmony with the lofty conception of the Roman Catholic church. "This protest is no mere formality, as one is inclined to consider it, but a possible

[51] Gunter, "Das evangelische Kaisertum," *Historisches Jahrbuch*, XXXVII, 379; Meiern, *Acta Pacis Westphalicae*, IV, 499–500.

[52] Gunter, "Das evangelische Kaisertum," *Historisches Jahrbuch*, *op. cit.*, XXXVII, 379.

[53] *Ibid.*, p. 380; Pastor, *op. cit.*, XIV, Part I, 101 n.

[54] Pastor, *op. cit.*, XIV, Part I, 101.

[55] Hergenröther, *Handbuch*, III, 744.

[56] Menzel, *op. cit.*, VIII, 244; see also Hiltebrandt, "Preussen und die römische Kurie in der zweiten Hälfte des siebzehnten Jahrhunderts," *Quellen und Forschungen aus italienischen Archiven und Bibliotheken* (herausgegeben vom Koenigl. Preussischen Institut in Rom), XI, 321.

[57] Ranke, *Die römischen Päpste* (1873 ed.), II, 373; Malet, *Histoire diplomatique de l'Europe aux XVIIe et XVIIIe siècles*, I, 161–62.

loophole left for the Catholics to recover the lost properties and rights of their church."[58] A recent liberal Catholic view is as follows: "This protest was, however, the expression of a feeling that cherishes the communion of religious values more highly than all the other wordly interests of humanity";[59] in other words, it was an expression of the spiritual, and not temporal, objectives of the church.

7. IF THE PAPAL PROTEST HAD BEEN OBSERVED

No power ever was known to have appealed to the pope in order to test the validity of the Peace of Westphalia or any part thereof.[60] According to the papal breve, no one was bound to observe the provisions of the Treaty that were injurious to the church "although they be fortified by an oath." The pope was acting in harmony with canon law, whereby he could grant a dispensation against fulfilling an oath if the obligation of observing such prevents the realization of a greater good.[61] But no power made use of the papal protest and appealed to the pope. If such powers as Austria, Bavaria, and the ecclesiastical princes had taken advantage of the papal protest and refused to abide by the terms of the Treaty, the war would have been resumed or the entire Treaty in its fundamental aspects would have had to be revised.[62] But the Catholic powers, as already observed, had for practical, secular reasons agreed to the insertion of a clause that nullified all protests against the Peace—above all, those of the pope. It is an interesting commentary that, of all the German prelates, the Archbishop of Trier was the first, and also the last, to publish the protest of Innocent X.[63] Politics had been secularized even among the ecclesiastical princes.

[58] Koch, *Geschichte des deutschen Reiches*, II, 526.

[59] Ehrhard, *Der Katholizismus und das zwanzigste Jahrhundert*, p. 172.

[60] Hergenröther, *Katholische Kirche und christlicher Staat*, p. 709; *Cambridge Modern History*, IV, 415.

[61] Perathoner, *Das kirchliche Gesetzbuch*, p. 465.

[62] Döllinger, *Kirche und Kirchen*, p. 62; Hergenröther, *Katholische Kirche und christlicher Staat*, p. 709.

[63] Baur, *Philipp von Sötern, Kurfürst zu Trier*, I, 291; Pastor, *op. cit.*, XIV, Part I, 101.

Chapter Twelve

IF THERE HAD BEEN A MORE SAGACIOUS POPE?

IT IS interesting to conjecture what the outcome might have been if Innocent X had accepted the inevitable and realized that church unity and the Protestant lands were gone, if not forever, at least for a long time to come. Urban VIII and Innocent X might have been shrewder politicians if they had abandoned the Catholic cause in those lands in which Protestantism had been a success since the early sixteenth century anyway, and had recognized the loss of church lands that could in no case be regained. If they had been willing to adopt such a policy, they could have co-operated harmoniously with the Catholic secular rulers, and the nuncio could have exerted a much greater political influence as a mediator among the Catholic representatives of the Congress. The papal Curia would not have accustomed the Catholic princes to act without the guidance of the church when disposing of church affairs. Moreover, it would have been possible to exact more ameliorating concessions for the Catholics in Protestant lands.

It had been regarded as regrettable that the Catholics under the leadership of Rome did not at Münster consolidate their power by entering with the papacy a convention that would have been equal, or even superior, to the treaties of Münster and Osnabrück in importance.[1]

Innocent X might have anticipated that protesting against the Peace of Wesphalia would be futile, for the opposition of Paul IV to the Peace of Augsburg had not prevented the Cath-

[1] Meaux, *La réforme et la politique française*, II, 679.

olic princes from confirming it in 1566 with the consent of the legate Commendone and on the advice of Petrus Canisius.[2] The protest of Innocent X was even less efficacious; anticipation of the protest did not delay for an instant the ratification of the Peace of Westphalia. The popes were sadly accustoming themselves to speaking without being heard by, or receiving any deference from, the Catholic princes;[3] the popes should have been binding these rulers to papal interests, instead of making it difficult for them to co-operate with the papacy owing to divergent interests.

It is interesting to recall that Henry IV of France (1589–1610) had arranged in his "Grand Design," according to the testimony of his Protestant minister Sully, to have the Roman pontiffs recognized as the arbiters of Europe, even including the Protestant powers. The pope was to be president of the Christian republic. If the Peace of Westphalia did not make provision for such an arrangement, it was, above all, to the detriment of the papacy.[4] We may not agree with Meaux, who, writing in 1889, had not had his optimism concerning a League of Nations tempered by the experience of the world since 1920. But, if the papacy had taken a practical view of existing conditions and would not have had to defend its time-honored theory of world religious unity under hierarchical control, some sort of a compromise arrangement might have been made that would have been to the advantage of the papacy and the church.

But postulating an attitude of this character on the part of the papacy is taking too much for granted. We must also recall that part of the fault of making European arrangements that were detrimental to the papacy rested, above all, with Cardinal Richelieu and especially Cardinal Mazarin, who stressed a European settlement to the advantage of Louis XIV. Both these cardinals had demanded from the pope a compliant attitude difficult to maintain. Richelieu had imperiously demanded certain fundamental objectives, which, if attained, would lead to

[2] See chap. iii. [3] Meaux, *op. cit.*, II, 679–80. [4] *Ibid.*, p. 680.

French dominance over the Austrian and Spanish Hapsburgs.[5] Mazarin, on the other hand, stressed minor matters, especially securing a cardinalate for his brother. His method of pursuing this object antagonized the pope to such an extent as to make impossible a harmonious co-operation to the advantage of general European Catholic interests. Moreover, Mazarin neglected to manipulate the settlement at Münster in a manner that would have advantaged the interests of the Catholic religion as well as the national honor and interest of France.[6] Mazarin was merely playing the game of secularizing politics. State interests were uppermost in his mind. The church was merely a tool for state purposes.

But the fault lay also with the popes themselves. In the coming decades and centuries the papacy had to carry on negotiations with the dissident states, and even to make use of them for its own defense; for example, the papacy was dependent on the military efforts of Protestant England and Prussia to relieve it from the humiliating fate imposed on it by Napoleon.[7] To revert once more to the seventeenth century, these Protestant states were already at that time more than half of the states of Europe; they were necessary for the equilibrium of Europe. In the face of this manifest necessity, why was the papacy so disinclined to recognize this? Why did it follow a policy that shunted itself off to the obscure edge of affairs where it had little power to exert any influence?[8]

However, this was a critical epoch demanding as head of papal affairs a more capable, more imaginative, and more sagacious man than Innocent X. The European crisis required a man of the caliber of Gregory VII or Innocent III. Such a man, through a powerful personality, might have achieved a position of statesmanlike conciliation for the papacy. The papacy need-

[5] *Ibid.*, pp. 490–509. [6] *Ibid.*, p. 680.

[7] *Ibid.*, pp. 680–81; for the foreign relations of the papacy from 1648 to 1815 see: Hergenröther, *Handbuch*, IV, 6–16, 297–362; Schmidlin, *Papstgeschichte der neuesten Zeit*, I, 1–144; Veit, *Die Kirche im Zeitalter des Individualismus*, IV, Part I, 1–243, 323–64; Part II, pp. 4–48; Pastor, *Geschichte der Päpste*, XIV, Part I, 7–8.

[8] Meaux, *op. cit.*, II, 680–81.

ed such a man then and in the ensuing century and a quarter, a period filled with the rivalries and wars of states with great personalities as rulers—Louis XIV, William of Orange, Maria Theresa, Joseph II, Frederick II, Peter the Great, and Catherine the Great. It was a period of great ministers, generals, statesmen, and men of letters and philosophical thought. But the papacy withdrew into the shadows, into obscurity, from which it did not stand out until after the French Revolution.[9]

The political humiliation of the papacy did not liberate souls, it turned them over to the secular power. In the Protestant states the prince became the religious head; in the Catholic states, the church, which the prince had not instituted, existed nevertheless by virtue of the sovereign's will. That was why he strove to subject it. The Catholic nations had to submit to a régime in ecclesiastical affairs that was similar to state control of church affairs in the Protestant states; this régime was not in harmony with Catholic theory either, and rendered the Catholic religion sterile.

After 1648 the Catholic church continued to decline in Germany. It still had many church lands left. The college of imperial cities was dominantly Protestant, but in the two other colleges the Catholics had a majority, that is, in the college of princes and the college of electors. By virtue of this last, the election of the emperor was in Catholic hands; and until the Empire was destroyed by Napoleon in 1806, there were only Catholic emperors. Nevertheless, after 1648 the Catholic church was inactive in German affairs; it took no part in the great War of Liberation (1813–14) and the movement for national resurrection and national unification in the nineteenth century. Was this because of its decline in patrimony? Its income was still the most affluent in Europe. The Catholic church in Germany was in the control of the state; under Joseph II (1765–90) of Austria the system of Josephism was perfected, and Bavaria adopted it. The ecclesiastical states of Germany scorned the pope and his spiritual jurisdiction until their de-

[9] *Ibid.*, pp. 681–82; Hegenröther, *op. cit.*, IV, 2–4.

struction as temporal rulers by Napoleon in 1803. These facts explain, in large part, why the German Catholic church was struck with paralysis after 1648.[10]

In France, the liberty of conscience granted under Henry IV, and preserved by Richelieu, was annihilated by Louis XIV in 1685, when the Edict of Nantes was revoked. Then France became religiously sterile; and the French church declined, like the papacy, and remained in such a state until the Revolution.[11]

If the papacy had taken a more statesmanlike stand in 1648, the church itself, although giving up some of its claims, might well have had a more cheering and fruitful history. But the papacy did not alter its policy to meet changed circumstances. It continued its unyielding attitude after 1648, futilely protesting against all subsequent treaties that infringed on its historic rights and asserting its claims to determine the dividing line between religion and politics, between spiritual and secular affairs.[12] But finally, in 1929, even Pius XI entered the Lateran Accord with Mussolini; the pope gave up all his former claimed rights in international politics by stating that the papacy "wishes to remain extraneous to all temporal disputes between states and to international congresses held for such objects, unless the contending parties make concordant appeal to its peaceful mission."[13] It is interesting, but fruitless, to conjecture what might have been the outcome if in 1648 there had been ruling a pope who could, with clarity of vision, foresee that by the twentieth century the Vatican would be occupied by a pontiff who realized that the future sphere of activity of the Roman Catholic church and the papacy lay, not in the field of politics, but in spiritual and social leadership.

[10] Meaux, *op. cit.*, II, 682–83; Hergenröther, *op. cit.*, IV, 67–74, 196–99, 400–402; Seppelt, *Papstgeschichte*, II, 153–90.

[11] Meaux, *op. cit.*, II, 683–84. [12] See chaps. xvii and xviii. [13] See chap. xviii.

Chapter Thirteen

THE MEANS TAKEN TO MAKE THE PEACE PERMANENT

1. MOST POWERS OF EUROPE INCLUDED IN THE TREATY

VARIOUS measures were taken to make the Treaty absolutely secure against protests. The Swedish plenipotentiaries endeavored to give weight to the clause against protests by including in the Treaty as their allies all the princes of Europe; it was a bit ironical that, besides Spain, only the pope and his agelong infidel enemy, the sultan, were not signatories of the Treaty.[1] Even the kings of England and Poland, and the Grand Duke of Moscow, who had had no part in the war and had not participated in the negotiation at Münster and Osnabrück, were included as signatories of the Treaty. The English Parliament had in May, 1646, communicated with the queen of Sweden to urge her to keep the rights of the elector of the Palatinate intact;[2] the elector Frederick V (1610–20) of the Palatinate had been the son-in-law of James I (1603–25) of England, and now England pressed Sweden to safeguard the interests of the son, Charles Louis (1648–80). After the spring of 1646 the English king was always included as the ally of the Swedes in both the Swedish and imperial peace projects and in the joint peace projects;[3] in September, 1648, the same arrangement was incorporated in the French-imperial peace project.[4]

King Wladislaus IV (1632–48) of Poland sent his minister-resident, Matthias of Krakau, to Münster, in June, 1646, to

[1] *Instrumentum Pacis Caesareo-Suecicum*, Art. XVII, par. 10, 11; Walther, *Universal-Register*, p. xlix; Hanser, *Deutschland nach dem dreissigjährigen Kriege*, p. 79.

[2] Meiern, *Acta pacis Westphalicae*, IV, 18.

[3] *Ibid.*, III, 73; IV, 589, 835; V, 467, 937; VI, 6, 111, 171, 394.

[4] *Ibid.*, VI, 553.

protect Poland's interests in connection with the cession of Pomerania to the Swedes; Poland had interests in Pomerania since it was contiguous to her own lands.[5] After April, 1646, Poland was always included as Sweden's ally in the peace projects.[6]

Ever since May 18, 1595, when the Grand Duke of Moscow had made the Treaty of Teusin with Sweden concerning the rights of the Baltic Sea Lapps,[7] he continued diplomatic relations with Sweden, though not without warlike interruptions.[8] After May, 1647, the Grand Duke was always included as the ally of Sweden in the Swedish-imperial peace projects at the Congress.[9]

It was important that all these signatory powers be given the protection of the Treaty. Each of the Protestant powers of Europe, and, to a less degree, the Catholic princes, had dealt with religious questions in a more or less sovereign way. They had in some cases, as in France, granted heretics the right to worship. Furthermore, the Catholic sovereigns had in the past participated in the secularization of church lands by signing such treaties as the Peace of Passau (1552) and the Peace of Augsburg (1555). The Peace of Wesphalia was even more offending and injurious to Catholic interests. Moreover, if the pope could release Catholic princes from observing treaties made with heretics, then all powers might suffer, for the whole structure of public law in Europe might be seriously shattered. Therefore the Treaty was made to include all the powers, except Spain, the pope, and the sultan.

2. MEASURES TAKEN TO PREVENT THE PRINTING AND DISTRIBUTION OF THE PROTESTS; THE IMPERIAL "PATENT"

On December 17, 1648, the deputies of the Empire assembled and, among other things, discussed means of executing the

[5] *Ibid.*, III, 775.

[6] *Ibid.*, pp. 62, 73; IV, 589, 835; V, 139, 467, 937; VI, 6, 111, 171, 394, 553.

[7] *Ibid.*, I, 163–64; Geijer, *Geschichte Schwedens*, II, 293; Bain, *Scandinavia*, 135.

[8] Bain, *op. cit.*, pp. 179–81; Bain, *Slavonic Europe*, pp. 189–90; Geijer, *op. cit.*, II, 93–98.

[9] Meiern, *op. cit.*, IV, 589; V, 467, 938; VI, 6, 111, 171.

Peace and providing for the observance of its terms. The ambassador of the elector of Bavaria suggested that some measures should be taken to prevent the printing, distribution, and sale of such things as the Burgundian Protest and similar protests.[10] The chancellor of the elector of Mainz remarked that

> many infamous libels and slanderous writings against the Peace were being scattered, as for example, a protestation under name of Burgundian, was publicly sold here, in which were contained many things which our most gracious and merciful masters could not tolerate if brought before them. Such writings served no other purpose than to arouse ill will and distrust among the Estates. Moreover, because these protests are in all cases forbidden in the *Instrumentum pacis*, therefore, we beg that the imperial power again prohibit the booksellers and printers from printing them under heavy penalty and from selling them if brought from other places. The copies should be confiscated, and other severe and unremitting punishments should be administered.[11]

To these remarks the imperial plenipotentiary, Volmar, replied that

> the Emperor had already issued an order prohibiting the distribution of the pamphlets; but he would issue an imperial decree [*placet*] which would be made public and would earnestly prohibit and forbid such distribution, since neither His Imperial Majesty nor they [the princes] took any pleasure in such libels.[12]

On June 27, 1650, at the Congress of Nürnberg, which had met to execute the terms of the treaties, the Emperor issued a "Patent," or proclamation, informing all princes, officers, and subjects in the Empire that a Peace with Sweden had been signed; and in order to prevent new misunderstandings and disorders, nothing was to be said or done contrary to the Peace, "whether by disputations, sermons, or other contraventions," on pain of punishment.[13]

3. THE TREATIES DECLARED LAWS OF THE EMPIRE, 1654

At the Diet of Regensburg (1653–54) both the Peace of Osnabrück and the Peace of Münster were incorporated, word for

[10] *Ibid.*, VI, 738, 739. [11] *Ibid.*, pp. 739, 740. [12] *Ibid.*, p. 741.

[13] Meiern, *Acta pacis executionis publica*, II, 436, 437; also Meiern, *Acta comitalia Ratisbonensia publica*, Vol. II, Appendix, pp. 71–72, par. 6; pp. 77–78, par. 34; Pastor, *Geschichte der Päpste*, XIV, Part I, 101, n. 4, wrongly cites Meiern, *Acta pacis Westphalicae*, VI 794.

word, in the degree of the Imperial Diet (*Reichsabschied*, or *Reichstag-recess*) and declared fundamental laws of the Empire.[14]

4. IMPERIAL EXECUTION OF THE CLAUSE AGAINST PROTESTS

The breve of Innocent X was reissued at least twice after 1648. We have observed that the breve, although dated November 26, 1648, was not released for distribution until August 20, 1650; the nuncios of each country were to be the agencies for making known the contents. By September 7, 1650, in accordance with papal instructions the breve was printed in Vienna by order of Camillus Melzio Melzius, Archbishop of Capua, apostolic nuncio at the imperial court; he had orders to have it affixed to all church doors throughout Austria.[15] According to Conring, the breve was solemnly issued at Rome, January 3, 1651.[16]

Emperor Ferdinand III, in spite of his ecclesiastical piety, suppressed and forbade the distribution of the protest with great vigor; he did so without first remonstrating with the pope or appealing to him in any way.[17] The Württemberg ambassador at the Congress of Nürnberg stated in October, 1650, that the bull (breve) of September 7, 1650, had actually been posted in Vienna but had been torn down at the express command of the emperor.[18] A Vienna printer, who had printed the breve, was imprisoned and forced to pay a fine of 2,000 thalers.[19] Although

[14] Abschied der Röm. Kayserl. Majestät und gemeiner Stände auf dem Reichstag zu Regensburg, Meiern, *Acta comitalia Ratisbonensia publica*, Vol. II, Appendix, pp. 4–69.

[15] Meiern, *Acta pacis executionis publica*, II, 780–84; on page 784 "Melzio" is misprinted "Mettii." Page 780 gives the impression that the breve was printed a second time, September 7, 1650; since the papal authorization of its publication had not occurred before August 20, 1650, this must have been the first printing.

[16] Conring, *Opera*, II, 563–65. This date is given by several secondary works: Charvériat, *Histoire de la guerre de trente ans*, II, 628; Kaemmel, *Deutsche Geschichte*, I, 683; Stacke, *Deutsche Geschichte*, II, 281. Garampi, *Raggualio della Paca di Vestfalia*, does not cite a publication at this time.

[17] Grauert, *Christina Königinn von Schweden*, I, 252.

[18] Meiern, *Acta pacis executionis publica*, II, 781.

[19] Hanser, *op. cit.*, pp. 80–81; Philipps, *Kirchenrecht*, III, Part I, 477; Hergenröther, *Handbuch, Kirchengeschichte*, III, 745; Menzel, *Neuere Geschichte der Deutschen*, VIII,

the printing and posting of the breve was forbidden in the Empire, the emperor permitted it to be posted in his hereditary possessions;[20] but this did not alter the situation. When later, at the Reichstag of Regensburg (1653–54), the Peace of Westphalia was solemnly ratified by the Empire, as just observed,[21] Monsignor Scipio Delci, Archbishop of Pisa and apostolic nuncio in Vienna, "did not neglect to go there [Vienna] personally; and on May 17, 1654, he presented a new solemn protest, and this was then registered in the chancery of Mainz";[22] but here again there were no results.

5. FEELINGS OF FERDINAND III CONCERNING THE PROTESTS

However, it can safely be said that, although Ferdinand III undoubtedly executed the terms of the Treaty in Vienna and in the Empire, he was probably not wholly resigned to the policy that he was forced by circumstances to adopt. The Venetian ambassador at Vienna in the summer of 1650, in discussing the peace negotiations and subsequent events, stated that, when the nuncio handed the protest to the Emperor, he received it with no evil will,[23] probably feeling that it was well to have it, so that, if in the future a favorable opportunity arose and he wished to break his oath, he could do so.[24] But the fact is that the emperor issued his patent and punished at least one offender, the printer of the breve; and as far as we know, neither the emperor nor any other power has made use of the protest of the pope against any part of the Peace of Westphalia.

244; Laurent, *Etudes sur l'histoire de l'humanité*, IX, 247; Zwiedeneck-Südenhorst, *Deutsche Geschichte im Zeitraum der Gründung des preussischen Königtums*, I, 67.

[20] Hurst, *History of the Christian Church*, II, 556; Kaemmel, *op. cit.*, I, 683.

[21] Meiern, *Acta comitalia Ratisbonensia publica*, Vol. II, Appendix, pp. 71–72, par. 6; pp. 77–78, par. 34.

[22] Garampi, *op. cit.*, p. 10; Londorp, *Acta publica*, VII, 717–18; Meiern, *Acta comitalia Ratisbonensia publica* does not contain the protest.

[23] Fiedler, *Die Relationen*, XXVI, 375; "che non mal volontieri la riceve," also cited by Pastor, *op. cit.*, XIV, Part I, 101, n. 4, but he gives the wrong page (395) in Fiedler.

[24] Ward, in *Cambridge Modern History*, IV, 415, Hergenröther, *Katholische Kirche und christlicher Staat*, p. 709.

Chapter Fourteen

THE CONTEMPORARY CONTROVERSIAL LITERATURE: PART I. THE FORE-RUNNERS OF WANGNERECK

1. NATURE AND IMPORTANCE OF THE LITERARY CONTROVERSY

A MODERN author, Egon Friedell, closes his discussion of the Thirty Years' War as follows:

> That purpose of secularizing all human activities and relations, which we have recognized as the essence of the Reformation, also seizes the Catholic world. Whereas in the sixteenth century denominational convictions and emotions still had such absolute sway in the souls of the people as to crowd out all national, social, and patriotic feelings and considerations, the very reverse now comes to pass: all of Europe is completely actuated by politics, is secularized, rationalized. The Middle Age has ended.[1]

The Peace of Westphalia signified the secularization of politics. During the war there had begun an intense literary controversy, which became even more violent during the peace negotiations, and lasted for some years thereafter. The main point at issue was the lawfulness and possible permanence of a peace that was to be made with heretics and did injury to Catholic interests. Such a discussion was inevitable; it is an invariable accompaniment of all movements bringing fundamental changes in the organization and practice of human society.[2] It was a contest between the constitutional lawyers, theologians, and publicists of the seventeenth century, who represented three groups of opinions: (1) the irreconcilable Catholics, (2)

[1] Friedell, *Kulturgeschichte der Neuzeit*, II, 14; Friedell, *A Cultural History of the Modern Age*, II, 15.

[2] Ritter, "Das römische Kirchenrecht und der westfälische Friede," *Historische Zeitschrift*, CI, 254–55.

the moderate Catholics, and (3) the Protestants, whose respective ideas will be considered in the next section.

In this contest the Roman Catholic church still claimed to have final authority in human affairs; it was defending its position against the claims of the state, which had, since the fourteenth century, increasingly asserted its own authority or claim to determine the scope of its own affairs and attend to them without any ecclesiastical interference. The claims of the church as supreme authority in most human affairs had been recognized for many centuries. But the Protestant Reformation gave increasing impetus to the state to assert its absolute and final authority in church and other affairs. The conflict dated back more than a century, and the bitterness with which it was carried on before and during the negotiations at Münster and Osnabrück is an indication of the supreme importance of the struggle. The fight had not yet been won. The Protestants were contending for a principle that they had advocated for several generations; there was nothing particularly new in their viewpoint. Neither was there anything new in the viewpoint expressed in the writings of the irreconcilable Catholics. The greatest ingenuity was manifested in the arguments of the moderate Catholics, representing the interests of the Catholic princes that had to find some legal bases that would justify the concessions detrimental to Catholicism that were being demanded by the victorious powers—France, Sweden, and their German Protestant allies.[3]

To the alert, informed people of the time the struggle that was being waged between the old and the new ideas was quite as important and significant as the similar struggles that have taken, and are taking, place in modern times concerning the rights of the crown as opposed to those of parliament; the rights of the intrenched upper classes in eighteenth-century France as opposed to the democratic or revolutionary rights of the nation; the rights of capitalistic society as opposed to the claims of the collectivists; the rights of individual nations as opposed to the

[3] *Ibid.*, p. 256; see also chap. xvi, below.

general interests of the world and humanity as expressed in the League of Nations, the World Court, and the disarmament movement. In other words, this battle of these seventeenth-century pamphleteers was the literary aspect of a tremendous struggle to change the trend of modern history, to make possible the secularization of politics.

2. THE THREE GROUPS OF DISPUTANTS

In the literary conflict three distinct groups of disputants or pamphleteers were noticeable: (*a*) There were, first, the "irreconcilables" or the extreme Catholics, who steadfastly insisted on maintaining all the rights of the Catholic church intact. They opposed the signing and denied the legality of any treaty that injured the historic claims and rights of the church in any respect, and were willing to have the Thirty Years' War go on indefinitely rather than make any concessions, whether permanent or even temporary. (*b*) The moderate Catholics held some ideas in common with the extreme or irreconcilable Catholics, but felt that, in the face of the existing situation produced by the prolonged and devastating war, which had ceased to be religious, some sort of conciliatory attitude must be taken to make possible the establishment of a much needed peace. (*c*) The Protestant writers were defending the rights of the secular rulers, Catholic as well as Protestant, to regulate church affairs regardless of the interests of the Catholic church. These writers pointed out historic precedents that justified the conclusion of a permanent peace such as was being negotiated at Münster and Osnabrück.

Most of these writers were scholastic in their thinking; they already had their conclusions to start with, and sought arguments to substantiate them. They were controversialists, advocates, such as we in American and European life have become familiar with during the World War and in post-war controversies concerning the League of Nations, the Soviets, reparations, debt-cancellation. The writings of Heinrich Wangnereck, chief of the irreconcilables, were in many ways determinative for all subsequent writings: those of the other irreconcilables, such as Adam Adami; those of the moderate Catholics, such as Vervaux and Caramuel; those of the Protestants, such as Conring and Dorsche. Wangnereck's arrangement of topics was followed by each of the others in approving or attacking his views.

Some of the writings that we shall consider were manuscripts, manifolded by copyists for distribution; a still greater number were printed, in some cases to the extent of hundreds of copies.[4] The circle of readers might be a very small group, e.g., the members of the extreme or moderate Catholics assembled to confer at Münster.

3. ON WHAT THE EXTREMIST AND MODERATE CATHOLICS AGREED AND DISAGREED

Both the irreconcilable and moderate Catholics agreed as to fundamental principles, but they differed sharply in the application of those principles to the practical problems incident to terminating the Thirty Years' War and drawing up the peace terms. During the war and during the peace negotiations the Protestants had demanded two things: (1) freedom of worship, i.e., the right to believe, teach, and preach their doctrines, hold religious services, and formulate their own church organizations and regulations; (2) the right to share all the endowments and properties of the church, that is, all the funded incomes for church offices and the actual lands of monasteries, bishops, and archbishops.

With reference to the first demand of the Protestants the two Catholic groups were agreed. The heretics should not be tolerated; they should be exterminated by the constant co-operation of the ecclesiastical and secular goverments. But the extremists stressed especially the subordination of the state to the church. The co-operation desired did not rest on the equal rights of the two powers but on the duty of the state authority to conduct its legislative and executive actions in accordance with the orders of the ecclesiastical authority on pain of excommunication and

[4] Steinberger, *Die Jesuiten*, p. 196.

removal from office. The extremists, to find a basis for this teaching, appealed to the medieval law concerning heretics and to the eternal moral law that forbids giving aid to or co-operating with sinners. Heresy being the most serious offense in the eyes of God, the state must not give aid to sinners by tolerating heresy. It was the duty of the secular ruler to exterminate heresy. But the moderates, like Caramuel, maintained that there was no positive divine command whereby the princes were compelled to persecute a definite religious belief.

Concerning the demand of the Protestants that they be given some of the ecclesiastical lands, the extreme Catholics asserted that in conformity with divine law the church alone was responsible for the control and disposal of these lands; the secular rulers had no authority whatever in the matter. But this theoretical statement could not be applied in the face of an existing situation determined by the superior force of arms of the German Protestants, the Swedes, and their Catholic ally, France. The Catholic princes were confronted now, in the years 1647–48, with the same conditions that had led to the ceding of church lands to the heretics by the Peace of Augsburg (1555) and the Peace of Prague (1635).[5]

4. THE RELATION OF THE PEACE OF AUGSBURG TO THE CONTROVERSY

All the important considerations in this great literary debate centered around the legitimacy of the Peace of Augsburg, which was a fundamental step in the long development toward the secularization of politics. We have seen in an earlier chapter that the final attitude of the papacy had been in favor of accepting the Peace of Augsburg provisionally and for an indefinite time. At the Diet of Augsburg in 1566 the Jesuit Petrus Canisius, supported by two other Jesuits, had expressed an opinion at the request of the papal legate Commendone; this opinion was that the Peace of Augsburg was not in conflict with the decrees of the Council of Trent, and that, although the pope

[5] Ritter, "Das römische Kirchenrecht," *Historische Zeitschrift*, CI, 258–61.

did not sanction this Peace, he permitted the Catholics in the Augsburg Reichstag to confirm and observe it so long as they did not have power to do otherwise.[6] So the Catholics did not regard the Peace of Augsburg as final; they had agreed to it only under compulsion; it was to be tolerated only as long as necessary. Naturally the Protestants condemned such an attitude; but they, as well as the Catholics, violated the Peace of Augsburg, and this was one of the fundamental causes of the Thirty Years' War.[7] Once the war had started, the whole question as to the validity of the Peace of Augsburg was opened again. At every attempt at drawing up a peace—in the Edict of Restitution, 1629, in the Peace of Prague, 1635, at the Diet of Ratisbon (Regensburg), 1640–41, and finally at the Congress of Westphalia, 1645–48—the validity of the Peace of Augsburg was questioned by the extreme Catholics and defended by the Protestants, who after 1647, for opportunist reasons, had the support of the moderate Catholics.[8]

5. THE FORERUNNERS OF WANGNERECK: LAYMANN AND FORER

In this chapter and the two following chapters of this treatise we shall center our attention mainly on the literary productions during and after the Westphalian negotiations; but a brief consideration of some of the fundamental works appearing previously will be of interest, since their content was closely related to the ideas defended and attacked in the later works. We shall first consider the *Pacis Compositio*, which appeared in 1629.

In that year Emperor Ferdinand II (1619–47) had issued the Edict of Restitution. It declared: (1) that all ecclesiastical properties seized by the Protestants since 1552 were to be restored to the Catholics, (2) that the holding of ecclesiastical

[6] Braunsberger, *Beati Petri Canisii S.J. Epistolae et Acta*, V, 229–55, letters 1314–18. See also chap. iii, above.

[7] Duhr, *Geschichte der Jesuiten in den Ländern deutscher Zunge*, II, Part I, 1–13; *Cambridge Modern History*, IV, 109, 110.

[8] *Cambridge Modern History*, IV, 111–13, 252–53, 397; Duhr, *op. cit.*, II, Part I, 460–91; Steinberger, *op. cit.*, pp. 10–13, 28–37, 76–168.

offices by Protestants in these lands was illegal, (3) that Catholic rulers might expel all Protestant subjects that do not give up their heresy.[9] This Edict caused great jubilation among the Catholics but great alarm and fear among the Protestants.[10] This fear was accentuated by the appearance, also in 1629, of the *Pacis Compositio*.[11] This book was written by Jesuits in Dillingen, the chief of whom was Father Paul Laymann (1575–1635), professor of canon law in the University of Dillingen. He was assisted by Father Laurenz Forer and probably others. Forer was confessor of Heinrich V von Knöringen, Bishop of Augsburg (1598–1646). The Bishop had fostered the writing of the book,[12] and its purpose was to correct the false ideas of the Catholics concerning the Peace of Augsburg and to present the facts to the advantage of the church. It was a legal justification of the practical measure taken by Ferdinand II in issuing the Edict of Restitution. Laymann, who especially possessed great legal knowledge and lucid style, defended the legality of the Edict of Restitution and refuted all arguments against it.[13] Forer, who had held positions at the universities of Ingolstadt and Dillingen, was the author of a mass of controversial writings against the Lutherans; these works were incisive and incontrovertible, and therefore greatly feared.[14] The book asserted that the Peace of Augsburg did not have the nature of a constitution but was a pragmatic sanction or temporary arrangement,[15] and that the princes were not permitted to tolerate heresy or

[9] *Cambridge Modern History*, IV, 111; Duhr, *op. cit.*, II, Part I, 460–61; Ritter, *Deutsche Geschichte*, III, 425–26; Riezler, *Geschichte Baierns*, V, 340–45.

[10] Duhr, *op. cit.*, II, Part I, 461.

[11] For full title see Bibliography under Laymann and Forer; Steinberger, *op. cit.*, p. 11, n. 5. A second edition, greatly enlarged, also 1629; German edition, 1630. Backer and Sommervogel, *Bibliothèque des écrivains de la compagnie de Jésus*, IV, 1590.

[12] Steinberger, *op. cit.*, pp. 10–11.

[13] *Ibid.*, p. 11; Duhr, *op. cit.*, II, Part I, 464.

[14] Dudik, "Correspondenz Kaisers Ferdinand II, und seiner erlauchten Familie mit P. Martinus Becanus und P. Wilhelm Lamormaini, kaiserlichen Beichtvätern S.J.," *Archiv für österreichische Geschichte*, LIV, 249.

[15] Laymann and Forer, *Pacis Compositio* (German ed., 1630), pp. 100–117.

enter agreements tolerating heresy,[16] arguments affirmed and denied often in works subsequently discussed.

The Catholics welcomed this book of clarifying and assuring statements, since it was a veritable arsenal of legal weapons against the Peace of Augsburg. For many decades there had been no such powerful attack on this Peace. But the Protestants took great offense at this book.[17] They showed their irritation by writing at least eight literary counterattacks, some of which appeared in more than one edition.[18] But the "Dillingen Book," as the Protestants called it,[19] remained so powerful in its influence that at the Reichstag of Regensburg (Ratisbon) in April, 1641, they demanded that it be stamped out.[20] And during the Congress of Westphalia the Swedes called it a peace-odious (*fried-hässigen*) book. Another evidence of the bitter[21] feeling connected with the authorship and appearance of this "Dillingen Book" is the reputed statement of Gustavus Adolphus that he "would like to see three L's suspended from the gallows: Lamormaini, Laymann, and Laurentius."[22] The last two, Father Paul Laymann and Father Laurenz Forer, were authors of the *Pacis Compositio;* and Lamormaini was the very influential Jesuit confessor of Emperor Ferdinand II (1619–37), who had the reputation of being "master of the imperial will" and the real director of the imperial policy.[23]

6. THE OPINION OF FATHER LAURENZ FORER

Forer did not confine his literary efforts to the co-authorship of the *Pacis Compositio*, but in the years 1634–36 he presented four

[16] *Ibid.*, pp. 118–26.

[17] Duhr, *op. cit.*, II, Part I, 464; Steinberger, *op. cit.*, pp. 11–12, 29.

[18] Backer and Sommervogel, *op. cit.*, IV, 1590, No. 27; Steinberger, *op. cit.*, p. 12, n. 1.

[19] Meiern, *Acta pacis Westphalicae*, II, 97, 571.

[20] Londorp, *Acta publica*, V, 206.

[21] Meiern, *op. cit.*, I, 821; see also II, 560; IV, 74.

[22] B. Dudik, "Correspondenz Kaisers," *Archiv für österreichische Geschichte*, LIV, 248; Steinberger, *op. cit.*, p. 35, n. 2.

[23] Dudik, "Correspondenz Kaisers," *Archiv für österreichische Geschichte*, pp. 228–55; Steinberger, *op. cit.*, pp. 3, 15, 16; Stieve, "Lamormaini," in *Allgemeine deutsche Biographie*, XVII, 572.

written opinions to the counsels of Emperor Ferdinand II (1619–37) and of Maximilian of Bavaria. These manuscripts, which were never printed, are found in the Bavarian state archives.[24] Two of these documents were certainly written by Forer himself; the third may have been written by him; the fourth expressed opinions coinciding with his own. The significance of these manuscripts lies less in their content than in the comments that Forer made in his own handwriting on the front and back of these writings; these comments throw some light on the circumstances explaining secularization of politics in the seventeenth century.

1. One of these manuscripts, dated 1635, was copied by another hand on the basis of Forer's original draft, which is also preserved in the same folder. Its title is a query, "Is it permitted permanently to promise the heretics permission to engage in public worship?" Forer naturally answers this negatively,[25] and adds a note: "I have offered this memorandum to many imperialists and Bavarian counselors, but it did not please."

2. A second pamphlet bears the title, "Does there exist the extreme necessity of extending a guaranty to heresy?"[26] Here again Forer answers "no," and adds in his own hand: "Written in 1636 and offered to the imperial and Bavarian counselors; they did not thank me."

3. A third manuscript, which may have been written by Forer, is entitled: "Reasons why it should not have been denied, and should not be denied now, that the Swedish war is a religious war."[27] To this is added a note in Forer's hand: "In the year 1635, I have communicated to the Bavarians and the imperialists, but sang to deaf [ears]."

[24] Bayerisches Hauptstaatsarchiv, München, *Jesuitica in genere*, fasc. 25, No. 370.

[25] Forer, *An liceat promittere haereticus, etc.* For full title see Bibliography, manuscripts section, under Forer.

[26] Forer, *An sit extrema necessitas, etc.* For full title see Bibliography, manuscripts section, under Forer.

[27] Forer, *Causae ob quas nec debuerit, etc.* For full title see Bibliography, manuscripts section, under Forer.

4. The last manuscript, by an unindentified author,[28] is a discussion pertinent to the situation of the day but bespeaking Forer's own opinion. In his own hand Forer added two comments: "Exhortation to the father confessor of the emperor, P. Lamormaini, in the year 1634. For this he expressed to me no great thanks"; and "N.B. What is herein advised against, was granted even more freely and ruinously in the Peace of Münster, and the emperor burdened his conscience to an extreme."[29] The first and fourth of these pamphlets are extreme Catholic arguments against permanently granting religious freedom;[30] the third advocated the elimination of all heretics from the imperial armies.[31] To us the main significance lies in Forer's having presented these pamphlets while counseling against making any concessions in the religious sphere but getting no sympathetic response in the two main Catholic courts of Germany, in Munich and Vienna. The explanation of this lies in the fact that during the second half of the Thirty Years' War the conviction grew in Catholic ranks that, in order to oppose the foreign foes of Germany, that is, France and Sweden, a combination of the Protestants and Catholics was urgently necessary; and in order to secure Protestant co-operation the Catholics had to make great concessions in religious matters to the Protestants.[32] In other words, politics had to be secularized for national considerations.

[28] Theodori Montani, *Iurisconsulti et Theolog: Discursus de Manifesto Caesari, dato 30, Aug. 1634.*

[29] Steinberger, *op. cit.*, p. 26, n. 1, lists these four pamphlets in a different sequence and gives the title of only the fourth in the sequence presented here. The comments of Forer are given in Latin.

[30] *Ibid.*, p. 25, n. 4. [31] *Ibid.*, p. 26, n. 3. [32] *Ibid.*, p. 27.

Chapter Fifteen

THE CONTEMPORARY CONTROVERSIAL LITERATURE: PART II. THE WRITINGS OF WANGNERECK

I. HEINRICH WANGNERECK (1595–1664), CHAMPION OF THE CATHOLIC EXTREMISTS

THE most important of all the writers on the extreme Catholic side was Heinrich Wangnereck; he was the outstanding defender of the strictly legalistic Catholic view of granting no compromise to the heretics. He was a native of Munich, a member of the Society of Jesus since 1611. He had spent most of his life as a teacher of various subjects in the German university at Dillingen, on the Danube; and after 1642, with a few years of interruption, until his death he was academic chancellor of the Jesuit Academy at Dillingen.[1] In 1645 he was given charge of the Jesuit mission in the imperial free city of Lindau am Bodensee, an overwhelmingly Protestant city. And it was at these two places, Dillingen and Lindau, where he lived and wrote during the stirring times of the literary warfare described in these chapters.[2] He was a disputative person, with a penchant for polemics against Protestantism, which he deeply hated as heresy. He was an impractical doctrinaire; he would overstate his arguments with such excessive ardor that his Jesuit superiors carefully avoided appointing him to offices through which he might gain political influence. On the other hand, his energy and determination qualified him especially to carry on the difficult task of legalistic propaganda.[3]

[1] Steinberger, *Die Jesuiten und die Friedensfrage*, p. 13. [2] *Ibid.*, p. 14. [3] *Ibid.*

2. WANGNERECK'S WRITINGS

The writings of Wangnereck which are concerned with the subject of this treatise were produced in the years 1640–48, under four titles, although a fifth is possible but not probable. In 1640 he wrote a work *Quaestio ardua.*[4] It was to be a theological basis for refusing all concessions to the Protestants, including the demanded amnesty.[5] Since the Edict of Restitution of 1629 the war had gone against the emperor and the Catholics. The Peace of Prague (1635) had been a compromise satisfying no one; after another half-decade of war the emperor was appealed to by the college of electors, meeting at Nürnberg (1640), and the Reichstag, meeting at Regensburg (1640–41), to procure a new settlement. It was clear that the emperor would need to cede to France and Sweden lands of his own or church lands.[6] It was under these circumstances that the indefatigable Bishop Heinrich V of Augsburg urged Wangnereck to write against ceding to the heretics any church lands or rights of toleration.[7] The pamphlet appeared anonymously and only in manuscript copies, since it was the object of Bishop Heinrich and of Wangnereck to have it circulate only among Catholic extremists.[8] To meet new conditions with reference to the theological aspects of the negotiations at Münster a revision of the *Quaestio ardua* appeared toward the end of the year 1646 under the title *Judicium theologicum.*[9] This pamphlet was in form and content far superior to the ordinary theological tracts of the time.[10] It was regarded as excellent propaganda material; and therefore Wangnereck's supporters, with the encouragement of the elector Anselm Kasimir of Mainz, concluded that it would

[4] *Ibid.*, p. 168. See Bibliography, manuscripts section, for fuller title.

[5] Steinberger, p. 30; Duhr, *Geschichte der Jesuiten in der Ländern deutscher Zunge*, II, Part I, 472.

[6] Ritter, *Deutsche Geschichte*, III, 615–16; *Cambridge Modern History*, IV, 252–55, 384.

[7] Steinberger, *op. cit.*, p. 30; Duhr, *op. cit.*, II, Part I, 473.

[8] Steinberger, *op. cit.*, pp. 31, 169.

[9] Full title in bibliography; Steinberger, *op. cit.*, p. 63, n. 2.

[10] Pastor, *Geschichte der Päpste*, XIV, Part I, 83–84.

be wise to publish the revised pamphlet under the new title. It was published without Wangnereck's knowledge, and under the pseudonym "Ernestus de Eusebiis" and with a fictitious place of publication.[11] In the years 1647 and 1648 it was repeatedly reprinted without change in different printing shops.[12] It soon became evident after the first appearance of *Judicium theologicum* that "Ernestus de Eusebiis" was a pseudonym; and the authorship was attributed to various persons, including the nuncio Chigi, who later became Pope Alexander VII.[13] It was not until 1663 that it became definitely known to those not in the restricted circle of extreme Catholics that the author was Wangnereck; this fact was made public by Hermann Conring.[14]

In June or July, 1647, Wangnereck may have published a third pamphlet, *Vehiculum Judicii theologici*, without date or place of publication. This was an answer to an attack on the *Judicium theologicum* that had been published in March, 1647, by Caramel y Lobkowitz, the father confessor of Emperor Ferdinand III.[15] Steinberger holds, however, that Wangnereck's authorship of the *Vehiculum* is not to be regarded as probable. Moreover, the form and content of this pamphlet is of no consequence; it is a restatement or amplification of the *Judicium theologicum*.[16]

In the second half of August, 1647, Wangnereck published an additional pamphlet entitled *Ponderatio*, or less frequently known as *Instrumenti pacis*.[17] This appeared under the pseudonym "Theophilus Generosus Genuinus Germanus," but it is

[11] Steinberger, *op. cit.*, pp. 69–71; Pastor, *op. cit.*, XIV, Part I, 83; Ritter, "Das römische Kirchenrecht," *Historische Zeitschrift*, CI, 261; Duhr, *op. cit.*, II, Part I, 474.

[12] Steinberger, *op. cit.*, p. 63, n. 2; p. 71, n. 5.

[13] *Ibid.*, pp. 64–66.

[14] Conring, *Opera*, II, 470, n. (*a*); Steinberger, *op. cit.*, p. 66; Duhr, *op. cit.*, II, Part I, 474.

[15] Steinberger, *op. cit.*, pp. 78–81, 85.

[16] *Ibid.*, p. 85; Ritter, "Das römische Kirchenrecht," *Historische Zeitschrift*, CI, 257–58.

[17] Both of these shorter titles are a part of the full title, which is found in the Bibliography.

clear by now that its author was Wangnereck.[18] In the *Ponderatio* Wangnereck, in order to give no trace of the identity of the authorship of this work and the *Judicium theologicum*, used the mask of pseudonymity in the *Ponderatio* and alluded to "Ernestus de Eusebiis" as a third person, a literary trick that was very successful.[19]

In the *Ponderatio* Wangnereck gave citations from *Judicium theologicum* to show that the peace terms as formulated were in defiance of the fundamental principles of the Catholic church.[20] He also opposed granting toleration to Calvinists.[21] The *Ponderatio* had no appreciable influence on the trend of the peace negotiations; however, the extreme Catholics could use it to show the moderate Catholics how the peace project, as sanctioned by the emperor, was in conflict with the strictly legal principles of the Roman Catholic church. But Emperor Ferdinand III had already, as a consequence of the theological opinions presented to him by Caramuel and his other spiritual advisers, given his sanction to the fundamentals of the peace project. Maximilian of Bavaria had also thrown his great influence in favor of the Peace, after his theologians, especially Vervaux, had advised him that the extreme conditions of the time required concessions to the Protestants at Catholic expense. Moreover, Maximilian's conscience had been quieted by the attitude of his advisers that one does not need to keep his promised word with heretics, an attitude that is objectionable to us moderns.[22]

In the early weeks of the year 1648 Wangnereck replied to Vervaux's *Notae in Judicium theologicum* by a pamphlet entitled *Responsum theologicum*.[23] It was printed anonymously early in 1648 by the Catholic extremists but with Wangnereck's consent.[24] The aim of the extremists was to have the tract read only by Catholics, therefore it was printed privately. Although it soon became widely known in all German Catholic circles, it

[18] Steinberger, *op. cit.*, pp. 89–90, 176.
[19] *Ibid.*, p. 90.
[20] *Ibid.*, p. 90.
[21] *Ibid.*, p. 90.
[22] *Ibid.*, pp. 90, 91, n. 4; pp. 196–97.
[23] Full title in Bibliography.
[24] Steinberger, *op. cit.*, pp. 112, 113, 177.

did not become known in the Protestant circles for a considerable time. Even Maximilian of Bavaria did not know of it until November, 1648; perhaps, because it was so critical of his policy, it was designedly kept from reaching the elector's hands.[25] Here again Wangnereck resorted to anonymity to protect himself against the wrath of the elector of Bavaria; and once more, as in the *Ponderatio*, he referred to "Ernestus de Eusebiis" as a disinterested third person.[26] In the *Responsum theologicum* he called Vervaux, the author of the *Notae*, "Irenicus" because of his pacific ideas; he himself scorned all such pacifists and questioned Vervaux's honesty.[27] A far worse offense was his attack on Maximilian of Bavaria for having signed the Treaty of Ulm with Sweden and France in March, 1647; this attack led to serious consequences for Wangnereck, as we shall see later.[28]

3. WANGNERECK'S MAIN IDEAS

In this brief treatment we cannot state all the ideas presented by Wangnereck in his *Judicium theologicum*, which contains all the ideas of his other works. He is very repetitious, but he is always clear-cut. Naturally he is opposed to the secularization of politics, that is, the power of the secular princes to determine the sphere of their power, even to the point of regulating church affairs and disposing of church lands. In stating his opposition he breathes the spirit and reasserts the arguments of the political theories of Innocent III and Boniface VIII. He is the seventeenth-century advocate par excellence of absolute papal power in all matters of religion and church rights. He wishes no yielding, not the slightest compromise, no matter how long the war need be continued to safeguard all the rights of the church. In Section IV, Point IV, of his *Judicium theologicum*,[29] he asserts that the emperor and the princes of the Empire usurped a power that was not in their province when they regulated religious affairs in the Peace of Münster, or Westphalia. His specific criticisms can be grouped in three statements.

[25] *Ibid.*, pp. 113–14, 139, n. 1.
[26] *Ibid.*, p. 115.
[27] *Ibid.*, pp. 115–16.
[28] *Ibid.*, pp. 116–17, 141–60.
[29] Conring, *op. cit.*, II, 500–501.

a) *The princes granted heretics the right to worship.*—This cannot be granted in any degree, even under pressure of necessity; that belongs solely to Peter and his successors, whose duty it is to drive off the wolves (heretics) that interfere with the pasturing of the sheep of Christ.

b) *The princes abrogated church jurisdiction* when they decided that certain bishoprics and other ecclesiastical offices shall cease to exist and that Catholic lands and subjects be turned over to lay princes. The Peace of Westphalia, like the Peace of Augsburg, is null and void in this respect.

c) *The princes proposed to renounce, annul, or suspend all ecclesiastical rights or decrees that were at variance with the terms of the Peace of Augsburg and the Peace of Westphalia.*—This referred to the clause against protests, which we have already considered, and, if applied, would mean that the church would forever forfeit its rights concerning heresy, its lost lands, churches, and ceded subjects. Wangnereck did not know the expression "secularization of politics," but he attacked its implication and its supporters. He had no patience with those advocating a peace that would he prejudicial to the interests of the Catholic church but advantageous to the secular princes. He scorned the policy of Emperor Ferdinand III, who sacrificed the lands and jurisdiction of the church in order to secure a peace that safeguarded his own Hapsburg possessions. Wangnereck opposed Maximilian of Bavaria because he was willing to grant an armistice to heretics and was working for a stable peace with the heretics in order to make sure that his newly acquired electoral dignity and territory, the Upper Palatinate, would remain unshaken in his possession. Wangnereck scorned those ecclesiastical princes like John Philipp von Schönborn, Archbishop of Mainz, who, being weary of war and desirous of peace, sacrificed the interests of mother church to the advantage of heretics. He contemned ecclesiasts like Caramuel and Vervaux, who advised their masters Ferdinand III and Maximilian, respectively, that under the pressure of circumstances a peace with heretics could be signed, even with prejudice to the church. Against

Caramuel and his like he wrote his *Ponderatio;* against Vervaux he composed his *Responsum theologicum.* A peace with heretics was anathema to him. Heretics were to be tolerated, not by secular authority, but solely by papal authority—and that merely as the church tolerated Jews, usurers, and prostitutes.[30]

4. WANGNERECK AND THE EXTREME CATHOLICS

It was natural that the extravagant, irreconcilable views of Wangnereck should find ready support among the Catholic extremists. In form and content his pamphlets were far superior to the ordinary theological opinions appearing in print, and were therefore well suited for propaganda purposes. The extreme Catholics, headed by Anselm Kasimir, elector of Mainz, and Franz Wilhelm von Wartenberg, had had his works printed; the copies of the *Judicium theologicum* found a ready sale and did much to add to the ranks of the extreme Catholics many persons who had previously been friendly to the idea of a conciliatory peace.[31] Although the writings of Wangnereck did not alter the outcome of the peace negotiations, they had the effect of binding the extreme Catholics together, giving them a gauge whereby they could judge the concessions that the emperor and the other moderate Catholics were willing to make to the Protestants.[32]

It was quite to be expected that Pope Innocent X, who had instructed the nuncio Chigi to protest against any peace terms prejudicial to Catholic interests,[33] should commend Wangnereck for his spirited, orthodox writings and interfere on his behalf when Caraffa, the general of the Jesuit Order, disciplined him at the urgent demand of Maximilian of Bavaria.[34] However much Chigi favored the contents of Wangnereck's writings and wished them to be known to all good Catholics, he, as well as others, was surprised and disappointed when, in 1646, the

[30] *Judicium theologicum*, sec. II, point 9, par. III; Conring, *op. cit.*, II, 513.

[31] Steinberger, *op. cit.*, pp. 69–73, 196.

[32] *Ibid.*, pp. 90–91.

[33] See above, chaps. iv and xi.

[34] See section 6 below. Steinberger, *op. cit.*, pp. 75, 146–59, 164, 203–4.

Judicium theologicum was published, for he felt that the Swedes and other Protestants would use these weapons against the Catholics; and subsequent events proved that this judgment was quite correct.[35] But Chigi stood by Wangnereck when he later incurred the wrath of Maximilian of Bavaria and secured Pope Innocent's relieving interference on behalf of the courageous polemist.[36] Count Peñaranda, the Spanish ambassador at Münster, regarded the printing of the *Judicium theologicum* as being important enough to send copies to the court of Madrid.[37]

It is quite easy to understand the hearty support that was given Wangnereck by the so-called "triumvirate"—Count Franz Wilhelm von Wartenberg, Adam Adami, prior to Murrhardt, and Johann von Leuchselring (Leuxelring). Concerning the first two and other ecclesiastical princes, a modern authority has said they "were contending less for the faith than for their secular possessions."[38] If the proposed peace terms were to be executed, Wartenberg would lose to the Swedes his bishoprics of Minden and Verden; and his bishopric of Osnabrück would be held alternately by a Catholic and a Protestant. During the war he had been driven from all these possessions by the Swedes; at the Peace Congress, being without lands himself, he represented Archbishop Ferdinand of Cologne. However, he was so insistent and persistent in defending Catholic rights that, as Trauttmannsdorff affirmed, he very appreciably checked the progress of the negotiations. But it must be said to his credit that he was more insistent in defending papal interests than his own; in fact, this was true to such a degree that the elector Ferdinand of Cologne found it necessary to deprive him temporarily of his right to vote when the matter of granting the electorate to Bavaria was decided in October, 1647; this action was taken by the elector Ferdinand through the influence of his

[35] Steinberger, *op. cit.*, pp. 73–75, 196; Pastor, *op. cit.*, XIV, Part I, 84.

[36] Steinberger, *op. cit.*, pp. 133–37, 151–54.

[37] Letters of Peñaranda, *Coleccion de documentos ineditos*, LXXXIII, 95; Steinberger, *op. cit.*, pp. 73, 196–97.

[38] Heigel, "Das westfälische Friedenswerk," *Zeitschrift für Geschichte und Politik*, V, 436–37.

brother, Maximilian of Bavaria.[39] Adami, prior of Murrhardt, and the persons he represented would also sustain losses of church territory and offices if the proposed peace were executed. At Münster, Adami represented the abbots, the heads of the collegiate churches, and the imperial prelates in the Swabian circle; he gladly adhered to the ideas of Wangnereck in the vain hope of preventing these various lands of his own and his constituents from being ceded permanently to the Duke of Württemberg.[40] Adami had himself written a pamphlet entitled *Anti-Caramuel*,[41] under the pseudonym "Humanus Erdeman Oecomontano"; it was written in the spirit of Wangnereck against making any concessions, and he published it when only half completed, having learned that Wangnereck was also contemplating a refutation of Caramuel.[42] Leuchselring represented at Münster the Catholic interests of Augsburg; he was an ardent person, devoted to the Catholic cause. When he, Wartenberg, and Adami, were derisively called "triumvirs," he scornfully called all other Catholics "trimmers" (*Lavierer*).[43] Being an ardent Catholic, he could not agree to granting Protestants a status of parity with Catholics in his city of Augsburg; Wangnereck's arguments were the best preventive of such concessions.

5. PROTESTANT CRITICISM OF WANGNERECK

The Catholic extremists, who, as has been observed, gladly based their contentions on Wangnereck's writings, proved to be very annoying to the Protestants and to the moderate Catholics. The printing and the distribution of the "poisonous" *Judicium*

39 Meiern, *Acta pacis Westphalicae*, IV, 777; F. Philippi, in *Allgemeine deutsche Biographie*, XLI, 190–91; Steinberger, *op. cit.*, pp. 58, 61, 71–72, 113, 143.

40 Israel, *Adam Adami und seine Arcana Pacis Westphalicae*, pp. 29–30, 117, 118; Steinberger, *op. cit.*, p. 64; Ritter, "Das römische Kirchenrecht," *Historische Zeitschrift*, CI, 264–65.

41 Full title in Bibliography, under Adami.

42 Israel, *op. cit.*, pp. 113–17; Steinberger, *op. cit.*, pp. 127–29.

43 Vogel, *Der Kampf auf dem westfälischen Friedenskongress um die Einführung der Parität in der Stadt Augsburg*, p. 12; Steinberger, *op. cit.*, p. 64; Odhner, *Die Politik Schwedens*, p. 112; Israel, *op. cit.*, p. 66.

theologicum with its "erroneous, highly injurious principles" released a great storm among the Protestants.[44] They resented especially the cocksure way in which "Ernestus" rejected all the claims of the evangelical powers. From the Catholic, strictly legal, standpoint he was undoubtedly on firm ground in stating that the Protestants had no right to church lands acquired during the Thirty Years' War. But he was especially offensive in attacking the legality and permanence of the Peace of Augsburg, which had been sanctioned in 1566, at least for the time being, by Peter Canisius (1521–97), the first German Jesuit, founder of the Jesuit Order in Germany, and one of the most eminent and effective promoters of the Catholic Reformation in Germany.[45] By declaring that the Peace of Augsburg, after having been in effect more than ninety years, was invalid, Wangnereck gave the Protestants a point of attack more advantageous than any that they themselves could formulate. Therefore, some of them demanded that the pamphlet *Judicium theologicum* be burned by the common hangman.[46]

The Swedes complained that "no more poisonous writing than the *Judicum theologicium*, especially in reference to this question (of religious difficulties), could have been issued by the devil himself, because it undermines all fundamentals of the Peace of Augsburg that have not been entirely nullified by it." The Swedes were especially embittered by the extravagant statement in the same sentence that "the Catholics will not come to a permanent agreement with the Protestants concerning church lands, and can tolerate the Protestants only in the sense that Jews, usurers, and prostitutes are endured."[47]

In a long session of the Protestant and imperial negotiations

[44] Meiern, *op. cit.*, IV, 654; Steinberger, *op. cit.*, p. 76.

[45] Braunsberger, *Petric Canisii Epistolae*, V, 229–55; Braunsberger, *Petrus Canisius, ein Lebensbild*, pp. 162–65; Metzler, *Der Heilige Petrus Canisius und die Neuerer seiner Zeit*, p. 34; Drews, *Petrus Canisius, der erste deutsche Jesuit*, pp. 121–23; Steinberger, *op. cit.*, p. 76; Baumgarten, in Wetzer and Welte, *Kirchenlexikon*, II, 1796; Benrath, in Herzog-Hauck, *Realencyklopädie*, III, 709. See also above, chap. iii.

[46] Steinberger, *op. cit.*, p. 76.

[47] *Judicium theologicum*, sec. II, point IX, par. III; Conring, *op. cit.*, II, 513; Meiern *op. cit.*, IV, 34; Steinberger, *op. cit.*, pp. 76–77.

at Osnabrück devoted to a consideration of ecclesiastical differences (February 16, 1647),[48] the Saxe-Altenburg representative, Wolfgang Konrad von Thumbshirn, urged that an inquisition be instituted against the author of the "malicious pamphlet" (*Judicium theologicum*);[49] and one of the most irreconcilable Protestants, Heinrich Langenbeck, the representative of Brunswick-Lüneburg-Celle, complained that the *Judicium theologicum* was "worse than the 'Dillingen Book,' " and "even annuls the Peace of Augsburg."[50]

6. THE MODERATE CATHOLICS AND WANGNERECK

Not only were the Protestants fearful of the nullifying influence of Wangnereck's writings, but the moderate Catholics manifested the same concern. They saw clearly that a spirit of conciliation and a willingness to yield to the demands of the Protestants, who were still in control of superior forces, were absolute essentials if peace were ever to be achieved. At the same session of February 16, 1647, Count Trauttmannsdorff, the conciliatory imperial ambassador, in responding to the remarks of von Thumbshirn and Langenbeck, called the "*Judicium theologicum* a bacchanalian work" (the writing of a drunken man).[51] According to another account,[52] Trauttmannsdorff is said to have remarked that this work is made up of "scholastic stupidities." On another occasion, in June, 1647, when the disturbing influence of all of Wangnereck's writings was being discussed by Trauttmannsdorff before the assembled Catholic representatives at Münster, he urged them not to delay the conclusion of peace, and to keep in mind the thwarting influence of "all kinds of scholastic disputations," whereby he undoubtedly meant the various works of Wangnereck.[53] Later, in September,

[48] Meiern, *op. cit.*, IV, 56–77. [49] *Ibid.*, p. 73; Steinberger, *op. cit.*, p. 77.

[50] Meiern, *Acta pacis*, IV, 74; Steinberger, *op. cit.*, pp. 11, 29, 77.

[51] Meiern, *op. cit.*, IV, 74; Steinberger, *op. cit.*, p. 77.

[52] Steinberger, *op. cit.*, p. 77, n. 7. Benedict Carpzov, *Discussio brevis*, fol. 2*b* (which I have not seen).

[53] Meiern, *op. cit.*, IV, 622–23; Pfanner, *Historia pacis*, p. 455; Steinberger, *op. cit.*, pp. 91–92.

1647, when a group of moderate Catholics (from Bavaria, Salzburg, Bamberg, Würzburg, Mainz, and Cologne) were endeavoring to consolidate the peace prospects created by Bavaria's giving up her armistice with Sweden and again allying with the emperor, Volmar, who had succeeded Trauttmannsdorff as imperial representative at the Congress, said that the "*Judicium theologicum*, the *Vehiculum*, and *Ponderatio*, were chiefly raillery [*cavillationes*] and foolish dreams."[54] The ideas of Trauttmannsdorff and Volmar were in harmony with those of the imperial court at Vienna, where there was a readiness to make great concessions to the Protestants;[55] above all, at the Vienna court there had been an ill temper owing to the assertion of "Ernestus de Eusebiis" that the emperor and the imperial states had no right to dipose of the ecclesiastical lands through such a peace treaty.[56] The father confessor of Empress Maria, the Capuchin Father Quiroga, in expressing an opinion concerning the *Judicium theologicum*, said of Wangnereck, "according to my judgment he is not a theologian and not a politician [*politicus*]."[57] At this date, the year 1647, it was not known who "Ernestus de Eusebiis" was.

The person that was responsible for taking definite action against Wangnereck was Maximilian of Bavaria. His Jesuit theologian, Johann Vervaux, had persuaded him that he and Emperor Ferdinand III might sign a peace prejudicial to Catholic interests because necessity demanded it, but that, if better times should ultimately return, the concessions made to the heretics need no longer be observed.[58] Inasmuch as Maximilian held such equivocal views, and since he was leader of the moderate Catholics, who earnestly wished peace, he found the writ-

[54] Sattler, *Geschichte des Herzogthums Würtenberg* (*sic*), VIII, 205; Steinberger, *op. cit.*, p. 77; Duhr, *op. cit.*, II, Part I, 474.

[55] Steinberger, *op. cit.*, pp. 24–25, 36–37, 39–40, 58–59, 77.

[56] *Judicium theologicum*, sec. III, point V; sec. IV, point IV; Conring, *op. cit.*, II, 496, 500–501; Steinberger, *op. cit.*, p. 77, n. 10; p. 78.

[57] Steinberger, *op. cit.*, p. 78, n. 4.

[58] *Ibid.*, p. 91, n. 4, quotes letters of Chigi to the papal secretary of state, dated Münster, October 4 and November 15, 1647; see also *ibid.*, pp. 196, 197.

ings of this unknown "Ernestus de Eusebiis" a block to successful peace negotiations.[59] When in January, 1648, Maximilian learned through Vervaux that it was Wangnereck, head of the Jesuit mission at Lindau, who was producing these peace-blocking writings,[60] he decided to take action. On January 3, 1648, he wrote a letter to Caraffa, the general of the Society of Jesus. After having called attention to the injuries that were threatened to the general welfare and to the Society of Jesus by writings of the type of the *Judicium theologicum*, he asked the general to take steps to hold Wangnereck in check.[61] Caraffa was in a dilemma. He himself was an opportunist and acted as a moderate Catholic;[62] he undoubtedly agreed with his predecessor, Vitelleschi, general of the Order from 1615 to 1645, who, after reading Wangnereck's *Quaestio ardua*, commended its author for his erudite work but requested that for the good of the Order the pamphlet remain unpublished.[63] Maximilian was a generous patron of the Jesuit Order; not to heed his urgent request that Wangnereck's pen be made inactive might lead to unpleasant consequences. On the other hand, Caraffa did not wish to offend his immediate superior, Pope Innocent X, and Chigi, who did not wish Wangnereck's useful political activities curtailed.[64] So Caraffa instructed Keppler, the provincial of Upper Germany, to deprive Wangnereck of his office, send him elsewhere, and keep him from writing any more pamphlets.[65] But papal influence forced Caraffa to revoke his orders; and moreover, because Innocent X was displeased with Vervaux's *Notae in Judicium theologicum*, Caraffa had to demand an accounting from Vervaux, who soon assured the Jesuit general that he would refrain from further polemical writing; this statement was sent by Caraffa to the papal Curia.[66]

[59] *Ibid.*, p. 132. [60] *Ibid.*, p. 132, n. 4; p. 133.

[61] *Ibid.*, pp. 133, 198 (contains Maximilian's letter to Caraffa).

[62] *Ibid.*, pp. 99–100; Pastor, *op. cit.*, XIV, Part I, 84, n. 4, and 85.

[63] Steinberger, *op. cit.*, pp. 32, 195. [64] *Ibid.*, pp. 136–38.

[65] *Ibid.*, pp. 134-35; Pastor, *op. cit.*, XIV, Part I, 84.

[66] Steinberger, *op. cit.*, pp. 136–38.

Maximilian, being a good politician, bowed to the papal rebuff. But when in November, 1648, he finally became aware of Wangnereck's *Responsum theologicum*, perhaps nine months after its publication,[67] he was deeply hurt.[68] Wangnereck was still permitted to write, whereas Vervaux's pen had been stopped. Wangnereck's new treatise assailed Vervaux's opinions and accused him of bad faith; but what was still worse, it attacked Maximilian's peaceful policies, especially the signing of the Treaty of Ulm in March, 1647, with France and Sweden, and the conciliatory policy that Maximilian and the other moderate Catholics had been following ever since.[69] Maximilian felt that quick action must be taken. The treaties of Münster and Osnabrück had been signed October 24, 1648; the circulation of such polemical works as the *Responsum theologicum* would undermine the confidence necessary to execute the treaties. The Congress of Münster was still in session; and on November 18, 1648, Maximilian wrote to Johann Philipp von Schönborn, Archbishop of Mainz, expressing his feeling that the whole situation should be presented not merely to the plenipotentiaries of the emperor and the moderate Catholic states but also to the Protestants. The Protestants should be assured of the willingness of the Catholic states to treat the *Responsum theologicum* in harmony with the provisions of that article of both treaties of Münster and Osnabrück, which punishes, as a breach of the Peace, every attack on the finally achieved work of conciliation.[70] The elector Johann Philipp von Schönborn in his answer of November 20, 1648, stated that he was in fundamental agreement with Maximilian, and went a step further in declaring that the *Responsum theologicum* contained "just those hos-

[67] *Ibid.*, pp. 112–13, 138–39. [68] *Ibid.*, p. 115.

[69] *Ibid.*, pp. 115–16, 138–40, 200–201.

[70] *Ibid.*, pp. 141–43. Peace of Münster, par. 114, in Walther, *Universal-Register*, p. lxxxv; Peace of Osnabrück, Art. XVII, par. 4, in Walther, *ibid.*, p. xliii. "Those that act contrary to this transaction or common peace through counsel of deed, or resist the execution and restitution . . . . , whether they be ecclesiastical or secular, should be subject to the imperial laws regulating a breach of peace," which means, should be placed under the ban (Gundling, *Vollständiger Discours über den westphalischen Frieden*, p. 586).

tile dogmas and presuppositions that are repugnant to the principles of our faith and religion," a viewpoint that was held against him by the ultra-Catholics for a long time afterward. This was what Johann Philipp thought in theory. But in practice he held that the decision should be postponed until a full clarity of view had been attained, inasmuch as Bishop Franz Wilhelm von Osnabrück and others of the extreme Catholic princes were involved in the matter; as a consequence, Maximilian finally declared himself in agreement with the policy of playing a waiting game, as his Mainz colleague desired.[71]

In Maximilian's letter to Johann Philipp he shows himself more as an experienced practical politician who does not wish, by rigid theory, to jeopardize anew the work of many years of costly labor. But on November 19, 1648, in a letter of complaint which he addressed to Caraffa, the general of the Society of Jesus, he shows, above all, what deep wounds his pride had suffered. In words of bitterness and irritation, and with the greatest emphasis, he demands an exemplary punishment for the Lindau superior, "this exceedingly bold person." His words seem like an ultimatum; if this outrageous insult were not effaced in good time, Maximilan's treatment of the Order would be in accordance with its deserts. A list of the offending passages in the *Responsum theologicum* (a compilation of Vervaux) accompanied the letter.[72] Caraffa, realizing that Maximilian was in dead earnest, and fearing similar protests from John Philipp von Schönborn and the emperor, visualized that the *Responsum theologicum* might be publicly burned in one or more places by the common hangman and a copy suspended from the gallows, the worst treatment that could be given any literary production.[73] To avoid such injury to the reputation of the Society of Jesus and to Wangnereck, Caraffa had Wangnereck imprisoned temporarily, deprived him of his active and passive vote in the Society, and forced him to beg Maximilian's pardon for the offense inflicted.[74] Wangnereck pacified Maximilian by

[71] Steinberger, *op. cit.*, p. 143.

[72] *Ibid.*, pp. 143–45, 200–201.

[73] *Ibid.*, p. 145.

[74] *Ibid.*, p. 146, n. 4, and p. 202.

affirming that the offensive part of the *Responsum theologicum* had been inserted by an unknown hand;[75] but his short incarceration terminated abruptly in February, 1649, through the interference of Innocent X and Chigi.[76] Wangnereck never completed the writing of his so-called *Apologeticum*, although 210 pages had been written; moreover, its publication never took place, having been prevented by a higher authority.[77] However, he planned a visit to Rome, which could, in the mind of Maximilian, be quite as dangerous, for he would be able to influence the papacy to take action against the Peace of Westphalia; and in response to Maximilian's request, the new general of the Society of Jesus, Francesco Piccolomini (1582–1651), who had succeeded Caraffa in December, 1649, although kindly disposed toward Wangnereck, postponed his mission to the papal Curia.[78] The year 1650 was still a time of uncertainty with reference to the stability of the Peace; it was not until June, 1650, that the arrangements were completed at Nürnberg for the full execution of the terms of the Westphalian settlement.[79] But that action did not clearly settle the question of the moral admissibility of the Peace. Pope Innocent X on August 20, 1650, ordered that his protest *Zelo Domus Dei* be issued against the Peace by all the nuncios.[80] Under the circumstances it is easy to understand why Maximilian was still worried, when in the first half of the year 1651 Wangnereck succeeded in getting to Rome in an official capacity and discussed, with Cardinal Capponi, means of strengthening the Catholic church in Germany; such action meant undermining the treaties of peace. It is also known that Wangnereck spoke unfavorably of his antagonist Caramuel to the members of the papal court.[81]

This discussion shows clearly how both the Protestants and the moderate Catholics feared the influence of the ardent and intemperate Wangnereck in combating the peace terms that only long wearisome negotiations had made possible. The mod-

[75] *Ibid.*, pp. 149–50.

[76] *Ibid.*, pp. 151–54.

[77] *Ibid.*, pp. 130, 155–57, 182.

[78] *Ibid.*, pp. 159–60.

[79] *Cambridge Modern History*, IV, 415.

[80] Pastor, *op. cit.*, XIV, Part I, 99.

[81] Steinberger, *op. cit.*, pp. 164–65.

erate Catholics, who made the ultimate signing of peace possible, he regarded as his main enemies. Of them he says: "What is said of them can be taught, but it is only academic wisdom; practical counsels and theologians are now needed."[82] He surely regarded himself as one of the practical theologians; but the verdict of history has gone against him. The changes of time required concessions to the new principles of government. He did not understand the new principle of state and national sovereignty. He was of German birth, had lived all his life in Germany, but had no German feeling; as his opponent Caramuel asserted, "he has no consideration for the distress of Germany, which he does not love."[83] The German Jesuit historian, Bernhard Duhr, writing in the twentieth century, and commenting on the *Responsum theologicum*, remarks that one can see

> what confusion and harm must result from adhering to medieval viewpoints in completely changed conditions. When only the Catholic religion existed, such fundamental principles could be defended; but as soon as the force of circumstances had helped the non-Catholic confessions to secure great and permanent possessions, it was no longer possible to adhere to these views if one did not wish to proclaim a general war and place into the hands of the other confessions weapons with which to fight the Catholics. If, according to the views of Wangnereck, the Catholics may not conclude a permanent peace with the Protestants, the Protestants must expect that the Catholics could break every peace as soon as they secured power enough to feel justified in repressing the Protestants with the prospects of success.[84]

[82] *Judicium theologicum*, sec. II, point X; Conring, *op. cit.*, II, 495.

[83] Caramuel, *Sacri Romani Imperii Pax* (1648 ed.), p. 97, No. 99.

[84] Duhr, *op. cit.*, II, Part I, 482.

Chapter Sixteen

THE CONTEMPORARY CONTROVERSIAL LITERATURE: PART III. THE OPPONENTS OF WANGNERECK

1. THE MODERATE CATHOLIC LITERARY OPPONENTS OF WANGNERECK

THE best known of Wangnereck's writings was the *Judicium theologicum;* it also did the cause of peace the most injury. It was the task of the moderate Catholic writers to weaken or, if possible, to destroy the influence of this work. The first moderate Catholic writers to attack the extremist ideas was the Spanish Johann Caramuel y Lobkowitz (1606–83), originally a member of the Cistercian Order, later a Benedictine. He was an ambitious person and had received many offices and much recognition for his services to the Roman Catholic church, including the important position of suffragan bishop (*Weihbischof*) of Mainz. Since 1645 he had been an agent of Philipp IV of Spain at the court of Vienna, where he became court preacher and court counselor in 1646. His services were so satisfactory that the emperor bestowed two rich Benedictine abbeys on him—Montserrat-Emaus in Prague, and another in Vienna. Although Caramuel was an ardent opponent of heresy and a strong supporter of the Roman Catholic church, he used his great learning and independence of thought in answering the *Judicium theologicum* in such a way as to justify Ferdinand III and Maximilian of Bavaria in concluding a peace that involved the toleration of heretics and the cession of church lands.[1]

[1] Steinberger, *Die Jesuiten und die Friedensfrage*, pp. 17, 77–84, 105, n. 1; Stieve, in *Allgemeine deutsche Biographie*, III, 780; Kaulen, in Wetzer and Welte, *Encyclopädie*,

Caramuel's work appeared in the early months of 1648 under the title *Sacri Romani Imperii Pax licita demonstrata*,[2] i.e., "The Peace of the Holy Roman Empire Presented as Legal." This work had been ready to print as early as the spring of 1647 but did not appear, owing to the opposition of Anselm Kasimir, electoral archbishop of Mainz, and the nuncio Fabio Chigi.[3] But after the death of Anselm in October, 1647, it was possible to have the work published in the spring of 1648. At first it appeared anonymously and without place of publication, but later in the year it appeared in a second edition with additions; a third edition appeared in 1649, somewhat revised. In the second and third editions his name was affixed, as was the place of publication, Frankfurt.[4] Copies soon reached the courts of the princes and were circulated at Münster and Osnabrück. Since the purpose of the work was to create a sentiment for peace in opposition to the influence of the *Judicium theologicum*, it naturally offended the nuncio and the extreme Catholics, who called Caramuel, along with Vervaux, a "half-heretic," reserving the label "absolute heretic" for the Protestant Dorscheus.[5] But Conring, a Protestant writing with a specific purpose, commended the work.[6]

In the *Pax licita*[7] Caramuel maintains that the proposed Peace of Westphalia is not a usurpation of authority that is not granted the emperor and the other princes. Existing circumstances compel the princes to make concessions to heresy and cede church lands to heretics, just as similar circumstances had led to the signing of the Peace of Augsburg, which was also a

---

II, 1934; Paquot, *Mémoires pour servir à l'histoire littéraire des dix-sept provinces des Pays-Bas*, II, 175–85; Tabaraud, in Michaud, *Biographie universelle*, VI, 651–53.

[2] A second and third edition appeared in the course of the year 1648. Steinberger, *op. cit.*, p. 82, n. 4, and p. 84.

[3] Steinberger, *op. cit.*, pp. 79–80.

[4] *Ibid.*, pp. 80–84, 129.

[5] *Ibid.*, pp. 82–84, 105. For Dorcheus, see below, next section.

[6] Conring, *Opera*, VI, 620: "Commendo quoque, Caramuelis librum, de pace licita, numquam hie liber iterum execudetur."

[7] Caramuel, pp. 209–21, Nos. 332–35; citations are to the third and enlarged edition of the year 1648. See the second title under Caramuel in the Bibliography.

compromise peace. He affirms that, since the power of the Protestants is so very great, and will not grow less, to refuse to make the concessions demanded now may easily result in even greater losses to the Catholics later. He asserts that, since Catholic subjects have the right to migrate from Protestant lands to Catholic lands, the Peace of Augsburg and the Peace of Westphalia actually liberated Catholics from heresy, instead of turning them over to heresy, as "Eusebiis" wrongly affirms. He asserts that the emperor is acting wisely when inserting the clause in the Treaty whereby he renounces all right of disregarding the promises of the Treaty. If he refused to insert this clause, the Protestants, who wish a lasting peace, would not sign a treaty at all. He affirms that the church lands are a constituent part of the German sovereign dominion and belong to the princes. The emperor may turn over to the heretics some church lands that he cannot protect; by so doing he is protecting the church against probably greater losses. Finally, the emperor needs no papal authority to dispose of church lands; he acts on the basis of divine and natural laws, and now especially he needs no permission of any kind when he is granting what he cannot prevent.

Caramuel's treatise was not a logical or consistent argument in all its parts; but it was essentially what Ferdinand III desired, the argument of a devout Catholic which supported a policy of concessions to heretics at the expense of the church in order to secure peace. Furthermore (although not stated by Caramuel), it implied a policy of protecting the Hapsburgs against the eventuality of ceding their own personal possessions to the victorous enemies.[8]

Another moderate Catholic writer, who was even more modern in his viewpoint, was Johannes Vervaux (1585–1661), who had come to the Bavarian court in 1631 as father confessor of the electress Elisabeth; since 1635 he acted in the same capacity for Maximilian.[9] In spite of the statutes of the Jesuit Order to the contrary, he engaged in a widely ramified political activity in

[8] Steinberger, *op. cit.*, pp. 78–79. [9] *Ibid.*, p. 20.

the service of his prince,[10] whose full confidence he possessed. Maximilian gave him the right freely to express his opinions on a wide range of subjects, but Vervaux kept in mind the sensitive princely pride of his ruler and was cautious not to give advice contrary to the elector's views. But we must remember that whatever Vervaux did and wrote was a matter of conviction and that he and Maximilian were kindred spirits.[11] Vervaux, having been born in Lorraine, found it easy to advise Maximilian to adopt a policy enabling him to co-operate politically with France, even though France were the ally of Sweden and the German Protestants.[12] Maximilian had used Vervaux in the preliminary and final negotiations resulting in the signing of the Treaty of Ulm in March, 1647, by Bavaria, France, and Sweden.[13] That treaty being signed, Vervaux, as spiritual counselor of Maximilian, advocated that it be used as a stepping-stone to a general peace.[14] When it became necessary for Maximilian to break the armistice with Sweden in September, 1647, Vervaux advised that he continue the alliance with France.[15] His whole policy was entirely in accord with that of his master; he wished to enable Maximilian to secure terms of peace favorable to Bavaria with the aid of France, Sweden, and the Protestants, and to induce the Catholic princes, especially Emperor Ferdinand III, to make compromises toward peaceful ends. This policy is reflected in his writings, and as a consequence the extreme Catholics regarded him as injuring real Catholic interests.[16]

Vervaux's part in the literary conflict of the Westphalian Peace era falls in the second half of the year 1647 and consists of two pamphlets written at the request of Maximilian and appearing under the common title *Notae in Consilium theologicum*, and having the special titles (1) *Notae Communes seu primae* and (2) *Notae particulares seu secundae bezw.* [*beziehungsweise*]

[10] *Ibid.*, pp. 20–21.

[11] *Ibid.*, pp. 21–22.

[12] *Ibid.*, pp. 21–22.

[13] *Ibid.*, pp. 25, 40–48.

[14] *Ibid.*, pp. 93–94, 97–98.

[15] *Ibid.*, pp. 98–99.

[16] *Ibid.*, pp. 99–100, 104, 118, 119; Pfülf, "Ein Beitrag, etc.," *Stimmen aus Maria-Laach, Katholische Blätter*, LVI, 528–34.

Arcana.[17] This work appeared in the garb of a theological opinion; it was never printed except when the *Notae Communes* were incorporated in the *Responsum theologicum* to enable Wangnereck to combat them.[18] This writing of Vervaux was prepared to enable Maximilian to have a clear view of the peace-hindering work of Wangnereck and also to distribute copies to the Catholic plenipotentiaries whom Maximilian wished to influence in favor of an early peace. The pamphlet was distributed secretly only to Catholics, but probably through the indiscretion of a Catholic diplomat it was not wholly unknown in the Protestant camp.[19] Although it did not cause the extreme Catholics to change their attitude, it was a factor in giving the moderate Catholics a program with which to oppose the unconciliatory views of Wangnereck.[20] The copy used by the author was among the Westphalian Peace papers of the Austrian plenipotentiary, Dr. Johann Crane, and is today found in the Vienna archives.[21] The title of this particular copy reads *Notae in Consilium* [=*Judicium*] *Theologicum Ernesti de Eusebiis super Quaestione an Pax Qualem desiderant Protestantes sit secundam se illicita.* It is written by at least four, possibly five, different copyists, who probably worked in shifts under pressure to combat the antipeace activities of Wangnereck through his writings. The *Notae* appeared anonymously; that Vervaux is the author has been learned from the reports of the nuncio Chigi to the papal secretary of state Panciroli.[22]

To us the significance of the *Notae* lies in about three of the sentence headings, which Vervaux amplifies, usually briefly; these headings are quite modern, when contrasted with the medieval views of Wangnereck, which the *Notae* were supposed to combat.

Nota V says: "The heretics are infamous on the basis of divine law; to deny that the Protestants are infamous is not a

[17] Steinberger, *op. cit.*, pp. 67, 101–2, 111, 173.

[18] *Ibid.*, p. 112.

[19] *Ibid.*, pp. 102–4, 173–74.

[20] *Ibid.*, pp. 103–4, 120.

[21] Cod. Vindob. 15154, fol. 659*a*–74*a*; see Steinberger, *op. cit.*, p. 173.

[22] Steinberger, *op. cit.*, pp. 173–74.

direct co-operation with heresy."[23] Nota VIII: "To defend non-Catholics is nothing evil in itself."[24] But a modern person cannot agree with Vervaux when he says in Nota IV, paragraph 3, that "the peace that is guaranteed the heretics is not permanent or absolute, but is a peace that can become only transitory."[25] Although this sentence is "reprehensible" (*verwerflich*) as Steinberger says, it undoubtedly contributed much toward easing the conscience of the pious Maximilian, who in this case of extreme necessity had to make a peace that did great injury to the Catholic church but could, when conditions changed advantageously in the future, be abrogated.[26] However we may judge Vervaux's *Notae*, they were a factor in securing the co-operation of Maximilian and other Catholic princes in negotiating a peace that produced the secularization of politics. On the other hand, they offended the nuncio Chigi, especially on account of the sentence that the emperor in the face of necessity could take for granted the consent of the Holy See to the ceding of ecclesiastical lands.[27]

2. THE PROTESTANT OPPONENTS OF WANGNERECK

During the critical negotiations at Münster and Osnabrück there appeared many pamphlets by Protestants, who attacked the extreme views of Wangnereck and aimed to bring about an early and permanent peace. We shall content ourselves with discussion of the writings of only two of these Protestant controversialists: Johann Georg Dorsche (1597–1659) and Hermann Conring (1606–81).

In the years 1647 and 1648 appeared four treatises by Dorsche (Dorscheus), a Lutheran preacher and polemical writer on theology, of Strassburg, who combated with equal bitterness both Catholics and Calvinists.[28] He was especially ardent in attack-

[23] *Responsum theologicum*, pp. 37–38.

[24] *Ibid.*, p. 68.

[25] *Ibid.*, pp. 18–19.

[26] Steinberger, *op. cit.*, p. 91 and n. 4.

[27] *Responsum theologicum*, pp. 99, 103, 115–16, 156; Steinberger, *op. cit.*, p. 104, n. 6.

[28] Steinberger, *op. cit.*, p. 105; Holtzmann and Krause, "Dorsche," *Allgemeine deutsche Biographie*, V, 363.

ing the writings of "Ernestus de Eusebiis," and was the only one among the Protestant writers that did not try to protect himself by resorting to anonymity or pseudonymity.[29] The most important of his four treatises, for our purposes, is entitled: *Anticrisis theologica, opposita Judico theologico Ernest de Eusebiis . . . . super Quaestione: An pax qualem desiderant Protestantes sit secundum se illicita?*[30] This treatise and three others on the subject (all similar in content), must have been in completed form in manuscript at the end of the year 1647.[31] The papal nuncio Chigi thought he discovered that Dorsche's publications corresponded in thought and even language with Vervaux's *Notae.* Chigi held that in Dorsche's work Catholic interests were being injured by a Protestant who was applying Catholic doctrines, that is, those of the moderate Catholics, of whom Chigi disapproved.[32] The writings of Dorsche seem to have had a certain influence; at least the nuncio Chigi in his report of March 6, 1648, speaks of the writings of Dorsche and urged Wangnereck to answer him briefly, an action that was left, however, to another hand, Father Melchior Cornaeus.[33]

Dorsche appeals to historic precedent to refute the assertion of Ernestus de Eusebiis that the secular powers were usurping a power they did not possess in negotiating the Treaty of Westphalia. He builds up an argument favoring the secularization of politics, showing that in past times the secular rulers had the right to deal with ecclesiastical affairs. Charles V and Ferdinand I were supported by good ecclesiastical opinion in believing that, as emperors, they had the right to call church councils to regulate matters of religion; moreover, they were acting within their rights when signing the Peace of Augsburg. The German ecclesiastical princes had sustained this view. Dorsche commented further that thus far there had been no absolutely

[29] Steinberger, *op. cit.*, p. 108.

[30] Haag, *La France protestante*, V, 463; Backer and Sommervogel, *Bibliothèque des écrivains*, VIII, 983.

[31] Steinberger, *op. cit.*, p. 108.

[32] *Ibid.*, p. 109.

[33] *Ibid.*, p. 102, n. 3, and p. 109.

clear opinion as to who had final authority over church lands. Certainly such authority could not be based on canon law. It was fully as correct to assume that secular rulers had jurisdiction in 1647 and 1648 over church lands because the existing distressed conditions granted the emperor and the imperial states a certain authority over church matters. According to the ideas of Pope Innocent III the emperor and the imperial states were not under obligation to ask papal advice in all affairs. Just as under certain circumstances a tax may be levied on ecclesiasts without the sanction of the pope, just so a cession of church lands might take place.[34]

There is no evidence that Dorsche influenced Catholics to accept his views, but he gave a theological and philosophical justification to the Protestant princes in insisting on the execution of their program.

Of all the Protestant treatises written against the *Judicium theologicum*, the most significant was that of Hermann Conring (1606–81), the most learned polyhistor of the seventeenth century.[35] He was not only an evangelical theologian of wide reputation, but he held successively chairs of natural philosophy, of medicine, and of politics at the University of Helmstedt, in Brunswick-Lüneburg, where he remained from 1620 until his death in 1681. He was also a physician of wide experience, a counselor to the queen of Sweden, to the Duke of Brunswick, and to the king of Denmark. His literary activity embraced many fields of human knowledge; he wrote important works on medicine, anatomy, political economy, theology, and jurisprudence; he is called the founder of the history of German law.[36] He also played a determinative part in the era of literary controversy here considered. He held that the broad religious and political claims of the pope were not substantiated in the original sources of ecclesiastical history and the works of the church fathers; he rejected

[34] Dorsche, *Anticrisis theologica*, pp. 42–56.

[35] Henke, in Herzog-Hauck, *Realencyklopädie*, IV, 267.

[36] Stobbe, *Hermann Conring, der Begründer der deutschen Rechtsgeschichte*, pp. 7–8; H. Bresslau, *Allgemeine deutsche Biographie*, IV, 446–51.

the infallibility of the church and the pope and the vicegerency (*Staathalterschaft*) of the pope; he thought papal intervention or meddling (*Einmischung*) in state affairs threatened the freedom of the German Empire.[37] He wrote a work entitled *Pro pace perpetua Protestantibus danda Consultatio Catholica: Auctore Irenaes Eubolo, Theologo Austriaco.*[38] In the Preface of the 1657 edition of this work he states that before he had written the *Consultatio Catholica* he had read all the important controversial literature on the subject, the *Judicium theologicum* of "Ernestus de Eusebiis," the *Vehiculum Judicii theologici*, the *Responsum theologicum*, the *Instrumenti Pacis Ponderatio*, and others of this kind.[39]

The *Consultatio Catholica* is regarded quite generally as having contributed greatly to the promotion of the conclusion of the Peace of Westphalia.[40] The great influence of the work is accounted for by the fact that he resorted to a literary trick; in the first place the title of the book indicated supposedly that it was written by a Catholic, as did the use of the term "heretic" in alluding to the Protestants; in the second place, the pseudonym indicated that the author was an Austrian theologian, and therefore a Catholic. This latter device was used by Conring especially in consideration of the yielding spirit that had already been manifested concerning the Protestant demands in the peace negotiations by the Vienna court, supported by the opinion of its theologians. Actually the "Austrian theologian" was not a Catholic at all, much less a Catholic theologian. In the Preface to the 1657 edition of the *Consultatio Catholica* Conring apologizes for the use of this trick because he knew that any treatise coming frankly from the pen of a Protestant would have no influence on the Catholics, whom he was, above all, anxious

37 Stobbe, *op. cit.*, pp. 32–33.

38 Conring, *op. cit.*, II, 472–90.

39 *Ibid.*, p. 470. This is Conring's statement in 1657; the last two works mentioned appeared, however, in 1648 after Conring had published the *Consultatio Catholica.*

40 Steinberger, *op. cit.*, pp. 123–25; J. P. Niceron, *Mémoires pour servir à l'histoire des hommes illustrés dans la république des lettres*, XIX, 260; Backer and Sommervogel, *op. cit.*, VIII, 983, quotes Niceron; V. Placius, *Theatrum anonymorum et pseudonymorum*, pseud. No. 966.

to persuade to accept a conciliatory and permanent peace.[41] No matter how capable the arguments presented by a Protestant, they would be lost on individuals of Catholic sympathies. A Protestant might just as well save his energies. So to Conring the end justfied the deceitful means.

The writing of the *Consultatio Catholica* occurred in the last week of 1647 in strict secrecy. At first it was circulated only in manuscript copies in Münster and Osnabrück, among all groups favoring peace. Later, in 1648, it was published through Jacob Lampadius, the representative of Brunswick-Lüneburg, who was a friend of Conring. Conring asserted that Lampadius had arranged for the publication of the treatise without knowing who the real author was.[42] Steinberger doubts the possibility of this; he thinks that Conring, like many Catholic writers, such as Wangnereck, Caramuel, Vervaux, and Cornaeus, wrote at the order of someone in authority, presumably the Duke of Brunswick-Lüneburg.[43] Another historian, Grauert, asserts that Conring was commissioned by Ferdinand III to refute the protest of Innocent X, in order to prove to the Roman court that its protest would be fruitless.[44]

In the introduction to the *Consultatio Catholica* it was stated that, although there was a difference of opinion among many respected Catholic rulers concerning the establishment of a permanent peace with heretics, and although some very important Catholic theologians declared that such a peace was not permitted, he himself, Ireneus Eubolus, the Austrian theologian, felt that the best interests of Germany, and especially of the Catholic church, were dependent solely on the early conclusion of a conciliatory peace.[45] He opposed Wangnereck's general idea that the secular rulers were usurping power when they dealt with matters of heresy and church property.[46] He offered a new

[41] *Opera*, II, 470–71; Steinberger, *op. cit.*, p. 123.

[42] *Opera*, II, 470; Steinberger, *op. cit.*, p. 124.

[43] Steinberger, *op. cit.*, p. 124.

[44] Grauert, *Christina, Königinn von Schweden*, I, 252, cites Conring, *op. cit.*, II, 531 ff.

[45] Conring, *op. cit.*, II, 473.

[46] *Ibid.*, pp. 483–84.

political justification for the acts of the emperor and the imperial princes, and showed them how they might have peace, preserve their secular interests, and still remain good Catholics. He stressed the supreme interests of the state, asserted the divine-right-of-kings theory, affirmed that the emperor and princes had legal authority to determine everything necessary for the existence of civil society, and that this authority was given them by God. Wangnereck did the princes an injustice when he asserted that they "were usurping a jurisdiction that did not belong to them," for the German church must, under all circumstances, recognize these rulers as princes and judges constituted for the church by God. Whoever rejected that, sinned against majesty (committed lèse majesté).

The princes, in establishing the proposed peace, were not exceeding the limits of their authority. They were assuming no power over spiritual affairs; such matters were left wholly in the hands of the ecclesiasts. The civil rulers, as protectors of the civil rights of all subjects, were, in drawing up the Treaty, merely using their legal rights to protect heretics and the Catholic church against injustice, which power must rest solely in secular hands, otherwise that power cannot function successfully.

Since that was a time of confusion and distress, there was great public need for the princes to take measures that limited ecclesiastical jurisdiction concerning temporal affairs; but there would be no suspension of the spiritual jurisdiction of the bishops. The bishops were now being deprived merely of secular jurisdiction, which had been granted them by the arbitrary laws of the princes in former centuries. The princes were now under the stress of circumstances, merely resuming their powers in these secular respects.

If, as "Ernestus de Eusebiis" contended, the lands of the German church were subject to the church and the pope as supreme administrator, the emperor and the imperial states had no actual control over these lands. This would be a nullification of the entire German system of government, and was therefore scandalous. (Such a statement was an appeal to the spirit of political independence of the secular powers.)

The ecclesiastical princes, when they lost control over heretics and church properties, were giving up merely civil rights, not spiritual or divine powers. These civil powers had originally been granted by the secular powers, which through the Treaty were merely resuming their original authority over secular affairs. He clinchingly added, "When discussing this point we should always remember the words of the Savior, 'Render unto Caesar that which is Caesar's.' "

The rights of the church and religion rested on divine law. The bishops, besides being spiritual rulers, had also been secular princes, and as such had sovereign rights in the Holy Roman Empire; and they, like secular princes, could take secular measures concerning the church, but they were acting solely on the basis of princely law.

In view of these facts, papal consent to the proposed Peace was not necessary; the emperor and the princes, secular and ecclesiastical, had authority to make disposition of the purely temporal matters in question.[47]

Conring, a Protestant, writing under the mask of a Catholic, hoped to contribute to the conclusion and permanence of the Peace by persuading the moderate Catholics to regard the expediency of signing and observing the proposed compromise treaty terms. To accept his arguments, as the princes did in practice, meant that politics was secularized, that the secular authority determined what was secular and took measures to assert its authority. If, because of confused conditions, the state found it necessary to resume jurisdiction over affairs that had for a long time been looked after by ecclesiastics, the state was not usurping authority. It was merely making arrangements for the welfare of civil life and signing a peace providing for such resumption of its own authority.

In the mind of Conring the conclusion of the Peace was not necessarily a guaranty of its being observed, in the face of the

[47] *Ibid.*, p. 484.

papal protest made public in August, 1650.[48] In 1657 he published an argument against the breve (bull, as he calls it) *Zelo Domus Dei* of Innocent X. This argument was entitled *Animadversio in Bullam Innocenti X.*[49] In this work of eleven chapters he wrote more boldly than when he was writing with a pseudonym. He asserted that "a person, even if he is a Roman Catholic, is permitted, without prejudice to his faith, not to observe papal bulls, much more to reject them, because they are burdened with faults," "that the declaration of Innocent was unnecessary," "quite unusual," "without any precedent," "not useful even to the Roman Curia itself, whether for the present or the future," "is injurious to the Roman Catholic church itself and to the Catholic parts of Germany."[50] After condemning further aspects of the papal protest Conring added in the final chapter that "all that have any relations with Rome have the right with a clear conscience and, according to moral law, are obliged not to observe the bull of Innocent X."[51] In other words, the papacy, in protesting against the Peace of Westphalia, was interfering in affairs that were wholly in the hands of the secular rulers. In making the assertions in these two treatises Conring showed himself the most precise and advanced of all the political theorists.[52] He stated the theory of secularization of politics as it was put into practice in the middle of the seventeenth century and subsequently.

3. THE LITERARY CONTROVERSY AND THE SECULARIZATION OF POLITICS

In summary it should be pointed out that Wangnereck was stating the political ideals of a vanishing age in which papal supremacy had been asserted and enforced in all religious affairs and in many secular affairs as well. Standing for the legal prin-

[48] Pastor, *op. cit.*, XIV, Part I, 99.

[49] Full title in Bibliography. Conring, *op. cit.*, II, 517–66.

[50] Conring, *op. cit.*, II, chaps. i–iv, 517–33.

[51] *Ibid.*, II, 561–63.

[52] Schröckh, *Christliche Kirchengeschichte seit der Reformation*, III, 403, states: "Conrings Schrift . . . . gehört unter die vorzüglichern."

ciples of that age, he could not modify those principles to meet the needs of a new era in which secular interests were dominant. His support came from those having a vested interest in conditions as they had been for half a millennium. But his theories could not cope with the new theories more in harmony with the new conditions. Such ideas were offered by Caramuel and Vervaux; they made it possible for their sovereigns and moderate Catholic allies to feel that, as good Catholics, they were actually promoting the best interests of the church if they abandoned the rigid theories of the Middle Ages and adopted a more conciliatory, more adjustable, theory that would meet a situation that might be only temporary.

But Conring, the Protestant, writing as a Catholic, went further than either of them. He stated in a precise way that the state has authority in all affairs affecting the church except purely spiritual affairs, which has come to be the modern theory and practice. The state, which has supreme interests, must, in the face of a great public need, exercise ecclesiastical jurisdiction of a temporal kind, such as protecting the interests of both the Catholics and the heretics. The state has interests superior to those of doctrinal differences. He applied the theories of politics that existed before the times of Gregory VII and Innocent III. He once more widened the scope of politics, and also justified its secularization.

4. THE SECULARIZATION OF POLITICAL THEORY

The main purpose of this treatise has been to trace the secularization of politics in practice. This section is to present, with less detail, the parallel secularization of political theory, or the secularization of politics in theory.

As James Bryce has said: "The Middle Ages were essentially unpolitical."[53] But this does not mean that there were no medieval political theorists. There were many—Augustine, Thomas Aquinas, Dante, Marsiglio of Padua—to mention only the most outstanding. These and other medieval thinkers could not get

[53] Bryce, *Holy Roman Empire*, p. 91.

away from the idea that human society had a divine purpose, that one of its main functions was to promote or protect religion and morals, and that the head of the state was responsible to the Supreme Being. The political theorists held this view regardless of whether they believed in a universal state with the pope as head (all kings and princes being responsible to God through the pope) or held the divine-right-of-kings theory, which maintained that the secular rulers were responsible directly to God, not indirectly through the pope. Whether papalists or regalists, these theorists "believed firmly in the divine nature of the state; they looked upon the ruler as God's representative and servant, but only so far as he really in fact carried out the divine purpose of righteousness and justice."[54]

Beginning with Machiavelli (1469–1527), there appeared a number of theorists who did not regard politics as a branch of theology but who, following the theories of antiquity, regarded the state as an end in itself, with objectives that must be pursued regardless of theology or ecclesiastical demands. To consider the theories of all these thinkers would go beyond the convenient limits of this treatise. We shall need to content ourselves with a brief statement of the ideas of Machiavelli, Hobbes, and Grotius, with incidental references to others holding fundamentally similar views.

Niccolò Machiavelli was the first political theorist of modern times to be entirely secular in his methods and theories. The source of his political inspiration was antiquity, in which politics had been wholly secular. He took all his illustrations from classical antiquity, drawing little or nothing from medieval times, or canon law, or the history of the Christian nations. He dealt in a practical way with the problems and objectives of the secular ruler and the ways in which he should exercise power. Principles of religion and morality were relegated to a subordinate place in both theory and practice. He rejected the medieval idea of the

[54] Carlyle, *History of Medieval Political Theory in the West*, III, 181-83; Pollock, *History of the Science of Politics*, pp. 33–42; Murray, *The History of Political Science*, pp. 131–71; Allen, *A History of Political Thought*, pp. 1–444.

divine nature of the state; he ignored the conception that the secular ruler was God's representative and servant.[55]

To be sure, as a student of the theory and practice of government, he regarded religion as a potent social force, a restraining agency, and therefore an aid in governing a state. He recognized that established religious ceremonies must be held in veneration by the ruler.[56] But such considerations were merely those of expediency. The secular authority, whether a monarch or the council of a republic, was to exercise full power in its own right, with no dependence on any religious authority. The principles of government were to be based on experience, and should be of such nature as to insure the supporting good will of the subjects or citizens. There was to be no dependence on papal or ecclesiastical sanction.[57]

Machiavelli ignored the medieval attitude and boldly condemned the popes (1) for having advanced their own material interests, and those of their relatives, under cover of advancing church interests; (2) for having used questionable means in securing political advantages in Rome and Italy; (3) for neglecting the administration of religion, thus causing a decline in religious interest and a loss of papal influence in religious affairs; and (4) for having forsaken their chief interest, religion, and having tried to dominate politics in Italy, with the unfortunate result of keeping Italy divided and of preventing her union under either a prince or a republic, a development that would have precluded the domination of Italy by foreigners.[58] In his *Prince* Machiavelli lays down, on the basis of experience, the principles of action that must be followed by a prince if he is to succeed as a ruler. In ignoring all considerations of religion and morality (except as expedients) he produced a book that was "the most

[55] Kojouharoff, "Niccolò Machiavelli," *National University Law Review*, X, No. 2, 38–39, 53; Morley, *Miscellanies*, IV, 50.

[56] *Discorsi sopra la prima deca di Tito Livio*, Book I, chaps. xi and xii.

[57] *Ibid.*, chap. x.

[58] *Ibid.*, chap. xii; *Florentine History*, pp. 29–31; Kojouharoff, "Niccolò Machiavelli," *National University Law Review*, X, No. 2, pp. 38–39.

direct, concentrated, and unflinching contribution ever made to the secularization of politics."[59]

The greatest English disciple of Machiavelli was Thomas Hobbes (1588–1679). He was more systematic than Machiavelli and much more clear-cut and specific in developing the modern idea of secular sovereignty.[60] In a forceful style he advocated the principles of absolute sovereignty, probably being influenced in holding these views as a consequence of the Civil War and revolution that he witnessed in England. This revolution had ecclesiastical, as well as political, aspects; and he became convinced that religion as well as politics must be in the power of one person, the king.[61] He does not deal with continental or international affairs at all. He makes no reference to the problems arising out of the Thirty Years' War and the difficulties of negotiating peace, which led Conring to formulate the most significant arguments in favor of the secularization of political theory.[62] Hobbes's arguments and discussions are concerned with the powers of the sovereign, the British king.

In the *Leviathan* he maintained that the sovereign is absolute, not responsible to anyone—is judge of all that is necessary for the peace and defense of his subjects. The sovereign himself, or through his appointed officials, is judge of all opinions and doctrines, this being necessary to peace, to prevent discord and civil war. The sovereign has the right to decide all controversy.[63]

[59] Morley, *op. cit.*, IV, 50.

[60] Jean Bodin (1530–96) may be regarded as having contributed to the development of the secularization of political theory in so far as he founded the doctrine of the sovereignty of the secular state. But inasmuch as his doctrines are confused, incoherent, and inconsistent, and since he avoided any awkward considerations of papal influence in politics, we shall omit a discussion of his ideas in this treatise. For a justification of this decision the reader is referred to J. W. Allen, "Jean Bodin," in Hearnshaw (ed.), *The Social and Political Ideas of Some of the Great Thinkers of the Sixteenth and Seventeenth Centuries*, pp. 42–62; Hearnshaw, *Bodin and the Genesis of the Doctrine of Sovereignty*, in R. W. Seton-Watson (ed.), *Tudor Studies*, pp. 109–32; Shepard, "Sovereignty at the Crossroads, a Study of Bodin," *Political Science Quarterly*, XIV, 580–603.

[61] Fritz, article "Hobbes" in Wetzer and Welte, *op. cit.*, VI, 45.

[62] See chap. xvi, sec. 2.

[63] *Leviathan*, pp. 159–84; *Philosophical Rudiments concerning Government and Society*, pp. 78–79.

Since the sovereign has "the right of judging what doctrines are fit for peace," therefore he is himself pastor of the people and no one may lawfully teach religion to the people except by permission and authority of the sovereign. All pastors derive their right of teaching and preaching from the sovereign.[64] The pastors execute their charges by authority of the civil sovereign; but the king, and every other sovereign, receives his authority directly from God and is therefore the supreme pastor. The sovereign has the right to perform all manner of pastoral functions, to preach, baptize, administer the sacrament of the Lord's Supper, to consecrate religious edifices, to "sit in judgment and hear all manner of cases."[65] The sovereigns may make any laws that they deem fit for the government of their subjects, for all civil and ecclesiastical affairs, because "both State and Church are the same men." Sovereigns "may, as many Christian kings now do, commit the government of their subjects in matters of religion to the Pope, but then the Pope is in that point subordinate to them, and exerciseth that charge in another's dominion *jure civili*, in the right of the civil sovereign; not *jure divino*, in God's right; and may therefore be discharged of that office, when the sovereign, for the good of his subjects, shall think it necessary."[66] "The civil sovereign appoints the judges, and appoints the Canonical Scriptures; for it is he that maketh them laws. He has supreme power in all cases," civil and ecclesiastical. "These rights are incident to all sovereigns, whether monarchs or assemblies."[67] These citations show that Hobbes, in stating the theory of the absolute sovereignty of the civil power over secular and spiritual affairs, is more precise than Machiavelli in expounding the theory of the secularization of politics. Through his writings the secularization of political theory may be regarded as having been achieved in England. Subsequent

[64] *Leviathan*, pp. 537–39. [65] *Ibid.*, pp. 540–41. [66] *Ibid.*, p. 546.

[67] *Ibid.*, pp. 546–47. For illuminating comment on Hobbes as a political theorist see: Laird, *Hobbes*, pp. 225–36, 273–317; Catlin, *Thomas Hobbes as Philosopher, Publicist and Man of Letters*, pp. 49–50; Tönnies, *Thomas Hobbes: Leben und Lehre*, pp. 236–70, especially pp. 256–59; Stephen, *Hobbes*, pp. 220–36; Dewey, "Motivation of Hobbes's Political Philosophy," in *Studies in the History of Ideas*, I, 88–115.

outstanding political theorists in Great Britain accepted the ideas of Hobbes in advocating the idea of absolute sovereignty, the exercise of secular authority free from ecclesiastical influence. To be sure, Jeremy Bentham (1748–1832) hardly referred to Hobbes; but Bentham's followers, James Mill (1773–1836), George Grote (1794–1871), and John Austin (1790–1859) very definitely showed the influence of Hobbes.[68]

On the Continent a contemporary of both Hobbes and Conring, Hugo Grotius (1583–1645), also contributed in a determinative way to the secularization of political theory. His ideas were different from those of Hobbes but were similar to those of Conring inasmuch as he affirmed that both state and international law must be free from the influence of the papacy and theology.[69] Later writers, especially Rousseau (1712–78) followed along the same groove in holding that sovereignty resided only in the body politic and had no legal limitations from whatever source.[70]

So, by the middle of the seventeenth century, as a consequence and a concomitant of the Thirty Years' War and the Civil War in England, through the writings of Conring, Grotius, and Hobbes the secularization of political theory may be said to have been achieved.[71]

[68] Robertson, *Hobbes*, pp. 232–33; Morley, "Life of James Mill," *Fortnightly Review*, O.S., XXXVII, 500; Halévy, article "James Mill," *Encyclopedia of the Social Sciences*, X, 480–81; Dewey, "Austin's Theory of Sovereignty," *Political Science Quarterly*, IX, 31–94; Tönnies, *op. cit.*, pp. 269–70; Laird, *op. cit.*, pp. 272–317.

[69] Grotius, *Freedom of the Seas*, pp. 15–17; Lee, "Hugo Grotius," *Proceedings of the British Academy*, XVI, 57; D. J. Hill, "Introduction to Grotius," *The Rights of War and Peace*, p. 9; Hearnshaw, "Grotius," in *Social and Political Ideas of Some of the Great Thinkers of the Sixteenth and Seventeenth Centuries*, pp. 141, 143.

[70] F. W. Coker, article "Sovereignty," in *Encyclopedia of the Social Sciences*, XIV, 267; Morley, "Life of James Mill," *Fortnightly Review*, XXXVII, 500.

[71] For a suggestive treatment of the philosophical aspects of the modern problem of sovereignty see Schmitt, "Soziologie des Souveränitätsbegriffes und politische Theologie," in *Hauptprobleme der Soziologie, Erinnerungsgabe für Max Weber*, II, 3–35.

Chapter Seventeen

THE SECULAR POWERS AND PAPAL CLAIMS FROM 1648 TO 1815

THE pope was defeated in 1648; but his high claims remained the same until 1929, when Pius XI (1922——) signed the significant Lateran Accord with Mussolini. After the middle of the seventeenth century the pope repeatedly took occasion to protest whenever the states of Europe reaffirmed the terms of the Peace of Westphalia or in other ways violated the claimed ecclesiastical or secular rights and authority of the papacy or the Catholic church. But all such protests were without effect.

I. THE PROTEST AGAINST THE PEACE OF NYMWEGEN, 1678, 1679

At the close of Louis XIV's war with Holland (1672–79), which involved much of Europe and caused Catholic Austria and Spain to combat Catholic France as allies of Protestant Holland, France and the Empire signed the Peace of Nymwegen, February 5, 1679. The papal nuncio, Bevillacqua, who had been empowered to act as mediator by Innocent XI (1676–89),[1] was a mediator only in a restricted way. The Protestant powers were not willing to accept Bevillacqua as a papal mediator but were willing to recognize him as a royal representative, that is, as a representative of the temporal head of the Papal States. It took considerable negotiating on the part of Austria to overcome the unwillingness of the Dutch government to provide the nuncio with a pass, because that government did not

[1] Londorp, *Acta publica*, X, 524–25.

wish, in an official document, to mention the name of the pope. Much preliminary negotiation was also necessary to provide a Catholic chapel so that the nuncio and his suite could worship in the Protestant Netherlands, and that other Catholics could have easy access to the nuncio's headquarters.[2] Bevillacqua had received instructions from the papal court "to be careful not to communicate with the heretics, this being forbidden by the Holy See. And if by chance it were possible to achieve anything for the benefit of the church, [he should] make use of the Catholic ambassadors."[3] In this last task he was unsuccessful; and as mediator he rendered little, if any, service and did not sign the peace terms.[4] Both the nuncio and the papacy were, however, naturally in touch with the negotiations that were being carried on; and for our purpose the significant phase of the diplomatic proceedings is that in the second article of the Peace of Nymwegen, signed by France and the Empire on February 5, 1679, the terms of the Peace of Münster were reaffirmed.[5] In anticipation of such an eventuation the papal court considered the feasibility of issuing a new protest against the Peace of Westphalia and finally decided that it could not be avoided.[6] Consequently on October 8, 1678, copies of two protests were sent to Bevillacqua, along with a note that a renewal of the protest was inescapable.[7]

Bevillacqua, in pursuance of his instructions, issued a concise declaration of a general character on October 30, 1678, which showed that the papal attitude toward the Peace of Münster

[2] Pastor, *Geschichte der Päpste*, XIV, Part II, 709–10; Quaranta, "Un legato del papa al congresso di Nimego," *Nuova Antologia*, settima serie, CCCXXVIII, 462.

[3] Quaranta, "Un legato del papa," *Nuova Antologia*, CCCXXVIII, 457; Pastor, *op. cit.*, XIV, Part II, 714.

[4] Pastor, *op. cit.*, XIV, Part II, 715–16, 721; Martin, *Histoire de France*, XIII, 542, 543, n. 2.

[5] Londorp, *op. cit.*, X, 692; Du Mont, *Corps universelle*, VII, Part I, 377; *Actes et mémoires des négociations de la paix de Nimegue* (3d ed.), III, 408 (in French III, 424).

[6] Pastor, *op. cit.*, XIV, Part II, 723.

[7] Bojani, *Innocent XI. Sa correspondance avec ses nonces*, I, 370. Pastor, *op. cit.*, XIV, Part II, 723, n. 7, states that these were copies of the protests of Chigi, and cites the Vatican Archives.

had not changed. He declared that he did not wish that any of his past or future actions as mediator at this peace conference should be interpreted as indicating that he on his part was trying to meddle in the affairs of the Protestant princes or that he was in any way giving his direct or indirect sanction to the terms of the Peace of Münster. He also requested that the Catholic representatives register this protest in their acts.[8] He had also been instructed to protest especially against the Spanish treaty with Holland because it transferred Catholic territories into heretic hands,[9] and also against the treaty between the Empire and Sweden, even if this were merely a confirmation of the Peace of Münster, thereby continuing the injuries sustained by the Catholic religion.[10] He was further instructed that in this case a general declaration in the sense of the protest of the nuncio at Münster would suffice,[11] and the protest or declaration of October 30, 1678, met this aspect of his instructions.

When finally the Peace of Nymwegen between France and the Empire had been signed, February 5, 1679, Bevillacqua issued a longer protest against the Peace of Westphalia and against the Peace of Nymwegen in so far as it confirmed the Peace of Westphalia. He explained that, inasmuch as the fundamental characteristics of the Peace of Westphalia were the bases of the Peace of Nymwegen, he had absented himself from the signing of the Peace, since he did not wish, through his presence, to appear to be giving his sanction to the Peace of Westphalia. Furthermore, to avoid giving the impression that by his silence he was sanctioning that Peace he wished solemnly to declare that in harmony with instructions sent from the papal court in the form of a breve of May 14, 1678, he reaffirmed the protests issued by the nuncio Chigi on October 26, 1648, and by Inno-

[8] *Actes et mémoires des négociations de la paix de Nimegue*, III, 92 (Italian), 93 (French); Du Mont, *op. cit.*, VII, Part I, 374; Pastor, *op. cit.*, XIV, Part II, 723.

[9] Bojani, *op. cit.*, I, 370–71; Pastor, *op. cit.*, XIV, Part II, 723.

[10] Bojani, *op. cit.*, I, 370; Pastor, *op. cit.*, XIV, Part II, 723.

[11] Bojani, *op. cit.*, I, 370.

cent X on November 26, 1648. The date of the Latin protest (in the Latin form) is February 19, 1679.[12]

It is only fair for us to keep in mind that at this period there was no desire on the part of the papacy, the Curia, or the nuncio to hinder the conclusion of peace in any way. In a letter written February 25, 1679, to Cardinal Buonvisi (the nuncio at Vienna) the papal secretary of state, Cardinal Cibo, stated that the pope was content with a protest against the Peace of Nymwegen because it represented a renewal of the Peace of Westphalia; he wished nothing further, for he rejoiced over the conclusion of this terrible war and hoped that the Catholic princes could soon unite in repelling the barbarism that was threatening Catholicism in so many places, especially in Hungary and in Poland. The secretary stated further that Buonvisi, keeping this papal attitude in mind, should encourage the emperor to ratify the Peace of Nymwegen in case its terms were acceptable to him.[13] This was a situation quite different from that of 1648, when the nuncio and the extreme Catholics were given papal support in their opposition to the conclusion of a peace that was injurious to church interests. Now there was to be no thwarting of a peace that was merely reaffirming the previous injuries done the church.[14]

2. PROTEST AGAINST THE PRUSSIAN KINGSHIP, 1701

The pontificate of Clement XI (1700–1721), an ambitious, zealous protector of church interests, was filled with quarrels of various sorts with the sovereigns of Europe.[15] On a number of occasions he issued futile protests. On January 18, 1701, the elector Frederick III of Brandenburg, after long preliminary

[12] *Actes et mémoires des négociations de la paix de Nimegue*, III, 498–500 (Latin), 501–3 (French); Pastor, *op. cit.*, XIV, Part II, 723.

[13] Trenta, *Memorie per servire all storia politica del Cardinale Francesco Buonvisi*, I, 368–69; Pastor, *op. cit.*, XIV, Part II, 723, n. 7.

[14] Du Mont, *op. cit.*, VII, Part I, 374.

[15] Pastor, *op. cit.*, XV, 10; Hergenröther, *Handbuch*, IV, 10–11; Wetzer and Welte, *Kirchenlexikon*, III, 492; Ziekursch, *Papst Klemens' XI. Protest gegen die preussische Königswürde*, *Festgabe Karl Theodor von Heigel*, p. 367; Landau, *Rom, Wien, Neapel während des spanischen Erbfolgekrieges*, pp. 56–61.

negotiations and with the consent of Emperor Leopold I,[16] crowned himself and his consort as king and queen in Prussia; and in order to demonstrate the independence of the Prussian kingdom of every ecclesiastical authority, it was arranged that the act of anointing should take place after the coronation by a Lutheran and a reformed bishop appointed by the elector especially for the occasion.[17]

This action was offensive to the papacy because the elector had assumed the title and insignia of kingship, the disposal of which was, according to papal theory, wholly in the hands of the pope. For the first time in the history of the Christian states a kingdom had been created without there having been requested or secured the sanction of the papacy, the oldest organized power in European Christianity.[18] This procedure was also offensive because a Catholic emperor, Leopold I (1658–1705), had consented to the assumption of this title by a heretic prince; he had done this in return for the good will and military aid in the approaching contest centering around the Spanish Succession.[19] A further injury was sustained by the Catholic Teutonic Order, which, although it had not administered the land in question since 1525, had not relinquished its claim to the lands that Frederick was now aiming to rule as a kingdom.[20]

Into the motives that may have actuated Clement XI subse-

[16] Preussischer Kron Tractat mit Kaiser Leopold I. von 1700, in Rousset, *Supplément au corps diplomatique*, Vol. II, Part I, p. 463; Klüber, *Europäisches Völkerrecht*, I, 169; Gfrörer, *Geschichte des achtzehnten Jahrhunderts*, I, 63–67.

[17] Hiltebrandt, "Preussen und die römische Kurie," *Quellen und Forschungen*, XI, 350; Lehmann, *Preussen und die katholische Kirche seit 1640*, I, 378–79; Waddington, *L'acquisition de la couronne royale de Prusse par les Hohenzollern*, pp. 16–347; Reboulet, *Histoire de Clement XI. Pape*, I, 72; Lafitau, *La vie de Clement XI*, I, 76; Zwiedeneck-Südenhorst, *Deutsche Geschichte*, II, 365–68; Stettiner, *Zur Geschichte des preussichen Königstitels und der Königsberger Krönung*, pp. 80–96; Gfrörer, *op. cit.*, I, 67–70.

[18] Hiltebrandt, "Preussen und die römische Kurie," *Quellen und Forschungen*, XI, 354; Stenzel, *Geschichte des preussischen Staates*, III, 111; Buder, *Leben und Thaten des klugen und berühmten Papst Clementis des Eilften*, I, 175–78.

[19] Waddington, *op. cit.*, pp. 141–45; Reboulet, *op. cit.*, p. 73; Gfrörer, *op. cit.*, I, 66.

[20] Reboulet, *op. cit.*, p. 73; Erdmannsdörffer, *Deutsche Geschichte*, II, 140–41.

quently, we need not enter here.[21] The significant fact is that by April 16, 1701, Clement XI had addressed breves to all of the Catholic powers (the emperor, France, Poland, Venice, Bavaria, the Swiss Catholic cantons, the Catholic archbishops and bishops), solemnly warning them not to honor the Margrave Frederick of Brandenburg with his newly assumed title, because he was attempting to establish a kingdom on the property of the Teutonic Order, which had not relinquished its claim, and also because the rights of creating kings belonged only to the pope. In his breves he usually quoted the passage from Hosea: "You have ruled, but not through me, and you have become king, and I have not recognized you," this indicating how conscious Clement XI was of being divine vicegerent (*Statthalter*).[22] On April 18, 1701, in a secret consistory Clement XI informed his cardinals of the actions he had taken and the reasons therefor.[23] Clement had made a mistake in issuing his protest, for it remained without force in the greater part of the world and strengthened the position of Prussia among the Protestant powers.[24] By 1703 most of the states of Europe, even including the ecclesiastical princes of Germany, had recognized the title, although the Archbishop of Salzburg waited till 1704 and the Archbishop of Cologne delayed until 1714. Before the death of Frederick I in 1713 all the Italian states had recognized his new title; Portugal had recognized it in 1704. France and

[21] Lehmann, *Preussen und die katholische Kirche seit 1640*, I, 379; Ziekursch, *Festgabe Karl Theodor von Heigel*, pp. 361–77; Friedensburg, "Die römische Kurie und die Annahme der preussischen Königswürde durch Kurfürst Friedrich III von Brandenburg," *Historische Zeitschrift*, LXXXVII, 407–31; Hiltebrandt, "Preussen und die römische Kurie," *Quellen und Forschungen*, XI, 340; Pastor, *op. cit.*, XV, 16, n. 2.

[22] Clementis XI, *Opera omnia*, Vol. II, *Epistolae et brevia selectoria*, pp. 43–50; Buder, *op. cit.*, I, 179–92 (in Latin and German); Hiltebrandt, *Preussen und die römische Kurie*, I, 107–8; Hiltebrandt, "Preussen und die römische Kurie," *Quellen und Forschungen*, XI, 354–55; Waddington, *op. cit.*, pp. 348–49, 447–48; Pastor, *op. cit.*, XV, 16; Lehmann, *op. cit.*, I, 379–80; Stettiner, *op. cit.*, p. 49; Schröckh, *Christliche Kirchengeschichte seit der Reformation*, VI, 361–62.

[23] Clementis XI, *Opera omnia*, Vol. I, *Orationes*, pp. 3–6; Pastor, *op. cit.*, XV, 16; Hiltebrandt, "Preussen und die römische Kurie," *Quellen und Forschungen*, pp. 355–56; Buder, *op. cit.*, I, 194–96.

[24] Waddington, *op. cit.*, pp. 356–57; Lehmann, *op. cit.*, I, 383; Stenzel, *op. cit.*, III, 111–12.

Spain waited until the close of the War of the Spanish Succession; Poland ceased resisting the change in 1764; the Teutonic Order expressed its dissent the last time in 1792.[25]

Until 1787 the intransigence of papal attitude was expressed by referring to the Prussian king in the official publication, the Roman *Staatskalender*, as the "Margrave of Brandenburg," for the pope had never even recognized the Protestant electors.[26] But in 1787 a significant change took place. In connection with the movement called "Febronianism," the Catholic church in Germany had had a vexing dissension as to the relative power of the archbishops and the two papal nuncios, one of them newly appointed in Munich and the other, the nuncio of Cologne, whose office had been recently revived. The four archbishops of Mainz, Trier, Cologne, and Salzburg had sent representatives to Ems to draw up the famous "Punctation of Ems" (1786). In this document the archbishops resisted the infringement of their metropolitan rights that would follow if the papal nuncios were to assert complete control of German ecclesiastical affairs. In the controversy that followed, Emperor Joseph II inclined somewhat against the nuncios, whereas the king of Prussia took an attitude against the "Punctation." This pleased Pius VI (1775–99); and, to strengthen this Hohenzollern friendliness, he considered favorably certain approaches that had been made by the Prussian king through an agent at the papal court, Abbé Ciofani, and in 1787 ordered the insertion of the title "king of Prussia" in the Roman calendar, thus abandoning the intransigent attitude that the papacy had observed for eighty-six years and withdrawing its protest.[27] On April 5, 1788, Pius

[25] Erdmannsdörffer, *op. cit.*, II, 141; Lehmann, *op. cit.*, I, 383–84; Stettiner, *op. cit.*, pp. 51–53; Waddington, *op. cit.*, pp. 357–82.

[26] Hergenröther, *op. cit.*, IV, 11.

[27] Biester, "Nimmt der Papst Behauptungen zurück?" *Berlinische Monatsschrift*, VIII (1786), 111–21, especially p. 116; Biester, "Von dem nunmehr auch im römischen Staatskalender befindlichen preussischen Königstitel," *Berlinische Monatsschrift*, IX (1787), 299–302, especially p. 301; Stettiner, *op. cit.*, pp. 71–73; Waddington, *op. cit.*, pp. 357–58; Hiltebrandt, "Preussen und die römische Kurie," *Quellen und Forschungen*, XI, 359; Ehrhard, *Der Katholizismus und das zwanzigste Jahrhundert*, pp. 192–93; Hergenröther, *op. cit.*, IV, 202–3; Ott, "Congress of Ems," *Catholic Encyclopedia*, V, 410.

VI wrote the first letter that a pope ever wrote to a "king of Prussia."[28]

3. PROTESTS AGAINST THE TREATY AND THE CONVENTION OF ALTRANSTÄDT, 1709–12

In 1709 and 1710 Clement XI expressed his condemnation of the Treaty of Altranstädt (signed September 24, 1706; ratified January, 1707). The circumstances explaining this papal action are as follows: Charles XII (1697–1718) of Sweden had invaded Saxony and forced Frederick Augustus II (1694–1733), the Strong, the elector of Saxony, to sign this treaty. The elector had in 1697 embraced Catholicism in order to become king of Poland in addition to being elector of Saxony.[29] In signing the Treaty of Altranstädt, Augustus II gave up the Polish throne (which was to be given to the Swedish candidate, Stanislaus Lesczinski)—and, what is more important, the elector and his successors were to maintain the Lutheran religion inviolate in Saxony in accordance with the Treaty of Westphalia. Augustus promised that no religious changes would be made, that Catholics would not be permitted to erect schools, academies, colleges, and monasteries, and that no churches would be conceded to the Catholics.[30] When the papal Curia heard of this Treaty, the pope doubted for a long time that the elector, a recent convert to Catholicism, had signed this agreement with a free will; such doubt was cleared up when the elector's representative, Baron de Schenk, appeared at the papal court in 1707 to explain that the responsibility lay with the Saxon negotiators.[31]

After Charles XII had later been defeated by Russia at Poltava in July, 1709, Augustus could once more assume his title of king of Poland. In September 21, 1709, Clement did his part

[28] Comte de Hertzberg, *Recueil des deductions*, II, 473–75; Stettiner, *op. cit.*, pp. 72–73.

[29] Erdmannsdörffer, *op. cit.*, II, 81.

[30] Du Mont, *op. cit.*, VIII, Part I, 204–6, par. XIX; *Theatrum Europaeum*, XVII, 139–43; Erdmannsdörffer, *op. cit.*, II, 243, Böttiger, *Geschichte des Kurstaates und Königreiches Sachsen*, II, 338–39.

[31] Alexandre, *Ad historiam ecclesiasticam supplementum*, II, 76, 77.

to enable Augustus to break his agreement concerning religious affairs. He sent a breve condemning the Treaty of Altranstädt because it sanctioned arrangements in the Peace of Westphalia, which the pope had long ago condemned.[32] Augustus, on April 2, 1710, sent an apologetic letter to Clement in which he expressed his devotion to the pope and asserted that the responsibility of the negotiations at Altranstädt was not his, but his negotiators'. However, Saxon religious conditions remained unaltered.

Clement XI also protested against the Convention of Altranstädt signed September 12, 1707, under duress by Emperor Joseph I (1705–11) with Charles XII of Sweden, who, after remaining in Saxony, was threatening to become involved in war with the emperor, an entanglement that Joseph wished to avoid in view of the European military situation produced by the War of the Spanish Succession (1702–14). So Joseph bought the good will of Charles by signing a peace that obligated the emperor to tolerate the Protestants in Silesia as they had been tolerated previous to 1648. All innovations to the advantage of the Catholics since that date were to be canceled. Protestants were to have the right to worship, build schools and churches, hold consistories, and fill public office.[33]

In some authorities it is recorded that Clement XI sent Joseph a breve on September 10, 1707, for the purpose of dissuading him from signing such a treaty.[34] But there is strong doubt as to its genuineness because there is no record of it in the *Epistolae* of Clement XI; neither can the original be found in the Vienna archives or the papal secret archives.[35] Wherever

[32] Clementis XI, *Opera*, Vol. II, *Epistolae*, pp. 645–48; Pastor, *op. cit.*, XV, 36, n. 3.

[33] Du Mont, *op. cit.*, VIII, Part I, 221–25; *Theatrum Europaeum*, XVIII, 91–93; Grünhagen, *Geschichte Schlesiens*, II, 403–6; Buder, *op. cit.*, I, 1097–1100; Zwiedeneck-Südenhorst, *op. cit.*, II, 469–70; Menzel, *Neuere Geschichte der Deutschen von der Reformation bis zur Bundes-Acte*, IX, 447–48; Immich, *Geschichte des europäischen Staatensystems*, p. 213; Klopp, *Der Fall des Hauses Stuart*, XII, 440.

[34] Buder, *op. cit.*, I, 1097–1100, which has a German translation of the breve; Krones, *Geschichte Österreichs*, IV, 85.

[35] Klopp, *op. cit.*, XII, 442, n. 2; Pastor, *op. cit.*, XV, 36, n. 3. Landau, *op. cit.*, p. 281, however, states that the letter was in Clement's own hand and was handed to

the original may be, or whatever its contents may have been, Joseph I answered Clement with an apologetic letter explaining that he had, on the advice of theological counsel, chosen a lesser evil to ward off a greater when he signed this treaty making concessions to Protestants in his own hereditary lands. He closed with an expression of regret for what had happened, and promised to permit no further injury to Catholic interests, and would even attempt to repair the injury done the church.[36]

As a small phase of the War of the Spanish Succession, Joseph I had other difficulties, of a political nature, with Clement XI incident to occupying Parma and Piacenza, two small duchies in northern Italy over which the pope had suzerainty. When those difficulties had been terminated, Joseph, in order to pacify the pope, issued a decree against the apostasy of Catholics to the Protestant faith in Silesia, an occurrence that was annoyingly frequent.[37] But this was not adequate or satisfactory to Clement, for in a breve of June 4, 1712, to Charles VI (1711–40), successor of Joseph I, he condemned once more the Convention of Altranstädt. Expressing his sorrow over the injury done the Catholic cause through the tolerance of heretics in Silesia, he rejected the Convention, declared it null and void, and admonished the emperor to do his utmost to make it ineffective.[38] But this breve remained without force.[39]

4. PROTEST TO THE CITY OF COLOGNE, 1709

In 1709 (February 16) Clement XI, in a letter to his nuncio at Cologne, expressed his disapproval of a treaty drawn up January 16, 1709, between the free imperial city of Cologne (not the electorate) and the king of Prussia, whereby the Prussian am-

Joseph by the nuncio in Vienna; that the original is in the K[önigliche] K[aiserliche] Staatsarchiv, Abteilung Romana; and that doubt as to its authenticity is without foundation. *Die europäische Fama*, LXXIII, 80–81.

[36] Klopp, *op. cit.*, XII, 442–44 (Joseph's letter in German), 551–53 (in Latin); Landau, *op. cit.*, pp. 281–82; Pastor, *op. cit.*, XV, 36.

[37] Menzel, *op. cit.*, XI, 461; Pastor, *op. cit.*, XV, 36, n. 3.

[38] Clementis XI, *Opera*, Vol II, *Epistolae*, pp. 1689–92; Pastor, *op. cit.*, XV, 36, n. 3.

[39] Krones, *op. cit.*, IV, 85.

bassador was allowed freedom of worship in his residence at Cologne.[40] This agreement had been the outcome of riotous demonstrations in 1708 against the Prussian representative at Cologne, Herr von Diest, whose house had been stoned by Catholic students as a protest against the practice of a heretical religion in the city. In retaliation the king of Prussia ordered the detention of some Cologne ships in his territories and the arrest and detention of citizens of Cologne. After an ineffective royal appeal to the emperor, and an intervention by Protestant princes, an agreement was reached whereby the city of Cologne granted certain rights of free exercise of the evangelical faith in the residence of the ambassador within the city of Cologne.[41] Against this treaty the apostolic nuncio in Cologne protested January 23, 1709;[42] and Clement XI, in caustic words concerning this offense against the Catholic religion, approved his action by sending him a breve, February 16, 1709.[43] It was only a formal and ineffective protest. Catholic historians ordinarily do not mention the incident.

5. PROTEST AGAINST THE TREATY OF BADEN, 1714

After all the powers had signed the Peace of Baden, which closed the War of the Spanish Succession, Clement XI, in a consistory held January 21, 1715, protested against all those parts of the Peace of Utrecht (August 13, 1713), the Peace of Rastadt (March 7, 1714), and the Peace of Baden (September 7, 1714) that were prejudicial to the interests of the Catholic church. Article III of the Peace of Baden stated that the treaties of Westphalia, Nymwegen, and Ryswick were adopted as a basis and foundation of the Peace.[44] So in this respect the papal protest was merely a new protest against the terms of the Peace of

[40] Clementis XI, *Opera*, Vol. II, *Epistolae*, pp. 586–89; Rousset, *op. cit.*, II, Part II, 75; Buder, *op. cit.*, II, 258–60.

[41] Faber, *Europäische Staats-Cantzley*, XIV (1710), 208–14; Buder, *op. cit.*, II, 245–49.

[42] Faber, *op. cit.*, pp. 242–50; Buder, *op. cit.*, II, 250–57.

[43] Clementis XI, *Opera*, Vol. II, *Epistolae*, pp. 586–89; Faber, *op. cit.*, XIV, 250–53; Rousset, *op. cit.*, II, Part II, 75; Buder, *op. cit.*, II, 258–60.

[44] Du Mont, *op. cit.*, VIII, Part I, 437.

Westphalia. But Clement XI further protested because the Peace of Baden recognized a ninth electorate (which had been erected for the benefit of Hanover in 1692)[45] and because it recognized the kingship of Prussia,[46] granted certain Catholic territories to Protestant princes,[47] and disposed of Naples and Sicily as though the pope had no suzerain rights over these realms.[48] He further protested against the arrangements made in Switzerland to the advantage of the Protestants and the disadvantage of the Catholics.[49] Previously, at the wish of Clement XI, Passionei, the papal nuncio at the Congress of Baden, had formulated a protest against the Peace of Baden, which was, after the conclusion of the treaty, to be deposited in legal form with the magistrate of Baden; but this officer refused to have it rendered valid in law through notaries, and therefore Passionei went to Luzern and deposited it in its archives, where it still remains.[50]

6. PROTESTS CONCERNING PARMA AND PIACENZA, 1723–48

In the years 1706–7 Emperor Joseph had a dispute with Clement XI concerning papal suzerainty over the duchy of Parma and Piacenza,[51] but that matter was temporarily settled. During the Congress of Cambray (1723–24) the powers of Europe agreed that the duchy of Parma and Piacenza should, on the extinction of the male line, succeed to Don Carlos, one of the sons of the ambitious Spanish queen, Elisabeth Farnese (1714–66), who regarded herself as the heir of the House of

[45] *Ibid.*, p. 438, Art. XIII.

[46] *Ibid.*, p. 438, Art. XIX.

[47] *Ibid.*, p. 440, Art. XXIX.

[48] *Ibid.*, p. 403, Arts. V–IX of the Peace of Utrecht between Spain and Savoy; p. 440, Art. XXX, of the Peace of Baden.

[49] Clementis XI, *Opera*, Vol. I, *Orationes*, pp. 111–18; Alexandre, *op. cit.*, II, 82; Pastor, *op. cit.*, XV, 79–80.

[50] Lengefeld, *Graf Domenico Passionei*, p. 47; Galletti, *Memorie . . . . del Cardinale Domenico Passionei*, pp. 60–61; Pastor, *op. cit.*, XV, 78–79.

[51] *Cambridge Modern History*, VI, 586–87; Pastor, *op. cit.*, XV, 34–36. See sec. 3 of this chapter.

Parma and Piacenza, which threatened to become extinct on the death of the reigning duke.[52] The pope had been undisputed suzerain over these territories for two centuries; and therefore in April, 1723, Innocent XIII (1721–24) sent Abbé Rota, the auditor (secretary of the Parisian nuncio, Bartolomeo Massei, to present to the Congress of Cambray a solemn protest against this disregard of his suzerain rights.

The protest stated that these rights had been secured in a peaceful manner and that Paul III had given this duchy as a fief to Peter Aloysius and the House of Farnese. As soon as the holder of a fief died, his first-born son was always sent on a solemn mission to the Holy See requesting a renewal of the investiture. All holders of this fief had annually faithfully paid the fees (*Zinsen*) as a permanent testimony of papal suzerainty over the duchy.[53] But this protest was not regarded, and in 1725 Emperor Charles VI granted the duchy as an eventual fief to Don Carlos of Spain in the event that Duke Anton of Parma (1697–1731) should die without male heirs.[54] Once more, in a consistory of the year 1726, Benedict XIII (1724–30) presented the cardinals with a statement of the situation, and declared his intention of having the papal nuncios continue to present at the Catholic courts papal opposition to such unjust infractions of papal rights, and declared that the papal Curia would publicly abominate such unjust treatment that was evidence of maliciousness and discord.[55] When in January, 1731, the old Duke of Parma died, Clement XII (1730–40) issued a breve (June 20, 1731) by which he declared that by right of escheat the duchy reverted to papal possession.[56]

[52] Erdmannsdörffer, *op. cit.*, II, 371–73, 412; Reumont, *Geschichte Toscanas*, I, 472–73; *Cambridge Modern History*, VI, 138–39. Immich, *op. cit.*, pp. 247, 255, 259.

[53] Rousset, *op. cit.*, III, Part II, 175–78, especially p. 177; Pastor, *op. cit.*, XV, 414–15.

[54] Du Mont, *op. cit.*, VIII, Part II, 121–22, peace between Charles VI and Philip V, signed at Vienna, June 7, 1725; Art. IV; Ranke, *Päpste*, III, 124.

[55] Faber, *op. cit.*, XLVII, 646–48.

[56] Brosch, *Geschichte des Kirchenstaates*, II, 76–77; *Cambridge Modern History*, VI, 149–50; Armstrong, *Elisabeth Farnese*, pp. 253–56.

The papal commissioner, Monsignor Oddi-Spinola, who had been appointed to take possession of the escheated duchy, posted the papal brief on various church doors in Parma and elsewhere. But this was no longer a time when papal breves instilled respect in the emperor and kings. Austrian troops appeared in the duchy and tore down the breves from the church doors.[57] Clement XII now issued a protest breve, sending it to all European courts; but it remained without effect. A certain Count Borromeo Arese took possession of the duchy for Don Carlos with the sanction of Emperor Charles VI. Count Stampa, the commander of the Austrian troops that had moved into the duchy, declared the papal breves and protests null and invalid; he asserted that no one need be bound by them or value their contents. Emperor Charles VI received the oath of allegiance of the guardian of Don Carlos, who was still a minor, and formally bestowed possession of the duchy on the guardian in December, 1731. Representatives from all parts of the duchy swore allegiance to the young Don Carlos without showing the slightest consideration for the papal protests and admonitions. Monsignor Oddi-Spinola protested anew, from Bologna, against all these proceedings. The next year Don Carlos appeared personally and took possession of his duchy without being in the least concerned about the suzerainty of the pope.[58] At the close of the War of the Austrian Succession (1740–48), by the Peace of Aix-la-Chapelle, Parma and Piacenza were transferred to the second son of Elisabeth Farnese, Don Philippe of Bourbon, Don Carlos having become the king of the two Sicilies in 1734;[59] on this occasion Pope Benedict XIV (1740–58) renewed the protest of his predecessors, but this also remained ineffective.[60]

57 Brosch, *op. cit.*, II, 77; *Cambridge Modern History*, VI, 150.

58 Brosch, *op. cit.*, II, 77; *Cambridge Modern History*, VI, 150; Armstrong, *op. cit.*, pp. 256–57.

59 Wenck, *Codex juris gentium recentissima*, II, 345–46, Art. VII; Krones, *op. cit.*, IV, 239; Reumont, *op. cit.*, II, 61; *Cambridge Modern History*, VI, 167, 239, 249–50; Armstrong, *op. cit.*, p. 390.

60 Brosch, *op. cit.*, II, 103.

7. PROTESTS AGAINST THE HANOVERIAN ELECTORATE, 1742–45

When the elector of Bavaria was elected emperor as Charles VII (1742–45) at Frankfurt in January, 1742, the papal nuncio, Doria, issued two protests in the name of Benedict XIV (1740–58). The first protest, which was issued January 23, 1742, the day before the election, declared that, inasmuch as the Holy See had never sanctioned the admission of the non-Catholic Duke of Hanover as one of the imperial electors, his admission to and participation in the intended imperial election was invalid.[61]

The second protest of the nuncio Dorio was issued January 24, 1742, the day of the election. In this protest he renewed the papal protest against the Peace of Westphalia, which the newly elected emperor was expected to observe but which Innocent X and all succeeding popes had rejected in so far as it injured church interests. He protested especially against Article XIV of the Peace, by which the elector palatine had been restored to the full possession of his rights as elector. In response to repeated papal requests the Catholic electors had promised to put an end to this situation; however, under the pretext of not wishing to disturb the electoral proceedings, nothing had been done. But the papacy hoped that in the present election this situation would be terminated.[62]

The nuncio also stated that he was forced to issue such a protest in harmony with the protests of the Holy See and his nuncios as well as with the protest made at the Congress of Münster and those that had been issued at all subsequent elections of a new Roman king.[63] The use of the expression "Roman king" instead of emperor is significant, inasmuch as, according to papal theory, the Roman king was not recognized as emperor until crowned by the pope, a procedure that had not been observed since the coronation of Charles V at Bologna in 1530. Although this protest remained ineffective, it caused consider-

[61] Faber, *op. cit.*, LXXXIII, 132–37; Adelung, *Pragmatische Staatsgeschichte Europas*, III, Part I, 48, n. 5; Moser, *Teutsches Staats-Recht*, VIII, 405–7.

[62] Faber, *op. cit.*, LXXXIII, 135.

[63] *Ibid.*, pp. 135–36.

able discussion in the electoral college at its meeting almost a year later, December 10, 1742. The elector of Hanover complained because the elector of Mainz had accepted and registered this protest at all and had given the nuncio a confirmation of the registration thereof. He also requested that such protests should, in the future, not be accepted in any case. The elector of Mainz requested that the college regard this acceptance of the protest purely as a formality, a mere private acceptance. The electors of Saxony and Brandenburg thoroughly disapproved of the whole proceeding, whereas the representatives of the remaining or Catholic electors (Treves, Cologne, Bavaria, and the Palatinate) declared that they had received no instructions on this point.[64]

This discussion had evidently produced the results desired by the electors, for at the new imperial election of 1745 (when Francis I [1745–65] was elected) the nuncio was ignored to such an extent that he did not publicly assume the title of a nuncio and did not even appear at the coronation.[65] In this election the electoral college was divided; Francis I had not been elected unanimously. Benedict XIV claimed that he had the right to decide whether the election had been conducted legally or not. When the nuncio wished to present the customary protest against the confirmation of the Peace of Westphalia and the ninth electorate (Hanover), the college of electors forbade all the notaries of the city of Frankfurt, on pain of punishment, to assist in the slightest the proposed registering of the nuncio's protest. Not being able to achieve his purpose, the nuncio left Frankfurt.[66]

8. PROTEST AGAINST THE TREATY OF VIENNA, 1815

At the Congress of Vienna, which was quite indifferent to the affairs of the Catholic church,[67] the papacy once more lost many territorial rights and suffered a disregard of some of its historic

[64] *Ibid.*, XCIV, 1–11. [65] Adelung, *op. cit.*, V, 94. [66] *Ibid.*, p. 153.

[67] Veit, *Die Kirche im Zeitalter des Individualismus*, Part II, p. 47; *Cambridge Modern History*, IX, 662–63. Hergenröther, *op. cit.*, IV, 357.

claims. France was allowed to retain Avignon and Venaissin, which had been in papal possession since the fourteenth century but which the French Republic incorporated as integral parts of France in 1791.[68] The Papal States, although restored to the pope, were decreased by the loss of Ferrara and of other small territories north of the Po River, which were given to Austria as ruler of Venetia.[69] It is certain that the size of the Papal States would have been reduced, even to a greater extent if Napoleon had not escaped from the island of Elba and re-established himself on the French throne.[70]

The Congress sanctioned the final secularization of German ecclesiastical lands which had been accomplished by Napoleon in 1803, with the aid of such Catholic German states as Austria and Bavaria (in the face of energetic papal and ecclesiastical opposition), in order to indemnify the German princes that had been dispossessed of the left bank of the Rhine to the advantage of France in the Peace of Lunéville in 1801.[71] By this secularization the Catholic church lost lands in Germany with over 3,000,000 population and 21,000,000 gulden annual income.[72] The Congress also recognized the dissolution of the Holy Roman Empire, which had occurred in 1806.[73]

Against these acts of the Congress of Vienna the experienced and capable Cardinal Hercules Consalvi, former papal secretary and now nuncio at the Congress, issued two protests on June 14, 1815; each protest was sent with an accompanying note of prot-

[68] Veit, *op. cit.*, Part II, p. 36; *Cambridge Modern History*, IX, 564, 576, 661; Nürnberger, *Zur Kirchengeschichte des neunzehnten Jahrhunderts*, I, Part I, 106; Mollat, *La question romaine de Pie VI à Pie XI*, pp. 41–43, 103, 105, 115, 121.

[69] Veit, *op. cit.*, Part II, p. 36; *Cambridge Modern History*, IX, 603, Nürnberger, *op. cit.*, I, Part I, 106; Mollat, *op. cit.*, p. 121.

[70] Nys, "Le droit international et la papauté," *Revue du droit international*, X, 529.

[71] Schmidlin, *Papstgeschichte der neuesten Zeit*, I, 206–14; König, *Pius VII. Die Säkularisation und das Reichskonkordat*, pp. 1–68; Doberl, "Die Säkularisation und die päpstliche Diplomatie (1798–1803)," *Historisch-politische Blätter*, LXIX, 760 ff.; Nürnberger, *op. cit.*, I, Part I, 106–7; Veit, *op. cit.*, Part II, pp. 16–21; Heigel, *Deutsche Geschichte*, II, 301–4, 421–48.

[72] Veit, *op. cit.*, Part II, p. 19.

[73] Heigel, *op. cit.*, II, 663–72; *Cambridge Modern History*, IX, 269, 607–8.

estation to the representatives of each of the important negotiating powers. These protests and notes were similar in content and purport to the notes that he had repeatedly sent in October and November, 1814, to Prince Metternich and others for the purpose of stating the papal viewpoint concerning the intentions of the Congress.[74]

In one of these notes Consalvi protested against the cession of Avignon and the Venaissin to France with the assertion that the papal signature to the Peace of Tolentino of February 19, 1797 (by which Pius recognized the cession of these papal lands to France), had been forced upon him after he had solemnly declared his neutrality, a procedure contrary to every human law, and that therefore such a treaty or pact that is the result of such an attack is null and void. The note also protested against the loss of Ferrara and Comacchio and lands north of the Po River, taken from the pope and given to the emperor of Austria and his successors as rulers of Venetia, which the Congress had also ceded to the Hapsburgs.[75]

The second protest, issued the same day, was a protest against what had been done to the injury of the rights and interests of the Holy See and the German church through the secularization of church lands and the failure to re-establish the Holy Roman Empire, which had been "the center of political unity, consecrated by the august character of religion."[76] In his

[74] Klüber, *op. cit.*, IV, 314; VI, 427 n., 428 n., 430–33; Gams, *Geschichte der Kirche Christi im neunzehnten Jahrhundert*, II, 379; Ruck, *Die römische Kurie und die deutsche Kirchenfrage auf dem Wiener Kongress*, p. 166; van Duerm, *Correspondance du Cardinal Hercule Consalvi avec le Prince Clement de Metternich*, pp. 45–54, 71; *Cambridge Modern History*, IX, 603; Schmidlin, *op. cit.*, I, 142; Veit, *op. cit.*, Part II, p. 42; Brück, *Geschichte der katholischen Kirche im neunzehnten Jahrhundert*, I, 293; Brosch, *op. cit.*, II, 284.

[75] Barbèri, *Bullarii Romani continuatio*, XIII, 399–404; Angeberg, *Le congrès de Vienne et les traités de 1815*, II, 1450–51, 1453–56, 1924–29; Klüber, *op. cit.*, VI, 437–46; Roskovany, *Monumenta catholica*, II, 96–99; van Duerm, *op. cit.*, pp. 71–79; Müller, *Das Friedenswerk*, I, 267–72; Schmidlin, *op. cit.*, I, 144; Brück, *op. cit.*, I, 293; Gams, *op. cit.*, II, 379–81; Flassan, *Der Wiener Kongress*, II, 167; Mollat, *op. cit.*, p. 121.

[76] Barbèri, *op. cit.*, XIII, 404–7; Klüber, *op. cit.*, IV, 319–28; Angeberg, *op. cit.*, II, 1451–53, 1922–24; Ruck, *op. cit.*, pp. 166–68; Müller, *op. cit.*, I, 272–74; Brück, *op. cit.*, I, 293; Veit, *op. cit.*, Part II, p. 42.

notes Consalvi stated that the pope, in taking an attitude of protestation against the further spoliation of the church, was following the example of "Innocent X after the Congress and the Peace of Westphalia in 1649 [*sic*], Clement XI after the Treaty of Altranstädt in 1707, and of Baden in 1714, and of Benedict XIV in 1744" (which should be 1742), just as their representatives in the said congresses protested against all innovations prejudicial to the church and to the rights of the Holy See contained in those treaties.[77] Subsequently, in an allocution delivered in a consistory of September 4, 1815, Pius VII (1800–1823) declared that he fully approved all the acts of Cardinal Consalvi and that these protests had the force of a papal bull.[78] The pope in his allocution of September 4, 1815, expressed his gratitude to the heretical Alexander I of Russia, King Frederick William III of Prussia, King Charles of Sweden, and the prince regent of England for their support in securing a restoration of the Papal States (except Ferrara) to the pope.[79]

Through the final act of the Congress of Vienna the church lost more property and claimed rights than at any time since the signing of the Peace of Westphalia. The statesmen at Vienna were not disturbed by the threat of protest against the Treaty; they did not deem it necessary to plan any action to make the protests ineffective; they even complied with Consalvi's request that his protests be inserted in the protocol, it being clear that such action on the part of the nuncio was merely a formality.

[77] Klüber, *op. cit.*, IV, 325; VI, 441; Müller, *op. cit.*, I, 270–71; Barberi, *op. cit.*, XIII, 402, 405; Angeberg, *op. cit.*, II, 1456, 1923, 1929.

[78] Barbèri, *op. cit.*, XIII, 394–99; Klüber, *op. cit.*, IV, 312–18 (in German); Müller, *op. cit.*, I, 281–84 (in German); Ruck, *op. cit.*, pp. 77, 78, 168–70 (extracts); Meyer, *Zur Geschichte der römisch-deutschen Frage*, I, 491; Schmidlin, *op. cit.*, I, 144; Veit, *op. cit.*, Part II, pp. 42–43; Brück, *op. cit.*, I, 293; Nürnberger, *op. cit.*, I, Part I, 107; Gams, *op. cit.*, II, 381; Flassan, *op. cit.*, pp. 167–68.

[79] Barbèri, *op. cit.*, XIII, 396–97; Klüber, *op. cit.*, IV, 315–16; Gams, *op. cit.*, II, 382.

Chapter Eighteen

PAPAL PROTESTS AGAINST THE LOSS OF THE PAPAL STATES, 1860–1929

ONE of the British representatives at the Congress of Vienna, Lord Castlereagh, remarked that Cardinal Consalvi excelled all other members of the Congress in diplomatic success.[1] In spite of the fact that Consalvi could not prevent the legalization of the great territorial losses that the church had sustained during the French Revolution and the Napoleonic era in France and Germany, Catholics nevertheless also regard him as having been diplomatically very successful in so far as he secured for the Holy See a restoration of the Papal States, which the pope had owned continuously since the eighth century and which had essentially retained the same boundaries since 1631, except for the period of the French Revolution and Napoleon.[2]

These States were the last temporal possessions of the pope (until the Lateran Accord of 1929 restored them in part). From the standpoint of papal theory it was essential that the papacy, as head of an international or world ecclesiastical organization, should retain control of these lands so that the pope would be

[1] Cardinal Wiseman, *Recollections of the Last Four Popes*, pp. 61, 113; Fischer, *Cardinal Consalvi*, p. 297; Allies, *Life of Pope Pius the Seventh*, p. 357.

[2] Schmidlin, *Papstgeschichte der neuesten Zeit*, I, 144; Wunderlich, *Das Pontificat Pius VII*, pp. 37–39; J. F. Schaefer, in article "Consalvi," *Catholic Encyclopedia*, IV, 265; Franz Werner, in article "Consalvi," in Wetzer and Welte, *Kirchenlexikon*, III, 953; MacCaffrey, *History of the Catholic Church in the Nineteenth Century*, I, 55, 209; Lulvès, "Der Lateran Vertrag zwischen dem Heiligen Stuhle und Italien," *Preussische Jahrbücher*, CCXVI (1929), 61; Goyau, "Un an de politique pontificale, Consalvi au congrès de Vienne," *Revue des deux mondes*, fifth period, XXXV (1906), 135–63.

able to function in the spiritual realm without being dependent on any secular ruler.[3]

But papal temporal authority could not withstand for many decades the nationalist amalgamation of the separate political divisions of the Italian peninsula under the leadership of the House of Sardinia. In the year 1860 approximately three-fourths of the Papal States (the Romagna, the Marches, Umbria) were incorporated into the new Kingdom of Italy; and on September 20, 1870, the last province, Rome, met the same fate.[4] From the great powers the pope could expect no effective aid in regaining his lands. When Austria, Russia, and Prussia met at an international congress in Warsaw in October, 1860, they adhered to the principle of non-intervention in Italian affairs.[5] In 1870 the powers also took no action, "fearing to burn their fingers."[6]

I. PROTESTS IN THE YEARS 1860–61

In the years 1860–61 Pius IX (1846–78) issued an almost unbroken chain of protests against these spoliations,[7] although we shall mention only the most important, for in all of them there is a repetitiousness in content and a similarity in spirit. On January 19, 1860, he addressed an encyclical to all Catholic clergy, protesting against the absorption of the Romagna by the king of

[3] Weber, article "Kirchenstaat," in Wetzer and Welte, *op. cit.*, VII, 679–80; Duchesne, *Beginnings of the Temporal Sovereignty of the Popes*, pp. 263–64; MacCaffrey, *op. cit.*, I, 435; see also Ausset, *La question vaticane, 1914–1928*, pp. 2–6; Gibbons, *The Faith of Our Fathers*, p. 144, but see also p. 58; McCarthy, *Pope Leo XIII*, pp. 244–45; Ellison, "The Pope's Temporal Sovereignty a Providential Fact," *Catholic World*, LXXIV, 557–66.

[4] Mollat, *La question romaine*, pp. 291–326, 357–66; Jarrige, *La condition internationale du Saint-Siège*, pp. 80–90; Stern, *Geschichte Europas seit den Verträgen von 1815*, IX, 71–74, and X, 440–41.

[5] *Europäischer Geschichtskalender*, I (1860), 228–33; *Annual Register, 1860*, [p. 235]; Mollat, *op. cit.*, p. 326; Stern, *op. cit.*, VIII, 455–56, and IX, 80.

[6] Jarrige, *op. cit.*, p. 92; Whitely, "The International Position of the Pope," *North American Review*, CLXXVII, 603; Barry, "Leo XIII, a Retrospect," *Dublin Review*, CXXXIII, 230; Ward, "Vatican and Quirinal," *Fortnightly Review*, LXXII, 463.

[7] Schrader, *Der Papst und die modernen Ideen*, Heft 1, p. 117, n. 1.

Sardinia.[8] On March 26, 1860, in a breve, he excommunicated, without specifying individuals, all those that had engaged in an attack on the Papal States, and at the same time he sent a protest to all powers against the annexation of the Romagna to Sardinia.[9] On September 28, 1860, Pius IX addressed an allocution to his cardinals concerning the invasion of his States, whereby he had lost about three-fourths of his temporal possessions. He declared that this rebellious action of the House of Sardinia (Savoy) was a breach of all the solemn treaties guaranteeing the sovereign independence of the Holy See. He also implored all princes to send him the aid necessary to defend his independence.[10]

After King Victor Emmanuel II (1861–78) took the title of king of Italy, February 18, 1861, Pius IX protested that such action was a usurpation of authority over papal territories; it was a spoliation of, and injury to, the sacred property of the church. He also said that the pope would never be able to recognize the title of king of Italy, which the king of Sardinia had arrogated to himself,[11] an adjustment that his successor, Pius XI (1922——), was able to make in 1929, however, as we shall observe later. On September 30, 1861, Pius IX, in an allocution, expressed himself once more very violently against the king of Sardinia and his predatory acts.[12]

2. PROTESTS AFTER 1870

Finally in 1870 the Franco-Prussian War made it feasible for the Kingdom of Italy to occupy the province of Rome and thus complete the unification of the peninsula (except, of course, for the lands demanded later by the Italian irredentists). On the same day that the royal Italian troops entered the papal capital,

[8] Schulthess, *Europäischer Geschichtskalender*, I (1860), 7; Schrader, *op. cit.*, Heft 1, pp. 118–19.

[9] *Europäischer Geschichtskalender*, I, 28; Schrader, *op. cit.*, Heft 1, pp. 106–14 (in Latin and German).

[10] *Europäischer Geschichtskalender*, I, 85–86; Schrader, *op. cit.*, Heft 1, pp. 119–21.

[11] *Europäischer Geschichtskalender*, II (1861), 219.

[12] *Ibid.*, p. 222; Schrader, *op. cit.*, Heft 3, pp. 160, 227.

September 20, 1870, a protest was issued once more, Pius IX having ordered that the only defense to be used "should consist of a protest, which would be suitable to establish the act of violence."[13] The papal secretary of state, Cardinal Antonelli, carrying out the instructions of the pope, issued a protest to each of the representatives of the foreign states accredited to the papal court. He declared the action of the "king of Florence" (where the Italian capital had been since 1865) to be an unworthy and sacrilegious confiscation of the sacred lands of the church. The act was null and void and could not prejudice the rights of sovereignty and possession of His Holiness and his successors.[14]

A little more than a month later, November 1, 1870, Pius IX addressed a protest to all Catholic clergy in which he confirmed the protest issued by the cardinal secretary of state in September. The pope declared that, in order not to be found remiss in the sacred duties of his high office, he protested against all usurpations of his temporal authority that had taken place recently or might take place in the future. All such usurpations he declared null and void. He asserted also that, because of such violence to his temporal authority, he was in a state of captivity, and therefore not in a position to perform the high duties of his office freely and without restraint. All persons that had participated in robbing him of his lands since 1860 he declared to be excommunicated.[15] Again, since he did not specify names, this excommunication appeared to be more formal than effective.

Pius IX also refused to accept the Law of Papal Guaranties of May 13, 1871, in which the Italian government declared the person of the pope to be sovereign and inviolable, guaranteed him an annual income of 3,225,000 francs to compensate him for

[13] Löffler, *Papstgeschichte von der französischen Revolution bis zur Gegenwart*, p. 97; Mollat, *op. cit.*, p. 364.

[14] *Acta Sancta Sedis*, VI, 56–60; *Europäischer Geschichtskalender*, XI (1870), 433, gives September 21, 1870, as the date of sending the protest to all the representatives in question; Mollat, *op. cit.*, pp. 365–66.

[15] Pius IX, *Acta*, V, Part I, 263–77, especially pp. 273, 275; *Acta Sancta Sedis*, VI, 136–45; *Europäischer Geschichtskalender*, XI (1870), 434; Mirbt, *Quellen zur Geschichte des Papsttums*, p. 466.

the loss of the income from the Papal States, and left him in possession of the Vatican palace, the Lateran palace, and the villa of Castelgandolfo, with their dependencies, and assured him free communication with the Roman Catholic clergy of the world and unrestricted exercise of his spiritual authority.[16]

In a breve of March 2, 1871, addressed to the papal vicar-general, Cardinal Patrizi, Pius IX rejected the Law of Papal Guaranties.[17] On May 15, 1871, he issued an encyclical to all the bishops of the Catholic church, rejecting the Law again, demanding that the temporal power of the Holy See be returned to him, and admonishing the princes to put forth a united effort to achieve this purpose.[18] He once more rejected the Law in an allocution at the consistory of October 27, 1871.[19]

In these several protests the pope made it clear that he could not accept the Law of Guaranties (1) because he could not accept the implication that he was dependent on another power, his position of spiritual leadership requiring that he be absolutely independent of any and all secular states; (2) because no guaranty by a secular state could secure for him the liberty and independence necessary to the exercise of his spiritual functions; (3) because this Law was not a treaty, or convention, but a unilateral arrangement, forced on him, and contained only rights granted by the state; (4) because the rights granted could be revoked by a mere vote of the Italian chambers; (5) because, although these rights were guaranteed by the conservative party in Italy, there was no guaranty that the parties of the left, such as the socialists, might not abolish it in the future; (6) because, to accept this Law would imply papal sanction of the loss of his temporal possessions, an attitude to which the pope could not accede; and (7) since this was only a one-sided

[16] *Europäischer Geschichtskalender*, XII (1871), 410–14; *American Annual Encyclopaedia*, XI (1871), 420; Albin, *Les grands traités politiques*, pp. 99–103; Mirbt, *op. cit.*, pp. 466–68; Mollat, *op. cit.*, pp. 366–67; Bompard, *Le pape et le droit de gens*, pp. 189–222; MacCaffrey, *op. cit.*, I, 433–35; Jarrige, *op. cit.*, pp. 92–94; Ausset, *op. cit.*, pp. 28–35, 147–53.

[17] *Europäischer Geschichtskalender*, XII (1871), 420–21.

[18] *Ibid.*, pp. 422–23.

[19] *Ibid.*, pp. 424–25.

guaranty, the pope could not appeal to the other powers to defend the papal rights thus guaranteed, for those powers had had no connection in granting them.[20]

This attitude of protest was maintained by all the popes down to 1929,[21] when the Lateran Accord was consummated between Pius XI and Mussolini. In this period (1870–1929) the papacy wished to have no legal connection with the Italian government. It wished to obliterate every appearance of subordination.[22] In 1878, after the death of Pius IX, the attitude of protest was carried to such an extreme that out of thirty-eight cardinals only eight voted to hold the conclave in Rome, whereas all the others thought that the election of the new pope should be held in some non-Italian place, Spain, Munich, and Malta being suggested. But on reconsideration the plan was regarded as unfeasible because, although the Italian government was willing to protect the cardinals in leaving Italy for the election, it would not promise to guarantee them a safe return to Rome.[23]

Down to the year 1929 (when Pius XI and Mussolini entered the Lateran Accord) the papal attitude of protest was also manifested (1) in the way the popes regarded the Italian kingdom and Catholic participation in Italian elections and (2) in the problems arising out of the consistently asserted claims of the pope as temporal sovereign. These aspects of the subject will be considered in the next two sections of this chapter.

[20] Based on the actual papal protests. See also Ward, "Vatican and Quirinal," *Fortnightly Review*, LXXI, 461–63.

[21] *Europäischer Geschichtskalender*, XXIII (1883), 427, 428, 429; O'Reilly, *The Life of Pope Leo XIII*, pp. 287, 291; Sforza, *Makers of Modern Europe*, p. 332; Goetz, "Papst Leo XIII.," in Marks und Müller, *Meister der Politik*, III, 397–98; McCarthy, *op. cit.*, pp. 244–45; encyclical of Benedict XV, "On Christian Reconciliation," *New York Times*, June 2, 1920, p. 17, and June 3, 1920, p. 14; Veit, *Die Kirche im Zeitalter des Individualismus*, IV, Part II, 143; Huddleston, "Vatican's New Place in World Politics," *Current History*, XIII, 208; Blind, "The Papacy and the New Italy, with Reminiscences of Garibaldi," *Westminster Review*, CLX, 263, 269; "Pope Leo XIII and His Successor," *Quarterly Review*, CXCVIII, 448.

[22] Ogg, "The Pope and the Italian Nation," *Chautauquan*, XXXVIII, 18.

[23] Cortesi, "The Vatican in the Twentieth Century," *International Monthly*, IV, 76–77; Schmidlin, *op. cit.*, II, 343.

3. PAPAL ATTITUDE TOWARD THE ITALIAN KINGDOM AND POLITICS

Pius IX and his successors (Leo XIII, Pius X, Benedict XV, and Pius XI) regarded themselves as prisoners in the Vatican palace. Pius IX, in spite of his financial distress, refused to accept the first annual payment that he was to receive from the Italian government (as provided in the Law of Papal Guaranties) in compensation for his loss of revenue from the Papal States. He, as well as his successors, avoided every act that might seem to imply giving papal consent to the spoliation perpetrated by the House of Savoy.

As early as February 29, 1868, Pius IX had, through the *Non expedit,* forbidden Catholics to participate in the elections of the Italian national state either as electors or as elected.[24] Once more the pope expressed himself on the point in a great audience of October 1, 1874, in which he declared that, by voting in the Italian national elections, Catholics were taking an oath to the new state and thus indirectly confirming and approving the annexation of the States of the Church.[25]

The Catholic laity did not regard the papal attitude with anything like approving unanimity, and only in the ultra-Catholic province of Bergamo (north-central Italy) was the papal injunction against voting observed at all. In other regions the Catholics voted in parliamentary elections in almost as great numbers as in local elections.[26] Leo XIII felt it necessary at various times to stress to Catholics the seriousness of observing the *Non expedit* (1886, 1895, 1902.)[27] Pius X, following the same policy, issued a statement, *Motu proprio*, December 18, 1903.[28] But by June 19, 1905, the same pope had greatly modi-

[24] Benigni, "Non expedit," in *Catholic Encyclopedia*, XI, 98–99.

[25] Löffler, *op. cit.*, p. 99; Benigni, article "Non expedit," in *Catholic Encyclopedia*, XI, 99; also article "Giacomo Margotti," in *Catholic Encyclopedia*, IX, 657.

[26] Ogg, "The Pope and the Italian Nation," *Chautauquan*, XXXVIII, 19.

[27] Benigni, article "Non expedit," *Catholic Encyclopedia*, XI, 99; *Quarterly Review*, CXCVIII, 449–55.

[28] *Europäischer Geschichtskalender*, XLIV (1903), 313–14; Benigni, article "Non expedit," *Catholic Encyclopedia*, XI, 99.

fied his attitude. In an encyclical, *Certum consilium*, issued to the Italian bishops, he allowed them to suspend the rule and grant good Catholics the right to vote in national elections if thereby they would prevent the election of a "subversive candidate."[29] This papal pronouncement increased the participation of Catholics in the Italian elections and strengthened the parties of the right. But the *Non expedit* remained theoretically in force; the papacy admitted only partial repeal,[30] until in November, 1919, Benedict XV finally abolished it.[31]

4. THE POPE AS A TEMPORAL SOVEREIGN

Although the pontiff had lost the territory over which he had ruled as sovereign of a temporal state, yet by general consent of the powers, including Italy, he was treated as a sovereign. He continued to exercise the right to send and receive diplomatic representatives; at certain courts the apostolic nuncio had precedence over other ambassadors. Even non-Catholic countries, such as Russia, Holland, and Prussia, maintained diplomats at the papal court. On special occasions Great Britain sent missions to the pope, as did the United States government in 1902, when it sent William Howard Taft to Rome to negotiate the purchase of the Catholic friars' lands in the Philippine Islands. A number of South American republics also had ministers accredited to the Vatican. After 1870 the pope still received royal honors, carried on negotiations with temporal sovereigns on equal terms, and remained a great factor in world-politics.[32]

[29] *Europäischer Geschichtskalender*, XLV (1905), 234–35, 342; Benigni, article "Non expedit," *Catholic Encyclopedia*, XI, 99; "Effect of the Passing of Pope Pius X," *Current Opinion*, LVII, 163, quotes *London Post.*

[30] Mollat, *op. cit.*, p. 407.

[31] Sforza, *op. cit.*, p. 142; Wood, "Three Pontificates," *Dublin Review*, CLXXVIII, 246–48; *Meyers Lexikon* (Leipzig), VIII (1928), 1375.

[32] Fenwick, "The Papacy in International Law," *American Journal of International Law*, VIII, 864–67; Whiteley, "The International Position of the Pope," *North American Review*, CLXXVII, 601–3; Nys, "Le droit international et la papauté," *Revue du droit international*, X, 502; James Murphy, "The Intellectual Activity of Leo XIII," *Catholic World*, LXXIII, 238, 244; Granvelle, "Foreign Policy of the Holy See: Part I,

The historic position of the papacy as a temporal authority was given recognition when in 1885 Germany and Spain selected Leo XIII as arbiter in a dispute concerning ownership of the Caroline Islands.[33] Again, in 1895, Haiti and Santo Domingo referred a boundary dispute to the same pope, though the terms of his decision do not seem to have been published.[34] In 1898, on the eve of the Spanish-American War, Leo XIII offered his friendly mediation to secure peace; Spain accepted the offer, but the United States rejected it.[35] On at least three other occasions Leo XIII or his agents acted as arbiters in international disputes.[36]

In 1815, at the Congress of Vienna, the pope was represented for the last time in a great political international assembly. He was not invited to the Congress of Paris in 1856 or to the Conference of Berlin in 1878, although at both of these congresses the powers discussed the means of persuading Turkey to respect the rights of its Christian subjects. When, however, Tsar Nicholas II (1894–1917) of Russia invited all the governments of the world to send representatives to the first Hague Conference in 1899, and also invited Pope Leo XIII to participate, the Italian government, through its minister of foreign affairs, Admiral Canevaro, notified the governments of the tsar and of Queen Wilhelmina, who was to be host to the Conference, that the Holy See must be prevented from participating in all questions,

---

Leo XIII; Part II, Pius X," *Contemporary Review*, XCIX, 452–62, 517–32. For a list of the thirty-six nations maintaining diplomatic representatives at the Vatican court in 1933, see Williams, *The Catholic Church in Action*, p. 181.

[33] *Europäischer Geschichtskalender*, XXVI (1886), 128, 131, 153; *Annual Register, 1885*, p. 64; Moore, *History and Digest of International Arbitration to Which the United States Has Been a Party*, V, 5043–46; Jarrett, article "Papal Arbitration," in *Catholic Encyclopedia*, XI, 455; Hergenröther, *Handbuch*, IV, 523; Darby, *International Tribunals*, p. 809; Müller, *Das Friedenswerk der Kirche*, I, 325–33.

[34] Moore, *op. cit.*, V, 5018; Darby, *op. cit.*, p. 823; Jarrett, "Papal Arbitration," *Catholic Encyclopedia*, XI, 455; Müller, *op. cit.*, I, 48.

[35] *Europäischer Geschichtskalender*, XXIX (1899), 303; Hoijer, *La solution pacifique des litigés internationaux avant et depuis la société des nations*, p. 40; Latané, *America as a World Power, 1897–1907*, pp. 23, 24.

[36] Roemer and Ellis, *The Catholic Church and Peace Efforts*, pp. 51–53.

for fear that such representation would be an acknowledgment of the temporal rights and power of the Holy See. The Dutch government, in issuing the final invitations to the powers, omitted sending an invitation to the papacy.[37]

Leo XIII, instead of protesting against the diplomatic slight that had been administered to him, conducted himself in such a way as to indicate that he was more pacifically minded than any of the powers assembled ostensibly in the interests of promoting peace. On April 11, 1899, in a discourse to the cardinals that was published in the press of the world, he commended the spirit of the Peace Conference and took it under his protection. When the Conference opened the second week in May, the *Osservatore Romano*, the official papal newspaper, at the instigation of the Vatican, published an article that was quite sympathetic with the Conference and contained no recriminations. In a letter to Queen Wilhelmina, in which the pontiff thanked her for her intention of inviting him to send representatives to the Conference, he expressed his hope that the movement might succeed in establishing a more peaceful era. He asserted that he as pontiff would do all in his power, under the abnormal conditions prevailing, to promote the cause of peace.

This dignified papal attitude caused the pope to be widely admired. The pontifical calmness was quite in contrast to the agitation manifested by Italy and its representatives at the Conference, whose chief aim seemed to be, not to promote the cause of peace, but to prevent the pope from being recognized as a sovereign, an action that might once more open up the Roman question. But Leo XIII tried to allay the fears and suspicions of the Italian representatives by ordering his intelligent internuncio, Mgr Tarnassi, to absent himself from The Hague for several weeks.[38] Naturally, since Italy had manifested such uneasiness over papal participation in the first Hague Conference,

[37] *Europäischer Geschichtskalender*, XL (1899), 247; Goyau, "La conférence de la Haye et le Sainte-Siège," *Revue des deux mondes*, CLIV, 590–606, 608; "The Peace Conference, and What Might Have Been" (editorial), *Catholic World*, LXIX, 577–83.

[38] Goyau, "La conférence de la Haye," *Revue des deux mondes*, CLIV, 606, 608–9; Granvelle, "Foreign Policy of the Holy See," *Contemporary Review*, XCIX, 458–59.

no invitation was extended to the pope in 1907, when the second Hague Conference convened.

The situation of the papacy after the spoliation of 1860 and 1870 and the enactment of the Law of Papal Guaranties (1871) had never received any formal international ratification. Therefore the papacy held that, if a Catholic ruler were to enter Rome to pay an official visit to the Italian king in the Quirinal palace, such ruler would be giving his moral sanction to the spoliation of the pontiff. All Catholic sovereigns respected this papal attitude. In 1871, Pedro II (1831–89), emperor of Brazil, avoided embarrassment by meeting Victor Emmanuel II (1861–78) at a station outside of Rome.[39] Francis Joseph I (1848–1916) of Austria, although bound to Italy by the Triple Alliance, always refused to return the royal visit made in Vienna in 1873 by Victor Emmanuel II. King Carlos I (1889–1908) of Portugal, for a similar reason, abandoned his plans to visit his relatives in Rome.[40] In 1919 the president of Brazil came to Rome and was admitted to the papal presence only through the subterfuge that he had not yet taken formal possession of his office, and on the strict understanding that it should not constitute a precedent.[41]

But the government of the French Republic did not manifest the same considerateness as did the monarchs of Austria and Spain, when in April, 1904, President Loubet made a return visit to the king of Italy. The foreign secretary of Leo XIII, Cardinal Rampolla, made a futile objection to carrying out the plan while it was still in the process of formulation, in 1903; and, once the visit had taken place, the successor of Leo XIII,

[39] J. T. Smith, "The Prisoner of the Vatican," *Munsey's Magazine*, XXXIV, 409. After diligent search, corroboration of this incident could not be found anywhere in the sources available to me. Pedro II was in Europe in 1871 and 1877, *Eminent Persons*, (London Times), V, 158; 1871 was accepted as the probable date of this incident on the basis of Schmidlin, *op. cit.*, II, 95.

[40] Murphy, "Germany and Russia at the Vatican," *Catholic World*, LXXVII, 428; Klein, "Breaking and Renewing Diplomatic Relations between France and the Holy See," *Catholic World*, CXII, 580; Coolidge, *Origins of the Triple Alliance*, pp. 209–16; "Pope Leo XIII and His Successor," *Quarterly Review*, CXCVIII, 442–44.

[41] *New York Times*, June 2, 1920, p. 17.

Pius X (1903–14), sent a confidential protest, dated April 28, 1904, to France and all the other states that had direct communication with his court. In this protest he pointed out that "through this official and festive visit to the king of Italy, taking place in one of the apostolic palaces [the Quirinal], the French president was publically sanctioning the spoliation of the pope." The papal organ, *Osservatore Romano*, commented that such a protest would not have been uttered if the interview had taken place in some other city of Italy, and that the pope did not imply by his action any protest against the *rapprochement* between France and Italy.[42] This protest, when it became public in a month, led to the withdrawal of the French ambassador to the Vatican.[43] The next year, in 1905, when France abrogated the Concordat of 1801 by unilateral action,[44] Pius X protested against this act on the ground that it was a violation of international law; but the protest was not heeded by France.[45] However, during the years 1920–21, the French government, needing the political support of the papacy in various European and world-questions, resumed diplomatic relations with the Vatican.[46] Since the World War all the great powers except the United States, and many lesser powers—thirty-six in all—have

[42] *Europäischer Geschichtskalender*, XLV (1905), 265–66; *Annual Register, 1904*, p. 9; "France and the Vatican" (editorial), *New York Nation*, LXXVIII, 406–7; "Chronique de la quinzaine," *Revue des deux mondes*, May 1, 1904, pp. 230–31; Klein, "Breaking and Renewing Diplomatic Relations," *Catholic World*, CXII, 580–81.

[43] "France and the Vatican" (editorial), *Nation*, LXXVIII, 407; Klein, "Breaking and Renewing Diplomatic Relations," *Catholic World*, CXII, 581; Buell, "France and the Vatican," *Political Science Quarterly*, XXXVI, 48–49.

[44] *Europäischer Geschichtskalender*, XLVI (1906), 207–11, 213, 214, 215; *Annual Register, 1905*, [pp. 259, 263–64, 265, 268]; Klein, "Breaking and Renewing Diplomatic Relations," *Catholic World*, CXII, 585.

[45] *Europäischer Geschichtskalender*, XLVI (1906), 234; Fenwick, "The New City of the Vatican," *American Journal of International Law*, XXIII, 373; Klein, "Breaking and Renewing Diplomatic Relations," *Catholic World*, CXII, 585.

[46] Buell, "France and the Vatican," *Political Science Quarterly*, XXXVI, 30–50; Huddleston, "The Revival of the Vatican," *Fortnightly Review*, CXIV, 67–77; Huddleston, "Vatican's New Place in World Politics," *Current History*, XIII, 203–10; Wood, "Vatican Politics and Policies," *Atlantic Monthly*, CXXVIII, 398–400; *Current History*, XII, 363–64, and XIV, 694–97.

been maintaining diplomatic representatives at the Vatican; and France also felt the need of having her representative present there when questions of importance to France were being discussed.[47]

Owing to the pleas of the Spanish and Belgian monarchs, Benedict XV issued an encyclical on May 20, 1920 (*On Christian Reconciliation*), which relaxed the papal attitude concerning the visits of foreign Catholic monarchs to the court of the king of Italy. As a consequence the Quirinal was visited in April, 1922, by the monarchs of Belgium; in July, 1922, by the president of the Argentine Republic; and in November, 1923, by the monarchs of Spain.[48]

During the World War (1914–18) Benedict XV (1914–22), who was "shepherd to peoples in both camps," endeavored assiduously to alleviate the evils of this titantic struggle. During each of the years 1914 and 1915 he made two appeals to the powers to compose their differences and seek peace.[49] On August 1, 1917, he offered his services as mediator to the belligerent powers.[50] The Central Powers answered the note.[51] The Allied governments ignored it except for the fact that President Wilson, who resented papal interference, answered

[47] *Literary Digest*, LXVI (September 25, 1920), 34; Williams, *op. cit.*, p. 181; Jarrige, *op. cit.*, p. 256.

[48] Wood, "Three Pontificates, a Retrospect," *Dublin Review*, CLXXVIII, 247; *New York Times*, June 2, 1920, p. 14, and June 3, 1920, p. 17; Buell, "France and the Vatican," *Political Science Quarterly*, XXXVI, 48; *Literary Digest*, LXVI (August 21, 1920), 24–25.

[49] (November 1 and December 24, 1914), *Europäischer Geschichtskalender*, LV (1914), 741–43; Müller, *op. cit.*, I, 422–25, 429–32; (January 22 and July 28, 1915), *Europäischer Geschichtskalender*, LVI (1915), 1003–4, 1006–7; Müller, *op. cit.*, I, 433–36, 444–46; Pace, "Pope Benedict XV," *Catholic World*, CXIV, 725–27; Löffler, *op. cit.*, pp. 187–89.

[50] *Europäischer Geschichtskalender*, LVIII (1917), Part II, 538–42; *Annual Register, 1917*, [pp. 205–6, 207–8]; Müller, *op. cit.*, I, 464–68; Pace, "Pope Benedict XV," *Catholic World*, CXIV, 727–29; Löffler, *op. cit.*, pp. 190–93; McMaster, *The United States in the World War*, I, 403–4.

[51] *Ludendorff's Own Story*, II, 131–32; Bassett, *Our War with Germany*, pp. 312–13; Löffler, *op. cit.*, pp. 193–94; Gebhardt, *Handbuch der deutschen Geschichte*, II, 814.

the note in such a way as to take all possibility of mediation out of the hands of the pope.[52]

The refusal of Great Britain, France, and Italy to pay any attention to the note of Benedict XV is in part explained by the fact that, when Italy made arrangements to enter the war through signing the secret Treaty of London (April 26, 1915), Article 15 provided that "France, Great Britain and Russia shall support such opposition as Italy may make to any proposal in the direction of introducing a representative of the Holy See in any peace negotiations for the settlement of questions raised by the present war."[53] Moreover, under the circumstances it is not strange that, when the Italian government confiscated the Palazzo Venezia, the seat of the Austrian legation at the Holy See, the Quirinal should pay no attention to the protest of Benedict XV against the violation of personal immunity and "most sacred rights" to receive ambassadors as guaranteed to him by the Law of Guaranties.[54]

5. THE LATERAN ACCORD OF FEBRUARY 11, 1929

The intransigent attitude maintained by the papacy since 1870 concerning the Kingdom of Italy, is, however, only one part of the truth. A reconciliation was desired by all the popes, since the time of Pius IX, if only it were possible to receive a recognition of papal rights in law as well as in fact. The popes had never been molested in the Vatican, and they all craved some sort of reconciliation. Leo XIII once said, "Let Italy take the first step and restore Rome to the Holy See; then the Holy See will relinquish its claims to its former possessions, and will

[52] House, *Intimate Papers*, III, 156; Jusserand, communication to the editor of the *American Historical Review*, XXXVII, 817–19; McMaster, *op. cit.*, I, 404–7; Bassett, *op. cit.*, pp. 313–14; Seldes, *The Vatican: Yesterday—Today—Tomorrow*, pp. 262–68.

[53] Temperly, *A History of the Peace Conference of Paris*, V, 390–91; for slightly different phraseology, see Cocks, *The Secret Treaties and Understandings*, p. 40; also *The New Europe*, VI (January 17, 1918), 27.

[54] *Europäischer Geschichtskalender*, LVII (1916), Part II, 297, 305–6; Fenwick, "The New City of the Vatican," *American Journal of International Law*, XXIII, 372.

live in peace with the kingdom as with all other states." This remark was never made in public, but often in private.[55]

Finally, after long negotiations, the Lateran Accord was consummated on February 11, 1929, between Pope Pius XI and Mussolini, as head of the Italian state, thus ending the irritating impasse that had existed between the Vatican and the Quirinal since September, 1870. Both parties were willing to make compromises. The pope recognized the Kingdom of Italy, thus removing from the Italian monarchy the stigma with which it had been regarded by non-Italian Catholics. The pope was willing to accept a cash sum and a stipulated amount of interest-bearing Italian bonds as compensation for his loss of income from the Papal States as they had existed in 1860.

The ultra-nationalist Fascist state, being in need of all the social and psychological support that it could secure, was willing to abrogate the unilateral Law of Guaranties and to make terms with the head of the great international Roman Catholic church, recognizing Roman Catholicism as the official religion of Italy and consenting to the giving of Catholic religious instruction in the schools of the nation. The pope was also given absolute sovereignty over a small state, with an area of about 110 acres, which Pius XI affirms is adequate to enable him to exercise his spiritual functions independently of a particular nation or group of nations. The pope now controls a "sort of spiritual District of Columbia," in which he has full authority.

The provision of the Lateran Accord that is far more pertinent to the subject of this treatise is the fact that in Article 24 the papacy has itself admitted the secularization of international politics, for the pope declares that the Holy See

wishes to remain and will remain extraneous to all temporal disputes between nations and to international congresses convoked for the settlement of such

[55] Crispoliti, "From Leo XIII to Pius X," *International Quarterly*, IX, 165; McCarthy, *op. cit.*, pp. 40–44; see also Vogüé, "Pope Leo XIII," *Forum*, XXII, 518–19; Crawford, "Leo the Thirteenth," *Outlook*, LXI, 774; *Edinburgh Review*, CXCVIII, 290.

disputes unless the contending parties make a concordant appeal to its mission of peace; nevertheless it reserves the right in every case to exercise its moral and spiritual power.[56]

This means that the papacy has finally recognized that its political activity, as interpreted by Gregory VII, Innocent III, and Boniface VIII, has come to an end. That the real realm of its influence lies in spiritual, moral, and broadly social fields. That in international politics its attitude will be one of neutrality; that it will not seek to enter the League of Nations, and that it would refuse to enter it even if an invitation were extended by courtesy.[57]

Thus in 1929 came to an end the long contest between the secular powers and the papacy. The head of the church at last relinquished his claims to be final authority in secular affairs. The counterclaims of the states that they should have full power to determine the sphere of politics, both national and international, had been recognized by the papacy. The pontiff had finally conceded that there is a sphere of human affairs in which he will take no part. Politics, national and international, had been secularized. The secularization of politics, which had in practice been established in 1648 by the Congress of Westphalia, but which had not been accepted as legal by the papacy, now, after almost three centuries of active and tacit protest, had at last been recognized by the papacy as a legalized situation in a solemnly sanctioned treaty. Politics was finally secularized in 1929, with the full and willing consent of the power that had for eight and a half centuries actively opposed it.

[56] Text of the Treaty, *Current History*, XXX, 552–57; Lulvès, "Der Lateran Vertrag," *Preussische Jahrbücher*, CCXVI, 69.

[57] Fenwick, "The New City of the Vatican," *American Journal of International Law*, XXII, 373–74.

Chapter Nineteen

THE PAPACY—VICTOR OR VANQUISHED?

THE reader may well have gained the impression that in the final eventuation of the long struggle against the secularization of politics, the papacy and the Roman Catholic church had suffered a humiliating defeat. In the minds of Wangnereck and his supporters in the seventeenth century that was true;[1] but, in the adjustments of later centuries, Catholic thinkers themselves have been able to look upon the secularization of politics as a blessing in disguise for the church. The original purpose and activity of the Catholic church were not political, but spiritual and moral. The assumption of political power by the church and papacy was only a temporary development, although the exercise thereof endured for many centuries. The entry of the church into the sphere of politics had been made necessary by the political confusion incident to the decline and ruin of the Roman Empire and the political chaos of feudal times. When the national monarchies of western and central Europe had developed adequate governing strength to take over the political functions of the state in an ever increasing degree, and when the church, against its will, was eliminated as a political influence, it was all the more able to confine itself to its original scope of activity: spiritual, social, and ethical leadership.

I. EXTRUSION FROM POLITICS AN ADVANTAGE TO THE PAPACY

In giving up its political rights and temporal authority the Catholic church has yielded nothing that is vital and funda-

[1] See chap. xv.

mental. In losing control of the Papal States the Holy See has got rid of its characteristics of caesaropapism, under which its spiritual power was too often subordinated to the secular. The pontiff, in terminating his protesting attitude when entering the Lateran Accord of 1929, has freed himself from a situation that had had a profoundly noxious influence on the ecclesiastical, religious, and moral situation, not only in Italy but elsewhere as well. Actually, in being freed from his secular power, the pope exerts a greater moral influence than formerly. In support of such affirmations the following citations from Catholic authors are pertinent: H. A. Brann, in discussing the "Relation of the Church to Human Progress," remarked, in 1889, "The Church may not be strong in temporals; but she is spiritually stronger."[2] William Barry, a Catholic divine and professor of theology, in discussing the significance of the pontificate of Leo XIII, just after his death in 1903, expressed the opinion that "when all is said, the nineteenth century leaves the Church visibly stronger than she was a hundred years ago, not merely, or chiefly in relation to politics, but as a spiritual power."[3] Frederick William, Bishop of Northampton (England), writing during the World War, in 1915, states the following: "Yet the Papacy, after all its vicissitudes, remains the supreme moral power in the world, with its dignity and obligations not lessened, perhaps even enhanced, by isolation from political entanglements."[4]

Non-Catholic and secular publicists and editors write in a similar vein. Dr. James Brown Scott, editor of the *American Journal of International Law*, writing in 1911, said:

> In the middle ages, the most powerful of emperors, barefoot and penitent, humbled himself before the Vicar of Christ; within the past generation, the man of "blood and iron" who had unified Germany torn by a thousand years of dissension and armed conflict, went, as it were, to Canossa; in our own day,

[2] *American Catholic Quarterly Review*, XIV, 648.

[3] "Leo XIII, a Retrospect," *Dublin Review*, CXXXIII, 248.

[4] "The Neutrality of the Holy See," *Dublin Review*, CLVII, 139. For further similar Catholic statements see: John K. Cartwright, "Contributions of the Papacy to International Peace," *Catholic Historical Review*, N.S., VIII, 167–68; Barry, "Benedict XV: Pontiff of Peace," *Dublin Review*, CLXX, 165.

and in a higher sense, the world bows before the Pontiff [Pius X] true to his mission, armed only with the sword of the Spirit and the breastplate of righteousness.[5]

The Italian, Salvatore Cortesi, in discussing papal affairs at the turn of the twentieth century, states that "several among the most enlightened" of the cardinals

acknowledge that the loss of the last inch of territorial domain has marked the starting point of the present extended spiritual power of the Roman Church. All her troubles, all her weaknesses of the past, from Charlemagne to our day, arose especially from her desire to maintain and augment the temporal power. With the cessation of this effort, the Pope, while presenting himself to the faithful of Christendom as despoiled, persecuted, and a prisoner, is in reality richer, freer and stronger. Freer and stronger, because in the full exercise of his spiritual ministry he has never enjoyed so much independence as at present, when he cannot be coerced with threats against his territory; the most eloquent proof of this being the famous "Kulturkampf" in Germany, which country, in other times, would certainly have ended the matter by an appeal to arms. Richer, because, since the popes have voluntarily shut themselves up in the Vatican, the offerings of the faithful have reached proportions not dreamed of before. To come to an understanding with the Italian government would be financially disadvantageous.[6]

James Gustavus Whiteley, discussing "The International Position of the Pope" in 1904, comments:

The loss of the temporal possessions has in some ways, however, added to the dignity and authority of the Pope. His power, relieved from temporal localization, has increased throughout Christendom. . . . . As Monsieur Revier remarks in his great work on International Law: "If the successor of Gregory and Innocent is not to-day the monarch of monarchs, the dispensor of crowns, the distributor of continents and oceans, he still personifies the greatest moral force of the world."[7]

And again,

The Pope, although deprived of his temporal possessions, still receives royal honors, sends and receives ambassadors, treats with temporal sovereigns on

[5] James Brown Scott, editorial, *American Journal of International Law*, V, 709.

[6] Cortesi, "The Vatican in the Twentieth Century," *International Monthly*, IV, 77–78; for a corroborative statement concerning the increased income and influence of the papacy, see Tuker, "The Papacy since the Events of 1870," *Fortnightly Review*, LXXXII, 665.

[7] Whiteley, "The International Position of the Pope," *North American Review*, CLXXVII, 606.

even terms, and is one of the great factors in the world's politics. It may even be said that his authority has been purified and increased since he has ceased to be a petty prince of Italy.[8]

The editor of the London *Spectator*, commenting in 1904 on the rumors as to the proposed policies of Pius X, the successor of Leo XIII, expressed the hope that the statement may prove well founded

that Pius X may make his Pontificate memorable by the abandonment of a policy that is certain to impair the vigour of the Roman Church. If the history of Latin Christianity is considered impartially we believe it will be admitted that the temporal power has done nothing but harm to the Roman Church. . . . . Had the Vatican been wise enough to refuse or discard its triple crown, its influence over its spiritual subjects would have been infinitely greater than it was throughout the centuries in which it was battling and intriguing, first to establish temporal sovereignty, and next to maintain that sovereignty undiminished. When the kingdom of Italy finally deprived the Pope of his temporal sovereignty, though leaving him complete spiritual independence and personal independence, the Holy See obtained an opportunity to renew its influence over the hearts and minds rather than the bodies of men. Unfortunately the Vatican had too long been concerned with serving tables, and with petty affairs of police and urban administration, to be able at once to cast aside those toys and rise to the height of the occasion.[9]

In the same year (1904) an Italian, discussing papal affairs as affected by the advent of Pius X, commented:

After the Popes sagaciously became and remained prisoners of the Vatican, they devoted themselves with calm and undisturbed mind to increasing the prestige of the Holy See, and succeeded in regaining for its spiritual ascendancy such a position as it had not enjoyed for ages. In consequence Italy now felt herself more restrained and bound in her relations with the Papacy when she saw how its increased splendor awoke in other nations an enlarged interest in the person and circumstances of the pontiff.[10]

Count Carlo Sforza, in chronicling his recollections of Pius XI, in 1930, observes that "the Church only appeared again as one of the leading moral forces in the world after she had lost all temporal power, and she lived in a régime of common liberty."[11]

[8] *Ibid.*, p. 603. [9] Editorial, *The Spectator*, XCII (1904), 951–52.

[10] Crispoliti, "From Leo XIII to Pius X," *International Quarterly*, IX, 163.

[11] Sforza, *Makers of Modern Europe, Portraits and Personal Impressions and Recollections*, p. 336; also quoted in *Current History*, XXXI, 1084, in "The Pope's Attitude toward Liberalism."

Washington Gladden, the eminent Congregationalist preacher, writing in 1903 in a symposium on the work and influence of Leo XIII, said that the great influence that the pope exerted, even among Protestants, was

> greatly assisted by the fact that Leo XIII had no temporal power to wield, but was compelled to confine his entire administration to the spiritual field. It is this fact that has made him the most powerful of all the Popes; all civilized rulers, Protestant as well as Catholics, have treated him with a respect never accorded to any of his predecessors.[12]

After contrasting the consequences of Pope Hildebrand's policy in general (and particularly with reference to the medieval German Empire) with the conciliatory policy of Leo XIII in terminating the *Kulturkampf* with William I and Bismarck, Dr. Gladden goes on to observe:

> How much more complete and permanent is this victory won by weapons that are not carnal, than any that Hildebrand ever won? How much stronger does the Roman Catholic Church stand, today, by virtue of Leo's peaceful policy, in all the nations of the earth, than it stood when by the vast assumptions of the medieval Pope it had arrayed against it the national feeling of every Christian people!
>
> The day will come, we may trust, when this lesson will be learned by Catholic theologians and Catholic rulers, and when it will be clearly understood that the power of the Christian Church must forever reside in its frank and complete abandonment of all pretensions to temporal power, in its fearless casting away of all carnal weapons, in its unhesitating and absolute trust in moral and spiritual forces. When that day shall come, the pontificate of Leo XIII will be pointed to as the one in which the true character of the Christian leadership of the world began to be clearly seen.[13]

2. THE PAPACY AND THE RECONSTRUCTION OF THE SOCIAL ORDER

The spiritual and moral gains of the papacy were achieved not merely as a consequence of having been extruded from the political sphere but—and this is even more significant—through

[12] Gladden, *North American Review*, CLXXVII, 354–55.

[13] *Ibid.*, pp. 355–56. For further similar and pertinent statements see: *American Review of Reviews*, LXV, 433; *Independent*, CVIII, 105; H. P. Fairchild, "What Does the Pope Want?" *New Republic*, LXV, 292; Ascoli, "The Roman Church and Political Action," *Foreign Affairs*, XIII, 449–50, 452; "Pope Leo XIII," *Quarterly Review*, CXCVIII, 287; Fawkes, "The Pontificate of Pius X," *ibid.*, CCXXVII, 478.

the aggressive and courageous leadership of Leo XIII and his three successors (Pius X, Benedict XV, and Pius XI) in attempting to reconstruct the social institutions of the modern world. This and the two following sections of this chapter will indicate the vigorous part that the papacy has played in fostering the rebuilding of the social order on sound ethical and Christian principles, in promoting the cause of universal peace, and, in recent years especially, in defending the right of the individual in safeguarding his conscience against the claims of the authoritarian or totalitarian state.

Leo XIII will long be remembered for imbuing the papacy with a change in attitude and motives. He felt that the church could not afford to carry on a policy of mere passivity. It could not be assuming an attitude of sullen resentment, of rancorous protest when the European continent was being altered fundamentally by great democratic forces. The papacy must engage in active leadership in the broad social sphere, which had been, and still was being, so significantly transformed by the Industrial Revolution. Since 1815 the liberal Catholic forces in many European lands had been carrying on only partially successful efforts to achieve needed social readjustments. It was Leo's hope to unite these forces under papal leadership, to animate them by a vivifying ideal that would enable the church to play its historic rôle as a potent social guide and force. Catholicism was to develop a social policy that was to dominate all other policies.

While still Bishop of Perugia he had, in his last three pastoral letters (of the years 1876, 1877, and 1878) expressed a challenging view concerning the relation of the Catholic church to the material and moral problems of the nineteenth century. As pope he issued many notable documents dealing with the broad social question. As a consequence he infused the papacy so fully with his objectives that it will probably not swerve from them for a long time.[14]

[14] Goetz, "Papst Leo XIII," in Marks and Müller, *Meister der Politik*, III, 386–95; Ward, "Leo XIII," *Fortnightly Review*, LXXX, 251–52; Vogüé, "Pope Leo XIII," *Forum*, XXII, 514–18; Schmidlin, *Papstgeschichte*, II, 365–73.

Leo XIII was neither the first Catholic nor the first among his contemporaries to see the significance of the labor problem with a new viewpoint. But he was the first of those in authority over any of the great organizations of the world to take a definite stand concerning the social question, giving it a revolutionary tinge. He combined the Catholic and social movement as an indissoluble unit. As to viewpoint, he made Catholicism one of the most advanced social organizations in the world.[15]

Throughout the long pontificate of Leo XIII he issued numerous encyclicals and other documents dealing with the social question.[16] In all of these he stressed the need for applying moral and religious forces to the solution of that question. His most significant encyclical was *Rerum novarum* (May 15, 1891). In this extended document of more than thirteen thousand words he deals with the condition of the working classes and the duties of the church to these classes.[17]

Into the details of this analysis of the misfortunes of the laborers we cannot go in this connection. Suffice it to say that he courageously points out that the present economic system has produced conditions that are "contrary to charity and justice," and that "a remedy for these conditions must be found quickly." He asserts that "men have been given over . . . . to the callousness of employers and the greed of unrestrained competition." He mentions "rapacious usury" that is "still practiced by avaricious and grasping men." He declares "that a small number of very rich men have been able to lay upon the masses a yoke little better than slavery itself."[18] He opposes socialism

[15] Goetz, article "Papst Leo XIII," in Marks and Müller, *op. cit.*, III, 399–400; Veit, *Die Kirche im Zeitalter des Individualismus*, IV, Part II, 146–47.

[16] Devas, "The Political Economy of Leo XIII," *Dublin Review*, CXXX, 294, and CXXXI, 132–52; Schmidlin, *op. cit.*, II, 368–83; Löffler, *Papstgeschichte*, pp. 129–30; Veit, *op. cit.*, IV, Part II, 146–47.

[17] "Encyclical Letter of Pope Leo XIII" (in English), *American Catholic Quarterly Review*, XVI, 529–57. For discussion thereof see Keane, "The Encyclical *Rerum Novarum*," *American Catholic Quarterly Review*, XVI, 595–611; Baur and Rieder, *Päpstliche Enzykliken und ihre Stellung zur Politik*, pp. 44–50; Schmidlin, *op. cit.*, II, 373–77; Seppelt, *Papstgeschichte*, pp. 133–34.

[18] *American Catholic Quarterly Review*, XVI, 530.

as a proposed solution of society's ills,[19] and affirms that the social question cannot be solved "without the assistance of Religion and the Church," which through its leadership must bring about the co-operation of "the Rulers of the State, of employers of labor, of the wealthy, and of the working population themselves, for whom we plead."[20] He pronounces "irrational and false" "the idea that class is naturally hostile to class."[21] He declares that "it is shameful and inhuman to treat men like chattels to make money by, or to look upon them merely as so much muscle or physical power"; that it is a crime "to defraud any one of his wages that are his due."[22] He maintains that, if the ills of society are to be cured, the only remedy lies in "a return to the Christian life and Christian institutions."[23] As a consequence it should be the "first duty . . . . of the State to make sure that the laws and institutions, the general character of the administration of the Commonwealth, shall be such as to produce of themselves public well-being and private prosperity"; "the public administration must duly and solicitously provide for the welfare and comfort of the working people."[24] Therefore the state should protect the workers through regulations concerning the length of the working day, the labor of women and children, adequate conditions of labor, minimum wages, Sunday rest.[25] But not all responsibility rests with the state. Employers and employees should also each do their part by forming associations and organizations that would provide necessary relief and legal protection to those in need thereof. He urged the formation of a Catholic labor organization, to which he gave much attention.[26]

Into an analysis of the faultlessness or feasibility of this social program we need not enter. The essential fact for us is that Leo XIII, through his courageous and penetrating statement, emphatically announced that the Catholic church was deeply in-

[19] *Ibid.*, pp. 534–35.

[20] *Ibid.*, p. 535.

[21] *Ibid.* p., 536.

[22] *Ibid.*, p. 537.

[23] *Ibid.*, p. 541.

[24] *Ibid.*, p. 543.

[25] *Ibid.*, pp. 546–50.

[26] *Ibid.*, pp. 550–56.

terested in the welfare of the great mass of workers everywhere in the world. The document was at once called the "Workingman's Magna Charta" and the "Social Magna Charta of Catholicism," and its author was designated as the "Workingman's Pope."[27] Through the publication of this encyclical, the pope had proclaimed the idea that the Catholic church should once more become the social guide of the world, in non-Catholic as well as in Catholic nations.[28] He had formulated for the church a new social doctrine, better suited to modern society, a doctrine that would give the papacy new social and moral prestige. In *Rerum novarum* and his numerous other published documents on the social question, he had laid down the foundation principles for scientific and organized economic thinking and planning. He encouraged the formation of Catholic organizations for dealing with the problems of present society in a spirit of love and not material efficiency.[29] The pope was once more calling attention to the need of applying the historic principles of Christian ethics, such as had been applied in medieval and early modern times, when the papacy and church officers urged slave owners and feudal lords to give better treatment to their slaves and serfs.[30]

Whereas, since 1815 the interests of the papacy had often seemed identified wholly with the thrones of Europe,[31] now the pope was proclaiming a doctrine that identified the interests of the church with those of the masses, who seemed increasingly helpless in the face of the relentless forces of the Industrial Revolution. Leo's dauntlessness and insight were all the more significant because, while he was proclaiming the most liberal social and labor program in the history of the church and "was

[27] Barry, *The Coming Age and the Catholic Church*, p. 34; *Encyclopaedia Britannica* (14th ed.), XIII, 929; *Quarterly Review*, CXCVIII, 305; Schmidlin, *op. cit.*, II, 377.

[28] Crawford, "Leo the Thirteenth," *Outlook*, LXI, 773; Granvelle, "Foreign Policy of the Holy See," *Contemporary Review*, XCIX, 458, 460.

[29] Goetz, article "Papst Leo XIII," in Marks and Müller, *op. cit.*, III, 401.

[30] Hergenröther, *Handbuch*, II, 190–91, and II, 612–17, 822–24; Allard, article "Slavery," *Catholic Encyclopedia*, XIV, 37–38; Ryan, article "Charity," *ibid.*, III, 597–98.

[31] Vogüé, "Pope Leo XIII," *Forum*, XXII, 518.

leading his hordes as a unit into the social battlefield," the governing authorities of the Protestant churches were warning their young ministers against discussing the social question.[32]

It is true that in January, 1902, Leo XIII somewhat reversed his liberal policy, as expressed in *Rerum novarum*, when he issued the encyclical concerning "Christian Democracy in Italy," in which he condemned, as novelties, all such things as factory laws for children, old age pensions, minimum wages for agricultural laborers, the eight-hour day, trade guilds, and the encouragement of Sunday rest (because they approached socialism too freely) and counseled the popular Christian movement (*Populari*) in Italy to devote its energies to a restoration of the temporal power.[33]

However, that swerving from the part of courageous papal leadership was more than offset when Pius XI issued his encyclical "Reconstruction of the Social Order," or *Quadragesimo Anno*, if we designate it by its Latin title. This document was issued May 15, 1931, in commemoration of the fortieth anniversary of the publication of *Rerum novarum* by Leo XIII. In this document Pius wished once more to call to the attention of the Catholic church and of the world at large the characteristics and influence of his predecessor's noteworthy pronouncement, to clear away certain doubts that had arisen concerning it, and to expand and clarify its principles so as to fit modern economic and social conditions. Above all, he sought to assure the great mass of workers that the Catholic church is mindful of their distressing conditions and is seeking a solution of present problems through means other than those of violence and revolution.[34]

Into the details of this significant document[35] of more than

[32] Goetz, article "Papst Leo XIII," in Marks and Müller, *op. cit.*, III, 401; see also Hutchinson, "Religion vs. the World We Live In," *Forum*, LXXXIX, 81.

[33] Article "Leo XIII," *Encyclopaedia Britannica* (14th ed.), XIII, 929; Goetz, article "Papst Leo XIII," in Marks and Müller, *op. cit.*, III, 401–2; Schmidlin, *op. cit.*, II, 383.

[34] Arnaldo Cortesi, *New York Times*, May 24, 1931, sec. I, pp. 1, 3; John A. Ryan, *ibid.*, May 26, 1931, p. 6.

[35] Authorized English translation, *New York Times*, May 24, 1931, sec. II, pp. 1-3.

twenty-thousand words we cannot enter here, but it is enough to point out that Pius XI is clear-cut in his denunciation of the evils of capitalism, in his recognition of the broad claims of the workers, and in his suggestions of remedies to be applied to the great social and economic problems of this age. Although he admits that the condition of the workingmen has greatly improved, "especially in the larger and more civilized states," he also points out that in eastern Asia and elsewhere "the number of dispossessed laboring masses" has "increased beyond measure" and that the immense army of hired rural laborers, whose condition is depressed in the extreme, "have no hope of ever obtaining a share in the land." He therefore demands the uplifting of the proletariat.[36] He points out the injustice of present-day distribution as evidenced by the "immense number of propertyless wage-earners on the one hand and the superabundant riches of the fortunate few on the other,"[37] and urges that the laborers be "freed from that hand-to-mouth uncertainty which is the lot of the proletarian."[38]

He condemns the immense economic power that is "concentrated in the hands of the few . . . . who are frequently not the owners but only the trustees and directors of invested funds, who administer them at their good pleasure" and "are able to govern credit and determine its allotment, ... thus grasping in their hands the very soul of production, so that no one dare breathe against their will." He asserts that "this accumulation of power is a natural result of limitless free competition," which is now replaced by economic dictatorship. He condemns "economic nationalism," "economic imperialism," and "international imperialism in financial affairs."[39] He also denounces the "frightful perils to which the morals of workers . . . . and the virtue of girls and women are exposed in the modern factories."[40]

He regards our present industrial system as an agency for the

[36] *New York Times*, May 24, 1931, sec. II, p. 1, col. 8, and p. 2, col. 2.

[37] *Ibid.*, p. 1, col. 8.

[38] *Ibid.*, p. 2, col. 1.

[39] *Ibid.*, col. 5.

[40] *Ibid.*, col. 8.

destruction and disintegration of human character. He asserts that the true Christian spirit cannot be fostered by a system in which

> man's one solicitude is to obtain his daily bread in any way he can, and so bodily labor, which was decreed by Providence for the good of man's body and soul . . . . has everywhere been changed into an instrument of strange perversion; for dead matter leaves the factory enobled and transformed, where men are corrupted and degraded.[41]

He recognizes the right of labor to organize,[42] asserts the supremacy of human welfare over profits,[43] and implies the right of labor to participate in the management of industry.[44] He maintains that wages should be high enough to obviate any need for the labor of women and children and to make possible the accumulation of property by the worker.[45]

Whereas his predecessor condemned socialism, Pius now condemns both socialism and communism (two opposing systems),[46] but affirms that the remedies for these evils lie in the application of the "principles of right reason and Christian social philosophy regarding capital and labor" and that "their mutual co-operation must be accepted in theory and reduced to practice." "Free competition . . . . and economic domination must be kept within just and definite limits" and "brought under effective control of the public authority" in such matters as the state can handle. "The public institutions of the Nations must be such as to make the whole of human society conform to the common good, *i.e.*, to the standard of social justice." There must be "a return to Christian life and Christian institutions," for "Christianity alone can apply an efficacious remedy for the excessive solicitude for transitory things, which is the origin of all our vices."[47] He demands that, inasmuch as there are moral issues underlying these social and economic questions, they be brought within the supreme jurisdiction of the church, which

[41] *Ibid.*

[42] *Ibid.*, cols. 1 and 3; p. 3, col. 4.

[43] *Ibid.*, p. 2, col. 8.

[44] *Ibid.*, col. 3.

[45] *Ibid.*, cols. 1 and 2; p. 3, col. 1.

[46] *Ibid.*, p. 2, cols. 5 and 6.

[47] *Ibid.*, cols. 5, 7, and 8.

has the "God-given task of interposing her authority" in all those matters "that have a bearing on moral conduct."[48]

It is hard to estimate the influence of these two papal encyclicals (*Rerum novarum* and *Quadragesimo Anno*) in the field of recent social readjustments. Non-Catholics may regard as overstatements the affirmations of Pius XI when, in his own encyclical, he declares that *Rerum novarum* was responsible for the formulation and execution of many social laws that improved the conditions of wage-earners, women, and children.[49] One may also take with a grain of salt the affirmation of Arnaldo Cortesi that *Rerum novarum*

> was eventually adopted by legislation or at least practical usage, in almost all countries. . . . . It formed the basis of discussion by students of social questions all over the world until the principles it propounded had gradually gained general acceptance.[50]

But some influence was probably exerted. For instance, the Weimar Assembly, of 1919, acted in harmony with the thought of Leo XIII when, through the influence of the Catholic representatives, it inserted Article 139 in the German constitution, which provided that "Sundays and legal holidays remain under the protection of law as days of rest and spiritual edification."[51] To cite an instance of more recent date, the Storm Group of the Eastern Marches (*Ostmärkische Sturmscharen*), a semi-military organization in Austria, headed by Chancellor Schuschnigg (1934——), favors a program of social justice such as was advocated by Pope Pius XI in *Quadragesimo Anno*.[52]

It may seem to the reader that the author is stressing the social leadership of the papacy too fully or praising it too enthusiastically. The writer is quite aware that it has not been the

[48] *Ibid.*, p. 1, col. 6. See also Duthoit, "L'encyclique de Pie XI sur la question sociale," *Revue des deux mondes*, 8th period, IV, 156–74; *Literary Digest*, CIX (May 30, 1931), 5–6.

[49] *New York Times*, May 24, 1931, sec. II, p. 1, cols. 4–6.

[50] *Ibid.*, sec. I, p. 3, col. 1.

[51] Baur and Rieder, *op. cit.*, pp. 48–49.

[52] Emil Lengyel, "Austria Reacts to Outside Pressure," *New York Times*, October 20, 1935, Part IV, p. 6, cols. 3–4.

dominant Catholic countries, like Italy, Spain, Portugal, and France, that have been in the vanguard in alleviating the condition of the workers by establishing social-insurance reforms. That honor goes to Protestant Germany, Great Britain, and Scandinavia, though Protestant America has lagged behind all of them. It is also clear that in such Catholic countries as Spain, Austria, and Mexico the most active opponents of radical social reforms have been the Catholic clerical groups, collaborating with the conservative political parties. It is also obvious that in recent decades individual Protestant denominations, and the Protestant churches of the United States, working as the Federal Council of Churches in Christ of America, have been more active and more advanced (or radical) than the Catholic church in promoting social and economic reforms. Moreover, in the minds of many liberal and radical reform advocates the vigorous official opposition of the Catholic church to the birth-control movement brands the church as a permanently conservative social influence.

It is not the purpose of the author to attempt to evaluate the conflicting views concerning such contentious matters, but the significant fact remains that in promulgating a social program Leo XIII and Pius XI caused the papacy to become one of the most active agencies working for the reform of present society, and that such leadership, whether markedly or only moderately successful, could not have been undertaken with any prospect of success if the papacy had still been intent on playing a part in national and international politics, instead of stressing religious, moral, and social leadership.

3. THE PAPACY AS AN ADVOCATE OF PEACE AND DISARMAMENT

Throughout medieval and modern times the papacy had been a constant advocate of peace and had frequently acted as arbiter and mediator between nations to preserve or restore peace.[53]

[53] Roemer and Ellis, *The Catholic Church and Peace Efforts;* Beales, *The History of Peace*. pp. 25, 187–88, 241, 244.

But since 1870 the pope has been able to exert an even greater and more forceful influence because, having been deprived of all temporal possessions, he had a "relatively free position as a neutral, since he could not be accused of territorial ambitions with his temporal domains gone."[54] Leo XIII, or his representatives, acted as arbiter in at least five international disputes.[55] In his allocution of February, 1889, he strongly condemned resort to aggressive wars to settle disputes between nations.[56] In spite of not being allowed to accept the invitation of the tsar to attend the first Hague Conference, his actions and public pronouncements showed that he was more sincere in desiring genuine disarmament and peace achievements than the representatives of the secular powers.[57]

Pius X (1903–14) on March 27, 1905, in an address to the college of cardinals, and on other occasions as well, condemned the strident nationalism and policy of "Might makes right" which was pursued in such an accentuated manner by the nations of Europe.[58] In 1906 he sent a message to the Universal Peace Congress, favoring the peaceful arbitration of international disputes.[59] On a number of occasions his representatives acted as arbiters between South American states.[60] In one of his last utterances, in 1914, he appealed to the nations to cease their folly and arbitrate their differences.[61] But his peace efforts had no restraining influence on the forces and system producing the catastrophe of 1914. However, the world will long remem-

[54] Roemer and Ellis, *op. cit.*, p. 51.

[55] Müller, *Das Friedenswerk der Kirche*, I, 47, 48, 325–33; Roemer and Ellis, *op. cit.*, pp. 51–53.

[56] Roemer and Ellis, *op. cit.*, p. 52; MacLean, *The Permanent Peace Program of Pope Benedict XV*, p. 14.

[57] See above, chap. xviii, sec. 4.

[58] Müller, *op. cit.*, pp. 377–78, 392–93; *American Journal of International Law*, V (Supplement), 214–16; editorial, *American Journal of International Law*, V, 707–9; Roemer and Ellis, *op. cit.*, p. 54.

[59] Müller, *op. cit.*, pp. 345–46; Roemer and Ellis, *op. cit.*, p. 54.

[60] Müller, *op. cit.*, pp. 48, 49, 379; Roemer and Ellis, *op. cit.*, p. 54.

[61] Müller, *op. cit.*, p. 419; Roemer and Ellis, *op. cit.*, p. 54.

ber one of the last acts of the pontiff, namely, his refusal of the request of the Austrian emperor, Francis Joseph, to bless his cause by responding, "I do not bless war: I bless peace."[62]

We have already discussed the unsuccessful appeals made by Pope Benedict XV (1914–22) to persuade the belligerent powers to settle their differences through peaceful means.[63] Undaunted by his failure in this respect, he demonstrated his sincerity as a humanitarian by using the full forces of the papal and church organization to alleviate the horrors of war through negotiating the exchange of disabled prisoners and civilians of the occupied territories, the hospitalization of the sick in neutral countries (especially the tuberculous in Switzerland), the exchange of letters between the prisoners of war and their families, the securing of a day of rest on Sunday for prisoners, the securing of truces to bury the dead, the identification and marking of the graves of those that had fallen in the Dardanelles campaign. He was instrumental in making possible the provisioning of the inhabitants of devastated regions like Poland and Belgium and in repatriating the prisoners after the war. "The Pope had come to be looked on as the only neutral securely and permanently disinterested."[64] Toward the close of the war, and during the peace negotiations, he tried—fruitlessly, to be sure—to secure a just and stable peace, free from punitive and vengeful aspects.[65]

[62] McKenna, "Peace, the Keystone of the Papacy," *Catholic World*, CXXXIII, 518; MacLean, *op. cit.*, p. 9.

[63] See above, chap. xviii, sec. 4. See also Roemer and Ellis, *op. cit.*, pp. 54–56; Barry and Wood, "Benedict XV: Pontiff of Peace," *Dublin Review*, CLXX, 185; *Appeals for Peace of Pope Benedict XV and Pope Pius XI* (pamphlet, Catholic Association for International Peace), pp. 3–7; MacLean, *op. cit.*, pp. 6–8; McKenna, "Peace, the Keystone of the Papacy," *Catholic World*, CXXXIII, 518–19; *Literary Digest*, LXXII (February 4, 1922), 30–31; Hergenröther, *op. cit.*, IV, 808–10.

[64] Müller, *op. cit.*, pp. 421–22, 425–28, 432, 437–40, 446–49, 454–55; Cartwright, "Contributions of the Papacy to International Peace," *Catholic Historical Review*, VIII, 165–66; Roemer and Ellis, *op. cit.*, pp. 55–56; MacLean, *op. cit.*, pp. 9–10; Hayes, "Pope Benedict the Fifteenth," *Forum*, LXVIII, 259–60; Poynter, "Pope Benedict XV, the Popes Benedict, and the Papacy," *Fortnightly Review*, CXVII, 472–73; Wood, "Benedict XV: Pontiff of Peace," *Dublin Review*, CLXX, 190.

[65] MacLean, *op. cit.*, pp. 24–30; Hergenröther, *op. cit.*, IV, 809–10; Barry, "Benedict XV: Pontiff of Peace," *Dublin Review*, CLXX, 176.

Consistent with previous papal practice, Benedict XV frequently advocated the establishment of a league of nations that would settle all international disputes without resort to war.[66]

The failure of papal peace efforts during the World War was not a reflection on the papacy and its occupant. Protestants, as well as Catholics, recognized that Benedict had assiduously served the cause of humanity and had maintained the papacy and the church as a great moral authority in the world. Mankind's verdict will be in harmony with that of Lord Curzon, who described the pope as being a "firm advocate of the moral brotherhood of mankind." Even the Turkish nation set its flag at half-mast when he died, and later erected in Constantinople a magnificent monument to him, whom they designated as "The Benefactor of Humanity, the Pope of Peace."[67]

In Pius XI (1922——) Benedict XV has had a worthy successor as a fearless advocate of peace. His courage in making papal peace activities possible was shown when in 1929 he signed the Lateran Accord with Mussolini, thus showing that on the basis of good will a knotty, difficult question of long standing could be amicably settled.[68] By some he has been called "the greatest worker in the cause of peace." He has repeatedly spoken out fearlessly for the "re-establishment of an enduring world peace and a reign of concord among nations."[69] In a message to the cardinals, Christmas Day, 1930, he asserted that securing "peace is made difficult . . . . because the spirit of peace does not possess the intelligence and hearts of men"; because "of an unequal distribution of privileges and burdens, of rights and duties, of participation in their fruits which can only

[66] MacLean, *op. cit.*, pp. 16–20; Hergenröther, *op. cit.*, IV, 809.

[67] MacLean, *op. cit.*, p. 4; Barry, "Benedict XV: Pontiff of Peace," *Dublin Review*, CLXX, 176–77; *Catholic Encyclopedia*, XVII (supplement), 96; *New York Times*, January 30, 1922, Part V, cols. 2, 3.

[68] Ryan, "Pius XI," *Commonweal*, XV, 623–25; McKenna, "Peace, the Keystone of the Papacy," *Catholic World*, CXXXIII, 519–20; Haider, "The Vatican and Italian Fascism," *Catholic World*, CXXXVII, 401–2; Wellhoff, "Persons and Personages," *Living Age*, CCCXLV, 144.

[69] Roemer and Ellis, *op. cit.*, pp. 56–57.

be produced by their friendly collaboration"; because "there reigns a hard, egotistical nationalism, which is the same as saying hatred and envy"; because there is "competition and antagonism in the place of willing co-operation"; and finally, because there is "ambition for hegemony and mastery in the place of respect for all rights, even those of the weak and small." In conclusion he declared, "We will not, we cannot believe in the reality of these threats [of war in 1930] for we cannot believe that any civilized state could become so monstrously homicidal, and almost certainly suicidal."[70] Similar moral and humanitarian utterances may be found in his numerous allocutions, radio broadcasts, and other public pronouncements.[71]

Pius XI has been criticized as being remiss in his duties as moral leader, inasmuch as he has not condemned the aggression of Italy in Ethiopia, in harmony with the action taken by the great majority of nations represented at Geneva.[72] Whatever papal action may be taken, it must be remembered: (1) that the papacy is bound by the Lateran Accord of 1929 "to remain . . . . extraneous to all temporal disputes between nations . . . . unless the contending parties make concordant appeal to its mission of peace"; and (2) that Pius and his predecessors have, by previous pronouncements, deprecated all wars in general.

Because of the persistent and consistent advocacy of a peace program by Pius XI it is not surprising to find that Mr. Victor J. Dowling, a Catholic, and a former presiding justice of the appellate division of the supreme court of New York, made this remark in a baccalaureate address in June, 1931: "What the world needs is respect for some central authority which would

[70] *New York Times*, December 25, 1930, p. 1, col. 3; December 28, 1930, p. 11, col. 1, which contains the full text.

[71] *Ibid.*, 1932: February 16, p. 1, col. 2; February 29, p. 1, col. 5; March 2, p. 12, col. 7; April 4, p. 12, cols. 1, 2; 1933: March 14, p. 1, col. 1, and p. 11, col. 1; June 10, p. 3, col. 4; December 20, p. 15, col. 6; December 24, p. 1, col. 4, and p. 2, col. 5; 1934: November 1, p. 6, col. 3; December 25, p. 1, col. 7; 1935: March 27, p. 12, col. 3; September 8, p. 1, col. 6; *Register* (Denver, Colorado), September 15, 1935; *Commonweal*, XXI, 663–64, and XXII, 469.

[72] *Springfield* (Massachusetts) *Weekly Republican*, October 24, 1935, editorial, "Pope's Move for Peace [of October 17]."

be free from suspicion. The Pope might be the arbitrator between nations."[73] More remarkable is the suggestion of a Protestant (Congregational) pastor, the Rev. John M. Phillips, of Hartford, Connecticut, that Christians, of every denomination, and Jews, appeal to Pope Pius XI to lead a world-movement against war, to end war through a religious truce similar to those of medieval times.[74] Without entering into comments about the inaccuracies of the reference to the medieval Truce of God, or the difficulties in carrying out the suggestion,[75] the significant point is the assertion by a Protestant minister that "the Pope's position of authority makes him the most distinguished social leader of the day."[76]

In conclusion we can be safe in saying that, if the time ever comes when the utter futility, wastefulness, barbarity, and immorality of the war system will lead the nations to substitute a system of international co-operation for common purposes, it will be recognized by the scholars of that age that the papacy was, along with many others, one of the consistently moral influences working for this progressive social reform. And such a service can be rendered because, in the words of James Brown Scott, the papacy has "neither army nor navy nor territory. It has only a conscience and law under the control of a moral and spiritual conception."[77]

4. THE PAPACY AND THE AUTHORITARIAN STATE[78]

In recent decades, everywhere in the world, there has been a great increase in the claims of the state on the lives and destinies

[73] *New York Times*, June 9, 1931, p. 24, col. 1. The address was delivered before the College of New Rochelle.

[74] *Ibid.*, January 29, 1935, p. 6, col. 5.

[75] "The Truce of God" (editorial), *Christian Century*, LII, 168–69.

[76] *New York Times*, January 29, 1935, p. 6, col. 5.

[77] Scott, "The Progress of International Law during the Last Twenty-five Years," *Proceedings of the Society of International Law, 1931*, p. 23; also cited in Roemer and Ellis, *op. cit.*, p. 58, which wrongly gives the date of the *Proceedings* as 1932.

[78] For the ideas and phraseology of most of this section the author is indebted to Tillich, "The Totalitarian State and the Claims of the Church," *Social Research*, I, 405–

of individuals and all organizations within the state. This has gone so far that in some states, as in Russia, Italy, and Germany, attempts are being made to regulate the whole realm of human activity and thought. The same tendency is under way elsewhere, although it has not as yet been pursued to the same degree.

Wherever the authoritarian state has been established, there has been a sacrifice of democratic practices and institutions, a denial of all liberal rights, including freedom of thought and religion. In each of the three states mentioned above (Russia, Italy, Germany) there is a militant nationalism, dominated by the leaders of a party, which aims to unify and amalgamate the whole nation in the pursuit of common ideals. The authoritarian state itself is to give all the needed spiritual satisfaction. There is not to be any competing spiritual life. The concept of a dual sovereignty, shared by the church and the state, is no longer acceptable. The communists in Russia regard Christianity as a rival and unwholesome method of human social salvation, which has been controlled and interpreted by the bourgeois class and its instruments. The social goal of Christianity, social justice, has never been, and can never be, achieved. Therefore the Christian religion must be stamped out in order that communism may be unhampered in achieving its own social goal. To the Fascists in Italy the state is supreme; the nation must be absolutely devoted to the welfare of the state; between the state and the church there must not be any conflict in ideals, demands, or loyalties, so far as the members of the nation are con-

---

33; Dawson, "Religion and the Totalitarian State," *Criterion*, XIV, 1–16; Beaven, "The Meaning for Religions of the Trend toward Nationalism," *Annals of the American Academy of Political and Social Science*, CLXXIV, 65–75. For additional treatment of this topic see: "Twilight of the Gods" (editorial), *Living Age*, CCCXLV, 132–41; "Relations of Church and State Must Be Studied" (editorial), *Christian Century*, L, 868; "The Church and Christian Totalitarianism" (editorial), *ibid.*, LI, 214–16; Sarolea, "The Political Backgrounds of the German Kulturkampf," *Contemporary Review*, CXLVII, 406–15; "Pie XI et Hitler," *Mercure de France*, CCXLIX, 257–67; "Le catholicisme et la politique mondiale," *Revue des deux mondes*, 8th period, XXV, 272–301; Ascoli, "The Roman Church and Political Action," *Foreign Affairs*, XIII, 483–98; Hutchinson, "Religion and the World We Live In," *Forum*, LXXXIX, 81–87; "The Policy of Pius XI," *Round Table*, December, 1934, pp. 44–59; Mason, *Hitler's First Foes*.

cerned. In Germany the National Socialists are developing a new form of paganism based on racial and political considerations. Religion will be national in characteristics and aims and will be fully under the control of the authoritarian or totalitarian state.

In all three of these authoritarian states there is no room for a spiritual life, a communion with a Supreme God, through whom the spiritual life of all is unified and amalgamated to a common purpose. The state must have unconditional sway over all phases of human thought and action; it claims absolute authority in the totality of life. Even in the United States there is an increasing tendency to assert the supremacy of the state over the conscience of the individual; by a Supreme Court decision (1931), Professor Douglas Macintosh, of Yale Divinity School, was denied American citizenship because he refused to agree to bear arms if he felt that a given war were unjustified.[79] So the present state, in many countries, tends to claim authority over the totality of life. But the Christian church, in its Roman Catholic, Greek Catholic, and Protestant branches, also is based on the absolute character of its teaching. All the Christian churches have claims in common. They claim that man has a religious nature, which is divinely instituted and which requires some form of communion with God. These churches assert also that spiritual life must not be interfered with by any secular power. So long as the Christian churches are churches, they will cling to this claim. They must keep alive the idea that once humanity had an original unity, that unity will and must ultimately be reachieved, and that the church is an agency in achieving this objective. So there is an evident clash of authority between the authoritarian (or totalitarian) state on the one

[79] "Majority Opinion of the Supreme Court," *Christian Century*, XLIX, 89–92; "Dissenting Opinion of Chief Justice Hughes, Justices Holmes, Brandeis and Stone Concurring," *ibid.*, pp. 92–94; Morrison, "The End of the Macintosh Case," *ibid.*, XLVIII, 1302–3; Charles P. Howland, "Congress in Regimentals," *ibid.*, XLIX, 84–86; Ross, "Conscience and the State, The Roman Catholic View," *ibid.*, XLIX, 86–87; Ross, "Catholics and the Constitution," *Commonweal*, XV, 119–21, 242–43; "Conscience versus Citizenship," *Literary Digest*, CIX (June 6, 1931), 7; "Conscience versus Congress," *ibid.*, CXII (February 20, 1932), 20–21.

hand and the Christian church on the other. If the various branches of the church submit to the totalitarian-state idea, they will be allowing themselves to have other gods besides the one God.

With all of these European centralized states, and with others as well (Spain and Mexico), the papacy has had difficulties; but the breach seems widest at the present writing (November, 1935) in Germany. No one can accurately foresee the outcome, but it is one of the vexed questions the ultimate solution of which will have a bearing on the prestige and influence of the papacy. If the Catholic church and the papacy are to retain their original aim and beliefs, they cannot compromise with the totalitarian or authoritarian state, whose claims and objectives leave no room for loyalty to any other organization claiming absolute authority in one phase of life's activities.

5. CONCLUDING STATEMENT

All of the problems touched upon in the last three sections of this chapter, along with many others that might be mentioned, are a part of a complexity of interrelated world-wide problems, the solution of which may be centuries in the future. But if these problems are ever solved, it seems probable that the papacy, whose constructive social leadership is exerted not merely among the more than three hundred million members of the Catholic church, will be one of the factors contributing to the successful solution. And we may well be justified in concluding that if the papacy plays a part (1) in securing more equitable social and economic conditions for the great mass of workers, (2) in substituting peaceful methods of international co-operation for the present system of anarchy and war, and (3) in effectively safeguarding the consciences of individuals against the claims of the authoritarian state, such an achievement will be attributable, in part, to the broadening moral and spiritual leadership of the popes, which was made possible through the long process known as the "secularization of politics."

Chapter Twenty

RETROSPECT—PROSPECT

1. THE MEDIEVAL ATTEMPTED AND THE CONTEMPORARY ACHIEVED TOTALITARIAN STATE

IN THIS treatise we have surveyed a millennium and half of history—about one-fifth of recorded human history. We began with a consideration of the City of God of Augustine, the medieval version of the totalitarian state. When this ideal had been put into practice, it was the aim of the papacy to have no differentiation between church and state. The church, through its guiding and dominating head, the papacy, was to exercise control over every important phase of human political, social, and cultural affairs. Kings and princes were vassals of the pope and were to shape their policies in harmony with his demands, though this ideal was never achieved, owing to vigorous and prolonged resistance on the part of some of the lay powers.[1]

But when, after the thirteenth century, the papacy declined in personnel and objectives, the developing states asserted their independence of the papacy in politics and even began to control religious affairs. This tendency, observable for several centuries, was given a pronounced impetus by the Protestant Reformation, and resulted finally, at the close of the Thirty Years' War, in the effective collaboration of both Catholic and Protestant princes of Europe in secularizing politics absolutely. The princes did this by agreeing to ignore the protest of the pope against the Treaty of Westphalia. For a long time the pope refused to recognize the changed situation, persistently protesting whenever, through state and international action, his historic

[1] See chap. i.

rights and interests, and those of the church, were affected adversely. This remained the situation, with diminishing acuteness, however, until in 1929, when, through the Lateran Accord, the papacy agreed to

> remain extraneous to all temporal disputes between nations and to international Congresses convoked for the settlement of such disputes unless the contending parties make a concordant appeal to its mission of peace; nevertheless it reserves the right in every case to exercise its moral and spiritual power.

That Accord marked the end of papal antagonism to the secularization of politics. The pope agreed to remain out of international politics, except when invited to participate; but he would not yield his right and duty to moral and spiritual leadership in the world, and, as has been observed in the preceding chapter, since 1878 he has been increasingly active in broad constructive social leadership.

The state, freed from the restrictions imposed on it through the papacy (the medieval attempted totalitarian state), has in modern times, and especially in the last half-century, increased its activities and claims to authority everywhere in the world. In several countries of Europe there have been formed totalitarian states, and there are tendencies elsewhere in that direction. All ideas and activities, all pursuits and ideals, must yield if in conflict with the claims and actions of the sovereign, absolute state. The educational system, the agencies of research, art, literature, the theater, the cinema, and the press, are all coerced into the service of the all-powerful state. Freedom of conscience no longer exists in the totalitarian state. The old conflict between the state and the church, now so clear-cut in Germany, Russia, Italy, Spain, and Mexico, "is smouldering in every part of Christendom, no less in America than elsewhere."[2]

2. THE VIEW AHEAD

We have surveyed fifteen centuries of the relation of church and state. We have adduced evidence that Catholic, as well as

[2] "The Church and Christian Totalitarianism," *Christian Century*, LI, 214.

non-Catholic, authorities accept the view that the divorce of the papacy from interference in politics was an inevitable and constructive trend, enabling the papacy to give up its temporary political leadership, so that it could once more, and with greater advantage and success, stress its original purpose—religious, ethical, and social leadership. But today, under the rule of the totalitarian state, the freedom that is necessary for the healthy existence of religion is being imperiled once again. The present policies of the authoritarian state are a menace, not merely to spiritual life, but to all other cultural and scientific, social and educational, activities of human society. If state authoritarianism is not checked or thwarted, our cherished Western civilization faces a serious alteration or even breakdown. Unrestricted power of compulsion, as exercised by the state in many countries today, is probably setting the stage for a new, and perhaps a long, struggle between church and state. This contest will affect not merely religion and religious institutions. It will fundamentally affect all other cultural, educational, scientific, and research pursuits, which thrive only in an atmosphere free from coercion and restriction. Those who follow this conflict at present and in the years to come will find much of interest in the historic background that is disclosed in the movement called the "secularization of politics."

Bibliography

MANUSCRIPTS

Crivelli, Julius Caesar. *Corrispondenza di Roma, 1612–1656.* Manuscript volume, Bayerisches Geheimes Staatsarchiv, Munich, K[asten] Schw[arz] 515/25.

———. *Corrispondenza di Roma, 1648, 1649.* Manuscript volume, Bayerisches Geheimes Staatsarchiv, Munich, K[asten] Schw[arz] 313/13.

Forer, Laurentius. *An liceat promittere haereticis permissionem exercitii heretici in perpetuum.* Manuscript in Munich, Bavarian Hauptstaatsarchiv (formerly Reichsarchiv). *Jesuitica in genere*, fasc. 25, No. 370.

———. *An sit extrema necessitas quae cogat permittere haeresin.* Manuscript in Munich, Bavarian Hauptstaatsarchiv (formerly Reichsarchiv). *Jesuitica in genere*, fasc. 25, No. 370.

———. *Memoriale in Manus oblatum Smo Dno No Innocentio X nomine et iussu Serenissimi Maximiliani Electoris Bavarij, una cum letteris credentialibus a P. Laurentio Forero Societatio Jesu. Penultimo Decembris anno 1645. "Nunc in Germania Catholicam Religionem versari in extremo periculo."* Manuscript in Munich, Bavarian Hauptstaatsarchiv (formerly Reichsarchiv). *Jesuitica in genere*, fasc. 25, No. 370.

Forer, Laurentius (?). *Causae ob quas nec debuerit neque etiam nunc debeat negari hoc bellum Suecicum esse bellum religionis.* Manuscript in Munich, Bavarian Hauptstaatsarchiv (formerly Reichsarchiv). *Jesuitica in genere*, fasc. 25, No. 370.

Garampi. *Raggualio della Paca di Vestfalia, e dello va rie Proteste fattesi dalla S. Sede contra la medesima.* Manuscript, Fondo Garampi 94, Vatican Archives.

Montanus, Theodorus. *Discursus ad Caesaris confessarium Patrem Lamormaini Anno 1634.* Manuscript in Munich, Bavarian Hauptstaatsarchiv (formerly Reichsarchiv). *Jesuitica in genere*, fasc. 25, No. 370.

Urban VIII. *Instruttione del cardinale Ginetti per un Congresso de pacificazione general.* In Staatsbibliothek, Munich, Codex italiano, 98, fol. 60; copy of original manuscript in Vatican Secret Archives, XXXIX, 1049.

Vervaux, Johann. *Notae in consilium* [=*Judicium*] *Theologicum Ernesti de Eusebiis super quaestione an Pax qualem desiderant Protestantes sit secundum se illicita, 1647.* Manuscript, Vienna Archives, Codex Vindobonensis 15154, fols. 659*a*–674*a*.

———. *Notae in Responsum Theologicum Ernesti de Eusebiis ad Notas clancularias Irenici. Quibis annotantur columniae, Scommata et Iniuriae, quas commentitius iste Ernestus in Imperatorem Romanum, Imperiique Status, ac ipsam denique Pacem Monasterii et Osnabrugi his annis tractatam ac conclu-*

sam in Responso hoc suo theologico sparsim impudentissime evomit ac communiscitur. Manuscript in Bavarian Secret State Archives, K[asten] Schw[arz] 346176; composed of extracts from Wangnereck's ("Ernestus de Eusebiis") *Responsum Theologicum.* Is possibly written by Vervaux.

WANGNERECK, HEINRICH. *Quaestio ardua, An Pax, quam desiderant Protestantes, sit secundum se illicita?* 1640. In manuscript only, in Hauptstaatsarchiv, Munich. *Jesuitica in genere,* fasc. 25, No. 372.

PRINTED WORKS

NOTE.—Editorials and unsigned articles are listed under the periodical in which they appeared.

ABBOTT, WILBUR CORTEZ. *The Expansion of Europe, a Social and Political History of the Modern World, 1415–1789.* 2 vols. New York, 1924.

Acta Sanctae Sedis in compendium opportune redacta et illustrata, Vol. VI. Rome, 1870.

Actes et mémoires des négociations de la paix de Nimègue. 3d ed. 4 vols. in 7. La Haye, 1697.

ADAMI, ADAM. Writing under the pseudonym "*Humanus Erdeman Oecomontanus.*" *Anti-Caramuel sive Examen et refutatio Disputationis Theologico-politicae quam de potestate Imperatoris circa bona Ecclesiastica proposuit Ioannes Caramuel Lobkovits.* Humano Erdeman Oecomontano auctore. Trimonadi, 1648.

———. *Arcana Pacis Westphalia sive . . . . relatio historica de S. Rom. Imperii pacificatione Osnobrugo Monasteriensi.* Frankfurt, 1698.

———. *Relatio historica de Pacificatione Osnabrugo-Monasteriensi . . . . atque Actorum Pacis Vestphalicae.* Edited by J. G. VON MEIERN. Leipzig, 1737.

ADAMS, GEORGE BURTON. *The History of England from the Norman Conquest to the Death of John, 1066–1216.* London, 1905.

ADAMS, G. B., and STEPHENS, H. M. *Select Documents of English Constitutional History.* New York, 1902.

ADELUNG, JOHAN CHRISTOPH. *Pragmatische Staatsgeschichte Europens von dem Ableben Kaiser Carlo VI an bis auf die gegenwärtigen Zeiten aus sicheren Quellen.* 6 vols. in 7. Gotha, 1762–65.

ALBIN, PIERRE. *Les grands traités politiques recueil des principaux textes diplomatiques depuis 1815 jusqu'à nos jours.* Paris, 1916.

ALEXANDRE, NATALIS. *Ad historiam Ecclesiasticam supplementum.* 2 vols. Bassano, 1778.

ALLEN, J. W. "Jean Bodin," pp. 42–62 in F. J. C. Hearnshaw (ed.), *The Social and Political Ideas of Some of the Great Thinkers of the Sixteenth and Seventeenth Centuries.* London, 1926.

ALLEN, JOHN WILLIAM. *A History of Political Thought in the Sixteenth Century.* New York, 1928.

Allgemeine deutsche Biographie. 56 vols. Leipzig, 1875–1912.

ALLIES, MARY H. *The Life of Pope Pius the Seventh.* London, 1875.

ANDREAS, WILLY. *Deutschland vor der Reformation, eine Zeitwende.* Stuttgart, Berlin, 1932.

ANDREAS, WILLY. *Geist und Staat, Historische Porträts.* Munich and Berlin, 1922.

ANGEBERG, COMTE DE. *Le congrès de Vienne et les traités de 1815.* 5 parts in 2 vols. Paris, 1864.

ASCOLI, MAX. "The Roman Church and Political Action," *Foreign Affairs* (New York), XIII (1935), 441–52.

AUBERY, ANTOINE. *Histoire du Cardinal Mazarin.* 2 vols. Paris, 1695.

AUSSET, J. *La question vaticane, 1914–1928.* Paris, 1928.

AVENEL, VICOMTE G. DE. *Richelieu et la monarchie absolue.* 4 vols. Paris, 1895.

BACH, JOSEPH. "Jakob Balde, ein religiös-patriotischer Dichter aus dem Elsass," *Strassburger Theologische Studien,* Band VI, Heft 3 und 4. Freiburg im Breisgau, 1904.

BACKER, AUGUSTIN DE, and P. ALOYS DE. *Bibliothèque des écrivains de la compagnie de Jésus ou notices bibliographiques.* Nouvelle édition par CARLOS SOMMERVOGEL. 9 vols. Brussels, Paris, 1890–1900.

BAIN, ROBERT NISBET. *Scandinavia.* Cambridge, 1905.

———. *Slavonic Europe, a Political History of Poland and Russia.* Cambridge, 1905.

BARBÈRI, ANDREAS ADVOCATUS. *Bullarii Romani continuatio summorum pontificum Clementis XIII . . . . Gregory XVI,* Vol. XIII. Rome, 1847.

BAROZZI, NICOLO, and BERCHET, GUGLIELMO. *Relazioni dagli ambasciatori Veneti nel secolo decimosettimo,* Ser. III, Vol. I. Venice, 1877.

BARRY, WILLIAM. "Benedict XV: Pontiff of Peace," *Dublin Review* (London), CLXX (1922), 161–78.

———. *The Coming Age and the Catholic Church, a Forecast.* New York, 1930.

———. "Leo XIII., a Retrospect," *Dublin Review* (London), CXXXIII (1903), 225–48.

———. *The Papacy and Modern Times, 1303–1870.* London, 1911.

———. *The Papal Monarchy from St. Gregory the Great to Boniface VIII, 590–1303.* New York, 1907.

BARTLET, J. VERNON, and CARLYLE, A. J. *Christianity in History, a Study of Religious Development.* London, 1917.

BASSETT, JOHN SPENCER. *Our War with Germany, a History.* New York, 1919.

BAUMGARTEN, H. "Die Politik Leos X. in dem Wahlkampf der Jahre 1518 und 1519," *Forschungen zur deutschen Geschichte* (Göttingen), XXIII (1883), 521–70.

BAUR, JOSEPH. *Philipp von Sötern, geistlicher Kurfürst zu Trier, und seine Politik während des dreissigjährigen Krieges.* 2 vols. Speyer, 1914.

BAUR, LUDWIG, and RIEDER, KARL. *Päpstliche Enzykliken und ihre Stellung zur Politik,* Schriften zur deutschen Politik, Vol. V. Freiburg i. B., 1923.

BAZIN, M. A. *Histoire de France sous Louis XIII et sous le ministère du Cardinal Mazarin, 1610–1661.* 2d ed. 4 vols. Paris, 1846.

BEALS, A. C. F. *The History of Peace.* New York, 1931.

BEAVEN, ALBERT W. "The Meaning for Religions of the Trend toward Nationalism," *Annals of the Academy of Political and Social Science* (Philadelphia), CLXXIV (1934), 65–75.

BELTRANI, GIOVANNI BATTISTA. "Felice contelori e i suoi studi negli Archivi del Vaticano," *Archivio della Società Romana di Storia Patria*, II (1879), 165–208, 257–80; III (1880), 1–47. Contains an account of the archival researches on which the protest of Innocent X was based.

BERNHEIM, ERNST. *Mittelalterliche Zeitanschauungen in ihrem Einfluss auf Politik und Geschichtschreibung.* Teil I, *Die Zeitanschauungen.* Tübingen, 1918.

BIESTER. "Nimmt der Papst Behauptungen zurück?" *Berlinische Monatsschrift*, VIII (1786), 111–21.

———. "Von dem nunmehr auch im römischen Staatskalender befindlichen preussischen Königstitel," *Berlinische Monatsschrift*, IX (1787), 299–302.

BLIND, KARL. "The Papacy and the New Italy, with Reminiscences of Garibaldi," *Westminster Review* (New York), CLX (1903), 263–70.

BLUNTSCHLI, JOHANN KASPAR. *Die rechtliche Unverantwortlichkeit und Verantwortlichkeit des römischen Papstes, eine völker- und staatsrechtliche Studie.* Nördlingen, 1876.

BOJANI, F. DE. *Innocent XI. Sa correspondance avec ses nonces 21 Septembre 1676—31 Décembre 1679.* 3 vols. Rome and Paris, 1910–12.

BOMPARD, RAOUL. *Le pape et le droit de gens.* Paris, 1888. Also under title *La papauté en droit international.* Paris, 1888. Dissertation.

BOTTIGER, C. W. *Geschichte des Kurstaates und Königreiches Sachsen.* 2d ed. by TH. FLATHE, in HEEREN and UKERT, *Geschichte der europäischen Staaten*, Vol. II. Gotha, 1870.

BOUGEANT, G. H. *Histoire des guerres et des négociations qui precédèrent le traité de Westphalie, composé sur les mémoires du Comte d'Avaux.* 6 vols., Paris, 1744; also in 3 vols., Paris, 1757.

BOURNE, EDWARD GAYLORD. "The Demarcation Line of Alexander VI: An Episode of the Period of Discoveries," *Yale Review* (Boston), I (1892–93), 35–55.

———. *Essays in Historical Criticism.* New York, 1901.

BOURRILLY, V. L. "L'ambassade de la Forest et de Marillac à Constantinople, 1535–1538," *Revue historique* (Paris), LXXVI (1901), 297–328.

BRANDI, KARL. *Der augsburger Religionsfriede vom 25. September, 1555, kritische Ausgabe des Textes mit den Entwürfen und der königlichen Deklaration.* 2d ed. Göttingen, 1927.

———. *Gegenreformation und Religionskriege*, in ERICH MARCKS, *Deutsche Geschichte*, Vol. II, Part II. Leipzig, 1930.

BRANN, H. A. "The Relation of the Church to Human Progress," *American Catholic Quarterly Review* (Philadelphia), XIV (1889), 639–52.

BRAUN, CARL JOHANN HEINRICH ERNST EDLER VON. "Skizzen aus dem diplomatischen Leben und Wirken des sachsen-altenburgischen Gesandten am westphälischen Friedenscongresse, Wolfgang Conrad von Thumshirn, 1645–1649," *Mittheilungen der Geschichts- und Alterthumsforschenden Gesellschaft des Osterlandes* (Altenburg), IV (1858), 387–471.

BRAUN, PLACIDUS. *Geschichte der Bischöfe von Augsburg.* 4 vols. Augsburg, 1813–15.

BRAUNSBERGER, OTTO, S.J. (ed.). *Beati Petri Canisii Societatis Iesu Epistulae et Acta.* 8 vols. Freiburg, 1896–1923. Vol. V, pp. 229–55, contains six letters of P. Canisius and his two Jesuit associates concerning the Peace of Augsburg.

———. *Petrus Canisius, ein Lebensbild.* Freiburg, 1921.

———. "Pius V. und die deutschen Katholiken," in *Stimmen aus Maria-Laach, Katholische Blätter*, Ergänzungsband XXVII, Ergänzungsheft 108. Freiburg im Breisgau, 1912.

BREUCKER, GUSTAV. "Die Abtretung Vorpommerns an Schweden und die Entschädigung Kurbrandenburgs, ein Beitrag zur Geschichte des westfälischen Friedens," *Hallesche Abhandlungen zur neueren Geschichte*, Heft VIII. Halle, 1879.

BROCKHAUS, HEINRICH. *Der Kurfürstentag zu Nürnberg im Jahre 1640.* Leipzig, 1883.

BROM, GISBERT. *Archivalia in Italië Belangrijk voor de Geschiedenis van Nederland*, Part III (Derde Deel). ("Rijka Geschiedkundige Publicatiën uitgegeven in Opracht van Z. Exc. den Minister van Binnenlandsche Zaken, kleine Serie, XIV. ['s-Gravenhage, 1914], 297–497.) Contains a description of the contents of the library of Fabio Chigi (the late Pope Alexander VII [1655–77] in Rome; this work also contains important documents concerning the Westphalian negotiations.

BROSCH, MORITZ. *Geschichte des Kirchenstaates*, Vol. II. Gotha, 1882.

BROWN, HORATIO. *Venice, an Historical Sketch of the Republic.* 2d ed. London, 1895.

BRÜCK, HEINRICH. *Geschichte der katholischen Kirche im neunzehnten Jahrhundert.* Vol. I, *Deutschland.* Mainz, 1887.

BRYCE, JAMES. *The Holy Roman Empire.* New York, 1905.

BUCHOLTZ, F. B. VON. *Geschichte der Regierung Ferdinand des Ersten*, Vol. VII. Vienna, 1836.

BUDER. *Leben und Thaten des klugen und berühmten Pabsts Clementis des Eilften.* 3 vols. Franckfurt, 1720.

BUELL, RAYMOND LESLIE. "France and the Vatican," *Political Science Quarterly* (New York), XXXVI (1921), 30–50.

Cambridge Medieval History. Planned by J. B. BURY, edited by H. M. GWATKIN and OTHERS. Vols. IV–VII. Cambridge, 1923–32.

Cambridge Modern History. Planned by the late LORD ACTON, edited by A. W. WARD, G. W. PROTHERO, and STANLEY LEATHES. 14 vols. Cambridge, 1903–12.

CAPES, W. W. *The English Church in the Fourteenth and Fifteenth Centuries.* London, 1900.

CARAMUEL Y LOBKOWITZ, JOHANN. *Sacri Romani Imperii Pacis licitae demonstratae, variis olim consiliis agitatae, nunc demum medullitus discussae, et ad binas hypotheses reductae Prodromus et Syndromus sive additamentum.* Francofurti, 1648. Second edition of title following.

———. *Sacri Romani Imperii Pax licita demonstrata.* Frankfurt, 1648.

CARLYLE, R. W., and CARLYLE, A. J. *A History of Medieval Political Theory in the West.* 3 vols. New York, 1903–16.

CARTWRIGHT, JOHN K. "Contributions of the Papacy to International Peace," *Catholic Historical Review* (Lynchburg and Washington), N.S., VIII (1928), 157–68.

Catalogus Codicum Manu Scriptorum Bibliothecae Regiae Monacensis. Vol. VII, *Codices Manu Scripti Gallici, Hispanici, Italici, Anglici, Suecici, Danici, Slovici, Esthnici, Hungarici descripti.* Munich, 1858.

Catholic Encyclopedia. Knights of Columbus ed. 17 vols., including Index and Supplement. New York, 1913–22.

Catholic World (New York), LXXIV (1902), 557–66, "The Peace Conference and What Might Have Been" (editorial).

CATLIN, GEORGE E. G. *Thomas Hobbes as Philosopher, Publicist and Man of Letters: An Introduction.* Oxford, 1922.

CHARVÉRIAT, E. *Histoire de la guerre de trente ans.* 2 vols. Paris, 1876–78.

CHEMNITZ, BOGISLAV PHILIP VON. *Geschichte des königlichen schwedischen in Teutschland geführten Krieges,* Parts III and IV. Edited by J. J. NORDSTROM. Stockholm, 1855–59.

CHÉNON, EMILE. *Histoire des rapports de l'église et de l'état du Ier au XXème siècle.* 2d ed. Paris, 1913.

CHERUEL, A. *Histoire de France sous le ministère de Mazarin, 1651–1661.* 3 vols. Paris, 1882.

———. *Histoire de France pendant la minorité de Louis XIV.* 4 vols. Paris, 1879–80.

———. *Lettres du Cardinal Mazarin pendant son ministère, recueilliés et publiés par M. A. Cheruel.* ("Collection de documents inédits sur l'histoire de France," Vols. II, III.) Paris, 1879, 1883.

———. *Saint-Simon considéré comme historien de Louis XIV.* Paris, 1865.

Christian Century (Chicago): XLIX (1932), 89–92, "The Majority Opinion of the Supreme Court" (art. on Macintosh Case); XLIX (1932), 92–94, "The Dissenting Opinion of Chief Justice Hughes, Justices Holmes, Brandeis and Stone Concurring" (art.); L (1933), 866, "Relation of Church and State Must Be Studied" (art.); LI (1934), 214–16, "The Church and Christian Totalitarianism" (art.); LII (1935), 168–69, "The Truce of God" (art.).

CLEMENTIS XI. *Opera omnia.* Vol. I, *Orationis consistoriales, homiliae, bullarium;* Vol. II, *Epistolae et brevia selectora.* Francofurti and Romae, 1729.

COCKS, F. SEYMOUR. *The Secret Treaties and Understandings.* 2d ed. London, 1918.

Commonweal (New York): XIII (1931), 565–66, "Catholics and Social Reform" (editorial); XXI (1935), 663–64, "The Pope's Prayer for Peace" (art.); XXII (1935), 455, "The German Bishops Speak" (art.); XXII (1935), 469, "Pius Speaks on Ethiopia" (art.).

CONRING [CONRINGINO] HERMANN. *Opera. Curante commentariisque suis haec opera passim augente et illustrante Iohanne Wilhelmino Goebelio.* 7 vols. Vol. VII, *Index universalis res et verba.* Brunsvigae, 1730.

CONRING [CONRINGINO] HERMANN. *De Pace Civili inter Imperii Ordines Religione Dissidentes Perpetuo Conservanda Libri Duo.* 2d ed. Helmstedt, 1677. Appears in CONRING, *Opera*, II, 467–566. Contains the two works of Conring listed below and Wangnereck's *Judicium theologicum.*

———. *Pro pace perpetua Protestantibus danda Consultatio Catholica: Auctore Ireneaes Eubolo* [pseudonym] *Theologo Austriaco.* Frideburgi, 1648. In *Opera*, II, 472–90.

———. *Animadversio in Bullam Innocentii X Papae. Qua utrumque pactum Pacis Germaniae, & Monasteriensis pariter & Osnabrugense, irritum reddere ille est conatus.* Helmstedt, 1657. In *Opera*, II, 517–66.

COOLIDGE, ARCHIBALD CARY. *Origins of the Triple Alliance.* New York, 1917.

CORTESI, SALVATORE. "The Vatican in the Twentieth Century," *International Monthly* (Burlington, Vermont), IV (1901), 68–82.

COVILLE, HENRY. *Etude sur Mazarin et ses démêlés avec le Pape Innocent X, (1644–1648).* ("La Bibliothèque de l'École des hautes études, fasc. No. 210.") Paris, 1914.

CRAWFORD, F. MARIAN. "Leo the Thirteenth," *Outlook* (New York), LXI (1899), 773–80.

CREIGHTON, MANDELL. *A History of the Papacy from the Great Schism to the Sack of Rome.* 6 vols. London, 1901–3.

CRISPOLITI, FILIPPO. "From Leo XIII. to Pius X.," *International Quarterly* (Burlington, Vermont), IX (1904), 154–69.

CRUMP, G. C., and JACOB, E. F. *The Legacy of the Middle Ages.* Oxford, 1927.

Current Opinion (New York), LVII (1914), 163, "Effect of the Passing of Pope Pius X" (art.).

CURTIS, EDMUND. *A History of Medieval Ireland.* New York, 1923.

DARBY, W. EVANS. *International Tribunals.* 4th ed. London, 1904.

DAVIS, H. W. C. *England under the Normans and Angevins, 1066–1272.* New York and London, 1925.

DAWSON, CHRISTOPHER. "Religion and the Totalitarian State," *The Criterion* (London), XIV (1934), 1–16.

DEBIDOUR, A. *L'église catholique et l'état en France sous la troisième république, 1870–1906.* 2 vols. Paris, 1906–9.

———. *Histoire des rapports de l'église et de l'état en France, 1789–1870.* Paris, 1898.

DEMPF, ALOIS. *Die Hauptform mittelalterlicher Weltanschauung.* Munich, 1925.

———. *Sacrum Imperium, Geschichts- und Staatsphilosophie des Mittelalters und der politischen Renaissance.* Munich, 1929.

DEVAS, CHARLES STANTON. "The Political Economy of Leo XIII," *Dublin Review* (London), CXXX (1902), 293–315; CXXXI (1902), 132–52.

DEWEY, JOHN. "Austin's Theory of Sovereignty," *Political Science Quarterly* (New York), IX (1894), 31–54.

———. "Motivation of Hobbes' Political Philosophy," in *Studies in the History of Ideas*, I, 88–115. Edited by the DEPARTMENT OF PHILOSOPHY OF COLUMBIA UNIVERSITY. New York, 1918.

DOEBERL, M. *Entwicklungsgeschichte Bayerns.* Vol. I, 3d ed., Munich, 1916; Vol. II, 1st and 2d ed., Munich, 1912.

———. "Maximilian I, Bayerns grosser Kurfürst, in neuester Beleuchtung," *Forschungen zur Geschichte Bayerns* (Munich and Berlin), XII (1904), 208–19.

DÖLLINGER, JOHANN JOSEPH. "Kirche und Kirchen, Papstthum und Kirchenstaat," *Historisch-politische Betrachtungen.* Munich, 1861.

DORSCHE [DORSCHEUS], JOHANN GEORG. *Anticrisis theologica, opposita Judicio theologico Ernesti de Eusebiis . . . . super Quaestione: An pax qualem desiderant Protestantes sit secundum se illicita?* Argentorati [Strassburg], 1647, 1648. German edition, 1648.

DOYLE, A. P. "Leo XIII., the Great Leader," *Catholic World* (New York), LXXVII (1903), 574–80.

DREWS, PAUL. "Petrus Canisius, der erste deutsche Jesuit," *Schriften des Vereins für Reformationsgeschichte* (Halle), Vol. X (1892).

DROYSEN, J. G. *Geschichte der preussischen Politik.* 5 vols. in 14 parts. 2d ed. Leipzig, 1868–86.

DRUFFEL, AUGUST VON. *Briefe und Akten zur Geschichte des sechzehnten Jahrhunderts mit besonderer Rücksicht auf Bayerns Fürstenhaus.* 4 vols. Vol. IV, *Beiträge zur Reichsgeschichte, 1535–1555.* Ergänzt und bearbeitet von KARL BRANDI. Munich, 1896.

DUCHESNE, L. *The Beginnings of the Temporal Sovereignty of the Popes, A.D. 754–1073.* London, 1908.

DUDIK, B., O.S.B. "Correspondenz Kaisers Ferdinand II. und seiner erlauchten Familie mit P. Martinus Becanus und P. Wilhelm Lamormaini, kaiserlichen Beichtvätern S.J.," *Archiv für österreichische Geschichte* (Vienna), LIV (1876,) 219–350. Contains biographical data concerning Lamormaini and Forer.

DUERM, CHARLES VAN. *Correspondance du Cardinal Hercule Consalvi avec le Prince Clement de Metternich, 1815–1823.* Louvain, Bruxelles, 1899.

DUHR, BERNHARD, S.J. *Geschichte der Jesuiten in den Ländern deutscher Zunge.* 4 vols. Freiburg, Regensburg, 1907–28.

———. "Die Quellen zu einer Biographie des Kardinals Otto Truchsess von Waldburg, zugleich ein Beitrag zu seiner Charakteristik," *Historisches Jahrbuch* (Munich), VII (1886), 177–209.

DU MONT, JEAN. Baron von Carlscroon. *Corps universel diplomatique du droit des gens, 800–1731.* 8 vols. Amsterdam and The Hague, 1726–31.

DUNLOP, ROBERT. *Ireland from the Earliest Times to the Present Day.* Oxford, 1922.

DUNNING, WILLIAM ARCHIBALD. *A History of Political Theories, Ancient and Mediaeval.* New York, 1919.

DUTHOIT, EUGÈNE. "L'encyclique de Pie XI sur la question sociale," *Revue des deux mondes* (Paris), 8th period, IV (1931), 156–74.

EGELHAAF, GOTTLIEB. *Deutsche Geschichte im 16. Jahrhundert bis zum augsburger Religionsfrieden (Zeitalter der Reformation).* 2 vols. Stuttgart, 1889–92.

EGLOFFSTEIN, HERMANN FREIHERR VON. *Baierns Friedenspolitik von 1645 bis 1647, ein Beitrag zur Geschichte der westfälischen Friedensverhandlungen.* Leipzig, 1898.

EHRHARD, ALBERT. *Der Katholizismus und das zwanzigste Jahrhundert im Lichte der kirchlichen Entwicklung der Neuzeit.* 2d and 3d ed. Stuttgart and Vienna, 1902.

EHSES, STEPHAN. "Franz I. von Frankreich und die Konzilsfrage in den Jahren 1536–1539," *Römische Quartalschrift für christliche Alterthumskunde und für die Kirchengeschichte* (Rome), XII (1898), 306–23.

———. "Papst Urban VIII. und Gustav Adolf," *Historisches Jahrbuch* (Munich), XVI (1895), 336–41. Proves untrustworthiness of Gregorovius' *Urban VIII.*

ELLISON, THOMAS HENRY. "The Pope's Temporal Sovereignty a Providential Fact," *Catholic World* (New York), LXXIV (1902), 557–66.

ERDMANNSDÖRFFER, BERNHARD. *Deutsche Geschichte vom westphälischen Frieden bis zum Regierungsantritt Friedrichs des Grossen, 1648–1740.* 2 vols. in ONCKEN, *Allgemeine Geschichte.* Berlin, 1892, 1893.

ESMEIN, A. *Cours élémentaire d'histoire du droit français.* 11th ed. Paris, 1912.

Europäische Fama, Die, welche den gegenwärtigen Zustand der vornehmsten Höfe entdecket. Without place, 1708; 2d ed., 1711.

Europäischer Geschichtskalender. Herausgegeben von H. SCHULTHESS und ANDERE. Annual publication, 1861——, Nördlingen and Munich.

"EUSEBIIS, ERNESTUS DE," pseudonym for HEINRICH WANGNERECK, *q.v.*

FABER, ANTON [CHR. L. LEUCHT]. *Europäische Staats-Cantzley (1697–1759).* 115 vols. and 9 index vols. (Vol. LXXIX and following by J. C. KÖNIG and OTHERS.) Nürnberg, 1697–1760. Continued under the title *A. Fabers Neue Europäische Staats-Canzley,* and after Vol. XXXI under the title *Fortgesetzte neue europäische Staats-Canzley.* 55 vols. Ulm, Frankfurt, and Leipzig, 1761–82.

FAWKES, ALFRED. "The Pontificate of Pius X," *Quarterly Review* (London), CCXXVII (1917), 477–93.

FEDERN, KARL. *Mazarin.* Munich, 1922.

———. *Richelieu.* Vol. XVI in "Menschen, Völker, Zeiten, eine Kulturgeschichte in Einzeldarstellungen." Vienna, 1926.

FENWICK, C. G. "The New City of the Vatican," *American Journal of International Law* (New York), XXIII (1929), 371–74.

FICKER, G., and HERMELINK, G. *Das Mittelalter.* Part II of G. KRÜGER, *Handbuch der Kirchengeschichte für Studierende.* Tübingen, 1912.

FIEDLER, JOSEPH. *Die Relationen der Botschafter Venedigs über Deutschland und Österreich im siebzehnten Jahrhundert* ("Fontes Rerum Austriacarum," zweite Abtheilung, Vol. XXVI). Vienna, 1866.

FIGGIS, JOHN NEVILLE. *The Divine Right of Kings.* 2d ed. Cambridge, 1914.

———. *Studies of Political Thought from Gerson to Grotius, 1414–1625.* Birbeck Lectures. Cambridge, 1907.

FISCHER, ENGELBERT LORENZ. *Cardinal Consalvi, Leben und Charakterbild des grossen Ministers Papst Pius VII.* Mainz, 1899.

Fischer, Hans. *Beiträge zur Kenntniss der päpstlichen Politik während der westphälischen Friedensverhandlungen (Juli 1647 bis Ende Januar 1648).* Dissertation. Bern, 1913.

Fisher, H. A. L. *The History of England from the Accession of Henry VII to the Death of Henry VIII, 1485–1547.* London, 1919.

Flassan, G. *Der Wiener Congress.* Translated from the French by A. L. Herrmann. 2 vols. Leipzig, 1830.

Flick, Alexander Clarence. *Decline of the Medieval Church.* 2 vols. New York, 1930.

Fontenay-Mareuil, Marquis de. *Mémoires de Marquis de Fontenay-Mareuil.* In Michaud and Ponjoulat, "Nouvelle collection des mémoires pour servir à l'histoire de France," 2d ser., V, 272–87. Paris, 1837.

Frederick William, Bishop of Northampton. "The Neutrality of the Holy See," *Dublin Review* (London), CLVII (1915), 134–45.

Friedberg, Emil. *Die Grenzen zwischen Staat und Kirche und die Garantieen gegen deren Verletzung.* Tübingen, 1872.

Friedell, Egon. *A Cultural History of the Modern Age*, Vol. II. Translated from the German by Charles Francis Atkinson. New York, 1931.

———. *Kulturgeschichte der Neuzeit*, Vol. II. Munich, 1928.

Friedensburg, Walter. "Die römische Kurie und die Annahme der preussischen Königswürde durch Kurfürst Friedrich III. von Brandenburg (1701)," *Historische Zeitschrift*, LXXXVII (1901), 407–31.

Funck-Brentano, Frantz. "Le caractère religieux de la diplomatie du moyen âge," *Revue d'histoire diplomatique* (Paris), I (1887), 113–25.

Gärtner, Karl Wilhelm. *Westphälische Friedens-Cantzley.* 9 vols. Leipzig, 1731–38. Contains documents from the year 1641 to 1646.

Galleti, Petro Aloysio. *Memorie per servire alla storia della vita del Cardinale Domenico Passionei Segretario de' brevi e bibliotecario della S. Sede Apostolica.* Roma, 1762.

Gams, Bonifazius. *Geschichte der Kirche Christi im neunzehnten Jahrhundert mit besonderer Rücksicht auf Deutschland*, Vol. II, which is Vol. XI of De Berault-Bercastel, *Geschichte der Kirche.* Innsbruck, 1855.

Gebhardt, Bruno. *Handbuch der deutschen Geschichte.* 7th ed. Edited and revised by Robert Holtzmann. 2 vols. Berlin, 1930–31.

Geijer, Erik Gustav. *Geschichte Schwedens.* Translated from the Swedish by Swen P. Leffler. In Heeren and Ukert, *Geschichte der europäischen Staaten*, Vol. III. Hamburg, 1836.

Geist, Gustav. *Die Säkularisation des Bistums Halberstadt im westfälischen Friedenskongresse, auf Grund archivalischen Materials dargestellt.* Dissertation. Halle a. S., 1911.

Gfrörer, Friedrich August. *Geschichte des achtzehnten Jahrhunderts.* Herausgegeben von J. B. Weiss. 3 vols. Schaffhausen, 1862.

Gibbons, James Cardinal. *The Faith of Our Fathers.* Baltimore, 1917.

Gierke, Otto. *Political Theories of the Middle Age.* Translated with an Introduction by Frederick William Maitland. Cambridge, 1900.

GINDELY, ANTON. *Geschichte des dreissigjährigen Krieges*, in "Das Wissen der Gegenwart," Vols. I, III, V. Leipzig, 1882.

GOETZ, WALTER. *Maximilians II. Wahl zum römishen Könige 1562. Mit besonderer Berücksichtigung der Politik Kursachsens.* Dissertation. Würzburg, 1891.

———. "Papst Leo XIII.," in ERICH MARCKS and KARL ALEXANDER VON MÜLLER, *Meister der Politik* (2d ed.), III, 383–403. Stuttgart and Berlin, 1924.

GOYAU, GEORGES. "La conférence de la Haye et le Sainte-Siège," *Revue des deux mondes* (Paris), fourth period, CLIV (1899), 590–611.

———. *Histoire religieuse.* Vol. VI in Gabriel Hanotaux, *Histoire de la nation française.* Paris, 1922.

———. "Un an de politique pontificale, Consalvi au congrès de Vienne," *Revue des deux mondes* (Paris), fifth period, XXXV (1906), 135–63.

GRANT, A. J. *The French Monarchy, 1483–1789.* 2 vols. Cambridge, 1914.

GRANVELLE. "Foreign Policy of the Holy See: Part I, *Leo XII;* Part II, *Pius X,*" *Contemporary Review* (London), XCIX (1911), 452–62, 517–32.

GRAUERT, WILHELM HEINRICH. *Christina Königinn [sic] von Schweden und ihr Hof.* 2 vols. Bonn, 1837–42.

GROTIUS, HUGO. *The Rights of War and Peace.* "Universal Classics Library." Washington and London, 1901.

GRÜNHAGEN, C. *Geschichte Schlesiens.* 2 vols. Gotha, 1884–86.

GUNDLING, D. NICOLAI HIERONYMUS. *Vollständiger Discours über den westphälischen Frieden, aus richtigen und unverfälschten MSCtis ans Licht gestellet.* Frankfurt a. M., 1737. In the *Cambridge Modern History*, Vol. IV, Bibliography, p. 868, the title is *Gründlicher Discours über den Westphäl. Frieden* with Introduction by C. J. FENSTEL (Frankfort and Leipzig, 1736). The *Catalogue* of the Bibliothèque nationale, "Auteurs," LXVI, 1194, gives the same. So does HEINSIUS, *Bücherlexikon* (1812), II, 213.

GUNTER, HEINRICH. "Das evangelische Kaisertum," *Historisches Jahrbuch* (Munich), XXXVII (1916), 376–93.

HAAG, EUGÈNE and EMILE. *La France protestante.* 2d ed. Under the direction of H. BORDIER. 6 vols., complete to "Gasparin." Paris, 1877–88.

HAMMER-PURGSTALL, JOSEPH VON. *Geschichte des osmanischen Reiches.* 2d ed. 4 vols. Pesth, 1840.

HANOTAUX, GABRIEL. "Richelieu Cardinal et première ministre," *Revue des deux mondes* (Paris), fifth period, VIII (1902), 86–123.

HANSEN, GEORG. "Briefe des Jesuitenpaters Nithard Biber an den Churfürsten Anselm Casimir von Mainz, geschrieben auf seiner Romreise 1645/46," *Archivalische Zeitschrift* (Munich), N.S., IX (1900), 132–75.

HANSER, K. F. *Deutschland nach dem dreissigjährigen Kriege.* Leipzig and Heidelberg, 1862.

HASSALL, ARTHUR. *Mazarin.* "Foreign Statesman Series." London, 1903.

HAUCK, ALBERT. *Der Gedanke der päpstlichen Weltherrschaft bis auf Bonifaz VIII.* Leipzig, 1904.

———. *Kirchengeschichte Deutschlands. Vierter Teil, erste und zweite (doppel-) Auflage.* Leipzig, 1903.

Hayes, Patrick J. "Pope Benedict the Fifteenth," *Forum* (New York), LXVII (1922), 259–63.

Hearnshaw, F. J. C. "Bodin and the Genesis of the Doctrine of Sovereignty, pp. 109–32, in *Tudor Studies*, edited by R. W. Seton-Watson. London, 1924.

———. "Grotius," pp. 153–73, in *Social and Political Ideas of Some of the Great Thinkers of the Sixteenth and Seventeenth Centuries.* London, 1926.

Hearnshaw, F. J. C. (ed.). *The Social and Political Ideas of Some Great Thinkers of the Sixteenth and Seventeenth Centuries.* London, 1926. Chap. ii, "Jean Bodin," by J. W. Allen; chap. vii, "Thomas Hobbes," by E. L. Woodward.

Heffter, August Wilhelm. *Das europäische Völkerrecht der Gegenwart.* 8th ed. By F. Heinrich Geffcken. Berlin, 1888.

Heigel, Karl Theodor. "Das westfälische Friedenswerk von 1643 bis 1648," *Zeitschrift für Geschichte und Politik* (Stuttgart), V (1888), 411–43.

Hergenröther, Joseph. *Handbuch der allgemeinen Kirchengeschichte, neu bearbeitet von Johann Peter Kirsch,* Vols. II–IV. 6th ed. Freiburg im Breisgau, 1925.

———. *Katholische Kirche und christlicher Staat in ihrer geschichtlichen Entwicklung und in Beziehung auf die Fragen der Gegenwart, Historisch- theologische Essays und zugleich ein anti-Janus vindicatus.* Freiburg im Breisgau, 1872.

Hertslet, Edward. *The Map of Europe by Treaty, 1814–1891.* 4 vols. London, 1875–91.

Hertzberg, Comte de. *Recueil des déductions, manifestoes, declarations, traités et autres actes et écrits publics qui ont été redigés et publiés pour la cour de Prusse.* Par le ministre d'état, Comte de Hertzberg. Vol. II, *Depuis l'année 1778 jusqu'à l'année 1789.* Berlin, 1789.

Herzog, J. J., and Hauck, Albert. *Realencyklopädie für protestantische Theologie und Kirche.* 3d ed. 24 vols., including 2 supplementary vols. Leipzig, 1896–1913.

Hill, David Jayne. *A History of European Diplomacy in the International Development of Europe.* 3 vols. New York, 1905–14.

Hiltebrandt, Philipp. *Preussen und die römische Kurie, im Auftrage des königlichen preussischen historischen Instituts, nach den römischen Akten bearbeitet.* Vol. I, *Die Vorfriderizianische Zeit (1625–1740).* Berlin, 1910.

———. "Preussen und die römische Kurie in der zweiten Hälfte des siebzehnten Jahrhunderts," in *Quellen und Forschungen aus italienischen Archiven und Bibliotheken* (herausgegeben vom Koenigl. preussischen historischen Institut in Rom), XI, (1908), 317–59.

Hobbes, Thomas. "The Leviathan," in Vol. III of William Molesworth, *The English Works of Thomas Hobbes of Malmesbury.* 11 vols. London, 1839.

———. "Philosophical Rudiments concerning Government and Society," in Vol. II of William Molesworth, *The English Works of Thomas Hobbes of Malmesbury.* London, 1841.

HODGKIN, THOMAS. *The History of England from the Earliest Times to the Norman Conquest.* London, 1906.

HOIJER, OLAF. *La solution pacifique des litiges internationaux avant et depuis la société des nations.* Paris, 1925.

HOUSE, EDWARD MANDELL. *Intimate Papers of Colonel House, Arranged as a Narrative by Charles Seymour.* 4 vols. Boston, 1926–28.

HOWLAND, CHARLES P. "Congress in Regimentals," *Christian Century* (Chicago), XLIX (1932), 84–86.

HUBER, A. *Geschichte Österreichs,* Vol. V. Gotha, 1896.

HUBERT, EUGÈNE. *Les Pays-Bas Espagnols et la République des Provinces-Uniés depuis la paix de Münster jusqu'au traité d'Utrecht (1648–1713), La question religieuse et les relations diplomatiques* ("Mémoires d'académie royale de Belgique, Classe des lettres et des sciences morales et politiques et classe des beaux-arts," deuxiéme série, Tome II). Brussels, 1907.

HÜBNER, BARON DE. *Sixte-quint.* 3 vols. Paris, 1870.

HUDDLESTON, SISLEY. "The Revival of the Vatican," *Fortnightly Review* (London), CXIV, (1920), 67–77.

———. "Vatican's New Place in World Politics," *Current History* (New York), XIII (1920), 199–210.

HUME, MARTIN A. S. *Spain, Its Greatness and Decay, 1479–1788.* Cambridge, 1913.

HURST, JOHN FLETCHER. *History of the Christian Church.* 2 vols. New York, 1897–1900.

HURTER, F. VON. *Geschichte Kaiser Ferdinands II.* 4 vols. Schaffhausen, 1857–64.

HUTCHINSON, PAUL. "Religion versus the World We Live In," *Forum* (New York), LXXXIX (1933), 81–87.

IMMICH, MAX. "Geschichte des europäischen Staatensystems von 1660 bis 1789," in *Handbuch der mittelalterlichen und neueren Geschichte.* Herausgegeben von G. VON BELOW and F. MEINCKE. "Politische Geschichte," Abteilung II. Munich, Berlin, 1905.

IRELAND, JOHN, and OTHERS [COLEMAN, COYLE, THOMAS, GLADDEN, JOHNSTON, MENDES]. "Leo XIII., His Work and Influence," *North American Review* (New York), CLXXVII (1903), 321–64.

ISRAEL, FRIEDRICH. *Adam Adami und seine Arcana Pacis Westphalicae,* in "Historische Studien," veröffentlicht von E. EBERING, Heft 69, Berlin, 1909.

"Italian-Vatican Agreement of February 11, 1929" (full text), *Current History* (New York), XXX (1929), 552–66.

JACOB, KARL. *Die Erwerbung des Elsass durch Frankreich im westfälischen Frieden.* Strassburg, 1897.

JANSSEN, JOHANNES. *Geschichte des deutschen Volkes seit dem Augsgang des Mittelalters.* 13th–18th ed., enlarged and edited by LUDWIG PASTOR. 8 vols. Freiburg im Breisgau, 1896–1903.

JARRIGE, RENÉ. *La condition internationale du Saint-Siège avant et après les accords du Latran.* Paris, 1930.

JASTROW, J., and WINTER, GEORG. *Deutsche Geschichte im Zeitalter der Hohenstaufen, 1125–1273.* 2 vols. Stuttgart, 1897–1901.

JENKINS, HELEN. *Papal Efforts for Peace under Benedict XII, 1334–1342.* Dissertation. Philadelphia, 1933.

JORGA, N. *Geschichte des osmanischen Reiches.* 5 vols. Gotha, 1908–13.

JUSSERAND, JEAN ADRIEN ANTOINE JULES. Communication to the editor of the *American Historical Review* (Washington), XXXVII (1932), 817–19.

JUST, LEO. *Das Erzbistum Trier und die Luxemburger Kirchenpolitik von Philipp II. bis Joseph II.* Vol. I, in MARTIN SPAHN, *Die Reichskirche vom Trienter Konzil bis zur Auflösung des Reiches.* Leipzig, 1931.

KAEMMEL, OTTO. *Deutsche Geschichte.* 3d ed. 2 vols. Leipzig, 1911.

KAINDL, RAIMUND FRIEDRICH. *Polen.* 2d ed. In the series "Aus Natur und Geisteswelt." Leipzig, Berlin, 1917.

KASER, KURT. *Deutsche Geschichte im Ausgang des Mittelalters, 1438–1519.* Vol. II (1486–1519), *Bibliothek deutscher Geschichte.* Stuttgart and Berlin, 1912.

KATT, FRIEDRICH. *Beiträge zur Geschichte des dreissigjährigen Krieges.* Part I, *Die bayerisch-fransösischen Verhandlungen von der Zusammenkunft in Einsiedeln bis zur ulmer Capitulation (1639–1647).* Dissertation. Göttingen, 1875.

KEANE, RT. REV. JOHN J. "The Encyclical *Rerum novarum*," *American Catholic Quarterly Review* (Philadelphia), XVI (1891), 595–611.

KERVILER, RENÉ. *Abel Servien, négociateur des traités de Westphalia, l'un des quarante fondateurs de l'académie française, étude sur sa vie politique et littéraire.* Le Mans, 1877.

KLEIN, ABBÉ FELIX. "Breaking and Renewing Diplomatic Relations between France and the Holy See," *Catholic World* (New York), CXII (1921), 577–87.

KLOPP, ONNO. *Der Fall des Hauses Stuart und die Succession des Hauses Hannover in Gross-Britanien und Irland im Zusammenhange der europäischen Angelegenheiten von 1660–1714.* 6 vols. Vienna, 1875–77.

KLÜBER, JOHANN LUDWIG. *Acten des Wiener Kongresses in den Jahren 1814 und 1815.* 8 vols., with Vol. IX as Supplement. Erlangen, 1817–35.

———. *Europäisches Völkerrecht*, Vol. I. Stuttgart, 1821.

KOCH, M. *Geschichte des deutschen Reiches unter der Regierung Ferdinands III.* 2 vols. Vienna, 1865–66.

KÖNIG, LEO. *Pius VII. Die Säkularisation und das Reichskonkordat.* Innsbruck, 1904.

KOJOUHAROFF, CONSTANTINE D. "Niccolò Machiavelli," *National University Law Review* (Washington), Vol. X, No. 2 (1930).

KRAUS, VIKTOR VON. *Deutsche Geschichte im Ausgang des Mittelalters, 1438–1519*, Vol. I. Stuttgart, Berlin, 1905.

KRONES, F. *Handbuch der Geschichte Österreichs.* 5 vols. Vienna, without date.

———. *Österreichische Geschichte.* Neubearbeitet von K. UHLIRZ, "Sammlung Göschen." 2 vols. Leipzig, 1906–7.

LAFITAU, PIERRE-FRANÇOIS. *La vie de Clement XI, souverain pontife.* 2 vols. Padua, 1752.

LAIRD, JOHN. *Hobbes.* London, 1934.

LA JONQUIÈRE, VICOMTE DE. *Histoire de l'empire ottoman depuis les origines jusqu'à nos jours.* 2 vols. Paris, 1914.

LANDAU, MARCUS. *Rom, Wien, Neapel während des Spanischen Erbfolgekrieges. Ein Beitrag zur Geschichte des Kampfes zwischen Papstthum und und Kaiserthum.* Leipzig, 1885.

LATANÉ, JOHN HOLLADAY. *America as a World Power, 1897–1907.* "American Nation Series," Vol. XXV. New York, 1907.

LAURENT, F. *Etudes sur l'histoire de l'humanité,* Vols. VI, IX, and X. Paris, 1860, 1865.

LAVISSE, ERNEST. *Histoire de France depuis les origines jusqu'à la Révolution,* Vol. III, Part I, Paris, 1901; Vol. IV, Part II, Paris, 1902; Vol. V, Part II, Paris, 1904.

LAVISSE, ERNEST, and RAMBAUD, ALFRED. *Histoire générale du ive siècle à nos jours.* 12 vols. Paris, 1896–1901.

LAYMANN, P. PAUL; FORER, P. LAURENZ; and OTHERS. *Pacis Compositio, etc.* See next two entries.

LAYMANN, PAUL, and FORER, LAURENZ. *Pacis Compositio inter Principes et Ordines Imperii Romani Catholicos atque Augustanae Confessioni adhaerentes in comitiis Augustae anno M.D.L.V. edita. Quam Iurisconsulti quidam Catholici ex publicis Comitiorum Actis et Decretis, adversus complurium Acatholicorum scriptorum commenta quaestionibus illustrarunt anno M.D.C.-XXIX. Iussu et auctoritate Superiorum. Dilingae Impensis Caspari Sutoris,* 1629. For German edition (1630), see next title. In the 1629 edition see Appendix, pp. 38 ff. and 47 ff., for German and Latin version of the Peace of Augsburg.

LAYMANN, PAUL; FORER, LAURENZ; and OTHERS[?]. *Pacis Compositio, Das ist aussfürlicher und wolgegründeten Tractat von dem im Jahr 1555 auf dem Reichstag zu Augsburg . . . . aufgerichteten Religionsfrieden.* Dillingen, 1630.

LE CLERC, JEAN. *Négociation secrètes touchant la paix de Münster et d'Osnabrug, ou recueil général des préliminaires, instructions, lettres, etc. ... depuis 1642 jusqu'en 1648.* 4 vols. The Hague, 1725–26.

LEHENMANN, CHRISTOPH[ORUM]. *De Pace Religionis acta publica et originalia, das ist: Reichshandlungen, Schrifften und Protocollen über die Constitution des Religionsfriedens.* 2 vols. Franckfurt, 1631.

LEHMAN, MAX. *Preussen und die katholische Kirche seit 1640: Publicationen aus den K. Preussischen Staatsarchiven,* Theil I, "Von 1640 bis 1740." Leipzig, 1878.

LEMAN, AUGUSTE. *Urbain VIII et la rivalité de la France et de la maison d'Autriche de 1631 à 1635, mémoires et travaux publiés par des professeurs des facultés catholiques de Lille,* fasc. XVI. Lille and Paris, 1920.

LENGEFELD, SELMA VON. *Graf Domenico Passionei päpstlicher Legat in der Schweiz, 1714–1716.* Dissertation. Ansbach, 1900.

LEO XIII. "Encyclical Letter of Pope Leo XIII [*Rerum novarum*]," *American Catholic Quarterly Review* (Philadelphia), XVI (1891), 529–57 (in English).

LEROY-BEAULIEU. *De la colonisation chez les peuples modernes*, Vol. I. 5th ed. Paris, 1902.

LINDNER, THEODOR. *Die deutschen Königswahlen und die Entstehung des Kurfürstentums.* Leipzig, 1893.

LINDSAY, THOMAS M. *History of the Reformation.* Vol. I, *The Reformation in Germany from Its Beginnings to the Religious Peace of Augsburg;* Vol. II, *The Reformation in Switzerland, France, the Netherlands, Scotland, England, the Anabaptist and Socinian Movements and the Counter-Reformation.* 2d ed. Edinburgh, 1907.

LINGARD, JOHN. *The History of England from the First Invasion by the Romans to the Accession of William and Mary in 1688*, Vols. II–IV. Edinburgh, 1902.

Literary Digest (New York): LXXII (February 4, 1922), 30–31, "The Amazing Achievements of Pope Benedict" (art.); CIX (June 6, 1931), 7, "Congress versus Citizenship" (art.); CXII (February 20, 1932), 20–21, "Conscience versus Congress" (art.).

Living Age (New York), CCCXLV (1933), 132–41, "Twilight of the Gods" (editorial).

LODGE, RICHARD. *Richelieu.* "Foreign Statesmen." London. 1896.

LÖFFLER, KLEMENS. *Papstgeschichte von der französischen Revolution bis zur Gegenwart.* 2d ed. Munich, Kempten, 1923.

LONDON TIMES. *Eminent Persons.* 6 vols. 1892–97.

LONDORP, MICHAEL CASPAR. *Acta publica.* 4th ed. 18 vols. Frankfurt a. M., 1668–1721.

LORENTZEN, THEODOR. *Die schwedische Armee im dreissigjährigen Kriege.* Leipzig, 1894.

LORENZ, OTTOKAR. *Geschichte König Ottokars II. von Böhmen und seine Zeit.* Vienna, 1866.

LUCHAIRE, ACHILLE. *Innocent III: La croisade des Albigeois.* 2d ed. Paris, 1906.

———. *Innocent III: La papauté et l'empire.* Paris, 1906.

———. *Innocent III: Rome et l'Italie.* 3d ed. Paris, 1907.

———. *Innocent III: Les royautés vassales du Sainte-Siège.* Paris, 1908.

———. *Social France at the Time of Philip Augustus.* Translated from the 2d ed. of the French by EDWARD BENJAMIN KREHBIEL. New York, 1912.

LUDENDORFF, ERICH VON. *Ludendorff's Own Story, August 1914—November 1918*, Vol. II. New York, 1919.

LULVÈS, JEAN. "Der Lateran Vertrag zwischen dem Heiligen Stuhl und Italien," *Preussische Jahrbücher* (Berlin), CCXVI (1929), 61–76.

LUNT, W. E. (ed.). *The Valuation of Norwich.* Oxford, 1926.

MACCAFFREY, JAMES. *History of the Catholic Church in the Nineteenth Century, 1789–1908.* 2 vols. 2d ed. St. Louis, Missouri, 1915.

MCCARTHY, JUSTIN. *Pope Leo XIII.* ("Public Men of To-day.") London, 1896.

MACHIAVELLI, NICCOLÒ. *Discorsi sopra la prima deca de Tito Livio.* Milano, without date.

MACHIAVELLI, NICCOLÒ. *Florentine History.* Translated by W. K. MARRIOTT. "Everyman's Library," London, 1909.

———. *The Prince.* Translated by N. H. THOMSON. Oxford, 1897.

MCKENNA, HUGH. "Peace, the Keystone of the Papacy," *Catholic World* (New York), CXXXIII (1931), 513–20.

MACLEAN, DONALD A. *The Permanent Peace Program of Pope Benedict XV.* Washington: Catholic Association for International Peace, 1931.

MCMASTER, JOHN BACH. *The United States in the World War.* 2 vols. New York, 1919, 1920.

MALET, ALBERT. *Histoire diplomatique de l'Europe aux XVIIe et XVIIIe siècles,* Vol. I, Paris, without date.

MARCKS, ERICH, and MÜLLER, KARL ALEXANDER VON. *Meister der Politik, eine weltgeschichtliche Reihe von Bildnissen.* 3 vols. 2d ed. Stuttgart and Berlin, 1923–24.

MARSAND, ANTONIO. *I Manoscritti italiani della regia biblioteca parigina.* 2 vols. Paris, 1835, 1838.

MARSHALL, CHARLES C. "Pact Seen as a Blow to Religious Freedom," *Current History* (New York), XXX (1929), 547–52.

MARTENS, G. F. DE; MURHARD, F.; MURHARD, C.; PINHAS, J.; SAMWER, CH.; and HOPF, J., *Nouveau recueil général des traités, etc.* 20 vols. Göttingen, 1843–75.

MARTIN, HENRI. *Histoire de France depuis les temps les plus reculés jusqu' en 1789.* 4th ed. 16 vols. Paris, 1855–70.

MASON, JOHN BROWN. *Hitler's First Foes: a Study in Religion and Politics.* Minneapolis, 1936.

MAURENBRECHER, WILHELM. "Beiträge zur deutschen Geschichte, 1555–1559," *Historische Zeitschrift* (Munich, Berlin), L (1883–84), 1–83.

———. "Beiträge zur Geschichte Maximilians II. 1548–1562," *Historische Zeitschrift* (Munich, Berlin), XXXII (1874), 220–97.

———. *Geschichte der deutschen Königswahlen vom zehnten bis dreizehnten Jahrhundert.* Leipzig, 1889.

———. *Karl V. und die deutschen Protestanten, 1545–1555.* Düsseldorf, 1865.

MAZARIN. *Lettres du Cardinal Mazarin.* See CHERUEL.

MEAUX, VICOMTE DE. *La réforme et la politique française en Europe jusqu'à la paix de Westphalie.* 2 vols. Paris, 1889.

MEIERN, JOHANN GOTTFRIED VON. *Acta comitalia Ratisbonensia publica de MDCLIII et MDCLIV, oder Regenspurgische Reichstags-Handlungen von den Jahren 1653 und 1654.* 2 vols. Göttingen, 1738, 1740. Contains Peace of Osnabrück, Peace of Münster, the Nürnberg Reichstag Recess of June, 1650, and the Regensburg Reichstag Recess of 1654.

———. *Acta pacis executionis publica oder Nürnbergische Friedens-Executionshandlungen und Geschichte.* 2 vols. Hannover and Göttingen, 1736, 1738. For Index see J. L. WALTHER, *Universal-Register.*

———. *Acta pacis Westphalicae publicae oder westphälische Friedenshandlungen und Geschichte.* 6 vols. Hannover, 1734–36. For Index see J. L. WALTHER, *Universal-Register.*

MEISTER, ALOYS. *Deutsche Verfassungsgeschichte von den Anfängen bis ins 15. Jahrhundert, Grundriss der Geschichtswissenschaft zur Einführung in das Studium der deutschen Geschichte des Mittelalters und der Neuzeit*, Reihe II, Abteilung 3. 3d ed. Leipzig, Berlin, 1922.

MENTZ, GEORG. *Johann Philipp von Schönborn, Kurfürst von Mainz, Bischof von Würzburg und Worms, 1605–1673, ein Beitrag zur Geschichte des siebzehnten Jahrhunderts.* 2 vols. Jena, 1896–99.

MENZEL, KARL ADOLF. *Neuere Geschichte der Deutschen seit der Reformation*, Vol. II. Breslau, 1854.

———. *Neuere Geschichte der Deutschen von der Reformation bis zur Bundes-Acte*, Vols. VIII and XI. Breslau, 1839.

Mercure de France (Paris), CCXLIX (1934), 257–67, "Pie XI et Hitler" (art.).

METZLER, JOHANNES, S.J. *Der Heilige Petrus Canisius und die Neuerer seiner Zeit.* Vol. I in *Katholisches Leben und Kämpfen im Zeitalter der Glaubenspaltung.* Münster, 1927.

MEYER, OTTO. *Zur Geschichte der römisch-deutschen Frage*, Vol. I. Rostock, 1871.

MIRBT, D. CARL (ed.). *Quellen zur Geschichte des Papsttums und des römischen Katholizismus.* 4th ed. Tübingen, 1924.

MOELLER, WILHELM. *History of the Christian Church.* Vol. III, *1517–1648.* Edited by G. KAWERAU; translated from the German by J. H. FREESE. London, 1900.

MOLLAT, G. *La question romaine de Pie VI à Pie XI.* ("Bibliothèque de l'enseignement de l'histoire ecclésiastique.") Paris, 1932.

MOMMSEN, WILHELM. *Richelieu, Politisches Testament und Kleinere Schriften.* (Übersetzung von FRIEDA SCHMIDT; eingeleitet und ausgewählt von WILHELM MOMMSEN, in "Klassiker der Politik," Vol. XIV.) Berlin, 1926.

MONTAVAN, WILLIAM F. "The Catholic View of Papacy's New Status," *Current History* (New York), XXX (1929), 541–47.

MOORE, JOHN BASSETT. *History and Digest of International Arbitration to Which the United States Has Been a Party*, Vol. V. Washington, 1898.

MORLEY, JOHN. "Life of James Mill," *Fortnightly Review* (London), O.S., XXXVII (1882), 476–504.

———. *Miscellanies*, Vol. IV, New York, 1908.

MORRISON, CHARLES CLAYTON. "The End of the Macintosh Case," *Christian Century* (Chicago), XLVIII (1931), 1302–3.

MOSER, JOHANN JACOB. *Von der Garantie des westphaelischen Fridens; nach dem Buchstaben und Sinn derselbigen.* Without place, 1767.

———. *Teutsches Staats-Recht*, Vol. VIII. Leipzig, 1743.

MÜLLER, JOSEPH. *Das Friedenswerk der Kirche in den letzten drei Jahrhunderten, Die Diplomatie des Vatikans im Dienste des Weltfriedens seit dem Kongress von Vervins, 1598.* Vol. I, *Die Friedensvermittlungen und Schiedssprüche des Vatikans bis zum Weltkriege 1917, Sammlung ausgewählter Aktenstücke über die Friedenstätigkeit des Heiligen Stuhles.* Berlin, 1927.

MURPHY, J. T. "Germany and Russia at the Vatican," *Catholic World* (New York), LXXVII (1903), 427–35.

MURPHY, JAMES. "The Intellectual Activity of Leo XIII," *Catholic World* (New York), LXXIII (1901), 238–44.

MURRAY, ROBERT H. *The History of Political Science from Plato to the Present.* 2d ed. New York, 1930.

New Europe (London), VI (1918), 24–27, "The Secret Treaty with Italy, April 26, 1915" (art.).

New York Times. (As cited in footnotes.)

NICERON, JEAN PIERRE. *Mémoires pour servir à l'histoire des hommes illustrés dans la république des lettres, avec un catologue raisonné de leurs ouvrages.* 43 vols. Paris, 1729–45.

NÜRNBERGER, AUGUST JOSEPH. *Zur Kirchengeschichte des XIX. Jahrhunderts.* Vol. I, Part I, *Papsttum und Kirchenstaat (1800–1846)*; Part III, *1850–1870.* Mainz, 1897, 1900.

NYS, ERNEST. "Le droit international et la papauté," *Revue de droit international et de législation comparée,* X (Ghent, 1878), 501–38.

———. *Les origins du droit international.* Harlem, 1894.

———. "La papauté et le droit international," *Revue de droit international et de législation comparée.* 2d ser., VII (Brussels, 1905), 155–80.

ODHNER, C. T. *Die Politik Schwedens im westphälischen Friedenskongress und die Gründung der schwedischen Herrschaft in Deutschland.* Translated from the Swedish by E. PETERSON. Gotha, 1877.

OGG, FREDERICK AUSTIN. "The Pope and the Italian Nation," *Chautauquan* (Springfield, Ohio), XXXVIII (1903), 14–19.

OMAN, C. W. *Political History of England from the Accession of Richard II to the Death of Richard III, 1377–1485.* London, 1920.

O'REILLY, BERNARD. *Life of Leo XIII, from an Authentic Memoir Furnished by His Order.* Philadelphia, 1903.

OWEN, LEONARD V. D. *The Connection between England and Burgundy during the First Half of the Fifteenth Century.* Stanhope Essay. Oxford, 1909.

PACE, EDWARD A. "Pope Benedict XV," *Catholic World* (New York), CXIV, 721–31.

PAQUOT, JEAN NOËL. *Mémoires pour servir à l'histoire littéraire des dix-sept provinces des Pays-Bays.* 3 vols. Louvain, 1765–70.

PASTOR, LUDWIG. *Geschichte der Päpste seit dem Ausgang des Mittelalters.* 5th–7th ed. 16 vols. in 22. Freiburg, 1925–33.

PEÑARANDA. Letters of Peñaranda in *Coleccion de documentos ineditos para la historia de España,* Vols. LXXXII–LXXXIV. Madrid, 1884–85.

PERATHONER, ANTON. *Das kirchliche Gesetzbuch.* 4th ed. Bressanone (Brixen), 1926.

PERKINS, JAMES BRECK. *France under Mazarin; with a Review of the Administration of Richelieu.* 2 vols. Boston, 1886.

PFANNER, TOBIAS. *Historia pacis Germano-Gallo-Suecicae Monasterii atque Osnabrugae tractatae.* "Irenopolis," 1679.

PFANNKUCHE, AUGUST. *Staat und Kirche in ihrem gegenseitigen Verhältniss seit der Reformation.* Leipzig, Berlin, 1915.

PFLUGKH-HARTTUNG, J. VON. *Weltgeschichte: Geschichte der Neuzeit, das politische Zeitalter 1650–1815.* Berlin, 1908.

PFÜLF, OTTO. "Ein Beitrag zur Geschichte der bayrischen Friedensbestrebungen an der Neige des dreissigjährigen Krieges," *Stimmen aus Maria-Laach, Katholische Blätter* (Freiburg), LVI (1899), 521–34.

PHILIPPI, F. *Der westfälische Friede: Ein Gedenkbuch zur 250 jährigen Wiederkehr des Tages seines Abschlusses am 24. Oktober 1648.* Unter Mitwirkung A. PIEPER, C. SPANNAGEL, F. RUNGE. Münster, 1898.

PHILLIMORE, ROBERT. *Commentaries upon International Law,* Vol. II. Philadelphia, 1855.

PHILLIMORE, WALTER GEORGE FRANK. *Three Centuries of Treaties of Peace and Their Teaching.* Boston, 1918.

PHILLIPS, GEORG. *Kirchenrecht,* Vol. III, Part I. Regensburg, 1848.

PHILLIPS, WILLIAM ALISON. *Poland.* ("Home University Library.") New York, without date.

PIEPER, ANTON. "Beiträge zur Geschichte des 30jährigen Krieges," Part III (review of Gregorovius' *Urban VIII*), *Historisch-Politische Blätter für das katholische Deutschland* (Munich), XCIV (1884), 471–92.

PIUS IX. *Acta,* Vol. V, Part V. Rome, 1871.

PIUS X. "Pontifical Brief on International Peace, June 11, 1911," *American Journal of International Law* (New York), V, Supplement (1911), 214–16.

PLACCIUS, VINCENTIUS. *Theatrum anonymorum et pseudonymorum.* Hamburg, 1708.

"Policy of Pius XI, The," *Round Table* (London), December, 1934, pp. 44–59.

POLLARD, A. F. *The History of England from the Accession of Edward VI to the Death of Elizabeth, 1547–1603.* London, 1910.

POLLOCK, FREDERICK. *History of the Science of Politics.* London, 1890.

POLLOCK, FREDERICK, and MAITLAND, FREDERICK WILLIAM. *The History of English Law before the Time of Edward I.* 2d ed. 2 vols. Cambridge, 1911.

PONCET, RENÉ. *Les privilèges des clercs au moyen âge.* Paris, 1901.

POYNTER, J. W. "Pope Benedict XV, the Popes Benedict, and the Papacy," *Fortnightly Review* (London), CXVII (1922), 464–73.

PREVITÉ-ORTON, C. W. (ed.), *The Defensor pacis of Marsilius of Padua.* Cambridge, 1928.

PRIBRAM, ALFRED FRANZIS. *The Secret Treaties of Austria-Hungary, 1879–1914.* 2 vols. Cambridge, 1920–21.

PÜTTER, J. S. P. *Geist des westphälischen Friedens.* Göttingen, 1795.

QUARANTA, CLINIO. "Un legato del papa al congresso di Nimego," *Nuova Antologia* (Rome), settima serie, CCCXXVIII (1926), 453–63.

Quarterly Review (London and New York), CXCVIII (1903), 279–306, "Leo XIII" (art.).

QUIDDE, LUDWIG. *Die Entstehung des Kurfürstencollegiums, eine verfassungsgeschichtliche Untersuchung.* Frankfurt a. M., 1884.

RANKE, LEOPOLD VON. *Deutsche Geschichte im Zeitalter der Reformation.* 6 vols. Berlin, 1839–47.

———. *Französische Geschichte vornehmlich im sechzehnten und siebzehnten Jahrhundert*, Vol. II. Stuttgart and Tübingen, 1854.

———. *The History of the Popes . . . . in the Sixteenth and Seventeenth Centuries.* Translated by E. Foster. 3 vols. Bohn edition. London, 1880–83.

———. *Die römischen Päpste in den letzten vier Jahrhunderten.* 3 vols. Vol. I, 8th ed., Leipzig, 1885; Vol. II, 4th ed., Berlin, 1856.

RAYNALDUS, ODORICUS. *Annales ecclesiastici ab anno M C X C VIII ubi Card. Baronius desinit*, Vol. XXI, Part II. Romae, 1677.

REBOULET, SIMON. *Histoire de Clement XI. Pape.* 2 vols. Avignon, 1752.

REED, DOUGLAS L. "The German Church Conflict," *Foreign Affairs* (New York), XIII (1935), 483–98.

Register, The (Denver, Colorado), September 15, 1935.

REIMANN, EDUARD. "Papst Paul IV und das Kaiserthum," *Abhandlungen der schlesischen Gesellschaft für vaterländische Cultur*, Philosophish-historische Abtheilung, 1871, pp. 25–40.

———. "Die religiöse Entwicklung Maximilians II in den Jahren 1554–1564," *Historische Zeitschrift* (Munich, Berlin), XV (1866), 1–64.

———. "Die römische Königswahl von 1562 und der Papst," *Forschungen zur deutschen Geschichte* (Göttingen), VIII (1868), 1–19.

———. "Der Streit zwischen Papstthum und Kaiserthum im Jahre 1558," *Forschungen zur deutschen Geschichte* (Göttingen), V (1865), 291–335.

REUMONT, ALFRED VON. "Fabio Chigi—Papst Alexander VII.—in Deutschland 1639–1651," *Zeitschrift des Aachener Geschichtsvereins* (Aachen), VII (1885), 1–48.

———. *Geschichte der Stadt Rom*, Vol. III, Part II. Berlin, 1870.

———. *Geschichte Toscanas seit dem Ende des florentinischen Freistaats.* 2 vols. in HEEREN UND UKERT, *Geschichte der europäischen Staaten.* Gotha, 1876–77.

REUTER, HERMANN. *Geschichte Alexanders des Dritten und der Kirche seiner Zeit*, Vol. III. Leipzig, 1864.

Revue des deux mondes (Paris), 8th period, XXV (1935), 272–301, "Le catholicisme et la politique mondiale" (art.).

RICHARD, P. "Origines et développements de la secrétairerie d'état apostolique (1417–1823)," *Revue d'histoire ecclésiastique* (Louvain), XI, Part I (1910), 52–72, 505–29, 728–54.

RIEZLER, SIGMUND. *Bayern und Frankreich während des Waffenstillstands von 1647, Sitzungsberichte der philosophischen-philologischen und der historischen Classe der Königlichen bayerischen Akademie der Wissenschaften* (Munich), II, Heft III (1898), 493–541.

———. *Geschichte Baierns*, Vol. V. Gotha, 1903.

———. "Die Meuterei Johann's von Werth, 1647," *Historische Zeitschrift* (Munich, Berlin), LXXXII (1899), 38–97, 193–239.

RITTER, MORIZ. "Der augsburger Religionsfriede, 1555," *Historisches Taschenbuch* (Leipzig), I (1882), 213–64.

———. *Deutsche Geschichte im Zeitalter der Gegenreformation und des dreissigjährigen Krieges (1555–1648), Bibliothek deutscher Geschichte.* 3 vols. Stuttgart, 1889–1908.

———. "Das römische Kirchenrecht und der westfälische Friede," *Historische Zeitschrift*, Dritte Folge, Band V, Heft 2. ("Der Ganzen Reihe," Band CI.) Munich and Berlin, 1908, 254–82.

ROBERTSON, GEORGE CROOM. *Hobbes.* Philadelphia, 1886.

ROEMER, WILLIAM F., and ELLIS, JOHN TRACY. *The Catholic Church and Peace Efforts*, Pamphlet No. 14 of the Catholic Association for International Peace. Washington, 1934.

ROGER OF WENDOVER. *Flowers of History, Comprising the History of England from the Descent of the Saxons to A.D. 1235, Formerly Ascribed to Matthew Paris.* Translated from the Latin by J. A. GILES. 2 vols. London, 1849.

ROSKOVANY, AUGUSTUS DE. *Monumenta catholica pro independentia potestatis ecclesiasticae ab imperio civili.* Vol. II, Quinque-ecclesiis [Fünfkirchen], 1847.

ROSS, J. ELLIOT. "Catholics and the Constitution," *Commonweal* (New York), XV (1931), 119–21; Discussion, pp. 242–43.

———. "Conscience and the State, the Roman Catholic View," *Christian Century* (Chicago), XLIX (1932), 86–87.

ROUSSET, J. DE MISSY. *Supplément au Corps universel diplomatique du droit des gens.* 5 vols. Amsterdam, 1739.

RUCK, E. *Die römische Kurie und die deutsche Kirchenfrage auf dem Wienerkongress.* Basel, 1917.

SACCHINO, FRANCISCO. *De Vita & Rebus gestis P. Pietri Canisii de Societate Jesu, commentarii.* Ingolstadii, 1616. For the attitude of Canisius concerning the Peace of Augsburg.

SAROLEA, CHARLES. "The Political Background of the German *Kulturkampf*," *Contemporary Review* (London), CXLVII (1935), 406–15.

SATTLER, CHRISTIAN FRIDERICH. *Geschichte des Herzogthums Würtenberg* [*sic*] *unter der Regierung der Herzogen.* 13 vols. Tübingen, 1769–83. Contains important documents, especially Vol. VIII.

SAX, CARL RITTER VON. *Geschichte des Machtverfalls der Türkei bis Ende des 19. Jahrhunderts und die Phasen der "orientalischen Frage" bis auf die Gegenwart.* Vienna, 1908.

SCHÄFER, DIETRICH. *Deutsche Geschichte.* 8th ed. 2 vols. Jena, 1921.

SCHAFMEISTER, KARL. *Herzog Ferdinand von Bayern, Erzbischof von Köln als Fürstbishof von Münster (1612–1650).* Dissertation. Haselünne, 1912.

SCHERER, RUDOLPH RITTER VON. *Handbuch des Kirchenrechts*, 2 vols. Graz, 1885–98.

SCHEVILL, FERDINAND. *History of the Balkan Peninsula from the Earliest Times to the Present Day.* New York, 1922.

SCHMID, JOSEPH. "Die deutsche Kaiser- und Königswahl und die römische Curie in den Jahren 1558–1620," *Historisches Jahrbuch* (Bonn), VI (1885), 1–41, 161–207.

SCHMIDLIN, JOSEPH. *Papstgeschichte der neuesten Zeit.* Vol. I, *Papstum und Päpste im Zeitalter der Restauration (1800–1846)*, Munich, 1933; Vol. II, *Papstum und Päpste gegenüber den modernen Strömungen, Pius IX. und Leo XIII. (1846–1903)*, Munich, 1934.

SCHMITT, CARL. "Soziologie des Souveränitätsbegriffes und politische Theologie," in MELCHIOR PALYI, *Hauptprobleme der Soziologie, Erinnerungsgabe für Max Weber*, II, 3–35. (Munich and Leipzig, 1923.)

SCHNABEL, FRANZ. *Deutsche Geschichte im neunzehnten Jahrhundert.* Vol. I, *Die Grundlagen.* Freiburg im Breisgau, 1929.

SCHNITZER, JOSEPH. *Zur Politik des heiligen Stuhles in der ersten Hälfte des dreissigjährigen Krieges.* Sonderabzug aus der *Römischen Quartalschrift*, 1899, Heft 2. Rom, 1899.

———. "Urbans VIII. Verhalten bei der Nachricht vom Tode des Schweden-Königs." *Festschrift zum elfhundertjährigen Jubiläum des deutschen Campo Santo in Rom*, pp. 280–83. Herausgegeben von STEPHAN EHSES. Freiburg i. B., 1897. Confirms Pieper's and Ehse's criticism of Gregorovius' *Urban VIII.*

SCHRADER, CLEMENS. *Der Papst und die modernen Ideen.* Heft 1, *De Enzyklika Quanta cura und der Syllabus*, Vienna, 1864; Heft 3, *Pius IX. als Papst und als Koenig*, Vienna, 1865.

SCHRAMM, PERCY ERNEST. *Kaiser, Rom und Renovatio.* 2 vols. Leipzig, Berlin, 1929.

SCHRÖCKH, JOHANN MATTHIAS. *Christliche Kirchengeschichte seit der Reformation*, Vols. III, VI. Leipzig, 1805, 1807.

SCHRÖDER, RICHARD. *Lehrbuch der deutschen Rechtsgeschichte.* 5th ed. Leipzig, 1907.

SCHULTHESS. See *Europäischer Geschichtskalender.*

SCOTT, JAMES BROWN. "The Pontifical Letter of June 11, 1911, on International Peace" (editorial), *American Journal of International Law* (New York), V (1911), 707–9.

———. "The Progress of International Law during the Last Twenty-five Years," *Proceedings of the American Society of International Law, 1931* (Washington), pp. 2–34.

SELDES, GEORGE. *The Vatican: Yesterday—Today—Tomorrow.* New York, 1934.

SEPPELT, F. X. *Papstgeschichte von den Anfängen bis zur französischen Revolution.* 2 vols. Kempten and Munich, 1921.

SETON-WATSON, R. W. (ed.). *Tudor Studies.* London, 1924.

SFORZA, COUNT CARLO. *Makers of Modern Europe, Portraits and Personal Impressions and Recollections*, pp. 331–43 on Pius XI. Indianapolis, 1930.

———. "The Present Pope's Attitude toward Liberalism," *Current History* (New York), XXXI (1931), 1081–86.

SHEPARD, MAX ADAMS. "Sovereignty at the Crossroads: A Study of Bodin," *Political Science Quarterly* (New York), XLV (1930), 580–603.

SISMONDI, J. C. L. SISMONDE DE. *Histoire des français.* 21 vols. Brussels, 1836–44.

SMITH, A. L. *Church and State in the Middle Ages.* Ford Lectures, delivered at Oxford in 1905. Oxford, 1913.

SMITH, C. MARSHALL. *The Seven Ages of Venice, a Romantic Rendering of Venetian History.* London and Glasgow, 1927.

SMITH, JOHN TALBOT. "The Prisoner of the Vatican," *Munsey's Magazine* (New York), XXXIV (1906), 408–11.

SMITH, PRESERVED. *The Age of the Reformation.* New York, 1920.

SPECHT, THOMAS. "Cardinal Otto Truchsess von Waldburg, Bischof von Augsburg (1543–1573)," *Beilage der Augsburger Postzeitung*, 1897, Nos. 50, 51, 54.

———. *Geschichte der ehemaligen Universität Dillingen (1549–1804) und der mit ihr verbundenen Lehr- und Erziehungsanstalten.* Freiburg im Breisgau, 1902.

Springfield (Massachusetts) *Weekly Republican*, October 24, 1935.

STEINBERGER, LUDWIG. *Die Jesuiten und die Friedensfrage in der Zeit vom Prager Frieden bis zum Nürnberger Friedensexekutionshauptrezess, 1635–1650.* ("Studien und Darstellungen aus den Gebiete der Geschichte," herausgegeben von HERMANN GRAUERT, Band V, Heft 2 und 3.) Freiburg im Breisgau, 1906. Of prime importance.

STENTON, FRANK MERRY. *William the Conqueror and the Rule of the Normans.* London and New York, 1928.

STENZEL, G. A. H. *Geschichte des preussischen Staates.* 5 vols. Hamburg, 1830–54.

STEPHEN, SIR LESLIE. *Hobbes.* ("English Men of Letters.") New York, 1906.

STERN, ALFRED. *Geschichte Europas seit den Verträgen von 1815 bis zum Frankfurter Frieden von 1871.* 10 vols. Stuttgart and Berlin, 1913–34.

STETTINER, PAUL. *Zur Geschichte des preussischen Königstitels und der königsberger Krönung.* Königsberg, 1900. Program.

STIEVE, FELIX. *Abhandlungen, Vorträge und Reden.* Leipzig, 1900. "Kurfürst Maximilian I von Bayern" and "Gustav Adolf."

———. "Beiträge zur Geschichte des Verhältnisses von Staat und Kirche in Baiern unter Maximilian I. (1595–1651)," *Zeitschrift für Kirchenrecht* (Tübingen), XIII (1876), 372–96; XIV (1877), 59–64.

———. *Churfürst Maximilian I. von Bayern. Festrede, gehalten in der baierischen Akademie der Wissenschaften.* Munich, 1882. (Same in STIEVE, *Abhandlungen, Vorträge und Reden*, pp. 155–80. Leipzig, 1900).

———. *Der Ursprung des dreissigjährigen Krieges, 1607–1619.* Vol. I. Munich, 1875.

STOBBE, O. *Hermann Conring, der Begründer der deutschen Rechtgeschichte* (Rectorats Rede, Breslau, 1869). Berlin, 1870.

SUPAN, ALEXANDER. *Die territoriale Entwicklung der europäischen Kolonien.* Gotha, 1906.

TEMPERLEY, H. W. V. *A History of the Peace Conference of Paris.* 6 vols. London, 1920–24.

Theatrum Europaeum. Vols. III–VI. Frankfurt, 1639–52.

TILLICH, PAUL. "The Totalitarian State and the Claims of the Church," *Social Research* (New York), I (1934), 405–33.

TÖNNIES, FERDINAND. *Thomas Hobbes: Leben und Lehre.* 3d ed., Stuttgart, 1925.

TOUT, T. F. *The History of England from the Accession of Henry III to the Death of Edward II, 1216–1377.* London, 1905.

TRENTA, TOMMASO. *Memorie per servire alla storia politica del Cardinale Francesco Buonvisi Patrizio Lucchese.* 2 vols. Lucca, 1818.

TUKER, M. A. R. "The Papacy since the Events of 1870," *Fortnightly Review* (London), LXXXII (1904), 664–77.

TUPETZ, THEODOR. "Der Streit um die geistlichen Güter und das Restitutionsedict (1629)," *Sitzungsberichte der philosophisch-historischen Classe der kaiserlichen Akademie der Wissenschaften* (Vienna), CII (1883), 315–566.

VAST, HENRI. *Collection de textes pour servir à l'étude et à l'enseignment de l'histoire, les grands traités du règne de Louis XIV.* Publiés par HENRI VAST. 3 vols. Paris, 1893–99.

Vehiculum Iudicii theologici. Without place and date [1647 (?), see Steinberger, *op. cit.*, p. 85, n. 3].

VEIT, LUDWIG ANDREAS. *Die Kirche im Zeitalter des Individualismus, 1648 bis zur Gegenwart.* Vol. IV, Parts I and II, in JOHANN PETER KIRSCH, *Kirchengeschichte.* Freiburg im Breisgau, 1932, 1933.

VIOLLET, PAUL. *Histoire des institutions politiques et administratives de la France,* Vol. II. Paris, 1898.

VOGEL, HERMANN. *Der Kampf auf dem westfälischen Friedenskongress um die Einführung der Parität in Augsburg,* in *Blätter aus der augsburger Reformationsgeschichte,* Vol. II. Augsburg, 1889. Also separate edition, Munich, 1900.

VOGÜÉ, E. MELCHIOR DE. "Pope Leo XIII," *Forum* (New York), XXII (1897), 513–25.

VOSSLER, KARL. *Jean Racine,* in "Epochen der französischen Literatur," Vol. III, Part II. Munich, 1926.

WADDINGTON, ALBERT. *L'acquisition de la couronne royal de Prusse par les Hohenzollern,* in "Bibliothèque de la faculté des lettres de Lyon," Vol. IX. Paris, 1888.

WAHRMUND, LUDWIG. *Das Ausschliessungs-Recht (Jus Exclusivae) der katholischen Staaten Österreich, Frankreich und Spanien bei den Papstwahlen.* Vienna, 1888.

WALTHER, J. L. *Universal-Register über die westphälische Friedenshandlungen und die Friedens-Executionshandlungen.* Göttingen, 1740. An index to the two works of Meiern. Contains treatises of Münster and Osnabrück and "Lebensgeschichte der westphälischen Friedens-Gesanden."

WANGNERECK, HEINRICH. *Instrumenti Pacis a Dominis Plenipotentiariis Caesareis Statibus Sacri Romani Imperii Mense Iunio exhibiti Ponderatio.* Written under the pseudonym of "THEOPHILUS GENEROSUS GENUINUS GERMANUS." Without place, 1647.

———. *Responsum theologicum super Quaestione: An Pax, qualem desiderant Protestantes, quae nunc Monasterij & Osnabrugi tractatur, sit secundum se illicita? Pro Principijs Christianis, & Veteris Ecclesiae Catholicae, Summonrunque Pontificum a. SS. PP. Sententia, in Judicio Theologico, Ernesti de Eusebiis.* Without place, 1648.

———. *Responsum theologicum super Quaestione: An Pax, qualem desiderant Protestantes, quaeque nunc Monasterij & Osnabrugi tractatur, sit secundum se illicita?* Printed anonymously, without place, 1648.

WANGNERECK, HEINRICH ["ERNESTUS DE EUSEBIIS," pseud.]. *Judicium theologicum super quaestione an Pax, qualem desiderant Protestantes, sit secundum se illicita.* Ecclesiopoli, 1646, 1647, 1648. Three editions.

WARD, WILFRID. "Vatican and Quirinal," *Fortnightly Review* (London), LXXI (1899), 460–74.

WARING, LUTHER HESS. *The Political Theories of Martin Luther.* New York, 1910.

WEBER, A. "Cardinal Otto Truchsess von Waldburg, Bischof von Augsburg," *Historische-Politische Blätter* (Munich), CX (1892), 781–96.

WEECH, WILLIAM NASSAU. *Urban VIII.* Lothian Prize Essay for 1903. London, 1905.

WENCK, F. A. W. *Codex juris gentium recentissime.* 3 vols. Leipzig, 1781–95.

WESTERMAYER, GEORG. *Jacobus Balde, sein Leben und seine Werke, eine literarhistorische Skizze.* Munich, 1868.

WETZER, HEINRICH JOSEPH, and WELTE, BENEDICT. *Kirchenlexikon, oder Encyclopädie der katholischen Theologie und ihrer Hülfswissenschaften.* 2d ed. Edited by J. HERGENRÖTHER and F. KAULEN. 12 vols. and Index vol. Freiburg i. B., 1882–1903.

WHITELEY, JAMES GUSTAVUS. "The International Position of the Pope," *North American Review* (New York), CLXXVII (1903), 601–6.

WIDMANN, H. *Geschichte Salzburgs.* 3 vols. Gotha, 1907–14.

WILD, KARL. *Johann Philipp von Schönborn, genannt der Deutsche Salamo, ein Friedensfürst zur Zeit des dreissigjährigen Krieges.* Dissertation. Heidelberg, 1896.

WILLARD, JAMES F. *The English Church and the Lay Taxes of the Fourteenth Century.* ("University of Colorado Studies," Vol. IV, No. 4.) Boulder, Colorado, June, 1907.

WILLIAM OF MALMESBURY. *Chronicle of the Kings of England from the Earliest Period to the Reign of King Stephen.* London, 1847.

WISEMAN, CARDINAL. *Recollections of the Last Four Popes.* London, 1858.

WOLF, GUSTAV. *Der augsburger Religionsfriede.* Stuttgart, 1890.

———. Review of Leman's *Urban VIII et la rivalité etc.*, *Zeitschrift für Kirchengeschichte* (Stuttgart), XLIV (N. F. VII) (1925), 139–40.

WOLTMANN, KARL LUDWIG VON. *Geschichte des westphälischen Friedens.* 2 vols. Leipzig, 1808, 1809.

WOOD, L. J. S. "Benedict XV: Pontiff of Peace," *Dublin Review* (London), CLXX (1902), 178–212.

———. "Three Pontificates: A Retrospect," *Dublin Review* (London), CLXXVIII (1926), 227–53.

Wood, L. J. S. "Vatican Politics and Policies," *Atlantic Monthly* (Boston), CXXVIII (1921), 398–406.

Wright, R. F. *Medieval Internationalism, the Contribution of the Medieval Church to International Law and Peace.* London, 1936.

Wunderlich, Bruno. "Die neueren Ansichten über die deutsche Königswahl und der Ursprung des Kurfürstenkollegiums," in *Historische Studien* (veröffentlicht von E. Ebering), Heft 114. Berlin, 1913.

———. *Das Pontifikat Pius VII. in der Beurteilung der deutschen Mitwelt.* Dissertation. Leipzig, 1913.

Wurzbach, Constant von. *Biographisches Lexikon des Kaiserthums Oesterreich.* 60 vols. Vienna, 1856–91.

Wylie, James Hamilton. *The Council of Constance to the Death of John Hus.* London, 1900.

Zauner, Judas Thaddaeus. *Chronik von Salzburg, fortgesetzt von Corbinian Gaertner*, Vol. VIII. Salzburg, 1816.

Ziehkursch, Johannes. "Papst Klemens XI. Protest gegen die preussische Königswürde," *Festgabe Karl Theodor von Heigel zur Vollendung seines sechzigsten Lebensjahres*, pp. 361–77. Munich, 1903.

Zinkeisen, Joseph Wilhelm. *Geschichte des osmanischen Reiches in Europa.* 7 vols. Hamburg, 1840–63.

Zivier, E. *Polen.* Gotha, 1917.

Zwiedeneck-Südenhorst, H. von. *Deutsche Geschichte im Zeitraum der Gründung des preussischen Königtums.* 2 vols. Stuttgart, 1890–94.

Index

INDEX

INDEX

PRINTED IN U.S.A.

www.ingramcontent.com/pod-product-compliance
Lightning Source LLC
LaVergne TN
LVHW020532100826
845148LV00010B/1436

* 9 7 8 1 4 9 8 2 9 2 6 8 9 *